*This book is dedicated to Harry Specht
in appreciation of his friendship.*

C o n t e n t s

9. **Who Plans? Choices in the Process**
   of Policy Formation   245

P r e f a c e

Those who write about social welfare policy analysis encounter many opportunities to argue their own points of view. There are, too, temptations to slip prescriptions into the analysis because the subject matter deals with compelling issues of human welfare. We recognize that many readers would like a book that provides solutions to the weighty problems of social welfare, whether or not they agree with our views. If they agree, they can congratulate their wisdom; if they disagree, they can affirm their own position by dissecting our biases and our logic. In either case, a book that gives firm and sure direction generally provides more immediate gratification than one that analyzes the terrain and debates the hazards of the different roads that can be taken.

Nonetheless, we offer few explicit and firm prescriptions for specific social welfare policies. (In the few cases where we do prescribe, it is less by design than from an inability to resist temptation.) Readers are forewarned that they will not find many specific answers to questions of social policy in this book. Rather, we attempt in this text to share the intellectual challenges that are confronted in making social welfare policy choices. "Good" and "righteous" answers to fundamental questions in social welfare policy are not easily come by. Addressed seriously, these questions require a willingness to abide complexity, an ability to tolerate contradictions, and a capacity to critically appraise empirical evidence and social values. Professionals engaged in the business of making policy choices require patience, thought, and an intelligent curiosity.

To speak of policy choices implies that plausible alternatives exist. Our second objective in writing this book is to present and illuminate these alternatives. The book is organized around what we consider to be the basic dimensions of choice in social welfare policy. We place these dimensions of choice in a theoretical framework that provides a way of thinking about and analyzing social welfare policies that is applicable to a wide range of specific cases. With this framework, we explore policy alternatives, questions they raise, and values and theories that inform different answers. Ultimately the purpose of this book is to equip students to come to grips with the complexities of social choice and to appraise and further develop their own thoughts on social welfare policy.

This book has been written and revised over a period of years in which we have had many discussions (and sometimes disagreements) with our students. We are pleased with whatever benefit they may have derived from exposure to the ideas for the book, and we are grateful for the tolerance and critical comments they have offered in response. We thank the editors of *Social Work* and *Welfare in Review* for permission to use material that originally appeared in those journals.

In preparing this fourth edition, we have been gratified by the extent to which our basic concepts of social policy choice-making have remained applicable and useful since the book was first published in 1974. We are equally impressed with the significant change in the structure and content of U.S. social welfare programs. When we were preparing the first edition, social welfare was at the apex of thirty-five years of growth fueled by the expansion of entitlement programs. We are finishing this fourth edition at a time when government is in the process of reducing welfare expenditures, eliminating entitlements, shifting the delivery of welfare benefits to private providers, and generally questioning the extent of the public sector's responsibility to care for the needy and protect the vulnerable. In response to this historic shift, this edition adds a new chapter on the history, scope, and philosophy of the modern welfare state. Also, we have incorporated into our discussion important recent developments including an analysis of the major welfare reform legislation of 1996, the continued trend toward privatization, and new concepts concerning social capital, civil society, the communitarian ethos, and the enabling state.

We owe special appreciation to David A. Hardcastle, School of Social Work, University of Maryland at Baltimore; Creasie Finney Hairston, Jane Addams College of Social Work, The University of Illinois at Chicago; Wayne Vasey of the School of Social Work, University of Michigan, Ann Arbor; Wyatt Jones of the Florence Heller School for Advanced Studies in Social Welfare, Brandeis University; Eveline M. Burns of the School of Social Work, Columbia University; and Riva Specht, who edited the first edition. Each read and commented upon various editions of the manuscript and provided us with thoughtful criticisms and constructive suggestions. While their good advice helped us to clarify and improve this work, we must, of course, claim exclusive responsibility for whatever deficiencies remain. We also must thank Lissa Roos Parker, who provided great care and cheerful assistance in typing the manuscript, and Rikki Baum who assisted immeasurably with the preparation of the welfare reform section of Chapter 8.

It will become quickly evident to our readers that we, like other contemporary students of social welfare policy, have been considerably influenced by the writings of Eveline M. Burns and Richard H. Titmuss. Their impact on this field is of such magnitude as to be pervasive, and footnotes are an inadequate means of recognizing how much they have done to illuminate social welfare policy.

It is with great sadness that we report Harry Specht died in 1995, while this fourth edition of the text was still in its planning stage. Harry's contribution to this text was integral to its success. He was one of the most powerful and prominent intellectual voices in his generation of social work educators, and his spirit continues to challenge the profession to do its best; his personal warmth and good company are sorely missed. Finally, we must acknowledge our debts to those who bore the brunt of the moments of strain and weariness that all authors inevitably experience. Our wives and children demonstrated remarkable perseverance and good humor in supporting us as we tried to find our way through the dimensions of choice. To Barbara, Evan, and Jesse; and Kathy, Joshua, Benjamin, and Sean, mere thanks are not enough to express the extent of our gratitude and affection.

Chapter **1**

The Field of Social Welfare Policy

"I don't think they play at all fairly," Alice began, in rather a complaining tone, "and they all quarrel so dreadfully one can't hear oneself speak—and they don't seem to have any rules in particular: at least, if there are, nobody attends to them—and you've no idea how confusing it is all the things being alive: for instance, there's the arch I've got to go through next walking about at the other end of the ground—and I should have croqueted the Queen's hedgehog just now, only it ran away when it saw mine coming!"

LEWIS CARROLL
Alice's Adventures in Wonderland, 1866

Students entering the field of social welfare policy quickly come to feel somewhat like Alice at the Queen's croquet party. They confront a puzzling and complex landscape, with changing features and hazy boundaries.[1] Its knowledge base is fragmented and less than immediately related to the realities of day-to-day social work. Yet, the study of this terrain is central for those who work in the social services because, to a large extent, social welfare policy shapes the forms of practice that professionals use and determines the client systems they serve. To a significant degree, both the supply of and the demand for services such as social casework, substance abuse counseling, residential care, case management, and community development reflect social welfare policy choices.

The objectives of this introductory chapter are to provide a general orientation to the field of social welfare policy and to illustrate the interrelatedness of practice and policy analysis. By presenting the subject matter of social welfare in a clearly understandable form, we hope that students will become interested in and comfortable with it, and recognize the importance and power of policy studies. The purpose of this book, as the title suggests, is to develop an operational understanding of social welfare policy by identifying the dimensions of choice essential to the subject matter.

First, however, we want to explore three major perspectives—institutional, analytical, and political—that illuminate the field of social welfare policy. The focus on *institutions* defines what social welfare policy is about, and delineates some of its boundaries. The focus on *analysis* indicates different approaches to studying policy, and for relating policy knowledge to social work practice. The focus on *politics* explores the interrelationship between society and government in the field of social welfare.

Institutional Perspectives on the Study of Social Welfare Policy

Social welfare policy is an elusive concept, and one could easily exhaust an introductory chapter simply describing alternative approaches to its definition. We will not do this, nor will we review the ongoing discussion over the relationships among social policy, public policy, and social welfare policy.[2] Suffice it to say that no single definition is universally, nor even broadly, accepted. However, some effort must be made to stake the boundaries that form a common realm of discourse among those concerned with this subject. Seeking to skirt the conceptual swamp of social policy, public policy, and social welfare policy distinctions, we will focus instead on trying to delineate, using an institutional perspective, the broad range of functions that may be influenced by social welfare policies.

In defining the scope of social welfare policy it is helpful to examine the constituent terms, *social welfare* and *policy*, separately. The term *policy* is somewhat easier to formulate. In this text we will examine "policy" as an explicit course of action. In this sense, policy is akin to what Kahn calls a "standing plan," what Rein describes as the substance of planning choices, and what Mangum explains as "a definite course of action . . . to guide and determine present and future decisions."[3]

Throughout this book our concern will be on the decisions and choices that help determine the social welfare course of action. What binds and delineates these decisions and choices is that they relate to social welfare in all its various aspects. More specifically, they address the functioning of the major institutions in our society that organize and provide social welfare.

The second term of concern, *social welfare*, can be approached by examining the character and functioning of these fundamental institutions. All human societies organize their essential social functions—child-rearing; the production, consumption, and distribution of goods and services; social protection, and so forth—into certain enduring patterns of conduct. All societies, for example, maintain institutions with responsibilities and expectations for raising and training the young. In most cases, one primary institution seldom exhausts the patterns a society uses to deal with its essential functions. Although the family is the primary institution for socialization, for example, it is by no means the only one. Religious and educational organizations and social service agencies also assume some socialization responsibilities, although socialization is not their *primary* activity.

There are six fundamental social institutions within which the major activities of community life occur: kinship, religion, workplace, markets, mutual assistance, and government. As indicated in Table 1.1, all of society's basic day-to-day activities are organized in one or more of these spheres. And each of these social institutions, to one degree or another, also carries out important social welfare functions.

Kinship

The family has always been society's major institution for procreation, emotional support, and economic well-being. The family is also the key instrument of socialization, helping society to transmit prevailing knowledge, social values, and behavior patterns from one generation to the next. As an instrument of social welfare, the family frequently provides private arrangements for income security through life insurance policies, private savings and other kinds of investment, and gifts.

TABLE 1.1   Institutions, Organizations, and Functions

Social Institutions	Key Organizational Forms	Primary Functions	Social Welfare Functions
Kinship	Families	Procreation, socialization, protection, intimacy, emotional support	Care for dependent members, interfamilial financial support
Religion	Churches	Spiritual development	Sectarian welfare, health, education, social services, counseling
Workplace	Work organizations	Employment	Employee benefits
Marketplace	Producers (firms) and consumers (households)	The exchange of goods and services for money	Commercial social welfare goods and services
Mutual assistance	Support groups, voluntary agencies	Mutual aid, philanthropy	Self-help, volunteering, community social services
Government	National, regional, and local governments	Mobilization and distribution of resources for collective goals	Antipoverty, economic security, health, education, housing services

The full extent to which the family provide financial and in-kind assistance to its members, mostly between generations, is difficult to measure.[4] An early estimate by Robert Lampman put the value of interfamily transfers of cash, food, and housing at $86 billion in 1978.[5] A more recent calculation, based on a 1985 survey by the U.S. Census Bureau, estimates that family cash transfers alone totaled $18.9 billion. These figures suggest an average family aid payment of $3,006—children helping aging parents with nursing or medical care expenses, parents helping children to buy homes or deal with financial emergencies, or separated parents paying alimony and child support.[6] The adequacy of the child support system has increasingly been a concern as a large number of children live with single parents in poverty situations. Although nearly $12 billion was paid to custodial parents in 1995 for child support, another $18 billion—owed under court order—remained unpaid.[7]

The family is also a welfare-providing institution in that it assists dependent members in noneconomic ways. Elders often rely on adult children for shopping and personal care, and families help disabled relatives of all ages who otherwise might require state-sponsored residential care or in-home assistance. In 1982, for example, 2.2 million U.S. citizens provided unpaid help to 1.6 million disabled elderly relatives. Most of these caregivers were women, and most lived with the person needing assistance. A full 80 percent of all caregivers provided care seven days a week, on an average of four hours daily.[8]

Finally, the importance of the family is reflected in the way people seek out help when faced with critical problems. Responding to a 1980 Gallup poll asking where they sought "advice, assistance, or encouragement" when problems arose, far and away most respondents said "family members." (The second most popular choice was "friends," and farther down the list were professional helpers such as social workers, counselors, and psychiatrists.)[9]

CAPSULE 1.1:   Kinship Security

It is patterns of kinship which most often cover us in our undertakings, provide us market opportunities, and even shield us from the importunings of the state. We do not hope to receive tuition, childcare, or a kidney from a business associate, but we do from relatives. Marriage is that device which extends to us a social security network of obligated kin. . . .

Marriage provides a kind of capital. Married couples, more than single parents, have parents and grandparents as a resource. House loans, emergency aid, care payments, cash gifts, and job opportunities come disproportionately from these relatives. Over one-fourth of all new home purchases depend upon gifts from parents.

Having four parents and eight grandparents attached to every marriage broadens the base of economic support, for us as for the Inuit.

David W. Murray, "Poor Suffering Bastards: An Anthropologist Looks at Illegitimacy," *Policy Review, 68,* Spring 1994, 13.

Religion

Religious institutions manifest the spiritual aspect of human society through ceremonies and observances that form systems of worship. Beyond this, churches sponsor elaborate social welfare provisions ranging from informal support and counseling to multimillion-dollar health, education, and social service programs.

The Church of the Latter Day Saints (Mormons), for example, operates over 600 food production projects for the poor, including twenty canneries and

---

CAPSULE 1.2:   The Social Service Congregation

The black church—usually at the forefront of successful black movements in the United States—finds itself in the 1990s becoming more of a social service agency than a spiritual, soul-saving institution.

"We're called to be everywhere," said the Rev. J. Alfred Smith Sr., pastor of the 4,000-member Allen Temple Baptist Church in East Oakland. "We're doing a hell of a lot more than we were 10 years ago. Things have gotten worse for the masses."

With black neighborhoods increasingly beset by unemployment, crime, violent death, drug abuse, AIDS and family separation, ministers say they need more than a Bible and a pulpit.

St. Augustine's Episcopal Church of Oakland opened its doors more than 20 years ago to the Black Panthers' first breakfast program in the East Bay. The breakfast program has long been dissolved but the church now provides groceries for 70 families each month, in addition to supporting scout troops, after-school tutorial programs, drug and alcohol dependency counseling and the Caring Family Project.

"I do feel we are being pressed to do more social work," said the Rev. Charles Carter of St. Augustine's. "You can't speak to someone about God if they're hungry. You can't save minds unless you educate them. If you're

going to save their souls you have to save their bodies, too. They are tied together."

Black churches—since the first one rose in Philadelphia in 1787—have been a political and social force from the abolitionist movement to the civil rights era. "It (the church) is the only institution we own lock, stock and barrel," said the Rev. Amos Brown of San Francisco's Third Baptist Church in the Western Addition.

Andrew Billingsley, a professor at the University of Maryland and author of "Climbing Jacob's Ladder: The Enduring Legacy of African American Families," wrote: "In addition to what it does for its members, the black church as an institution has always reached out to serve important functions for the black community as a whole. It is in this respect both preserver of the African American heritage and agent for reform. Indeed, no successful movement for improving conditions of life for the African-American people has been mounted without the support of the church."

The 1990s have presented new challenges. With government spending on social programs shrinking, the black church has had to feed and clothe the hungry and the homeless, provide jobs, rein in young gang toughs, react to violence in the neighborhood, and share its space with government and other programs.

Gregory Lewis, "New Role Thrust on the Black Church," *San Francisco Examiner,* February 28, 1993, B1.

numerous meat-packing and dairy operations supplied by church-owned welfare farms. A recent estimate indicates that each year about 200,000 church members receive nearly 32 million pounds of commodities from Mormon storehouses and auxiliaries.[10] The Mormons also run Deseret Industries, which provides work and shelter for the elderly and handicapped, places members in jobs through church-sponsored employment offices, and organizes an extensive program of child welfare, foster care, and adoption services.[11]

Catholic, Jewish, and Protestant welfare organizations have similar explicit social welfare objectives, implemented both through professionalized agencies such as Catholic Charities and the counseling activities of priests, ministers, and rabbis. The range of church-related services has been broadened even further in recent years by "family ministries" and "family life education" programs focused on married couples and their children, premarrieds and singles, and people facing special problems such as alcoholism and divorce.[12]

Workplace

Workplace organizations—factories, farms, universities, service-providing firms—often promote the welfare of their members—their workforce—by providing job-related goods and services, along with regular paychecks. One's job is the most important single source of support for most U.S. citizens—both by providing the income necessary for everyday life, and through welfare arrangements attached to the job, generally known as fringe or occupational benefits. The word *fringe*, however, seriously understates the importance of these benefits, because their average value in 1993 exceeded $14,000 per employee, or about 41 percent of a typical worker's overall compensation.[13] These benefits provide a vital portion of an employee's work-related package of compensation, one that until quite recently was enlarging on a yearly basis (Figure 1.1). While wage income rose approximately 500 percent between 1965 and 1984, for example, supplemental employer contributions rose by 1,000 percent, with most of this nonwage compensation going into private pension schemes.[14]

Along with pensions, the most important fringe benefit is health insurance. Unlike most Western nations, which provide health benefits through public programs, U.S. citizens obtain their health benefits through their employment; in 1989 nearly two-thirds of all U.S. citizens under age 65 had employment-related insurance.[15] Many firms also provide benefits such as company cars, parental leaves, college tuition for the children of employees, gyms, legal and dental services, relocation assistance, and low-cost housing. Unions occasionally provide special benefits to supplement the public system of unemployment insurance. And many human services such as on-site child care and alcohol and drug counseling are provided as part of company-sponsored EAPs (Employee Assistance Programs). Although many companies have social workers and psychologists for such tasks, others rely on ordained ministers and priests to tend to their employees' emotional needs.[16]

An Armload of Perks

Some companies on the cutting edge are offering the following benefits to employees who may be able to buy them through payroll deductions or simply choose them as part of a flexible benefits plan. The percentage of companies offering each benefit was supplied by Hewitt Associates.

Long-term care insurance
10%

Elder-care benefits
24%

Group financial planning
2%

Auto insurance
8%

Health-insurance opt-outs
16%

Buying vacation time
11%

Selling vacation time
10%

The New York Times; Illustration by Niculae Asciu

FIGURE 1.1   An Armload of Perks.

Source: Kathleen Murray, "Going Cubicle to Cubicle to Sell Them Insurance," *The New York Times,* July 16, 1995, F10.

Some would argue that these benefits embody market exchanges—the basic package of compensation that workers frequently bargain for in lieu of wages—rather than social welfare. But even when fringe benefits are seen as an integral feature of a business/labor exchange, their tax-preferred treatment means they are to some extent publicly subsidized.[17]

Marketplace

Although there are several theoretical ways in which goods and services can be produced and allocated in society—centralized state control is one system, private altruism another—the most ubiquitous and successful economic institution in modern times for satisfying people's material desires is the private marketplace. Typically identified with capitalism, the market brings together buyers, sellers, and producers in satisfying, efficient transactions, its "invisible hand" allocating society's resources according to mutual needs and desires.

A primary component of the marketplace in industrial societies is the business firm that, together with nonprofit organizations and governments, creates and distributes all goods and services in this country. In recent years, an increasingly significant part of the corporate sector has engaged in the production and sale of social welfare goods and services. There are, for example, ten major child-care chains operating today, many on the franchise principle, running more than 1,000 child-care centers—about 5 percent of all centers nationwide. Even in more traditional social service areas such as child welfare institutions, group-home care, and residential treatment, more than half of all programs are run by proprietary establishments.[18]

The biggest profit-making operations of all are in the health field, where major corporations operate about 11 percent of all the hospital facilities in the country. Profit-making firms also own a major portion of the "nursing home industry" (thus, the "industry") and medical labs and clinics. One of the newest and fastest growing parts of the U.S. health care system—free-standing emergency centers—is almost entirely a commercial enterprise. Major private corporations such as Upjohn Labs have also expanded into the home-health field and drug and alcohol treatment services.

We don't want to give the impression that the profit sector is entirely the domain of major corporations. At one end of the market continuum are thousands of individual and small group entrepreneurs who directly provide health and social services. These include private practice psychiatrists, social workers, marriage and family counselors, and lay people who operate family day care and board and care homes. Currently, it is estimated that as many as 25 percent of the

---

CAPSULE 1.3:   Butchers, Brewers, and Markets

It is not from the benevolence of the butcher, the brewer, or the baker, that we expect our dinner, but from their regard to their own self-interest. We address ourselves, not to their humanity but to their self-love, and never talk to them of our own necessities but of their advantages.

Adam Smith, *The Wealth of Nations*, 1776.

members of the National Association of Social Workers are in private practice for at least part of their work week.[19] It is clearly the hope of many MSWs to go "solo," hang out their shingle, and "do good" providing services that clearly are in demand—most of which revolve around personal relationships, individual insecurities, and sex, alcohol and drug problems.[20]

Mutual Assistance

The fourth major institution of modern society—mutual assistance—is perhaps the most explicitly focused on social welfare activities. Variously characterized as charity, philanthropy, informal help, or social support, these arrangements express society's need for mutuality, its recognition of interdependence, and its desire to assist the less fortunate. Whether viewed as a function of altruism or of self-interest, mutual assistance constitutes an essential part of community life.

Most mutual assistance represents society's natural response to everyday need. Whereas traditions of self-help go far back in U.S. history, they increasingly constitute a critical resource for millions of people. One of the most notable developments of the past decade has been the reawakened interest in informal helping systems along with a reconceptualization of the ways in which professionals and lay helpers can work together.

How *do* friends, neighbors, and peers help? Neighbors check in on the sick and disabled, making sure all is well, sometimes helping with housework and cooking and shopping and babysitting. Friends provide loans and emergency living arrangements. Self-help groups—small, nonbureaucratic, nonprofessional—assist people facing common emotional problems. Working face to face with others who share and understand their predicament, millions of people achieve a positive sense of themselves and learn realistic strategies for problem-solving.

CAPSULE 1.4:   Tocqueville on Mutual Aid

Americans of all ages, all stations in life, and all types of disposition are forever forming associations. There are not only commercial and industrial associations in which all take part, but others of a thousand different types—religious, moral, serious, futile, very general and very limited, immensely large and very minute. Americans combine to give fêtes, found seminaries, build churches, distribute books and send missionaries to the Antipodes. Hospitals, prisons and schools take shape in that way.

If they want to proclaim a truth or propagate some feeling by the encouragement of a great example, they form an association. In every case, at the head of any new undertaking, where in France you would find the government or in England some territorial magnate, in the United States you are sure to find an association.

Alexis de Tocqueville, *Democracy in America,* 1835.

It is estimated that 12 to 15 million U.S. citizens belong to self-help groups.[21] Among the most common groups are:

Parents Without Partners (single parents and their children)
La Leche League (nursing and other new mothers)
Candlelighters (the parents of children with cancer)
Alcoholics Anonymous (recovering alcoholics)
Al-Anon (family members of alcoholics)
National Alliance for the Mentally Ill (families and friends of the seriously mentally ill)

Among the more esoteric are:

I Pride (interracial couples)
Parents of Near Drowners (POND)
Incompletes Anonymous (procrastinating students)
Beauties Anonymous
Helping After Neonatal Death (HAND)

CAPSULE 1.5:   The Twelve Steps

The twelve-step program, pioneered in the late 1930s by Alcoholics Anonymous, has been embraced by self-help groups dealing with over 200 separate problems, ranging from overeating and gambling to sex and love addiction.

The twelve "spiritual steps to personal growth," the guiding intervention for all "recovery," were formulated by Bill Wilson, AA's cofounder, in 1939. They are:

1. Admitting powerlessness over alcohol—that our lives had become unmanageable.
2. Coming to believe that a Power greater than ourselves can restore us to sanity.
3. Making a decision to turn our will and our lives over to the care of God, as we understand Him.
4. Making a searching and fearless moral inventory of ourselves.
5. Admitting to God, to ourselves, and to another human being the exact nature of our wrongs.
6. Being entirely ready to have God remove our defects of character.
7. Humbly asking God to remove our shortcomings.
8. Making a list of all persons we've harmed and being willing to make amends to them all.
9. Making direct amends to such people wherever possible except when to do so would injure them or others.
10. Continuing to take personal inventory and when we are wrong to promptly admit it.
11. Seeking through prayer and meditation to improve our conscious contact with God, praying only for knowledge of His will for us and the power to carry that out.
12. Having a spiritual awakening as the result of these Steps, carrying the message to others, and practicing these principles in all our affairs.

Adapted from Al-Anon Family Group, *One Day At A Time in Al-Anon*, New York, 1973.

Beyond self-help and informal support is the extensive and multifaceted system of voluntary associations that provides formal expression to the philanthropic impulse. Organized on a nonprofit basis, and aimed at addressing community welfare needs, over 41,000 voluntary agencies today provide an array of social services for disadvantaged children, families, adults, the elderly, and a variety of special-need populations. These agencies, generally small in size compared to government bodies, and governed by citizen boards of directors, coexist with a vast population of other nonprofits serving educational, health, research, and cultural purposes.[22]

Government

Governmental institutions, according to the *Encyclopedia of the Social Sciences*, deal with the "control of the use of force within a society and the maintenance of internal and external peace . . . as well as control of the mobilization of resources for the implementation of various goals and the articulation and setting up of certain goals for the collectivity."[23] Among the most important functions of the modern state, of course, is the mobilization and distribution of resources for welfare purposes. So important, and so huge, is the role of public activity in this area that the modern state is often defined principally as a "welfare state." And today's polity, at least in the industrial world, *is* organized to support welfare. Broadly, the modern state is organized to insure economic prosperity and social stability, and, more specifically, material security, minimum standards of health, education, and housing, and protection against the contingencies of modern life that interfere with people's well-being.

Evolving Institutions and the Welfare State

The nature of society's helping arrangements is critically influenced by the balance that exists among its institutional sectors. That is, the various systems of provision have distinctive characteristics and distinctive costs and benefits. The help that families provide, for example, is immediate, emphatic, caring, and unbureaucratic. However, family help can be onerous, emotionally exhausting, and costly for caregivers. Families can be wiped out financially by the needs of sick and dependent relatives. Family care, of course, is also limited by ties of marriage and blood. It provides nothing for those who are without families of their own.

Public services have their own pluses and minuses. Although they can be impersonal, inefficient, and bureaucratic, they can also ensure that all needy individuals are helped and that no one is allowed to fall below a certain minimum standard of living. They can redistribute societal resources and promote equality. They can reduce the stigma of private charity, making benefits a right rather than a handout.

Although social welfare activities are distributed among all the major institutions of society, the balance among them varies considerably. In an historical context, welfare functions evolved separately, institution by institution. In the simplest societies, most aspects of life revolve around the family—with religious, governance, economic, and mutual aid activities all organized through the kinship structure. As societies grow in complexity, individuals and groups begin to take on discrete social functions, and with increasing specialization there evolved independent religious, governmental, economic, and mutual aid organizations.

If each of the major social institutions of society serve at least some welfare functions, is it possible to think in terms of social welfare *itself* as an institution? This question, it turns out, is one of fundamental conceptual importance, although it is only in recent times that it has been posited. Prior to the current century, social welfare was a subject matter of relatively modest scope. It was only when prevailing social arrangements became unable to deal with the emerging needs of modern industrial life that the publicly organized system of social welfare enlarged. The first major spurt of government social welfare activity in the United States resulted from the recognition that the family, religious and economic institutions, and the instruments of voluntary mutual aid and local government were unable to address the enormous social distress caused by the Great Depression of the 1930s. This realization resulted in new demands being placed on government, especially national government. This change—frequently described as a shift from a residual model of social welfare to an institutional one—corresponded to the emergence of the U.S. welfare state.

The traditional (i.e., residual) view is that social welfare itself is not a significant societal institution, but rather a supplemental activity necessary only when the "normal" channels fail to perform appropriately. Viewed as a residual, temporary response to the failures of individuals and major institutions, social welfare is seen as a set of activities, that, although needed at times, is undesirable and expendable. Residualists argue that it is inappropriate to place social welfare on an equal standing with the primary institutions shown in Table 1.1.

Speaking at the Conference of Charities and Corrections in 1914, Dr. Abraham Flexner expressed one aspect of residual conception of social welfare in comparing social work with the recognized professions:

> *A good deal of what is called social work might perhaps be accounted for on the ground that the recognized professions have developed too slowly on the social side. Suppose medicine were fully socialized; would not medical men, medical institutions, and medical organizations look after certain interests that the social worker must care for just because medical practice now falls short? The shortcomings of law create a similar need in another direction. Thus viewed, social work is, in part at least, not so much a separate profession as an endeavor to supplement certain existing professions* pending their completed development.[24]
> [Emphasis added]

Competing with this conception is the institutional view of social welfare as a distinct pattern of activities serving not as a safety net to catch the victim after all else has failed but rather as an integral and "normal 'first line' function of modern industrial society."[25] Perceived as a basic social institution, social welfare carries none of the stigma of the "dole" or of "charity." It is seen, instead, as a primary means by which individuals, families, and communities fulfill their social needs.

Much of our understanding of these competing models depends on how we comprehend both the causes and the incidence of unmet needs in society. In both models, the major institutional structures of society are viewed as ineffective to some degree in meeting people's needs. The fundamental issues are these: To what extent is this an anomaly reflecting mainly the deficiencies of some individuals and a small margin of institutional malfunctioning? To what extent is it a normal consequence of institutional limitations and individual failure? An answer of "very much" to the first question and "very little" to the second relegates social welfare to the status of a residual safety net activity. Reverse these answers and social welfare emerges as a basic and distinct social institution.

The answers to these questions, however, remain equivocal. In this regard, Wilensky and Lebeaux's 1958 assessment is still accurate:

> *While the two views seem antithetical, in practice American social work has tried to combine them, and current trends in social welfare present a middle course. Those who lament the passing of the old order insist that the [institutional conception] is undermining individual character and the national social structure. Those who bewail our failure to achieve utopia today argue that the residual conception is an obstacle which must be removed before we can produce the good life for all. In our view, neither ideology exists in a vacuum; each is a reflection of broader cultural and societal conditions. With further industrialization the [institutional conception] is likely to prevail.*[26]

While the debate continues, it is difficult to ignore the vast importance of the social welfare enterprise in modern society, *and* the primary role of government in it. Although the development of social welfare as a separate institution doesn't entirely equate welfare with government—national government in particular— there is no denying that modern societies demand a major public role, a role that is most frequently conceptualized in terms of the welfare state.

Analytic Perspectives on the Study of Social Welfare Policy

Analysts tend to approach the field of social welfare policy in several interrelated ways. The major approaches to analysis can be characterized as studies of the three Ps: *process, product,* and *performance.* Each approach examines social welfare policy questions that are primarily relevant to the professional roles of planning, administration, and research. Professionals engaged in these activities devote most of their resources and energies to questions concerning the process, product, and performance of social welfare policy. In actual agency practice, all three roles may be performed by the same worker. In such cases the worker tends to draw equally on the knowledge and insights generated by all three modes of study. However, in most large agencies and programs, planning, administration, and research tasks are specialized, and practitioners tend to be more interested in the insights of one analytic approach than in others. Even when the roles of planner, administrator, and researcher are highly compartmentalized, however, requirements for handling "outside" tasks seep into the job.[27]

Similarly, it is important to underscore that these three approaches are overlapping and interrelated. This is a shorthand way of saying that conceptual distinctions tend to capture the core qualities of a phenomenon, but, by their very nature, do not well portray subtle and relative characteristics. Frequently, policy analysts may employ different combinations of approaches in their investigation. In *Fiscal Austerity and Aging,* for example, Carroll Estes and others trace the *process* of legislative development concerning the needs of the aged, describe the various programs that were *products* of this legislation, and evaluate their *performance*.[28]

Whatever the practice, however, it is theoretically useful to distinguish among these analytic approaches because each, at its core, addresses different types of questions, and the knowledge and insights generated are differentially applicable to major practice roles related to social welfare policy. At the conclusion of this chapter we will describe what we believe to be the policy-relevant tasks of the direct-service practitioner.

Studies of Process

Studies of process in social welfare policy focus on the dynamics of policy formulation with regard to sociopolitical and technical-methodological variables. Political science and history are two of the major academic disciplines on which process studies are based. Process study is most concerned with understanding how planning data and the relationships and interactions among the political, governmental, and interest group collectivities in a society affect policy formulation.

Studies of process are employed as points around which policy assessments are organized, usually in the form of case studies of the political and technical inputs to decision making. Process studies may vary in respect to the time dimension and levels of analysis with which they deal. That is, they may be long-range studies of the development of an entire social welfare system, or studies of the development of specific circumscribed programs. Examples of the former are James Leiby's historical analysis, *The History of Social Welfare and Social Work in the United States*[29]; Heffernan's political/economic analysis, *Introduction to Social Welfare Policy: Power, Scarcity, and Common Human Needs*[30]; and Piven and Cloward's sociopolitical analysis, *Regulating the Poor: The Functions of Public*

Welfare.[31] Analyses of specific programs include Martha Derthick's *Uncontrollable Spending for Social Service Grants,*[32] Linda Gordon's *Pitied But Not Entitled: Single Mothers and the History of Welfare 1890–1935,*[33] Gilbert and Specht's *Dynamics of Community Planning,*[34] and Theda Skocpol's recent *Boomerang: Clinton's Health Security Effort and the Turn Against Government in U.S. Politics.*[35]

Regardless of the time perspective, however, process studies generally deal with such questions as the societal context in which policy decisions are made, the behaviors, motivations, and goals of various actors who participate in the process, and the stages of the process of policy development. Process studies help illuminate how social context, social roles, and stages of development contribute to policy outcomes.

Studies of Product

The product of the planning process is a set of policy choices. These choices may be framed in program proposals, laws and statutes, or standing plans that eventually are transformed into programs. The analytic focus of product studies is on issues of choice: What is the form and substance of the choices that make up the policy design? What options did these choices foreclose? What values, theories, and assumptions support these choices?

Essentially, the analytic approach employed in this book is that of product study. Although widely employed in a variety of academic disciplines, product study is the least systematically developed form of social welfare policy analysis. Analyses usually focus on one or another issue of choice that is germane to a specific policy, but there is no systematic framework for placing the generic issues of policy design in a broad context. Examples of these issue-specific studies are cited in the following chapters as we attempt to explicate a generic view of social welfare policy from this analytic perspective. In Chapter 3 we will address the development and utility of this approach in greater detail.

Studies of Performance

Performance studies are concerned with the description and evaluation of the programmatic outcomes of policy choices. Studies of program outcome are more amenable to objective, systematic observation than studies of process and product because program boundaries are more sharply delineated. Performance can be measured through the collection of qualitative and quantitative data and through the application of a wide range of methodological tools from various academic disciplines. Research methodology as taught in the social science disciplines and in professional schools provides the major technological and theoretical knowledge and skill for these kinds of studies.

From this perspective, investigators ask two types of questions: First, how well is the program carried out. Second, what is its impact? With regard to the former, programs are monitored to see what they consist of, whether they are reaching their target population, how much they cost, and so on. Impact is measured as "the difference between pre-program behavior and conditions and post-program behavior and conditions which can legitimately be attributed to the intervention."[36] Some examples of performance studies are Rein's *Work or Welfare: Factors in the Choice for AFDC Mothers*,[37] Segal and Aviram's *The Mentally Ill in Community-Based Care*,[38] and Berrick and Gilbert's *With the Best of Intentions: The Child Sexual Abuse Prevention Movement.*[39]

Performance studies, of course, are frequently carried out by analytic staff attached to the legislative bodies responsible for policy oversight. The U.S. General Accounting Office, for example, monitors and assesses federal social programs on a regular basis for the U.S. Congress. Among their recent studies are evaluations of Head Start, public housing for the mentally disabled, and McKinney Act (Homeless) legislation.[40]

Intellectual debate is generally more vigorous in the arena of process studies than in work concerned with product and performance. That is not to say that there is no controversy with respect to product and performance studies. Rather, the issues at stake in the latter two arenas most frequently stem from the political, economic, and social context within which programs are developed, whereas the issues that underlie process studies are more likely to be related to intellectual and philosophical assumptions *about the social context itself.* For example, an analysis that is focused on a particular program's design might deal with such issues as whether there is utility in charging a fee for the use of a social service (as we do in Chapter 7), or whether there are advantages or disadvantages to offering benefits in cash versus in kind (as we do in Chapter 5). Analyses of performance seek to measure the effects, effectiveness, and efficiency of social welfare programs. In such studies, the purposes and objectives of the policies and programs are taken as a starting point. But in studies of process, analysts attempt to come to grips with such questions as: What large political and economic forces in society brought about these social welfare policies and programs? What are the factors that determine how communities meet changing social needs? The ways analysts deal with these questions are strongly influenced by their own cultural and philosophical values and by their *welt anzicht,* or world view.

The concepts used in this book to analyze the products of policy can be applied to social welfare programs in all societal contexts—capitalist, socialist, communist, or whatever. Similarly, the analytic methods used in the study of social welfare policy products (i.e., separating the components of choice in program design and examining the values and theories associated with these choices) do not vary in any considerable way from one social context to another. However, the study of process is heavily dependent on the analyst's basic intellectual and philosophical assumptions about the social context. The analyst is often guided by overarching ideas about the nature of human society; frequently, analysts may not even be aware of how these assumptions influence their own thinking.

Political Perspectives on the Study of Social Welfare Policy

The classic debate in the politics of social welfare pits individual versus collective values, values that offer starkly different expressions of the good society and the proper role of government within it (Table 1.2). Individualism, a philosophic orientation emphasizing the pursuit of individual (rather than collective) interests, embodies a faith in the opportunities afforded ordinary people to succeed in life by dint of their own aptitudes and ambitions. For many commentators, the widely held belief that achievement and effort go hand in hand constitutes the United States' basic ethos, the primary element of "American exceptionalism" accounting for our success as a prosperous, free nation.[41]

The collective perspective, on the other hand, reflects a very different understanding of proper conduct in society, one that recognizes the importance of common action on behalf of common goals. The collective impulse views social action—not individual action—as the key component of a society's well-being, and a necessary check on the divisiveness inherent in unchecked self-advancement.

The governing postulate of individualism—every person responsible for his or her own fate—represents the traditional vision of the American Dream. The postulate, always an essentially optimistic one, is built on a broadly held premise

TABLE 1.2   Political Perspectives on Social Welfare Policy

	The Individualist Perspective	The Collective Perspective
Political Ideology	Conservative	Liberal/Progressive
View of Social Problems	Problems reflect bad choices, personal dysfunction, culture of poverty	Problems reflect fundamental socioeconomic circumstances, barriers to access, lack of opportunity
View of Markets	Unregulated markets and private property insure prosperity and welfare	Unregulated markets create dangerous economic cycles, unemployment, urban blight, poverty and inequality, and environmental degradation
Responsibility of Government	Government should be small—a modest and decentralized adjunct to private institutions	Government should be large enough to advance social welfare on behalf of the broad community
Social Policy Agendas	Rely on private, voluntary, and religious arrangements; provide a minimum safety net focused on the poor	Rely on public leadership; provide broad program coverage to insure full opportunity, economic security, and basic social goods

that those who work hard and self-reliantly will be rewarded with material success. The implication, of course, is that those who fail in life fail due to personal inadequacy, lack of effort, or insufficient skill.

Individualism as a social philosophy finds its economic expression in the principle of *laissez-faire,* the theory that society works best when people can freely advance their own material self-interest within an unimpeded private marketplace. For conservatives, it is private action and private interests that result in an optimal level of welfare, with the entrepreneurial spirit successfully producing jobs, wealth, and great measure of economic security for all. As columnist George Will puts it, individualism and free-market capitalism have created "the most efficient anti-poverty machine the world has ever seen."

Politically, individualism is a fundamental element of conservatism. As is evident in the comments of Dwight Eisenhower, conservatism places primary value on the private institutions of society, with families, churches, and private associations viewed as basic institutions for "social intervention," not the state.

The rival perspective—the collective impulse—is represented in the economic and political ideas, parties, and movements of the left. Long associated with various strands of democratic socialism, progressivism, and social liberalism, collectivism holds that citizens—as a matter of right—are entitled to a "fair share" in society. For the left, society's problems are less the product of personal inadequacy than a consequence of socioeconomic malfunction. For much of this century, the core assumption of collectivism was that the problems of modern society were rooted in the greedy self-seeking of industrial capitalism. During the Progressive Era and the New Deal, for example, the left was preoccupied with confronting concentrated economic power and the problems of monopoly.

Nowadays, the collective approach is advanced less in the language of socialism and class conflict and more in the language of socioeconomic factors, opportunities, and social welfare. Although reconciled to the basic structures of capitalism, the left nevertheless still views individualism—in personal conduct and in markets—as a harmful instrument of inequality, social problems, and domination by social and economic elites.

CAPSULE 1.6:   The Individualist Perspective

All of us can sense a disturbing disposition on the part of many to seek solutions to their problems from sources outside themselves. Because life today is complex and interdependent, we seem always more ready to lean on government than upon ourselves. Such an approach can never retain the health and vigor of America. Rather, we must believe in and practice an approach founded on individual initiative, individual self-reliance, individual conscience, and individual voluntary effort.

Dwight David Eisenhower, 1957.

The politics of individuals and collectives, of right and left, confront each other most directly in their rival views of the role of government in society. Not surprisingly, individualists are suspicious of government action. Whereas Ronald Reagan, on several occasions, stated that "the best thing government can do is nothing," conservatives rarely reject the worth of public action *completely*. We need a military, and public roads, and basic education, and a structure of law to enforce the rules of fair play. But when it comes to social welfare, conservatives resist going beyond the minimum safety net required to protect the social order. They resist government action because public welfare is seen as undermining personal responsibility and impeding the marketplace. This was the rationale in 1935 for opposing social security—people wouldn't responsibly plan for their own futures if they were assured a retirement income—and it is the conservative rationale today for opposing health and social service initiatives.

The collective principle, on the contrary, unabashedly values government as the expression of the democratic will of the broad community, the one institution in society with the authority to protect the interests of all against the agendas of the few. For Franklin Roosevelt, "liberalism" was simply "plain English for a changed concept of the duty and responsibility of government toward economic life."[42] For the left, the mission of government is to counterbalance the market, to modify the power of selfish forces in favor of the whole, and to insure economic management for growth, employment, and fair wages. Whereas conservatives advocate minimum government, progressives stress active public responsibility to guarantee that basic human needs are addressed. In practice, progressive social policy is based on a broad egalitarian ethic, advancing an allocation of resources that reduces inequalities in society, whether they take the form of income differences, or excessive differences in education or health or housing.

CAPSULE 1.7:   The Collective Perspective

Little good is ever said for government as a whole. The public sector of the economy is seen, not as a course of wealth or form of income, but a burden on the economic system. We believe we are enriched by the production of automobiles, or cosmetics, but depressed and impoverished by expenditures on public education or food stamps for the always undeserving poor. [But] public services are not, in any respect, inferior to private goods and services. Clean streets are as much a part of our standard of living as clean houses. Public health measures are as likely to save lives as private hygiene. Our liberties are greatly enlarged by our public services—by good schools, good law enforcement, ample opportunities for recreation and self-development. Collective decision is, simply, an indispensable feature of public activity.

John Kenneth Galbraith, 1986.

Why Policy Analysis Is Relevant
to Direct Service Practitioners

We have observed that the study of social welfare policy may serve the interests of planners, administrators, and researchers. Another group of professionals also is responsible for carrying important policy-related functions. These are people who devote the major portion of their energies and resources to direct-service activities, such as caseworkers, probation officers, and group workers.

The practitioner directly involved in the provision of services to clients can play an important role in the formulation and execution of social service policies. Indeed, it is well recognized that the separation of policy formulation from policy execution is a delicate division, more characteristic of a porous membrane than of the solid line of bureaucratic hierarchy. Experienced practitioners often exercise considerable discretion in executing broad directives, and so shape as well as discharge organizational policies.

The importance of practitioner discretion for policy interpretation increases as organizations grow larger and more complex. Too frequently, however, the charge to the practitioner is delivered in oversimplified cliches to "get into the political arena" or to deal more effectively with "community elites."[43] Such demands can be demoralizing to professionals, particularly to those whose major energies are devoted to dealing with the problems of individuals and families. At best, a general call to arms without more specific instructions about which arms to use and how to use them is only temporarily inspiring; at worst, it is likely to leave many feeling inadequate.

A second reason for the direct practitioner's sense of inadequacy in policy formulation is that this task is not as well defined as others. In casework or probation, for example, the actual doing (counseling) and the objects of one's work (cases) are relatively clear. Many of the methods used in direct practice allow professionals to work within a series of fairly well-defined roles that usually have a high degree of consonance. The process by which policy is formulated, however, involves a wide range of roles that often strain against one another. Direct service, finally, tends to be *individual* practice—one social worker handling one case. Policy formulation, very differently, involves the efforts of many people.

In addition, the transmission of knowledge and skills in the field of social welfare policy is neither well-organized nor sharply defined. Participation in policy formulation requires expertise in a major area of service, and a comprehensive and extensive knowledge of a field. It also requires certain general analytic skills that may be taught to all in the helping professions. If policy formulation is seen as a process that entails many different tasks, roles, and transmissible analytic skills, then all professionals can learn to utilize the process and contribute to it in the most appropriate ways.

The fact that the direct-service practitioner's major functions are remote from the final decision points in the process of policy formulation makes many students less than enthusiastic to take courses in social welfare policy. Direct-practitioners are more inclined to concentrate on the development of interactional skills, on learning how to conduct themselves as professionals, and how to engage themselves with clients, colleagues, and community leaders and groups. The study of social choices and social values seems, to many, abstract and theoretical. But professionals who ignore social choices and social values in favor of developing practice skills are like musicians playing background music to a melody that seems to come from nowhere. Like musical themes, the directions and goals that are reflected in social welfare policy are neither accidental nor aimless; they develop because people make choices. One has to understand what the range of choices is, what values are implied in the alternatives, the framework within which these choices are made, the various means by which these choices are implemented, and the methodological tools that can be used to assess the consequences of these choices.

Although direct-service workers may be unconcerned with policy design, they are affected by it in important ways. In the long view, policy choices affect the technologies direct-service workers will use. Consider, for example, the ways in which changes in federal policies have affected the character and extent of the social services. The 1962 amendments to the Social Security Act placed great value on the provision of supportive casework services to welfare clients, and this choice was supported with substantial financial resources. In 1967 social welfare policy changed, and, along with the push for the separation of income and services, individualized therapeutic interventions were significantly deemphasized in favor of social services to reduce and prevent financial dependency. This was accomplished on a "matching" basis whereby the federal government paid $3 for every $1 spent by the states. Federal expenditures, in addition, were open-ended, meaning unlimited. As a result, federal social services costs by the early 1970s soared to more than $2 billion annually, up from practically nothing a decade earlier. Federal policy responded in 1974 with enactment of Title XX to the Social Security Act, which placed a "cap" (financial limit) on federal expenditures and required states to meet certain requirements. These included offering protective services to children and adults without regard to income, and spending at least 50 percent of their Title XX funds on people in the "categorical" programs (i.e., those receiving public assistance, such as Aid to Families with Dependent Children or Supplementary Security Income). In 1981, allocations for Title XX were reduced, and states were given virtually free reign in designing programs and targeting beneficiaries. Since that time the program's basic structure has remained virtually intact, although its ability to address social problems has been drastically reduced because funding has remained essentially fixed in dollar terms, which means a significant reduction in value terms. Federal spending after 1996 will be limited to $2.5 billion annually, considerably less than half the real, inflation-adjusted amount of 1981.

Later, we will examine some of the factors that were related to these changes in social choices and assess some of the values, theories, and assumptions underlying them. At this point we only want to illustrate how the kinds of social services that professionals offer, their magnitude, their clientele, and the conditions under which they are provided, are affected by public social policy. The direct-service practitioner who has the conceptual tools to analyze the dimensions of policy is more likely to be a participant in these changes rather than merely a product or victim of them.

Whether or not the direct practitioner *is* conversant with social welfare policy, the public *assumes* that those engaged in the provision of services can provide useful information about social welfare programs and their consequences. Legislators, politicians, and community groups turn to child welfare workers, probation officers, and mental health case managers for advice, and their advice is treated seriously—whether ill- or well-informed—because of their status as professionals. There is, then, at the very least, a professional obligation to be knowledgeable about policy matters.

Finally, many students now being trained as direct practitioners will, later on, become planners, administrators, and researchers because these positions are frequently filled within agencies on the basis of seniority. Direct-service professionals who will ultimately perform policy-related roles would be wise to link some part of their formal education to planning, organization, and analysis.[44] From a career point of view, it is essential that the direct practitioner have at least an appreciation of the dimensions of the field of social welfare policy, if not an intimate knowledge of its specializations.

Notes

1. See, for example, Martin Rein, *Social Policy* (New York: Random House, 1970), 3–20; Kenneth Bouding, "The Boundaries of Social Policy," *Social Work,* 12(1) (January 1967), 3–11; Richard Titmuss, *Essays on 'The Welfare State'* (London: Unwin University Books, 1963).

2. See, for example, David A. Gil, "A Systematic Approach to Social Policy Analysis," *Social Service Review,* 44(4) (December 1970), 411–26.

3. Alfred Kahn, *Theory and Practice of Social Planning* (New York: Russell Sage, 1969), 13; Rein, *Social Policy,* 211; Garth Mangum, *The Emergence of Manpower Policy* (New York: Holt, Rinehart, and Winston, 1969), 130.

4. See Neil Gilbert and Barbara Gilbert, *The Enabling State: Modern Welfare Capitalism in America* (New York: Oxford University Press, 1989), 18–19.

5. Robert Lampman, *Social Welfare Spending* (Orlando, FL: Academic Press, 1984), 27.

6. U.S. Bureau of the Census, *Who's Helping Out? Support Networks Among American Families*

(Washington, D.C.: U.S. Government Printing Office, 1988).

7. "Parents Fall Short on Child Support Payments," U.S. Census Bureau Press Release, May 13, 1995.

8. National Center for Health Services Research and Health Care Technology Assessment, *Research Activities,* July 1987, #87, 1–2.

9. Sheila Kamerman and Alfred Kahn, *Helping America's Families* (Philadelphia: Temple University Press, 1982).

10. "Mormons and the 'Sin' of Being Poor," *San Francisco Examiner,* December 19, 1982, A16.

11. Ibid.

12. Kamerman and Kahn, *Helping America's Families.*

13. Kathleen Murray, "Going Cubicle to Cubicle to Sell Them Insurance," *New York Times,* July 16, 1995, F10–11.

14. Gilbert and Gilbert, *The Enabling State,* 20.

15. U.S. General Accounting Office, *An Overview of the Working Uninsured,* Report #GAO/HRD-89-45, February 1989, 2.

16. Barnaby Feder, "Ministers Who Work Around the Flock," *New York Times,* October 3, 1996, C1. For a general discussion of EAPs, see Kathryn Troy, *Meeting Human Needs: Corporate Programs and Partnerships* (New York: Conference Board, 1986); and Paul Kurzman and Sheila Akabas (eds.), *Work and Well-Being: The Occupational Social Work Advantage* (Washington, D.C.: NASW Press, 1993).

17. Gilbert and Gilbert, *The Enabling State,* 20–21.

18. C.E. Born, "Proprietary Firms and Child Welfare Services," *Child Welfare,* 62(2), 1983, 109–118.

19. Harry Specht, "Social Work and the Popular Psychotherapies," *Social Service Review,* 64(3) (September 1990), 345.

20. Available evidence reflects a shift in professional social work toward private practice. National survey data reveal that the proportion of social workers reporting employment under profit-motivated auspices, mainly private practice, increased fourfold (3.3 percent to 12 percent) between 1972 and 1982. Findings from a Massachusetts survey in the mid-1980s indicate that 19 percent of the Licensed Independent Clinical Social Workers (the state's highest level of license for social work) were in private practice on a full-time basis and 26 percent on a part-time basis. See Gilbert and Gilbert, *The Enabling State,* 73; and Thomas McGuire, et al., "Vendorship and Social Work in Massachusetts," *Social Service Review,* 58(3) (September 1984), 372–83.

21. Phyllis R. Silverman, "Mutual Aid Groups," *Encyclopedia of Social Work,* 18th Edition, Volume 2, 1987, 171–75.

22. Ralph Kramer, "Voluntary Agencies and the Personal Social Services," in Walter W. Powell (ed.), *The Nonprofit Sector,* 1987, 240–45.

23. Roy Wallis, "Institutions," *Encyclopedia of the Social Sciences,* Volume 14 (New York: MacMillan, 1968), 410.

24. Abraham Flexner, "Is Social Work a Profession?" Presented at the Conference of Charities and Corrections, May 17, 1915.

25. Harold Wilensky and Charles Lebeaux, *Industrial Society and Social Welfare* (New York: Russell Sage, 1958), 138.

26. Ibid., 140.

27. For example, in Robert Perlman and Arnold Gurin, *Community Organization and Social Planning* (New York: John Wiley and Sons, 1972), an entire chapter is devoted to various ways in which the administrator of a direct-service agency is engaged in community organization and social planning tasks.

28. Carroll L. Estes, et al., *Fiscal Austerity and Aging* (Beverly Hills, CA: Sage Publications, 1983).

29. James Leiby, *The History of Social Welfare and Social Work in the United States* (New York: Columbia University Press, 1978).

30. Joseph Heffernan, *Introduction to Social Welfare Policy: Power, Scarcity, and Common Human Needs* (Itasca, IL: F.E. Peacock, 1979).

31. Frances Fox Piven and Richard A. Cloward, *Regulating the Poor: The Functions of Public Welfare* (New York: Pantheon Books, 1971).

32. Martha Derthick, *Uncontrollable Spending for Social Service Grants* (Washington, D.C.: Brookings Institution, 1975).

33. Linda Gordon, *Pitied But Not Entitled: Single Mothers and the History of Welfare 1890–1935* (New York: Free Press, 1994).

34. Neil Gilbert and Harry Specht, *Dynamics of Community Planning* (Cambridge, MA: Ballinger Publishing Co., 1977).

35. Theda Skocpol, *Boomerang: Clinton's Health Security Effort and the Turn Against Government in U.S. Politics* (New York: W.W. North & Co., 1996).

36. Howard Freeman and Clarence Sherwood, *Social Research and Social Policy* (Englewood Cliffs, NJ: Prentice-Hall, Inc., 1970), 13.

37. Mildred Rein, *Work or Welfare: Factors in the Choice for AFDC Mothers* (New York: Praeger Publications, 1970).

38. Steven P. Segal and Uri Aviram, *The Mentally Ill in Community-Based Care* (New York: John Wiley and Sons, 1978).

39. Jill Duerr Berrick and Neil Gilbert, *With the Best of Intentions: The Child Sexual Abuse Prevention Movement* (New York: Guilford Press, 1991).

40. See, for example, U.S. General Accounting Office, Early Childhood Programs, GAO/HEHS-94-169BR, May 1994; *Public Housing: Housing Persons with Mental Disabilities,* GAO/

RCED-92-81, August 1992; *Homelessness: McKinney Act Programs and Funding*, GAO/RCED-91-126, May 1991.

41. See Byron E. Shafer (ed.), *Is America Different? A New Look at American Exceptionalism* (New York: Oxford University Press, 1991).

42. Alan Brinkley, *The End of Reform: New Deal Liberalism in Recession and War* (New York: Alfred A. Knopf, 1995), 10.

43. Alan D. Wade, "The Social Worker in the Political Process," *Social Welfare Forum 1966* (New York: Columbia University Press, 1966), 52–67.

44. For a more detailed discussion of these curriculum issues, see Neil Gilbert and Harry Specht, "The Incomplete Profession: Commitment to Welfare vs. Commitment to Social Work," *Social Work, 19*(6) (November 1974), 665–74.

Chapter **2**

The Modern Welfare State

"The test of our progress is not whether we add more to the abundance of those who have much; it is whether we provide enough for those who have too little."
FRANKLIN DELANO ROOSEVELT
Second Inaugural Address, January 20, 1937

"You must rank me and my colleagues as strong partisans of national compulsory insurance for all classes for all purposes from the cradle to the grave."
WINSTON CHURCHILL
Radio Broadcast, March 21, 1943

"Central to any consideration of the 20th century is the huge steps taken in the direction of human well-being . . . in nutrition, in shelter, in the enjoyments, which no one should minimize, of a modern standard of living. Our century began with a small number of rich and a large, meager mass. The century is ending, in the fortunate countries at least, with a very large comfortable community."
JOHN KENNETH GALBRAITH
New Perspectives Quarterly, 13(1), Winter, 1996.

The contemporary welfare state, in its most prosaic terms, conveys the idea of significant government responsibility for social protection; in this sense, every modern industrial state is a welfare state. All utilize public intervention to ensure that neither bad luck nor economic distress nor social disadvantage fully determine the life chances of citizens. All have programs explicitly directed to combating misfortune and advancing opportunity and, as the U.S. Constitution states, providing "for the general welfare." And all spend substantially on social welfare—more than for any other single activity. In most, indeed, social welfare spending accounts for well over half of all government spending, whereas the majority of governmental civil servants work at planning and implementing social programs.

The Evolving Welfare State

Chapter 1 described the development of social welfare in the United States in terms of an evolution from a "residual conception" where helping was principally a function of families and charities to an "institutional conception" where the nation-state provides a broad range of social and economic protections. For Wilensky and Lebeaux, writing in 1958, the residual approach, represented by old-fashioned poor-law welfare—cash assistance for the poor—coexisted in the United States with an emerging institutional approach—something like the welfare state—which was represented by social insurance, public education, and other programs designed to help all individuals and families, not just impoverished ones.[1]

Whereas the residual to institutional pattern has characterized many societies, the road to the welfare state has followed different contours in different countries. In recent years, indeed, a significant body of scholarship has provided a portrayal of its distinctive features internationally.[2] Whatever their individual differences, however, all welfare states have evolved through a series of common historical sequences. These stages, presented in Table 2.1, provide a developmental overview of the welfare state from inception through retrenchment.

Inception

The welfare state was born over a century ago in an era of industrial change and great social and political ferment. For long periods prior to the end of the nineteenth century, of course, all nations had *some* public responsibility for welfare. The British Poor Law, for example, had replaced church responsibility for the relief of pauperism with government responsibility in 1603. But it was not until the invention of social insurance that traditional poor relief gave way to modern welfare.

Conceived in Germany in the 1880s, and very rapidly spread throughout the rich countries of the world, social insurance emerged in response to a common set of circumstances—the decline of rural agriculture, the transformation of farmers and peasants into industrial workers, and the jeopardy faced by increasing numbers of families as economic cycles of boom and bust disrupted their livelihood. Facing the issue of how to shield families from the hazards of industrial society, government leaders—often joined by labor and business—found an answer in social insurance.

The origins of welfare states throughout the world date to the enactment of these compulsory public programs. Recognizing the growing numbers of people who faced years of grinding destitution when they could no longer work, social insurance sought to *prevent* the most common risks of the industrial order—illness, old age and death, unemployment, and accidents—rather than dealing with them *after* the fact. On humanitarian and religious grounds, social insurance provided a minimum cash allotment to help people manage their lives with dignity, without the uncertainties and stigmas of private charity or poor relief. On

TABLE 2.1   The Evolving Welfare State

	Inception 1880s–1930s	Growth 1940s–1950s	Maturation 1960s–mid-1970s	Retrenchment Mid-1970s on
Political Developments	Growth of democracy; universal adult suffrage, development of union movement, social democracy, modern liberalism	Broad political consensus favoring increasing social spending; labor parties powerful in Europe, Democrats in the United States	New political constituencies advance civil and social rights for minorities, women, the disabled, and others	Conservative resurgence; tax revolt; weakening of unions, social democratic parties; welfare state delegitimized
Economic Developments	Golden era of unrestrained capitalism; economic dislocations of industrialization	Triumph of Keynesian economics after the Great Depression; powerful post World War II economic growth; low unemployment	Sustained prosperity and improved living standards through the mid-1970s; 1973 "oil shock" weakens Western economies	Slower economic growth; stagnating personal incomes; increased inequality; rise in European unemployment; strong demands on social security from an aging population
Key Social Policies	Poor law tradition gives way to new initiatives in social security (pensions, unemployment, health care); public spending reaches 5 percent of GDP	Growth in coverage of basic social security, health care, public aid programs, and family allowances	Broadened range of income, health care, and social service programs; public spending by mid-1970s averages 25 percent GDP in Europe, 20 percent in United States.	Few new programs; some erosion of public assistance safety net; modest curtailments in social security programs; spending levels stabilize
Role of Government	Beginning of national welfare leadership; decline of private institutions and localism	Broad expansion in national social financing, regulation, "universalization" of the constituency of the welfare state	New program emphasis on social and economic rights for minorities, excluded groups, and urban poverty populations; major increase in public employment	Reagan (U.S.) and Thatcher (U.K.) seek to reduce the size and scope of the welfare state; decentralization; privatization
Key Dates and Events: England and Europe	1886: Germany adopts health insurance; 1911: England enacts National Insurance Act; 1921: Austria adopts first family allowance	1941: British Archbishop Temple coins the phrase "welfare state"; 1943: Beveridge Plan provides welfare blueprint for post–World War II English society	1966: New Ministry of Social Security created in Great Britain; provides more generous supplementary benefits; 1971: New benefits to help the chronically ill	1979: Margaret Thatcher becomes Britain's Prime Minister, privatizes public housing and reduces pension payments
Key Dates and Events: United States	1913: Progressive federal income tax initiated; 1935: Social Security enacted	1953: Federal cabinet-level Department of Health, Education, and Welfare created	1964: War on Poverty initiated by Lyndon Johnson; 1965: Medicare and Medicaid enacted	1980: Ronald Reagan elected President; 1994: Republicans gain control of U.S. Congress; 1996: AFDC repealed

political grounds, it represented the growing strength of the working class in politics; given a greatly broadened franchise, ordinary people were able to demand, and secure, help from government. And the value of social insurance in promoting social harmony was not lost on the political and economic elites of the era. If workers had something to look forward to when they could no longer work, something to protect their families' futures, they would be far less likely to feel alienated from the labor force, resentful of their employers, or partial to radical politics.

The "birth" of the welfare state is usually traced to Germany's initiation of health insurance in 1883. Most of Western Europe soon followed Germany's lead, introducing health, accident, old age pension, and unemployment programs prior to World War I, with the United States belatedly enacting its national insurances during the Great Depression of the 1930s. Workman's compensation developed to meet the needs of industrial workers who were incapacitated by accidents. Health insurance responded to the risks of sickness. Pension insurance emerged to help those who grew too old or feeble to work.

The accumulation of these programs made social welfare something very different, in scope and in intent, from the traditional poor-law state with its focus on destitution and relief. Social insurance represented a recognition that private charity and family support—and help from friends and church members—simply weren't sufficient in the modern world. So governments took on new protective responsibilities, sponsoring, regulating, and financing insurance programs for certain risks and certain workers. The programs were compulsory; workers in particular job categories (at first, typically, manual workers and farmers), and often employers, *had* to participate. These workers, and their employers, had to pay at least a portion of the costs. And, most critically, social insurance provided a legal claim to benefits, making it an essential right of modern political life.

CAPSULE 2.1:   In the Beginning

Social insurance first took hold in the 1880s in Germany. Germany was, like the United States, industrializing very rapidly, a generation after England, but the historical context was different. The German government was dominated by a landed aristocracy, a proud ruling class, authoritarian but paternalistic, pious and public-spirited. It wanted modern industry, the basis of national wealth and imperialist power. Its leaders were displeased by the disorganization, exploitation, and misery of the English proletariat, however, and contemptuous of the English philosophy of liberalism and *laissez-faire* economics that seemed to justify it. Prince Otto von Bismarck, the prime minister, was sensitive to workers' grievances and in fact willing to pacify the workers through constructive measures for their welfare. In 1881 he introduced in the Reichstag a legislative program that ultimately created national health insurance (1883), accident insurance (1884), and disability and retirement insurance (1889).

James Leiby, *A History of Social Welfare and Social Work in the U.S.*, 1978, 197–98.

Although social insurance represents the *sine quo non* of the welfare state, its defining minimum, the emergence of modern welfare was accompanied by significant state action in other areas of social concern. State-sponsored public health and sanitation initiatives were common in the decades immediately before and after the turn of the century. Broad public education—especially at the secondary level—became commonplace by the outbreak of World War I. Workplace safety legislation and public housing were similarly widespread, and in the interwar period (1918–1939), child allowance programs were initiated throughout Europe providing cash help to ordinary families. Perhaps most significantly, the emerging welfare states all broadened their instruments of taxation—generally by imposing progressive taxes on income—to provide the wherewithal for their rapidly expanding responsibilities.

Finally, the evolving welfare state refined many of the old institutions and principles of poor relief. Called "public assistance" or "social assistance" in the modern era, these means-tested antipoverty programs, typically directed to particular groups of the needy, remained an essential safety net element in Europe and, far more so, in the United States, especially for those not connected to the labor market and therefore not covered by social insurance.

Growth

The years of the midcentury—the 1940s and 1950s—marked a period of significant expansion in the scope of social welfare activities, and the principle component of that growth, at least in terms of spending, was the elaboration of the social insurance initiatives of the earlier decades. Simply stated, once they had begun, the basic programs of income protection—for retirement, for the loss of a job, for accidents—progressively and insistently expanded in scope and coverage, shielding an increasing portion of the population, and absorbing an increasing slice of the budget. With the passage of time, programs that originally had been designed to address narrow circumstances and specific groups were liberalized, amended, and broadened toward universal coverage. At the same time, benefit levels, first established at near subsistence levels, were liberalized to meet mainstream standards of reasonableness.

In Germany, for example, the original programs of social insurance had been restricted to factory laborers. Within 25 years, however, most workers—farm and nonfarm, commercial and industrial—were covered. In England, the system of unemployment safeguards was broadened from its 1911 focus on seasonal employees to nearly the entire labor force. In the United States, the original Social Security Act, limited to retiring commercial and industrial workers and the unemployed, was regularly expanded, first to benefit widows and other survivors (1939), then to incorporate farm and domestic workers (1950), and later to protect the disabled (1956) and provide health care for the elderly (1965).

What this process of expansion produced was the inclusion of the middle class in the fabric of the welfare state. As social security benefits were universalized, all income groups grew to rely on public income support. As health, housing, and education programs became basic citizen entitlements, the welfare state drew in skilled workers and professionals. Even in the United States, where the public has always been ambivalent in its support of "welfare," social security drew in broad middle-class constituencies, as did less obvious welfare measures such as tax subsidies for home ownership and employer-sponsored health and retirement plans.

Maturation

Measured in terms of real spending, the growth of welfare states in the 1960s and early 1970s was unprecedented. By 1975, the nations of Western Europe devoted, on average, about a quarter of their Gross Domestic Product (GDP) to public social welfare; in the United States, the figure surpassed 18 percent. This increased spending partly reflected the continued expansion of the core social insurances (in significant measure, a consequence of the aging of the population in most all industrial nations) and partly reflected new initiatives aimed at improving the circumstances of the poor, minority groups, single women household heads, and others in society who had only a weak attachment to the labor force. As economic growth and prosperity advanced throughout the West, liberalized social attitudes created not only a new sensitivity to social injustices, but also a new readiness to support programs aimed at civil rights and economic opportunity. In Europe, for example, social policies broadened to aid the un- or underemployed through an assortment of job training, employment subsidy, and liberalized sickness and

---

CAPSULE 2.2:   The Golden Age

In the Golden Age, all the problems which had haunted capitalism in its era of catastrophe appeared to dissolve and to disappear. The terrible and inevitable cycle of boom and slump, so murderous between the wars became a succession of mild fluctuations thanks to—or so the Keynesian economists who now advised governments were convinced—their intelligent macro-economic management. Mass unemployment? Where was it to be found in the developed world in the 1960s, when Europe averaged 1.5 per cent of its labor force out of work and Japan 1.3 per cent? Only in North America was it not yet eliminated. Poverty? Of course most of humanity remained poor, but in the old heartlands of industrial labor what meaning could the *Internationale*'s 'Arise, yet starvelings from your slumbers' have for workers who now expected to have their car and spend their annual paid vacation on the beaches of Spain? And, if they fell upon hard times, would not an increasingly universal and generous Welfare State provide them with protection, undreamed of before, against the hazards of ill-health, misfortune, even the dreaded old age of the poor? Their incomes rose year by year, almost automatically. Would they not go on rising for ever? The range of goods and services offered by the productive system, and available to them, made former luxuries part of everyday consumption.

Eric Hobsbawm, *The Age of Extremes*, 1994, 267.

work initiatives. At the same time, many welfare states themselves became "virtual employment-machines," promoting full-employment policies and often providing, within the public sector, a significant source of new jobs.[3]

The welfare state expanded markedly in the United States as well, despite the United States' continuing reluctance to adopt the ideology of social welfare in any explicit fashion. Rising tax revenues in the early 1960s provided U.S. policymakers the opportunity to respond relatively painlessly (in a fiscal sense) to the heightened demands for social change created by the Civil Rights movement. The programs of the Great Society—job training, food stamps, Medicare and Medicaid, mental health, and social services—powerfully advanced the U.S. welfare state creating, in particular, policies directed toward improving the circumstances of African Americans, a group at that time still largely excluded from mainstream U.S. society. Their political exclusion was addressed by a variety of civil and voting rights enactments that, for the first time, enfranchised African Americans in the southern states. Housing and public accommodation laws significantly reduced long-standing patterns of segregation in schools, residences, offices, and public buildings. And, most germane to the welfare endeavor, new social legislation provided a range of services and benefits focused on the urban ghettos in which a large portion of African Americans lived.

Retrenchment

In 1973, the Organization of Petroleum Exporting Countries (OPEC), the oil producers' cartel, more than doubled the world price of crude oil, precipitating the "oil shock" that signaled the end of the economic golden age of the post–World War II era and the beginning of the "modern" period of slow growth, uncertain social progress, and increased questioning of the usefulness and affordability of social policy. In the 15 years prior to 1975, for example, social expenditures in Europe and the United States grew at an average of 6.5 percent per year. In the decade after, they grew at just 3.4 percent annually.[4]

Social welfare, throughout the West, even in the most advanced welfare states, has come under increased scrutiny as sluggish economies combined with increased demands for benefits—many of them driven by demographics—have produced high levels of economic insecurity, growing inequality in income and wealth, increasing class resentment, and a growing failure of tax systems to pay the cost of obligated spending. These social and economic failures have produced different political results in different welfare states. But in all countries, welfare has been under fire. In the social democracies of Europe, political regimes have been unable to contain the emergence of a level of unemployment unprecedented since the Great Depression. Whereas the core institutions of public social protection have remained largely intact, their cost has resulted in levels of deficit spending that increasingly threaten the basic fabric of the economy. Not one of the European welfare states—even those governed by the left—has been able to avoid reductions in social programs or benefit levels, and the magnitude of these cuts has accelerated rapidly since 1990.

CAPSULE 2.3:   Laying Off Nanny

Almost everywhere [in Europe today] there is a realization that the welfare-state ideal has gotten out of control.

From Britain to Italy, a drive is on to eliminate waste and corruption and to prune bloated bureaucracies. Tax incentives are being offered to the well-off to opt out of state pension schemes. Means testing is now commonplace. Services that once were free, such as hospital beds and child care, now attract charges. The age at which state pensions are paid is being raised.

Some of the reforms seems little more than common sense. Dutch students will soon be unable to travel free on public transport or to claim unemployment benefits as soon as they graduate. Private pension funds have been legalized in Italy after a 20-year debate.

Retirement at 58 will soon be a thing of the past in Germany, and "bad weather" payments for construction workers are to be scrapped. So is a Dutch program that paid jobless artists to paint.

No European country proposes to dismantle the "nanny state" entirely; the belief that it is government's duty to care for those in need is too deeply rooted, and grass-roots resistance is too fierce.

But even left-of-center politicians tacitly accept the need for change. In a gloomy speech to the European Parliament last week, socialist Jacques Delors, the European Commission president, warned that the European Community will have 30 million unemployed by 2000 if Europe does not become more competitive.

"Laying Off Nanny," *U.S. News & World Report,* October 25, 1993, 42.

In England and America, the reaction against social welfare has been virulent, and the scope of social policy change considerable. The victory of Margaret Thatcher's conservatives in Great Britain in 1979 and the election of Ronald Reagan in the United States in 1980 advanced explicit crusades against the welfare state. For Reagan and Thatcher, Newt Gingrich, and other New Right *laissez-faire*-ists, the decades of welfare growth were themselves viewed as a primary cause not only of economic decline but of community and family decay as well.

There are two ways of interpreting these recent changes in the character of the welfare state. One view is that they reflect the necessary corrective adjustment required in a period of fiscal retrenchment and demographic change. Economic growth has slowed considerably since the 1960s and early 1970s, budget deficits have soared, and unemployment rates have risen, even in those welfare states explicitly committed to full employment policies. The aging of the population, the most powerful single force pressuring outlays, is a near universal phenomenon, and one not likely to dissipate. These forces—structural forces—are having enormous impacts on the domestic policies of all the world's affluent nations. All are trimming social benefits over broad program areas in an oft-times undramatic but highly potent process of decrementalism.

In the United States, where cutbacks have been painfully noticeable, AFDC payments were reduced by half in real terms between 1970 and 1996,[5] housing benefits have been sharply cut, and public aid for noncitizens and drug and alcohol abusers has been slashed. Social security in the United States (and several European nations) has been trimmed by increasing the age for full eligibility. Even Sweden, the model of generous universal welfare, has extended wait times for unemployment and sickness eligibility, frozen children's benefits, and increased the pension retirement age.

The other interpretation of recent changes in the welfare state is that they represent something far more significant than modest corrective accommodations to financial and demographic trends. For many, recent changes in welfare represent a broad philosophical rejection of the conventional ideology of welfare entitlement. In the United States, for example, the reaction against the welfare state in the 1990s has come not only from the New Right, but from political moderates. Bill Clinton campaigned for the presidency in 1995 with a promise to "end welfare as we know it" by placing a two-year time limit on welfare receipt. And the Progressive Policy Institute (PPI), the policy arm of the Democratic Leadership Council (an organization Clinton helped organize in 1985), recommended measures to transform the very essence of social policy. The PPI blueprint for a new America advised:

> [T]he new administration must replace the welfare system with a new strategy for enabling America's poor. While the welfare state is organized around the goal of income maintenance, the enabling state should be organized around the goals of work and individual empowerment. Above all it should help poor Americans develop the capacity they need to liberate themselves from poverty and dependency. And it should do so directly, by-passing whenever possible public bureaucracies and service providers, and placing responsibility and resources directly into the hands of the people we are trying to help.[6]

The core ideas of the PPI report, according to Ben Wattenberg, represent "nothing less than a new public value system for Democrats, a move from the 'welfare state' to the 'enabling state.' "[7] These ideas resonate with the position taken by the Organization for Economic Cooperation and Development calling for a shift from a "passive" to an "active" society under which "the welfare system should be refocused and made less generous in terms of eligibility and benefits" and passive income supports should be replaced by measures designed to put people to work.[8] In England, the government's 1989 White Paper on Community Care similarly highlighted the "enabling role" of local social service providers, encouraging their use of private and voluntary providers.[9] Even in Sweden, Marklund observes, "the idea of welfare according to need has at least partly been replaced by incentive-oriented policies."[10]

What does a welfare philosophy based on work, self-help, private efforts, incentives, and personal responsibility mean for the future of social policy? Several of the essential characteristics of the conventional welfare state and the emerging "enabling" model are identified in Table 2.2.

TABLE 2.2   The Welfare State and Enabling State Compared

Welfare State	Enabling State
Expanding social rights	Linking rights to obligations
Focus on direct expenditures	Increasing indirect expenditures
Transfers in the form of service	Transfers in cash or vouchers
Delivery by public agencies	Delivery by private agencies
Policy focused on individuals	Family as unit of policy focus
Welfare benefits for consumption	Welfare benefits for investment
Reducing economic inequality	Restoring social equity

Source: Neil Gilbert, *Welfare Justice*, 1995.

Theories of Welfare Growth

Assuring significant economic protections to the mass of citizens has been one of the key achievements of the economically advanced nations of the twentieth century. The progress in approximately 100 years from the tentative, haphazard, and partial "welfare" of family, church, and volunteer-based charity to the systematic universal welfare of the modern state, of course, didn't emerge in an historic vacuum. State welfare was not simply an idea that suddenly won out over the hearts and minds of the leaders of the West. The welfare state, rather, although it was established on an intellectual foundation of considerable cogency and appeal, won out over alternative views of public responsibility because of two indispensable cophenomena: democracy and prosperity. Without universal suffrage, the dominant political *modus operandi* never would have become hospitable to the idea that the primary purpose of government was to serve the needs of people. Without material prosperity, the costly social insurances, health, housing, and social service programs of the modern era would simply not have been affordable.

In its political dimension, the welfare state developed hand-in-hand with electoral democracy. The expansion of voting rights to workers and to women—a process largely complete in Europe and the United States by 1918—increased demands for social protection and economic fair play. The universal adult franchise created a new electoral politics powerfully influenced by socialist ideology, working-class interest groups, and policy agendas promoting the responsibility of the state for collective well-being. According to "power resources" theorists, the expansion of social welfare paralleled the growing power of unions and parties on the left.[11]

In much of Europe, and to a degree in the United States, this broadened electoral participation shifted politics leftward. Social legislation that prior to World War I had seemed radical became the norm (first in Europe, then in the United States), with the atmosphere of progressivism most tangibly expressed in social services, workplace regulation (particularly the eight-hour workday), and social security. New labor-oriented parties strengthened in all the European countries, and the older liberal parties abandoned their traditional *laissez-faire* orientation.

By the time the Great Depression of the 1930s arrived, the response, most everywhere, was to expand the welfare state, with governments seeking to rescue their economies and assist their citizens through regulation, planning, and economic assistance.

For the standard-bearers of the welfare state—social democrats (in Europe) and New Deal/Great Society liberals (in the United States)—the major business of government became personal dignity and material well-being. Voters demanded welfare, whether or not they called it that, and modern political regimes aggressively advanced its instruments—income transfers, social services, minimum standards, and fair shares for all. From this perspective, the contemporary welfare state represents the hard-won political victory of ordinary working people over traditional economic and social elites.

One of the best-known explanations of the political dimension of the welfare state is that of T. H. Marshall, who interpreted the growth of welfare in terms of the historic evolution of the meaning of citizenship.[12] As industrial society developed, according to Marshall, the bonds tying people to their communities changed. In traditional preindustrial societies, human relationships were based on ascribed statuses; the individual's place in society was determined at birth and usually did not change. The social mobility and rapid change of modern societies, however, required a different form of social solidarity, and citizenship provided a "direct sense of community membership based on loyalty of free men endowed with rights and protected by common law." Civil, political, and social rights, according to Marshall, constituted the elements of citizenship, and these rights were perceived as developing through an evolutionary process. Civil rights (e.g., the right to trial by jury) develop first, political rights (the right to vote) next. These, in turn, lay the groundwork for social rights (the right to education and welfare).

Interestingly, Marshall did not believe that citizenship rights necessarily eliminated inequality; in fact, he argued that these rights often developed to ensure the stability of their social systems. The classic illustration, of course, is Bismarck's concession of social rights to German workers in the 1870s and 1880s. Bismarckian social legislation was quite explicitly intended to reduce the force of socialist demands for full civil and political rights.

Largely independent of politics is the economic dimension—the emergence and development of the welfare state as a corollary of modern industrialization. There is no question but that the phenomenal expansion of economic productivity that came with the Industrial Revolution created the means and the expectations for a welfare-oriented society. It was industrialization, of course, that created the very *need* for a new welfare system. Although politically oriented theories view the welfare state as a response to increasing demands from emerging political forces, economically oriented theories see welfare resulting from the essential character of modern industrial economies and their needs for labor, efficiency, and markets. One influential body of theory interprets welfare expansion in terms of "technological determinism," a theory that sees government action responding to the imperatives of economic modernization.[13] Industry's "need" for a highly educated, well-trained, reliable work force, for example, is seen as leading to health, welfare, and educational legislation to ensure the development and protection of that work force. This view posits that modern societies, whatever the exact nature of their political ideology, are converging in their essential features, increasingly mixing individual freedom and state controls.

A final explanation of the welfare state interprets the emergence of social programs as a facet of capitalist self-protection. Far from viewing the welfare state as a working-class victory, Marxists see social welfare as a strategic antidote to the instabilities of capitalism, a procedure for moderating class conflict and protecting the interests of commanding elites. In this sense, the welfare state is a "handmaiden" to capitalism, a way to regulate and control the conditions under which work is organized and wealth is distributed, a mechanism to pacify the working class and keep it subservient. *Regulating the Poor,* by Richard Cloward and Frances Piven, provides one powerful analysis of the U.S. system of social welfare from this perspective; James O'Connor's *The Fiscal Crisis of the State,* is another.[14] Marxism, of course, like technological determinism, is "grand" theory, useful for analyzing entire systems, but less helpful for looking at parts. And because Marxism is primarily focused on economics and class interest, it tends to ignore the independent influence of values, ideologies, and political institutions in the development of social welfare programs.

Is America Exceptional?

Although all welfare states share a variety of common attributes, they are markedly distinct in many of their essential aspects. They differ in size, in their relative emphasis on program fields, in their structure and financing, and in their underlying philosophical orientations. Some of the most dramatic of these differences separate the welfare states on both sides of the Atlantic, with the United States generally characterized as substantially less welfare oriented. The thesis of American exceptionalism, introduced in the previous chapter, has been widely advanced as a way of explaining the significant differences that exist between the United States and Europe.

Although both U.S. and European welfare states have sponsored large and complex systems of social insurance since World War II, the two traditions have diverged sharply in their underlying ideology and their protective breadth. European welfare states have been importantly motivated by a social ethos valuing equality and social solidarity, whereas the United States has cautiously developed its programs, emphasizing means-testing and private (philanthropic, as well as corporate) welfare provision.

These difference orientations have colored the spirit, the scope, and the magnitude of social welfare in their respective societies. Europe, with powerful labor organizations and social-democratic political parties, early on adopted a range of collectivist welfare policies, policies not only guaranteeing income security to employees unable to continue in the labor market, but also to ordinary, employed working-age families. The United States, more individualistic in its political culture, developed its social programs relatively late in the century, and never adopted many of the communalistic programs popular in other countries. Child allowances, national health care, broad labor market protections, and public housing and housing subsidies—all common features in Europe—have been either unknown, or of modest significance, in the United States. Furthermore, in the United States, national welfare authority has remained rudimentary, with great areas of responsibility left in the hands of state and local officials, officials often tending toward highly selectivist orientations.

Today's Welfare State

One of the great triumphs of the twentieth century has been the accommodation of capitalism and social justice—the development of productive stable market economies supported and advanced by the mass of ordinary citizens enjoying middle-class standards of living.

The world of developed market economies—the world of contemporary welfare states—posits the obligation of government to act when society's private institutions do not properly function. Organized public welfare is at the very core of Western societies, improving the daily lives of major segments of the population, and adding to the stability and humaneness of the economic order. Welfare states across the globe have not only substantially increased the level of economic protection, they have provided access to critical health and education services. Welfare safety nets generally insure basic levels of well-being to the poor, economic supports reduce the hardship of recession, and social insurance, for the first time in history, has largely severed the traditional linkage between old age and poverty. Although the nature of these achievements vary from country to country, all welfare states have succeeded in institutionalizing extensive structures of provision that have remarkably improved the well-being of society's most at-risk groups.

But what, exactly, *is* the welfare state? How *is* it to be defined? Although many definitions have been offered, perhaps the most substantive, in a programmatic sense, is that of Asa Briggs, who saw the essence of the welfare state in those governmental activities that were intended to "modify the play of market forces" to improve the well-being of citizens not able to manage on their own.[15]

Briggs specified three particular goals for the welfare state (see Table 2.3), and three corresponding forms of policy. The first goal is helping people maintain their economic security when various "social contingencies," such as unemployment, divorce, or old age, make normal self-support impossible. And one thing welfare state policy does well, and with considerable efficiency, *is* to buffer people from large drops in their standard of living when their income is interrupted. The largest welfare state programs indeed—the *first* pillar of all welfare states—are the social insurance policies that prevent economic insecurity by offsetting lost income.

TABLE 2.3   The Three Pillars of the Welfare State

Goals	Policies	Beneficiaries
Economic Security: Protect citizens from common life risks by replacing lost income	Social Security: social insurance against illness, unemployment, disability, retirement, death of a spouse	The working population, retirees, and their families and dependents
Material Sufficiency: Provide a basic floor of social protection	Public Assistance: cash relief and social services	The poor and disadvantaged
Basic Services: Insure access to critical goods and services	Education, health care, housing, nutrition	The broad citizenry

The basis of eligibility for these policies, it must be noted, is *not* chiefly poverty. These policies are *not* limited to those who are made poor by events beyond their control. The basis for governmental intervention, rather, is the loss of income from employment. Unemployed workers, for example, may not be impoverished, but they are generally entitled to unemployment insurance benefits; retiring workers may have reasonable earnings, yet they are entitled to retirement benefits. Social insurance programs protect against the range of conditions that results in a loss of job income. Because they are universal—because they cover everyone, regardless of income—social security programs are the costliest element in the budgets of all welfare states.

Briggs' second goal, "guaranteeing individuals and families a minimum income irrespective of the market value of their property," makes sure that people achieve at least a minimum level of material sufficiency. This is the antipoverty goal of the welfare state, and it is expressed in public assistance programs aimed at the poor. Some of these policies provide services, typically aimed at building skills and independence and helping the disadvantaged move into mainstream society, and some provide cash.

Poverty relief, of course, has always been implicit in poor law and public assistance legislation. In the United States, indeed, it was made a principal domestic priority by President Lyndon Johnson in 1964 when he declared "unconditional war on poverty in America." Antipoverty policies, in contrast to social security, are targeted on those who fall below a recognized minimum income. They are not meant to assist the broad spectrum of the population, but rather aid special groups with special needs. One of the most common ways of determining eligibility for these programs is by a means test, an administrative procedure that limits benefits to those whose incomes and assets fall below a certain, usually very modest, level. Because these programs are focused on the relatively small proportion of citizens who are poor, they are considerably smaller in magnitude than universal social insurance policies.

The third welfare state goal identified by Briggs, "ensuring that all citizens without distinction of status or class are offered the best standards available in relation to a certain agreed range of social services," means helping people secure those fundamental goods and services that society considers essential. The leading example of such a basic service, of course, is public education. Free public schooling at elementary and secondary levels is provided as a basic right of citizenship in all welfare states; parents are compelled to send children of specific ages to school. Higher education is typically not free, but governments often subsidize tuition and otherwise help students and their families meet college costs. Such help may or may not bear any relationship to financial need in the narrow sense, but it is given in recognition of the difficulties most families have in planning for—or borrowing for—the costs of college, and also in the faith that society as a whole benefits from encouraging more people to seek higher education. In addition to education, contemporary welfare states generally promote nutrition programs, day care, and housing. In most all welfare states (but *not* the United States), free, comprehensive, universal health care is a right of citizenship. In the United States this has never been a goal of public policy although a considerable amount is spent on health, especially for the elderly and the poor.

Although these three objectives serve to define a core public policy agenda in all advanced industrial economies, it is not entirely accurate to say that the institutional model has won the day. Despite its significance in contemporary life, the welfare state remains an ambiguous, vulnerable enterprise, retaining important elements of residualism. Eligibility requirements, for example, often reflect the concept of public intervention as a last resort, available only when personal resources have been exhausted. Although it is an essential political and economic institution in Western Europe, the United States, Canada, New Zealand, Australia, and Japan, the welfare state is nevertheless subject, as we have seen, to sustained political criticism, especially from the right.

A final word is important to add on the issue of *redistribution,* which is traditionally an important concern of the social democratic, progressive left. Briggs' model says little about the role of the welfare state in achieving redistribution in society, in promoting policies that seek some significant measure of socioeconomic equality. Little has been said about redistribution simply because, although not uncommon, it is hardly an *essential* feature of welfare states. Although a prominent theme among the early socialist theorists of "womb to tomb" social welfare—the British Fabians in particular—and still a guiding principle among the nations of Europe with powerful social democratic movements, particularly the countries of Scandinavia, it is not, nor has it been, universally characteristic. The organization of social welfare in the United States, Japan, Austria, New Zealand, France, and most welfare states, indeed, has largely followed the model pioneered by Germany, systems largely built on social insurance, with eligibility for benefits related to prior employment, and benefit levels related to prior salary or wages. Although egalitarian, redistributive principles have made *some* headway in all welfare countries (most all, for example, have universal child allowances and universal access to health care), the ideal of comprehensive, generous benefits for all, based on citizenship (à la Marshall), rather than a connection to work, is hardly dominant, and is becoming ever the less common.

Welfare Scope

The enormous scope of the welfare state in all the rich nations of the world attests to its fundamental role in late twentieth-century society. The clearest way of indicating this scope is to examine expenditures, the money outlays governments actually devote to addressing their welfare goals. Although this approach understates the size of the welfare institution because it omits private (nongovernmental) expenditures and indirect (nonspending) tax benefits, it nonetheless yields an impressive picture.[16] As Table 2.4 indicates, public social spending (excluding education) as a portion of GDP ranges from 16 percent (United States) to 40 percent (Sweden) among 14 major welfare states, with an average about 20 percent.

Table 2.5 focuses on the United States, showing the magnitude of the U.S. welfare effort since 1950. One of the most significant findings, not unexpectedly, is the significant increase in total spending—not only in absolute dollars, but in proportion to the overall economy (i.e., as a percent of GDP). The most rapid growth occurred between 1965 and 1975, when spending increased nearly fourfold and the GDP portion nearly doubled, from 11.5 percent to 19.1 percent. Since the mid-1970s, change has been far less dramatic, with virtually no GDP expansion

TABLE 2.4   Public Social Welfare Spending, Excluding Education, as a Percent of GDP, Selected Years

	1960	1970	1980	1990
Austria	15.9	18.9	23.4	24.7
Belgium	——	19.3	25.4	25.8 (1988)
Canada	9.1	11.8	14.4	18.6
Denmark	——	19.1	25.7	26.6 (1988)
Finland	8.8	13.6	21.4	27.1
France	13.4	16.7	23.5	26.0 (1988)
Germany	18.1	19.5	25.4	24.0 (1989)
Italy	13.1	16.9	19.7	23.4 (1988)
Japan	4.0	5.7	10.5	11.6
Netherlands	11.7	22.5	25.7	26.8 (1988)
Norway	7.9	16.1	21.3	28.7
Sweden	10.8	16.8	32.4	33.9
United Kingdom	10.2	13.2	19.4	20.3 (1988)
United States	6.8	9.5	13.7	16.8 (1992)
Average	10.9	15.8	21.6	23.7

Source: Figures for 1960–1990 (except for United States) from OECD, *New Orientations for Social Policy*, 1995, Paris, 57–60, and *OECD Economies at a Glance: Structural Indicators*, 1996, Paris, 105–111. U.S. figures from Ann Kallman Bixby, "Public Social Welfare Expenditures Fiscal Year 1992," *Social Security Bulletin*, 58(2), Summer 1995, 70.

TABLE 2.5   U.S. Public Social Welfare Spending, Selected Years

Spending	1950	55	60	65	70	75	80	85	90	93
Billions $	24	33	52	77	146	289	493	732	1159	1364
% GDP	8.8	8.5	10.3	11.0	14.2	18.2	18.1	17.8	18.5	21.1

Source: *Annual Statistical Supplement to the Social Security Bulletin,* 1996, 158.
The figures include education spending, and are therefore larger than those in Table 2.4.

between 1975 and 1990, and just a small increase since, mainly in response to the recession of the early 1990s.

Welfare Realms

Spending on social welfare, compared to the size of the overall economy, is the most widely used indicator of a country's welfare effort. And it *is* a very helpful indicator for representing, and for tracking over time, a nation's commitment to the welfare objectives we have identified. Nevertheless, figures of the sort represented by Table 2.5 have distinct limitations. As noted, they omit *private* spending on social welfare, whether organized on a for-profit or nonprofit basis, and they don't incorporate the value of all of the less-organized forms of social welfare provided informally through families, churches, and other mutual assistance arrangements. In addition, public spending tells us nothing about the scope of workplace employee benefits. These vitally important activities are hidden from view in any accounting system that simply reports direct government outlays.

Even when we focus on the *public* side of the welfare state, direct outlays provide an incomplete measure of the value of government programs. Regulatory programs, for example, although relatively inexpensive in terms of their direct costs, have enormous social and economic impacts. Affirmative action and antidiscrimination measures, for example, have significantly broadened job and educational opportunities for groups that have been excluded from full participation in U.S. life, while minimum wage and workplace safety laws have vastly improved working conditions.

The figures in Table 2.5, finally, don't provide any indication of the *kinds* of activities public dollars are supporting, or the groups or classes who are receiving help. It provides an *overall* social welfare price tag, but very little in the way of the particulars.

There are, of course, a variety of ways in which the U.S. welfare "product" might be detailed. Among the most common classification systems are those by functional fields (e.g., health, criminal justice, education), problem areas (e.g., domestic violence, homelessness, unemployment), and population groups (e.g., children, adolescents, the aged). There is considerable overlap among these

---

CAPSULE 2.4: "The Revolution No One Noticed"

While Americans were preoccupied with the turmoil of the 1960s—the civil rights movement and the war in Vietnam—a revolution no one noticed was taking place. For many years, the argument for increased attention to social welfare in America had followed clear lines: The United States was spending the largest portion of its budget for defense; programs for people who were poor, sick, aged, or minorities were underfinanced. Social welfare proponents contended that in order to be more responsive to the needs of its citizens, the nation should "change its priorities" and spend more for social programs to reduce poverty and less on wars like that in Vietnam. The argument ended with a call for a change in national priorities.

In a single decade America's national priorities were reversed. In 1965, national defense expenditures accounted for 43 percent of the federal government's budget; social welfare expenditures (social insurance, health, and public assistance) accounted for 24 percent. While the mass media focused on the war in Vietnam and Watergate, a revolution in national policy from "guns to butter" was occurring. By 1975, defense accounted for only 26 percent of the federal budget and social welfare expenditures had grown to 42 percent of the budget. Twenty years later, in 1995, social welfare expenditures account for about 55 percent of the federal budget. Health programs alone (primarily Medicaid and Medicare) comprise about 18 percent of the total budget. Only 18 percent of the 1995 budget is devoted to national defense. Social welfare is clearly the major function and major expenditure of the federal government.

Diana DiNitto, *Social Welfare, Politics and Public Policy*, 1995, 40.

realms. The line between functional fields and problems is rather fuzzy; it appears to be less substantive than definitional. The U.S. Social Security Administration's classification of social welfare expenditures indicates a functional division in terms of social insurance and public aid (i.e., income maintenance), health, education, and housing programs. But there is one special classification based on group affiliation (veteran's programs) and a residual category of "other" social welfare, which includes a problem area (juvenile delinquency) as well as group-classified programs such as child welfare.[17]

Spending Programs

When defined in terms of U.S. Social Security Administration categories, the realm of social welfare can be viewed in terms of its most important program components. As indicated in Table 2.5, the major element in the overall social welfare budget, not unexpectedly, is social insurance, a program that between 1950 and 1993 enlarged from $5 billion to $657 billion, and from 1.8 percent to 10.2 percent of GDP. Public assistance, the antipoverty component of welfare, quadrupled its GDP portion, from 0.9 percent to 3.4 percent, over the same period, while education doubled its share.

Table 2.6, not unexpectedly, shows substantial growth in all the major welfare state programs over the past 40 years. Not unexpectedly, because social welfare as

**TABLE 2.6   U.S. Public Social Welfare Spending
by Major Program Sectors, Selected Years**

Program	1950	60	65	70	75	80	85	90	93
Social Insurance									
Billions $	$5	19	28	55	123	230	370	561	657
% GDP	1.8%	3.8%	4.0%	5.3%	7.7%	8.5%	9.0%	9.0%	10.2%
Public Assistance									
Billions $	$2	4	6	16	41	73	98	181	221
% GDP	0.9%	0.8%	0.9%	1.6%	2.6%	2.7%	2.4%	2.6%	3.4%
Health & Medical									
Billions $	$2	4	6	10	17	27	39	66	75
% GDP	0.8%	0.9%	0.9%	0.9%	1.1%	1.0%	0.9%	1.1%	1.2%
Education									
Billions $	$7	18	28	51	81	121	172	277	332
% GDP	2.5%	3.5%	4.0%	5.0%	5.1%	4.5%	4.2%	4.5%	5.1%
Other									
Billions $	$7	7	9	14	27	42	54	74	79
% GDP	2.8%	1.3%	1.2%	1.3%	1.6%	1.3%	1.0%	1.3%	1.2%
TOTAL									
Billions $	$24	52	77	146	289	493	732	1159	1364
% GDP	8.8%	10.3%	11.0%	14.2%	18.2%	18.1%	17.8%	18.5%	21.1%

Source: Annual Statistical Supplement to the Social Security Bulletin, 1996, 156–68.
Social insurance includes Medicare; Public assistance includes Medicaid.

a public institution came into its own in the latter half of the twentieth century, emerging as the main focus of domestic policy in all the rich countries. What the table shows only indirectly, however, is the fact that the greatest portion of welfare growth reflects spending on the elderly, spending not only in the form of pension payments under social insurance, but also in the form of medical programs (Medicare and Medicaid) and public assistance. Of all the factors accounting for the transformation of modern public budgets, none match the increased size, and effective demands, of the elderly. At the federal level, indeed, almost *all* noninterest spending growth since 1960 can be explained by expanded benefits for the retired.[18]

The figures in Table 2.6 also indicate the very considerable degree to which the U.S. welfare state has become an instrument of middle-class social welfare. Social security, most notably, comprises a network of medical and income entitlements aimed at providing economic security over the life cycle of ordinary families, a network that absorbs just about half of all dollars spent on welfare. Though the public at large often views the welfare state as "welfare"—AFDC/TANF and food stamps and other parts of the safety net—these programs, in the aggregate, are exceedingly modest in size.

Another way of expressing this middle-class tilt is to note the very modest size of redistributive spending. In the United States, social policy—very much in the Bismarckian tradition of work-based social insurance—is closely linked to employment. Social security is the largest single program, and benefits under social security are strongly tied to previous earnings. Relatively affluent workers, in other words, become relatively affluent retirees. Programs that focus on the poor (public assistance) are small, and programs that aim to distribute basic services to all, regardless of income level (like national health care) are generally absent.

Social, Occupational, and Fiscal Welfare

The realms of welfare state policy may be seen from another perspective, one that goes beyond direct spending, and beyond a focus on the public sector. This approach, first designated by Richard Titmuss, sees not one but three complimentary systems of welfare: social, occupational, and fiscal.[19]

The *social* component discerned by Titmuss corresponds to the "direct expenditure" approach utilized by OECD and the U.S. Social Security Administration to organize the spending data in Tables 2.4, 2.5, and 2.6. Basically, they equate social welfare with the provision of a range of publicly sponsored goods and services—income support, health, social services, and the like. The *occupational* system, on the other hand, comprises the system of welfare associated with employment, chiefly the fringe benefit arrangements identified in the previous chapter. *Fiscal* welfare, finally, involves the income side of the budget coin. Specifically, it identifies those features of the tax-raising system, such as special tax deductions and credits, that advance explicit social objectives.

According to Titmuss, all three welfare systems share a fundamental social character and goal. That is, each constitutes a primary area of collective intervention aimed at meeting individual and societal needs. Although many question the appropriateness of defining the welfare system in such extensive terms, today there is broad recognition among policy scholars and analysts, as well as among policymakers themselves, not only of the important role played by each of these separate arrangements in affecting citizens' well-being but also the varying ways in which each of the systems affect one another. There is also considerable evidence that over the past several decades the scope of fiscal and occupational welfare has grown at least as rapidly as traditional social expenditures.

The Titmuss model illuminates the broad range of organized welfare and the artificiality of narrowly equating welfare with government outlays. For Titmuss, analyses of welfare that limit themselves to public outlays present distorted, and overly sanguine, views of the true character of the welfare state. One of the most obvious distortions can be seen in how the beneficiaries of organized welfare activities are identified. Because occupational welfare generally mirrors employment status, its benefits are distributed in much the same ways as wages and salaries. That is, health, pension, and other perquisites of employment are first and foremost a function of job status. One must be employed, or related to someone who is employed, to receive them. And because their value generally increases with income, managerial and professional workers are eligible for broader and more lucrative benefits than blue-collar or intermittently employed workers.

Although occupational welfare is restricted in scope, and inversely related to need, it is nevertheless extremely important to a broad segment of the population. In 1992, for example, benefits averaged $14,807 per employee, 41 percent of the average worker's total compensation.[20] Over half (51 percent) of all firms offer life insurance to employees' dependents, 85 percent cover their retirees' medical insurance, and 27 percent offer full hospital room and board.[21] Smaller numbers of firms offer programs such as adoption services, health promotion, legal assistance, child and elder dependent care, and drug and alcohol counseling and treatment. Today, fully one-third of the 65-plus population receives regular employee pensions.

For Titmuss, occupational welfare is a form of "collective intervention" because its scope and character reflect public policy. In other words, despite their nominal "private" character, job benefits are significantly influenced by government. Public policy in the form of special tax arrangements—notably the deductibility of employee benefit costs as a regular business expense—has been a powerful inducement for private employers to sponsor health and welfare programs. From the employees' point of view, fringe benefits are also specially advantageous, because benefits such as health insurance are not taxed, whereas an equivalent cash payment—provided as salary—would be. Other employer-provided fringe benefits, such as pension contributions, are tax deferred until retirement, at which time they are subject to several tax advantages. Thus, although these benefits have a cash value that is the equivalent of wages in the employment contract, this cash value is substantially tax exempt. To the extent that these benefits escape taxation they constitute government subsidies ("welfare," it might be argued), in the same manner as other social provisions.

The chief idea of Titmuss's third classification—fiscal welfare—is that the tax system itself serves as an important instrument of social policy, above and beyond its role as a source of revenue. Acting through a number of special tax measures, fiscal welfare advances welfare objectives in much the same fashion as direct spending. Federally financed public housing and housing allowances for the poor, clearly within the realm of direct social welfare, are akin to benefits derived from such fiscal measures as the income tax deduction for interest payments on home mortgages. Similarly, deductions and credits for charitable contributions, occupation-based health and pension plans, and child care are substantially equivalent to direct subsidies. As Titmuss stated, "The tax saving that accrues to the individual is, in effect, a transfer payment. In their primary objectives and their effects on individual purchasing power there are no differences. Both are manifestations of social policies in favor of identified groups in the population."[22]

In an effort to quantify the value of such fiscal measures and increase public awareness of their importance, Stanley Surrey, a one-time U.S. Treasury Department official, invented the concept of the "tax expenditure." According to Surrey, these are "deviations" from the normal tax code that serve to affect the private economy in ways that normally are achieved by spending. Surrey estimated the value of these deviations, which were not counted in ordinary budget tabulations, to be about one-quarter of the regular federal budget.[23] As a result of

Surrey's work, Congress in 1974 ordered an annual accounting of tax expenditures to accompany the regular federal budget.

The large number of people that benefit from tax expenditures, and the view that these provisions amount to a form of public subsidy, has led some analysts to claim that "everyone is on welfare."[24] For others, however, there are important differences between a system of fiscal measures such as tax expenditures and traditional social welfare. Irving Kristol, for example, challenges the view that these benefits are similar to direct social welfare provisions. To think of tax deductions as subsidies, he states, "implicitly asserts that all income covered by the general provisions of the tax law belongs of right to the government, and what government decides, by exemption or qualification, not to collect in taxes constitutes a subsidy."[25] In other words, allowing citizens to keep money they earned that is spent or invested in ways that benefit the individual or society is not the moral or functional equivalent of taking money from those who can afford to pay taxes and distributing it as cash benefits to those in need.

Tax expenditures—loopholes, to their detractors—are, of course, different in many ways from direct spending. For one thing, like occupational welfare, they tend to benefit better-off taxpayers the most. Often described as upside-down subsidies, they generally provide the greatest dollar value to those in the highest tax brackets. The deductibility of charitable contributions, for example, clearly helps voluntary hospitals, universities, and social services agencies, but it just as clearly reduces the tax liability of the rich far more than of ordinary taxpayers. Because the poor usually pay no federal income taxes at all, of course, they get no immediate benefit.

Whereas tax expenditures can be portrayed as returning funds to the private sector, lessening public intrusion, and foregoing public income to promote private action—all conservative preferences—Titmuss is clearly correct in his contention that tax policies constitute critical elements in social policy. Although the overall distribution of these indirect outlays does not help those most in need, taxation remains a key instrument for implementing public aims. Fiscal welfare and occupational welfare are analogous to regular spending, and all three systems must be assessed if one is to understand, or to affect, the nature of contemporary social welfare. Occupational, fiscal, and social welfare can each be assessed as a distinct phenomenon, but their interactions have a major bearing on the nature of the overall welfare system.

The occupational system, for example, frequently supplements public provisions, as with retirement pensions. In areas such as health insurance, it often provides support where government action is absent. Of course, meeting social needs through the occupational system discourages the development of public policy to meet the needs of those who are not employed. The repeal of the short-lived Catastrophic Medicare Bill of 1988 reflected, in large measure, the broad coverage provided by private "medi-gap" policies to retired workers. A major concern on the left, therefore, is that occupational welfare—welfare principally for the middle classes and well-to-do—undermines support for the mainline welfare state. Public provision is already a dubious public objective; an expanded occupational system, it is feared, may further reduce the constituency for government efforts on behalf of the disadvantaged.

The provision of social welfare transfers through indirect tax expenditures, such as deductions for mortgage interest and exclusions on employee benefits, has grown dramatically in recent decades. Between 1970 and 1995, for example, the number of tax expenditure items in the federal code increased by almost one-third, from 71 to 115. In the area of income maintenance alone, the value of benefits funded through indirect outlays grew at a faster rate than benefits financed through direct expenditures, rising from $25 billion in 1978 to $82 billion in 1995.[26]

Regulatory Welfare

There is a significant limitation in utilizing a conception of social welfare that is restricted to concrete benefits—be they occupational or public; income, goods, or services; or funded through outlays or through tax arrangements—because they ignore the importance of other sorts of vital interventions. At all levels of government, public activities that enhance community well-being involve more than simply the allocation, directly or indirectly, of income or services.

Social welfare objectives, most immediately, are also advanced by the regulatory powers of government. Regulatory powers, of course, have long been used to pursue health and safety goals in employment, day care, and housing and the licensing and certifying of residential facilities and hospitals. Today's social regulation, far broader in scope, advances a variety of explicit social objectives, many of which couldn't otherwise be pursued because of budgetary restrictions.

One such area of regulation imposes obligations on the private sector to help needy groups such as children and the handicapped, therefore reducing the need for direct public programs. Thus, for example, many state and local governments have enacted child-care ordinances affecting developers of commercial properties. In San Francisco, a typical instance, major developers must either provide on-site care for employees' children or else pay $1 per square foot into a special fund to support centers throughout the city.[27] At the state level, Massachusetts has extended access to health care throughout the commonwealth by requiring private businesses to provide medical insurance to all their employees. Other states require private insurance plans to cover a variety of populations and procedures. For example, employers may be obligated to extend insurance coverage to family dependents, such as newborns, as well as to handicapped workers, those needing alcohol treatment, and those requiring home health care. In the early 1980s, California prohibited insurance companies from denying coverage for the services of social workers, dentists, podiatrists, speech and hearing therapists, and professional counselors and psychologists.

Such mandated benefits—benefits by regulation—permit government to address social and health problems without having to spend money or raise taxes. Regulation, of course, is not without costs. The private sector pays in one fashion or another, either through higher insurance rates or higher consumer prices. Some regulations may even result in firms withdrawing benefits. It has been argued, for example, that state-mandated programs have caused many small employers to drop employee health coverage altogether.[28] In a similar vein, many contend that stringent rent control ordinances lead to a decreasing number of available rental units.

Social regulation also affects the realm of private life and families. In the 1980s, for example, a broad political consensus emerged in support of federal regulations to ensure fair child-support payments from absent parents. To increase payment levels and to enforce compliance with court-ordered child-support rulings, federal enactments powerfully strengthened the influence of government over family behavior. The 1984 Child Support Enforcement Amendments required states to establish procedures for withholding support payments from the wages of delinquent (i.e., nonpaying) parents. Later enactments required paternity determinations at birth and compelled states to establish and utilize uniform standards for child-support payments. Perhaps most important, the 1988 Family Support Act required states to withhold wages in cases in which court child-support orders were violated. Because the vast majority of absent fathers are not currently paying support for their children on a regular basis, these federal regulations are likely to increase the income level of one-parent households.

Such regulatory interventions can advance welfare state goals. Although someone winds up paying for each measure—be it employers, employees, or separated parents—such approaches substantially broaden the range of ways in which government can address problems. Regulatory substitutes for spending programs, especially attractive in an era of fiscal constraint and tax and spending limits, are likely to expand in importance in the years ahead.

Summary

It should be evident by now that social welfare is pluralistic and multifaceted, involving major institutional sectors, governmental levels, and societal realms organizing help to people through a complex enterprise of formal and informal, profit-making and altruistic, and private and public endeavors. It should be clear, as well, that the overall nature of social welfare in society is powerfully influenced by government. And this is the distinguishing feature of the modern welfare state: government stands as the single institution in society with the authority and resources to act broadly and comprehensively on behalf of the common good. Government alone is able to compel citizens (through taxes) to serve the interests of the broad community, to insure that isolated individuals—individuals apart from private and informal and personal networks of help—get assistance in time of need, to guarantee that no one falls beneath a minimum level of well-being, and to redistribute resources and promote equality.

Notes

1. Harold Wilensky and Charles Lebeaux, *Industrial Society and Social Welfare* (New York: Russell Sage, 1958), 138.

2. See, for example, J. Ambler (ed.), *The French Welfare State* (New York: New York University Press, 1991); R. Cos, *The Development of the Dutch Welfare State* (Pittsburgh: Pittsburgh University Press, 1993); Christopher Pierson, *Beyond the Welfare State* (University Park, PA: The Pennsylvania State University Press, 1991).

3. Gosta Esping-Anderson, *The Three Worlds of Welfare Capitalism* (Princeton, NJ: Princeton University Press, 1990), 149.

4. Organization for Economic Cooperation and Development, *The Future of Social Protection* (Luxembourg: OECD, 1988), 11.

5. Robert Pear, "Typical Relief Check in 1996 Was Worth Half That of '70," *New York Times*, November 19, 1996, A10.

6. Will Marshall and Martin Schram (eds.), *Mandate for Change* (New York: Berkeley, 1993), 228.

7. Ben Wattenberg, "Let Clinton Be Clinton," *Wall Street Journal*, January 20, 1993, 12.

8. Organization for Economic Cooperation and Development, *Economic Surveys: Netherlands* (Paris: OECD, 1991), 89, and OECD, "Editorial: The Path to Full Employment: Structural Adjustments for an Active Society," *Employment Outlook* (July 1989).

9. Maria Evandrou, Jane Falkingham, and Howard Glennerster, "The Personal Social Services: Everyone's Poor Relations But Nobody's Baby," in John Mills (ed.), *The State of Welfare: The Welfare State in Britain Since 1974* (Oxford: Oxford University Press, 1990).

10. S. Marklund, "The Decomposition of Social Policy in Sweden," *Scandinavian Journal of Social Welfare*, 1(1) (1992), 10.

11. See Paul Pierson, "The New Politics of the Welfare State," *World Politics*, 48(2) (January, 1996), 150–53.

12. T.H. Marshall, *Sociology at the Crossroads and Other Essays* (London: Heinemann, 1963).

13. See Reinhard J. Skinner, "Technological Determinism," *Comparative Studies in Society and History*, 18(1) (January 1976), 2–27; and J.K. Galbraith, *The New Industrial State* (London: Hamish Hamilton, 1967).

14. Frances Fox Piven and Richard A. Cloward, *Regulating the Poor: The Functions of Public Welfare* (New York: Pantheon Books, 1971); James O'Connor, *The Fiscal Crisis of the State* (New York: St. Martin's Press, 1973).

15. Asa Briggs, "The Welfare State in Historical Perspective," *European Journal of Sociology*, 2 (1961), 221–58.

16. For estimates that include tax expenditures and control for social factors related to need, see Neil Gilbert and Barbara Gilbert, *The Enabling State: Modern Welfare Capitalism in America* (New York: Oxford University Press, 1989).

17. Ann Kallman Bixby, "Public Social Welfare Expenditures, Fiscal Year 1992," *Social Security Bulletin*, 58(2) (Summer, 1995).

18. Rudolph Penner, "Federal Government Growth: Leviathan or Protector of the Elderly," *National Tax Journal*, 44(2) (December, 1991).

19. Richard Titmuss, *Essays on the "Welfare State,"* 2nd edition (London: Unwin University Books, 1958), 34–55.

20. Kathleen Murray, "Going Cubicle to Cubicle to Sell Them Insurance," *New York Times*, July 16, 1995, F10–11.

21. Ibid.

22. Titmuss, *Essays on the "Welfare State,"* 44.

23. Stanley Surrey, *Pathways to Tax Reform* (Cambridge, MA: Harvard University Press, 1973).

24. See, for example, Mimi Abramovitz, "Everyone Is on Welfare: The Role of Redistribution in Social Policy Revisited," *Social Work*, 8(6) (November/December, 1983), 440–45.

25. Irving Kristol, *Two Cheers for Capitalism* (New York: Mentor, 1978), 194.

26. *Budget of the United States Government*, Fiscal Year 1997, Analytical Perspectives, Section 5, 81–87.

27. *San Francisco Chronicle*, October 8, 1985, 10.

28. "How Mandated Benefits Boondoggle the Little Guys," *San Francisco Chronicle*, October 23, 1989, 1.

Chapter 3

A Framework for Social Welfare Policy Analysis

Even when armed with this much greater scientific knowledge, contemporary societies will, of course, face difficult choices between simultaneously held but competing values or objectives. . . . The precise balance between adequacy and equity in the determination of social insurance benefits, between equal access to minimum security and retention of the principle of local autonomy, between the interests of different social classes in allocating the costs of social security measures, or between the claims of family obligation and responsibilities to the wider community illustrate the nature of these ultimate and difficult value choices. Yet while there is no guarantee that democracies will act rationally in formulating their social policies, it is also abundantly clear that they cannot even be expected to do so unless they are made aware of the full implications of the choices available to them.

EVELINE M. BURNS
Social Security and Public Policy, 1956

Traditionally, courses in social welfare policy have emphasized the study of process and performance. In courses organized around process, students have learned about social, political, and technical processes in policy formulation, and in courses organized around performance they have learned about the details of social welfare programs in operation. A major advantage of the study of performance is its focus on factual and substantive material: it describes and evaluates programs. Here, too, lies its major shortcoming: the substance of social welfare programs is continually changing. Moreover, these programs are so numerous that one or two courses can cover only a segment of the field. Under the Title XX Amendments to the Social Security Act alone, for example, states offer more than twenty different categories of service (see Table 3.1).

As indicated in Chapter 1, a third approach to the study of this field is to focus on the set of policy choices that evolves from the planning process. From this perspective the analytic task is to distinguish among and to dissect the essential components of policy design rather than to examine the sociopolitical processes through which policy is developed or to evaluate policy outcomes. The basic components of policy design to which this task is addressed may be seen as dimensions of choice. In this chapter we present a framework for analyzing basic choices in the design of social welfare policy.

With this analytic approach, we will use program descriptions as examples to formulate and substantiate general concepts of policy design. Because we are mainly interested in illustrating the concepts that are useful in the analysis of social welfare policy, rather than in understanding the details of specific programs, there will be a certain eclecticism in the selection of these examples; we include large and small programs, pieces of programs, existing programs, and proposed programs, some of which may never leave the drawing boards and others that have not yet arrived on the public agenda.

As Eveline Burns has suggested, the major advantage of this approach is that it equips students with a convenient set of concepts that can usefully explain and illuminate a wide range of policies.[1] The broad application of our analytic framework is conveyed through the use of historical examples, such as the War on Poverty/Community Action and Model Cities Programs of the 1960s, and the Older Americans Act and the Seattle and Denver Income Maintenance Experiments of the 1970s, along with the most recent developments in welfare reform under the Personal Responsibility and Work Opportunity Reconciliation Act of 1996.

An analytic framework is an intellectual tool that helps to order reality by culling and distilling the essential elements of complex phenomena. Before elaborating the analytic framework around which this book is organized, let us say a few words about the general character of social welfare policy—our conceptual foundation on which the framework is constructed.

Benefit Allocations in the Social Market and the Mixed Economy of Welfare

In trying to construct an analytic framework that will help us understand the vast array of social welfare measures ranging from the Social Security Act of 1935 to the Personal Responsibility and Work Opportunity Reconciliation Act of 1996, we must grapple with the question: What are the common elements in social welfare policies? There is no single answer to this question with which everyone engaged in policy analysis will agree. Obviously, the apparent commonalities in the design of social welfare policy vary according to the level of abstraction on which the analysis is conducted. In this respect, an analytic framework is somewhat like a microscope; it provides a conceptual lens through which the phenomena under investigation may be studied. Like a microscope, most analytic frameworks do not have a wide depth of focus. Rather, they tend to lock on some level of abstraction that magnifies and draws our attention to a distinct set of concepts. The analytic framework we use in this book places social welfare policy in the context of a *benefit-allocation mechanism functioning outside the economic marketplace.* As Marshall has observed:

> *In contrast to the economic process, it is a fundamental principle of the Welfare State that the market value of an individual cannot be the measure of his right to welfare. The central function of welfare, in fact, is to supersede the market by taking goods and services out of it, or in some way to control and modify its operations so as to produce a result which it would not have produced itself.*[2]

To say that social welfare allocations are made outside the economic marketplace offers a rather nebulous picture of the conceptual domain within which social welfare policy operates. In order to clarify this domain we must draw a distinction between social and economic markets. This distinction rests on the principles and motives that guide the allocation of provisions. The social market of the welfare state allocates goods and services primarily in response to financial need, dependency, altruistic sentiments, social obligations, charitable motives, and the wish for communal security. In contrast, benefits in a capitalist society are distributed through the economic market, ideally on the basis of individual initiative, ability, productivity, and a desire for profit.[3] As illustrated in Figure 3.1, the social market contains both a public and a private sector. The public sector encompasses federal, state, and local governments, and accounts for the largest portion of goods and services distributed in the welfare state. Provisions allocated through the private sector of the social market include the informal efforts of family and friends, the services provided by voluntary agencies and, occasionally, by profit-oriented agencies. The last overlap with the activities of the economic market, which to some extent blurs the boundary between the private social welfare sector and the economic market.

The allocation of provisions in the social market involves both the financing and the delivery of benefits, and these roles are not always performed by the same unit. A public agency, for example, can hire its own staff to provide day-care

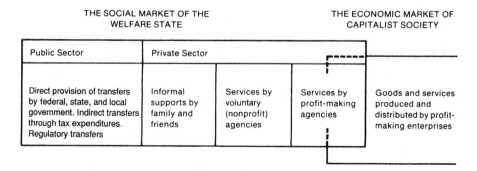

FIGURE 3.1   Social and Economic Markets of Welfare.

services for low-income mothers, or, through purchase-of-service arrangements, it may pay to have the service provided by a voluntary agency, a profit-making enterprise, or by members of the client's family. In this manner the roles of public, voluntary, profit-oriented, and informal units are variously combined. The resulting variety in the modes of benefit allocations constitute what is commonly referred to as the mixed economy of welfare.[4]

Although profit-oriented agencies still constitute only a small segment of the social market, their numbers have been growing since the mid-1960s. By the 1980s, proposals for the expansion of profit-oriented enterprises in the social market gained serious consideration. Robert Reich, for example, advanced a scheme for government and business partnerships aimed at integrating social welfare and economic development. Under this arrangement, he says, "we can expect that a significant part of the present welfare system will be replaced by government grants to businesses that agree to hire the chronically unemployed."[5] Public funds for social services such as day care, health care, and disability benefits would be allocated to businesses, eliminating the need for government administration. Joined in this way to business institutions, social welfare provisions serve an important purpose by contributing to the formation of human capital. Herein lies what is certainly the strongest attraction of such mergers—it confers on welfare activities the legitimacy and value of a productive force promoting growth in the market economy.

By the mid-1990s, proprietary agencies were prominently represented in many social service areas including homemaker/chore, day care, transportation, meals-on-wheels, and employment training.[6] The most conspicuous area of growth has been in nursing home care. Whereas about one-half of nursing home costs are paid with public (mainly Medicaid) funds, close to 82 percent of all nursing homes are operated on a for-profit basis.[7] As noted in Chapter 1, this area of service is typically referred to as the nursing home "industry;" the child care "industry" looms just over the horizon. By 1987 there were over 240,000 for-profit day-care centers with a combined revenue of $4.2 billion.[8] This penetration of profit-oriented agencies into the welfare state imbues the social market with the spirit of capitalism and inclines the *modus operandi* of social welfare allocations toward that of the market economy.

However, there is an aspect of mixing welfare services with the market economy that runs counter to the communal and charitable ethos that typifies the humanistic character of social welfare. The merger of welfare programs and private enterprise assumes a harmony among social and economic purposes that is not self-evident. Reward for merit and productivity is hardly consonant with support for benefits based on need and dependency. A system that encourages taking risks for financial gain is unlikely to invest serious effort in the pursuit of equality and security. The fundamental issue is how a capitalist society deals with conflicting objectives such as meeting need versus rewarding merit, promoting freedom versus providing security, and providing equality of opportunity versus ensuring equality of outcome.

The functioning of the social and economic markets in industrialized capitalist societies is based on a complex relationship between individual ambitions and collective responsibilities. It is a relationship that is filled with tensions and contradictions. Marshall suggests that these tensions help maintain a constructive balance between charitable and profit making impulses (or need and merit) and so contributes to a healthy society.[9] It is difficult to imagine that such a balance might be improved by an influx of profit-oriented agencies to commercialize the social market.

Some analysts believe that, because social welfare policies entail benefit allocations outside the market system, they provide for unilateral exchange or "social transfers" (from society to the individual) rather than reciprocal or "market exchange" (from buyer to seller).[10] Although we will analyze social welfare policies

---

CAPSULE 3.1:   Rights, Responsibilities, and the Communitarian Perspective

American men, women, and children are members of many communities—families; neighborhoods; innumerable social, religious, ethnic, work place, and professional associations; and the body politic itself. Neither human existence nor individual liberty can be sustained for long outside the interdependent and overlapping communities to which all of us belong. Nor can any community long survive unless its members dedicate some of their attention, energy, and resources to shared projects. The exclusive pursuit of private interest erodes the network of social environments on which we all depend, and is destructive to our shared experiment in democratic self-government. For these reasons, we hold that the rights of individuals cannot long be preserved without a communitarian perspective.

A communitarian perspective recognizes both individual human dignity and the social dimension of human existence.

A communitarian perspective recognizes that the preservation of individual liberty depends on the active maintenance of the institutions of civil society where citizens learn respect for others as well as self-respect; where

we acquire a lively sense of our personal and civic responsibilities, along with an appreciation of our own rights and the rights of others; where we develop the skills of self-government as well as the habit of governing ourselves, and learn to serve others—not just self.

A communitarian perspective recognizes that communities and polities, too, have obligations—including the duty to be responsive to their members and to foster participation and deliberation in social and political life.

A communitarian perspective does not dictate particular policies; rather it mandates attention to what is often ignored in contemporary policy debates: the social side of human nature; the responsibilities that must be borne by citizens, individually and collectively, in a regime of rights; the fragile ecology of families and their supporting communities; the ripple effects and long-term consequences of present decisions. The political views of the signers of this statement differ widely. We are united, however, in our conviction that a communitarian perspective must be brought to bear on the great moral, legal, and social issues of our time.

Preamble to the Communitarian Platform, in Amitai Etzioni (ed.), *The Responsive Community*, 2(1), Winter 1991/92, 4–5.

as unilateral designs for allocating benefits that are usually free or well-subsidized, it should be recognized that those on the receiving end often incur stringent obligations. As Zald points out, "Although many welfare recipients may not pay money for the service that they receive, they may pay much more: gratitude, political acquiescence, and the like. Thus the lack of reciprocity depends on specification of coin."[11]

Indeed, in the 1990s a new emphasis has emerged on delineating the responsibilities associated with citizen claims to social welfare benefits. In public discourse on social policy, a central question being asked is: If social welfare benefits are the rights of citizenship, what social responsibilities accompany these rights?[12] Lawrence Mead's analysis of the social obligations of citizenship opened the debate about how to weigh citizen's rights to public aid against their obligations to perform as dependable members of the community.[13] According to Mead, entitlement to social welfare benefits should be conditioned on the recipients' performance of expected behaviors, such as working in available jobs, contributing to the support of their families, learning enough in school to be employable, and respecting the law. This debate about the appropriate balance between individual rights and responsibilities was broadened by the Communitarian movement, which was launched in the early 1990s.[14]

Elements of an Analytic Framework: Dimensions of Choice

Although entitlements to welfare are increasingly being joined to individual responsibilities, benefits remain social transfers allocated outside the economic marketplace. Within the benefit-allocation framework, social welfare policies can be interpreted as choices among principles determining *what* benefits are offered, to *whom* they are offered, *how* they are *delivered*, and *how* they are *financed*. The elements of this framework, of course, are not physical structures of the sort a microscope might reveal. Rather, they are social constructs that are used in the intellectual processes of making choices. The major dimensions of choice in this framework may be expressed in the form of four questions:

1. What are the bases of social allocations?
2. What are the types of social provisions to be allocated?
3. What are the strategies for the delivery of these provisions?
4. What are the ways to finance these provisions?

A few words are in order about the genesis of this approach. Eveline Burns utilized this general framework in her seminal study, *Social Security and Public Policy*, focusing on four types of decisions that informed program design in the realm of social security: (1) those related to the nature and amount of benefits; (2) those concerned with eligibility and the types of risks to be covered; (3) those regarding the means of finance; and (4) those relevant to the structure and character of administration. Our analytic approach in this book seeks to extend the pathways of policy analysis charted by Burns, and others.[15] These dimensions of choice cut across the entire field of social welfare policy, rather than simply delineating choices specific to a single program sector.

We treat the bases of social allocations, types of social provisions, strategies of delivery, and modes of finance as "dimensions" of choice because each will be examined along three axes: (1) the range of alternatives within each dimension, (2) the social values that support them, and (3) the theories or assumptions that underlie them. This framework is illustrated in Figure 3.2.

Choices Regarding Allocations and Provisions

The first two dimensions of choice are expressed in the question, *Who gets what?* The *bases* of social allocations addresses the "who" of social welfare policy.

Social welfare policies always include some designation of beneficiaries, those whose welfare is to be enhanced through policy implementation. Although these policies are supposed to serve the abstract interests of society-as-a-whole—the elusive "public interest"—direct and immediate benefits are usually distributed differentially among segments of the population. We will have more to say about notions of the public interest in Chapter 9. For now, suffice it to say that few social welfare policies help everybody equally. Choices are required, and they are continually made as trade-offs among what policy planners think is desirable, what circumstances necessitate, and what the public will countenance.

Numerous criteria are used to determine who is eligible for social provisions. These criteria include marital status, employment status, residence, family size, IQ, health, age, education, length of military service, ethnicity, gender, religion, and income. Our concern in examining the bases of social allocations, however, is not to catalog the many possibilities that may be employed to define eligibility. Rather, the issues of choice we address focus on a set of general principles that informs the design of eligibility criteria. *The bases of social allocations refer to the choices among the various principles upon which social provisions are made accessible to particular people and groups in society.*

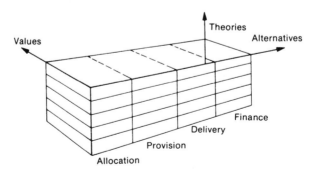

FIGURE 3.2 Dimensions of Choice.

The bases of social allocations are the guidelines for the operational definition of eligibility criteria. *What* people become eligible to receive involves policy choices about the nature of the social provision. In policy analysis the traditional choice has been whether benefits are offered in *cash* (money) or *in kind* (goods or services). There are, however, other types of benefits that are commonly distributed through social welfare policy, such as power, vouchers, and opportunities, which permit different degrees of consumer sovereignty than the in-cash/in-kind dichotomy. In Chapter 5 we analyze the range of alternatives in this dimension of choice. Our objective is to distinguish the various forms of social provision and their implications for consumers of social welfare benefits. Thus *questions about the nature of social provisions refer to the kinds of benefits that are delivered.*

Choices Regarding Delivery and Finance

The third dimension of choice addresses alternative strategies for delivering social provisions. Here the choices are not about "who" and "what," but rather about "how." That is, after decisions about the "who" and "what" of policy are resolved, arrangements must be made for getting the provisions selected to the eligible consumers. The ways delivery systems are designed to achieve this objective are of crucial significance to the first two dimensions of choice because it is through the delivery mechanism that policy guidelines regarding eligibility and the nature of provision are operationally expressed. Consider, for example, a proposal for new employment counseling services. Should they be centrally located in a downtown facility or dispersed in small neighborhood units? Should counselors be trained professionals or local residents? Should the services be offered if they duplicate others that exist? Should they be incorporated under a unified administrative umbrella that includes health and legal aid services? Should the services be provided by a government agency, a nonprofit organization, or a profit-making organization? These choices influence who gets served and the type of benefits they receive, policies about the nature of provisions and bases of allocations notwithstanding. Included among these design elements are overall composition of the service system, linkages among service units, location of facilities, caliber and adequacy of personnel, and public versus private auspices.

In examining the design of delivery systems, one usually discusses strategies to enhance the flow of services from providers to consumers, a point to which much of the literature in this area is addressed. Since the federal social service cutbacks of the 1980s, however, increasing attention has been given to strategies for rationing services and for contracting publicly funded activities to private agencies. When we examine this dimension of choice in Chapter 6 we will analyze strategies for facilitating service delivery, as well as considerations of public versus private auspices. *Delivery strategies refer to the alternative organizational arrangements among providers and consumers of social welfare benefits in the context of local community systems (i.e., neighborhood, city, and county), the level at which the overwhelming majority of providers and consumers come together.*

If social welfare policies are viewed as benefit-allocation mechanisms functioning outside the marketplace, choices must be made concerning the sources and types of financing. It is important to recognize the distinction between funding benefits and delivering them. To clarify where funding ends and delivery begins, it is helpful to think in terms of a simple flow chart. *Funding choices involve questions concerning the source of funds and the fashion in which funds flow from the point of origin to the point-of-service provision.* Delivery choices involve the organizational arrangements that move social provisions, either in cash or other forms, from providers to consumers.

Some of the major financing alternatives concern whether money is derived from public, private, or mixed sources; the level of government involved; and the types of taxes levied. Financing also involves the administrative conditions that govern funding arrangements such as grant-in-aid formulas, specification of purpose, and timing. This dimension of choice will be examined in Chapters 7 and 8.

Although the dimensions of allocation, provision, delivery, and finance will be analyzed separately in the following chapters, each with its own range of alternatives, it should be emphasized that most decisions are interdependent in the design of social welfare policies. For instance, a decentralized delivery system results when the social provision is in the form of power, as in policies for greater parental control of local education that transfer decision-making authority from middle-class professional bureaucracies to service consumers. Similarly, the basis of social allocations and methods of finance are closely interwoven when eligibility for benefits involves some form of payments as in subsidized user charges and contributory social insurance.

These four dimensions of choice encompass fundamental issues in the design of social welfare policies. The process through which these issues are resolved raises a different set of choices, choices that concern the design of decision-making arrangements. In Chapter 9 we explore the implications of alternative arrangements for social welfare planning.

An Example: The Transformation of Social Services

At this point we will tie the dimensions of choice to a concrete case so the reader can see how the framework is applied. The selected case involves the evolution of social services over the last four decades.[16] The focus is on social service provisions originally established under several titles of the Social Security Act: Titles I (Old Age Assistance), IV-A (Aid to Families With Dependent Children), X (Aid to the Blind), and XIV (Aid to the Permanently and Totally Disabled). Incorporated into Title XX of the Social Security Act in 1974, these provisions were refashioned in their current form in 1981 as the Social Services Block Grant. There are, of course, other sources from which social services emanate, such as the Adoption Assistance and Child Welfare Act of 1980, the Older Americans Act, first legislated in 1965, and the Anti-Drug Abuse Act of 1988. The reason that the Social Services Block Grant has been selected as the focal point of analysis is that it provides the largest single source of social service funds. In the most concrete sense, it represents the cornerstone of the structure of social services in the United States.

Any discussion of developments in the social services over the last thirty-five years must take into account the substantial increase in federal spending in this area. Between 1963 and 1971 federal grants to states for social services grew more than threefold, from approximately $194 million to $740 million. That was a moderate rate of growth compared with the precipitous rise from $740 million to $1.7 billion that occurred between 1971 and 1972. Of course, $1.7 billion was no trifling sum, but when state estimates for 1973 indicated a potential increase in expenditures to $4.7 billion, Congress enacted a $2.5 billion ceiling on federal expenditures for social services.[17] This ceiling on social service funding rose to $2.9 billion by 1981 but was reduced to $2.4 billion in that fiscal year when Title XX was redesignated as the Social Services Block Grant. Since then, federal spending on social services gradually rose, reaching $2.8 billion in 1990 and remaining at that level until 1995. Under the Personal Responsibility and Work Opportunity Reconciliation Act of 1996, annual federal funding for the Social Services Block Grant was reduced 15 percent.[18]

Although it is important to appreciate the growth of federal funding as a force in the general development of social services, the focus of this case study is on the substantive program changes that have accompanied the changing levels of federal support. In this analysis, the overall rise in federal expenditures can be seen as a quantitative backdrop to a qualitative transformation in the nature of the social services.

Social services experienced several significant changes since they first gained solid financial support in the 1962 social security amendments. There has been a consistent broadening of social service eligibility standards and an enlargement of the population receiving services. In 1962, eligibility was limited to public assistance recipients, former recipients, and others who, in light of their precarious life circumstances, were potential candidates for public assistance. The Bureau of Family Services defined "potential recipients" as those who might reasonably be expected to require financial aid within one year of their application for services. Whereas these standards offered the *possibility* of extending services beyond the immediate public assistance population, it was not realized in practice. At that early stage, both program funds and trained social service workers were in relatively short supply. Because political support for the 1962 amendments was predicated on the idea that intensive social work services would reduce the size of public assistance rolls, the recipient population clearly held first priority on service allocations. Despite those immediate limitations, the possibility of extending service eligibility was established in principle.

This principle was applied in the social security amendments of 1967. Under these amendments persons became eligible for social services if it was determined that they might become welfare recipients within the next five years. Even more significant was the introduction of the concept of "group eligibility," whereby residents of low-income neighborhoods and other groups (such as those in institutional settings) could become eligible for service.

By 1972, people who were not receiving welfare were well represented among the social service clientele, and their number was growing. One reason for this was that the 1967 amendments had provided a loophole through which states could squeeze many locally funded services into federally funded programs eligible for 75 percent cost reimbursement.

The Title XX Social Service Amendments of 1974 ushered in a new set of eligibility criteria that further extended entitlements. Under the enactment, the federal government designated three categories of people who were eligible for services: (1) *income maintenance recipients,* (2) *income eligibles,* and (3) *universal eligibles.* Income maintenance recipients were those receiving public assistance, including Supplementary Security Income and Medicaid; these recipients are poor according to already-existing means-tested standards. Title XX regulations required each state to target at least 50 percent of its federal funds for people in this category. Income-eligible recipients included those who earned up to 115 percent of their state's median income. States could offer services free of charge to those whose income did not exceed 80 percent of the state median. For those earning between 80 and 115 percent of the median, services could be offered on a subsidized basis for reasonable income-related fees. The universal category referred to services that were available free-of-charge to all without regard to income: information and referral services, protective services for children and adults, and family planning. In 1978, a fourth category, *group eligibility,* was added. This category allowed states to designate groups of people with similar characteristics—for example, the elderly and the institutionalized mentally ill—as service eligible if it could be shown that 75 percent of the group's members had incomes less than 90 percent of the state's median income.

When Ronald Reagan's 1981 Omnibus Budget Reconciliation Act superseded Title XX with the Social Services Block Grant (SSBG), federal eligibility requirements were eliminated altogether, leaving states free to exercise whatever standards of eligibility they desired. Despite the discretion afforded them, however, most states continue to employ much the same eligibility standards as before.[19]

As eligibility restrictions were eliminated, the scope and content of social provisions changed. Social services were originally advanced in 1962 as a way to prevent and reduce dependency—through intensive social casework services that presumably would rehabilitate the poor, changing their behavior in ways that would help them become economically independent.[20] Although social services also included other basic forms of provision such as homemakers and foster-home care, the essential feature was the provision of social casework. Although this was not specified in the law, "welfare professionals in the Bureau of Family Services knew more or less what they meant by 'services.' Fundamentally and at a minimum, it meant casework by a trained social worker."[21]

There is an intangible quality about casework service that makes the exact nature of the provision difficult to specify. This vagueness has led to the cynical observation that such service "is anything done for, with, or about the client by the social worker. If a social worker discusses a child's progress in school with an AFDC mother, a check is made under 'services related to education. . . .' When the discussion turns to the absent father and possible reconciliation, a check is made under 'maintaining family and improving family functioning.' "[22] In a similar vein, Handler and Hollingsworth characterized public assistance services as "little more than a relatively infrequent, pleasant chat."[23]

At its best, social casework is certainly a more skillful and nurturing enterprise than these comments suggest. But large caseloads, the demands of eligibility certification (while trying to establish a casework relationship), the diversity of clientele (many of whom did not need or want casework services but were forced to accept them), and the omnipresent bureaucratic regulations of public assistance were hardly conducive to effective practice.[24] In any event, whatever its powers and benefits, social casework was not a cure for poverty. The addition of almost one million recipients to the public assistance rolls between 1962 and 1966 dramatically proved this point.

The failure to reduce economic dependency combined with social casework's intangible quality made these services a prime target of congressional disillusion, a disillusion that was reflected in the 1967 Social Security Act amendments under which casework services were deemphasized. The 1967 amendments opened the way for a broader conception of social services. Before, federal grants for services went mainly to pay the salaries of social caseworkers.[25] In contrast, the regulations implementing the 1967 amendments "created such a comprehensive array of specific services that literally almost any service was federally reimbursable."[26] At the same time, greater emphasis was placed on the delivery of services far more tangible than social casework. According to Derthick, "a distinction soon began to develop between 'soft' and 'hard' services. Advice and counseling from a caseworker were 'soft' . . . and presumably less valuable than day-care centers, or drug treatment centers, or work training, which were 'hard,'" and which soon became much more widely available. She continues, "the changed conception and changed social context helped lay the basis for granting funds for a much wider range of activity than the daily routines of caseworkers."[27]

With the passage of the 1974 social service amendments, the movement toward services diversification reached new heights. Under Title XX, each state was free to support whatever social services it deemed appropriate for its communities. The only requirement was that these services be directed to one of five federally specified goals, goals which were so broadly stated as to encompass almost anything the imagination of social service planners could devise. In the first year of implementation, Title XX plans for the fifty states and the District of Columbia specified a total of 1,313 services.[28]

The substantive range of services today is illustrated in Table 3.1, which shows services grouped into the twenty-five categories devised by the federal government in 1990 for purposes of tabulation and analysis. Whereas many federal reporting requirements and regulations were eliminated in the 1981 conversion from the "old" Title XX to the "new" Social Services Block Grant (SSBG), there have recently been new requirements mandating annual reports, uniform definitions of services, and specific information on the number of people receiving services, the amount of SSBG funds going for each service, methods of service delivery, and

TABLE 3.1   Title XX Social Service Categories

Adoption services
Case management services
Congregate meals
Counseling services
Adult day care services
Child day care services
Employment, education, and training services
Family planning services
Foster care services for adults
Foster care services for children
Health-related and home health services
Home-based services
Home-delivered meals
Housing services
Information and referral services
Legal services
Pregnancy and parenting services for young parents
Prevention and intervention services
Protective services for adults
Protective services for children
Recreational services
Residential treatment services
Special services for the developmentally disabled, the blind, and the physical disabled
Special services for juvenile delinquents
Transportation services

criteria for eligibility. Today, some states offer the full twenty-five services, whereas two use all of their funds to support just one or two services. Some states have also attempted to mesh Title XX funds with other federal, state, and local social service dollars in order to consolidate their services and budgetary planning.[29]

Along with the increasing emphasis on tangible services and the diversification of social service content, a profound change in the purpose of the social services was taking place. The 1962 services were almost exclusively aimed at reducing poverty; under Title XX there developed a service network of broad scope largely concerned with maintenance and care, directed more at enhancing human development and the general quality of life than at reducing economic dependency.[30] The first major step in this direction was the 1967 divorce of income-maintenance functions from social service functions in the public assistance program.[31] In 1977, this administrative separation was reinforced at the federal level by placing income-maintenance programs under the Social Security Administration and joining social service and human development programs under the Office of Human Development Services (OHDS). This trend is reflected in Title XX's current emphasis on services that are not associated with notions of personal deficiency or inadequate character, such as transportation and meals-on-wheels for the elderly, homemaker services for the disabled, and day care for children of all backgrounds.

Along with the separation of financial aid from the provision of social services, responsibility for the delivery of services became more dispersed through the increasing use of purchase-of-service arrangements between public agencies and social service providers in the private sector. Under the 1962 amendments, state public assistance agencies were enjoined from using federal funds to purchase services directly from voluntary agencies. It was possible, however, to purchase these services indirectly, with grants to other public agencies, which could then "contract out." Opportunities for purchase of services from private sources were significantly broadened when the 1967 social security amendments authorized purchase arrangements for a wide array of activities. Although the amendments allowed state agencies to purchase services directly from private agencies, private-agency donations could not be used as the states' 25 percent matching share *if* those contributions reverted to the donor's facility.[32] This restriction was lifted in 1974. The growing reliance of voluntary agencies on government funding

---

CAPSULE 3.2:   Charities on the Dole

Those who expect America's charities to replace government as a provider of social welfare ought to look a little closer. They will find that the so-called independent sector, which receives between one-quarter and one-third of its funds from taxpayers, isn't so independent after all.

In fact, many social-service agencies actually receive most of their funding from government. Save the Children owes 60 percent of its budget to the generosity of taxpayers, Catholic Charities 65 percent, CARE 78 percent, and the United Cerebral Palsy Association more than 80 percent. Topping this list is the ineptly named Volunteers of America, which receives 96 percent of its $51-million budget from government sources. . . .

There are, of course, many small, innovative, and values-driven grass-roots charities that are addressing human needs much more efficiently than failed federal programs and social-service agencies. These groups mostly avoid government money, because they know that government support comes with strings attached.

These strings involve more than just paperwork and regulations. Government support also changes charities' incentives, giving them reasons to keep caseloads up instead of getting them down by successfully turning around peoples' lives. It distorts their missions. It turns lean, cost-effective organizations into bloated bureaucracies, and dilutes their spiritual or religious message. In instances where the Salvation Army decided to accept government funds (which constitute about 15 percent of its revenues), it stopped requiring church attendance as a condition of its assistance. Unfortunately, this experience is all too common. The charity that stays genuinely independent from government is still the exception.

Although charities are supposed to offer an alternative to government provision of social welfare, they have become so dependent on and aligned with government that they no longer represent a way out of the welfare state. If we place our faith in private non-profits as they are currently organized, we are in for a big disappointment. Before we can rely on charities to help us dismantle government, they must wean themselves off the dole.

Kimberly Dennis, "Charities on the Dole," *Policy Review, 5,* March/April 1996, 26.

was seen by some as a trend that robbed the voluntary sector of its traditional independence.

Over the last three decades Title XX's flexible service delivery provisos have generated an enormous expansion in the systematic use of public funds to purchase private/voluntary services. Given the virtual elimination of federal reporting requirements in the 1981 Social Services Block Grant, it is difficult to calculate the precise magnitude of purchase arrangements. It is estimated, however, that federal funds provide about 50 percent of all financial support for services provided by nonprofit agencies.[33]

These changes in the scope and delivery of provisions were accompanied by basic reforms in federal financing. Under the 1962 laws, federal financing was open-ended, with the states reimbursed for 75 percent of social service costs to recipients in the four public assistance categories: the aged, the blind, the disabled, and families with dependent children. The 1967 amendments expanded the range of services and clientele that might qualify for federal funds. With this expansion the definitions of "social services" and client-eligibility standards were loosely drawn. Whether a particular service for certain clients qualified for federal reimbursement was dependent in large part on local interpretation rather than on a clearly defined statutory formula. The most enterprising states made the boldest interpretations, claimed the greatest need, and received the largest proportional share of federal grants for social services. In the states' scuffle for federal funds, grantsmanship was the name of the game. Three states—New York, Illinois, and California—were the biggest winners, together receiving 58 percent of federal grants in 1972.[34]

This open-ended approach to financing underwent fundamental revisions with the 1974 Title XX amendments. The new legislation incorporated the social service provisions originally financed under the four public assistance categories (Titles I, IV-A, X, and XIV of the Social Security Act) into a single grant (Title XX) program. With the $2.5 billion ceiling that Congress placed on social services, financing was no longer open-ended. This limitation ushered in a change in allocative procedures that tied federal allotments to a formula based strictly on state population. Each state was thereby entitled to a proportional share of Title XX funds, but the receipt of these funds was contingent on meeting certain regulations and supplying a local matching share. When the Social Services Block Grant was enacted in 1981, the local share requirement was dropped along with most other federal regulations. SSBG allocations continue on a population basis, spreading funds in a way that yields a rough form of interstate equalization. However, this mode of finance is not especially sensitive to the greater needs of poorer states.

Application of the Framework

Now let us superimpose the dimensions of choice on the complex social service program changes that have occurred over the last three and one-half decades. Our approach to policy analysis provides a way of thinking about this program that extracts and organizes its major elements, making the whole more readily comprehensible. Using the framework we have outlined, the substance of social service policy may be divided into our four choice categories, which are summarized as follows:

1. *The bases of social allocations: Selective to universal.*
   In 1962, eligibility for social services was means-tested, effectively limited to recipients of the four categorical aid programs—Aid to Families with Dependent Children (AFDC), Aid to the Blind, Old-Age Assistance, and Aid to the Permanently and Totally Disabled. By 1974, eligibility criteria were broadened by the Title XX amendments to include many middle-income beneficiaries. The Social Services Block Grant, which revised Title XX in 1981, gave the states latitude to impose any eligibility criteria they wished. Because most states continue to employ the limited requirements of earlier years, it would be an exaggeration to say that in the 1990s there is universal access to social services. Nevertheless, there has been a pronounced trend from selective toward universal access.

2. *The nature of social provision: Intangible and limited to concrete and diversified.*
   In 1962, social services consisted primarily of social casework to help families improve their functioning and gain economic independence. What these services entailed, beyond some form of psychotherapeutic counseling, was only vaguely defined. More tangible forms of service were established in 1967, emphasizing employment training, day care, and family planning. Under the 1981 conversion to the Social Services Block Grant states may offer any kind of social service imaginable. By 1990, diversification of social services had grown to include twenty-five categories of provision.

3. *The delivery system: Public-and-linked-to-income-maintenance, to public, private, and free standing.*
   Up to 1967, social service and income maintenance functions were combined and delivered by the same administrative unit. Caseworkers distributed financial aid and also provided social services. After 1967 these functions were administratively divorced and performed by different workers, with an emphasis placed on hiring AFDC recipients to perform certain service roles related to day care and eligibility determination. Also, since 1975, an increased reliance on purchase-of-service arrangements by state and local governments has drawn an increasing number of private nonprofits into what was originally a delivery system of public agencies.

4. *Finance: Open-ended categorical grant to fixed-amount block grant.*
   In 1962 the federal government reimbursed states for 75 percent of all social service costs for recipients in the public assistance categories. When these services were incorporated into Title XX, a $2.5 billion expenditure ceiling (which slowly rose to $2.8 billion by 1995 and was lowered to $2.5 billion in 1996) was established with grants allocated to states according to a formula based strictly on population size. To qualify for grants, states were required to

supply a 25 percent local match. For all practical purposes, Title XX amounted to a block grant. In 1981, the Social Services Block Grant provided states almost complete discretion in use of these grants, and no longer required matching funds or reporting or planning requirements.

In specifying the dimensions of choice—the first step of a two-step process in social welfare policy analysis—we ask these questions: What benefits are to be allocated, and to whom? How are these benefits to be delivered and financed? These questions may be answered without reference to purpose. So now we turn to the second step in the analysis process—the "why" question, addressing the values, theories, and assumptions that inform social choices.

Distributive Justice in Public Assistance

Some answers to the "why" of social choice can be found in the explication of underlying values. Alva Myrdal explains the importance of illuminating the values embedded in policy designs:

> *An established tendency to drive values underground, to make analysis appear scientific by omitting certain basic assumptions from the discussion, has too often emasculated the social sciences as agencies for rationality in social and political life. To be truly rational, it is necessary to accept the obvious principle that a social program, like a practical judgment, is a conclusion based upon premises of values as well as upon facts.*[35]

The analysis of values and social welfare policy may be approached from at least two levels. At the broader level the analytic focus is on policy in the generic sense. Rather than examining each of its dimensions of choice and the values expressed therein, this level of analysis addresses broad purposes. Specifically, to what extent does the policy achieve distributive justice? At this level of generality three core values shape the design of policy: *equality, equity,* and *adequacy.* As we will see by examining the changing arrangements for financial aid under public assistance, these values are not always in harmony.

In addition to providing social services, the main function of categorical public assistance programs has been to provide financial assistance to the needy. When these programs were established under the Social Security Act of 1935, three categories of needy people were eligible for aid: the elderly under Title I, Old-Age Assistance (OAA); dependent children under Title IV, Aid to Dependent Children (ADC); and the blind, under Title X, Aid to the Blind (AB). A fourth category was added in 1950 under Title XIV, Aid to the Permanently and Totally Disabled (APTD).

In 1961, Aid to Dependent Children was changed to Aid to Families with Dependent Children (AFDC), reflecting an emphasis on maintaining the family unit. Legislation in 1988 required the states to provide financial aid to children of unemployed parents (AFDC-UP).

These four categorical programs were financed by the federal government and administered by the states, with each state contributing a variable matching share, the size of which was based on its wealth. A fifth public aid option, General Assistance (GA), is available for individuals who do not qualify for support under the federally financed programs. Funded entirely by states and localities, General Assistance is usually more parsimonious than the federal categories with regard to the duration and amount of assistance.

In 1965 a broad program of medical assistance for the poor was enacted, unifying the various arrangements for meeting medical costs that existed under the four categorical programs. Known as Medicaid, this program also allows the states to offer payments to the "medically indigent," people whose economic resources are insufficient to pay all their medical costs but who do not otherwise qualify as needy for cash assistance.

Through the early 1970s, Medicaid and the five categorical programs (OAA, APTD, AFDC, AB, and GA), along with food stamps, formed the general core of public assistance in this country. Within the framework established by federal legislation, the states had considerable latitude to design programs according to their own local norms and preferences. One reflection on this policy is the twenty-odd different agency names used by the fifty states to designate the bureaucracies administering the public assistance programs. These include Public Welfare, Social Services, Family and Children Services, Institutions and Agencies, Human Resources, and Economic Security, to name but a few. More profound variations exist with regard to standards of eligibility and levels of assistance. For example, in 1993, average monthly AFDC payments per family ranged from $748 in Alaska to $115 in Alabama, with the U.S. average of $337.[36] In more than half the states, AFDC payments equal less than the minimum required to meet basic needs according to cost standards that these states themselves had set.

The structure of categorical public assistance was dramatically altered by the Social Security Act amendments of 1972 under which Old-Age Assistance, Aid to the Blind, and Aid to the Permanently and Totally Disabled were replaced by the consolidated Supplementary Security Income (SSI) program (implemented in 1974). In contrast to the incorporation of the categorical social services under Title XX, which increased state administrative authority, the replacement of the financial aid categories by SSI brought these programs entirely under federal control. Administered by the Social Security Administration and supported totally by federal funds, SSI provides uniform cash assistance to the needy, blind, aged, and disabled throughout the country. Average monthly payments to SSI recipients more than tripled from $114 in 1975 to $363 in 1995. The highest amounts go to the blind, whose monthly payment averaged $396 in 1995.[37] (See Figure 3.3.)

AFDC was not included in the federalization. Until 1996, it continued to be administered by the states under federal regulations and to be jointly financed through open-ended federal matching grants. With the passage of the Personal

Public Assistance Categories, 1962

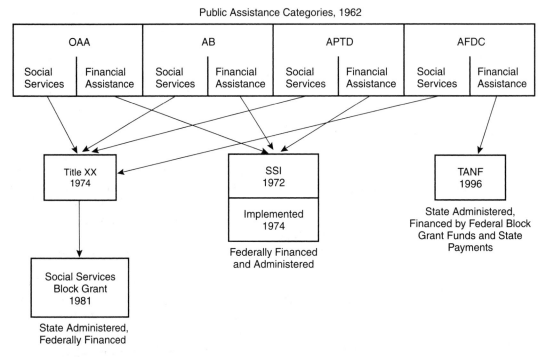

FIGURE 3.3   Reorganization of Public Assistance: Social Services and Financial Aid.

Responsibility and Work Opportunity Reconciliation Act of 1996, AFDC was replaced by TANF—the Temporary Assistance to Needy Families program. This unprecedented reform, substituting TANF block funding grant for AFDC's open-ended arrangement, effectively eliminated a national entitlement to public assistance—fulfilling President Clinton's campaign promise to "end welfare as we know it," if not exactly along the lines he envisioned.

Under TANF, states receive a fixed level of federal funds to provide income support to poor families with children based on the amount spent on AFDC in 1994.[38] It should be noted that because AFDC caseloads had been declining in most states, the initial block grant allocations for 1997 were higher than the amount states would have received under AFDC.[39] Future prospects, however, are more threatening. During a period of recession, for example, if caseloads rise and a state runs out of block grant funds, eligible applicants for public aid will have to be denied assistance unless a state has the political will to commit its *own* funds to the program.

Beyond capping the level of federal support that states might draw on to aid needy families, TANF introduced sweeping changes in the essential character of public assistance—among which time-limited welfare was the most radical measure. Under TANF, states are barred from providing federal cash benefits to

---

CAPSULE 3.3:   A Monster of His Own Creation

The Republican-controlled Congress [has now produced] a welfare reform bill that ends 60 years of guaranteed federal financial support to poor mothers and their children. It mandates that most welfare mothers work or attend school for their benefits and reduces federal support to the states while giving them a great deal more discretion in deciding who gets assistance and who does not.

How did we get to this point? Most people, whether they like or detest these radical changes, credit (or blame) the Republicans for them. But in fact, Bill Clinton is as responsible as the Republicans for what is happening to welfare in America.

It was Clinton who, as a candidate, single-handedly moved the welfare debate sharply to the right with his promise to "end welfare as we know it." Liberals could hear this wonderfully ambiguous phrase as a promise to improve the current system, and conservatives could hear it as a promise to dismantle it. But the overarching effect was to undercut support for the system among moderate voters. Hearing a Democrat repeatedly bad-mouth welfare gave credibility to the program's sharpest critics.

As he campaigned across the nation, Clinton introduced—and made politically acceptable—a radical idea: time-limited welfare. We said that welfare should "provide people with the education, training, job placement assistance, and child care they need for two years—so that they can break the cycle of dependency. After two years, those who can work will be required to go to work, either in the private sector or in meaningful community service jobs."

Although Clinton was usually careful to repeat the entire formulation, most voters heard only a promise of "two years and they're out"—and he did little to dispel this misimpression.

After Clinton won in 1992, his campaign rhetoric was considered a stroke of political genius—allowing him to define himself as a New Democrat without alienating old-style liberals. Perhaps.

But Clinton's rhetoric had another effect. Before his campaign, no major Republican proposal had even remotely suggested time-limiting welfare. Now, it is the core of the Republican bills passed by both the House and Senate.

Douglas J. Besharov, "A Monster of His Own Creation," *The Washington Post*, November 2, 1995, A31.

---

families for more than a total of five years during their lifetime, although up to 20 percent of recipients may be exempted from the limit due to hardship. States must also develop plans describing how TANF recipients will engage in work activities after being on the welfare rolls for two years.

In allocating financial aid outside of economic markets, public assistance programs like TANF and SSI represent an effort to alter the distribution of resources in society. In this effort one aim of public assistance is to further distributive justice—an undertaking that must come to grips with the values of *equality, equity,* and *adequacy.*

Equality

Although it is one of the foundation stones of distributive justice, equality is a value open to interpretation. At least two salient notions were differentiated by

Aristotle: *numerical equality* and *proportional equality*.[40] These concepts represent the egalitarian and meritarian elements of distributive justice. Numerical equality implies the same treatment of everyone—to all an equal share. Proportional equality implies the same treatment of *similar* persons—to each according to his or her merit or virtue. These interpretations of equality offer conflicting prescriptions for the treatment of dissimilar persons. With the concept of proportional equality, Vlastos points out, "the meritarian view of justice paid reluctant homage to the egalitarian one by using the vocabulary of equality to assert the justice of inequality."[41] To clarify this distinction and to reduce the definitional awkwardness, we will use the term equality in its numerical sense and will subsume the meaning of proportional *equality* under the value of equity.

Social welfare policy is influenced by the value of equality with regard to the outcome of benefit allocations. Specifically, the value prescribes that benefits should be allocated so as to equalize the distribution of resources and opportunities. In some policies this value is predominant, as, for instance, in the development of quota hiring plans for the equal allocation of work roles among different groups of people. In a modified version there are opportunity-oriented policies whereby the equal shares objective is recast in terms of *equal opportunity*. Fair housing legislation, for example, demands that people, whatever their racial and ethnic characteristics, receive the same treatment in their quest for shelter. It does not, however, ensure equal *results* for everyone.

In public assistance, the introduction of uniform federal grants under SSI was, in part, a measure to promote greater equality in financial aid across the country. The influence of the equality goal in shaping the design of public assistance is also evident in the extent to which money is shifted from wealthy states and individuals toward those that are poor. Although such redistribution takes place through public assistance, it falls considerably short of creating even a roughly equal share for all because distributive justice is also responsive to other values.

Equity

Equity denotes a conventional sense of fair treatment. There is a proportional quality to notions of fair treatment—if you do half the work you deserve half the reward. People's deservedness should be based on their contributions to society, modified only by special considerations for those whose inability to contribute is clearly not of their own making. Accordingly, there are many "equitable inequalities" that are normatively sanctioned, as in policies that offer preferential treatment for veterans and in unemployment benefits that vary in proportion to prior earnings.

In public assistance, equity is stressed through the doctrine of "less eligibility," first formulated by the English Poor Law Commissioners in 1834. In the Commissioners' words:

> *It may be assumed that in the administration of relief, the public is warranted in imposing such conditions on the individual relieved, as are conducive to the*

benefit either of the individual himself, or of the country at large, at whose expense he is to be relieved. The first and most essential of all conditions, a principle which we find universally admitted, even by those whose practice is at variance with it, is that his situation on the whole shall not be made really or apparently so eligible as the situation of the independent laborer of the lowest class. [Emphasis added.][42]

One reason for the extremely low level of public assistance in most states is the ingrained belief that aid should not elevate the conditions of recipients above those of the poorest workers. Here, the emphasis on equity supports the maintenance of incentives to work. It is interesting to note the historic shift that has taken place in the relation between incentives to work and public assistance as increasing numbers of women have entered the labor force.

In the 1960s and 1970s policymakers began a serious debate about the right of welfare mothers to collect public aid and remain at home with their children. The issue was not simply whether welfare benefits should be lower than the income one might earn in the paid labor force, but whether active measures should be employed to encourage welfare mothers to work. Reflecting the view that various incentives should be offered to encourage welfare recipients to seek employment, the 1967 amendments to the Social Security Act established the WIN (work-incentive) program to provide training and employment to "all appropriate individuals," which included welfare mothers with young children. Previously, work programs had been available on a much smaller scale mainly to fathers of families receiving aid under AFDC-UP. In addition, the provision of day-care services was authorized so that mothers would be free to work and, for an incentive, the first $30 of monthly earnings plus one-third of the remainder were exempted from determination of continued eligibility for assistance. (In 1981, the "30 plus one-third" earnings disregard was limited to only the first four months of employment, and in 1988 WIN was replaced altogether with the workfare provisions of the Family Support Act.)

Around the same time that the 1967 amendments were being implemented, other proponents argued for increasing the level of AFDC benefits for women who stayed at home. Casting this claim in the name of equity, they did not ask that dissimilar people, those who work and those who do not work, be treated equally and awarded similar standards of living. Rather, the argument was made that motherhood itself should be considered an occupation—one, indeed, that is more trying than most. This view was expressed by a ten-member panel (nine of whom were men) commissioned by the federal government to study the problem of U.S. workers. The panel recommended, among other things, that welfare mothers be subsidized to stay home and care for their children.[43] The case for this policy gains momentum when we calculate the substantial per capita costs of day-care services necessary to allow AFDC mothers the freedom to work.[44]

By 1996, the question of whether the interests of equity were best served by providing public assistance to subsidize the home-care of children or by expecting welfare mothers to seek paid employment in the labor market was resolved clearly in favor of the labor market option—welfare became "workfare." Indeed, as noted, the Temporary Assistance to Needy Families program not only expects welfare recipients to seek employment within two years, but sharply limits the number of years that poor families are eligible to receive public aid during their lifetime. The political consensus that motivated the shift from welfare to workfare was influenced in part by the more general movement of women's labor from the household to the market economy. Steadily on the rise, the labor force participation rate of married women with children under age eighteen almost doubled from 39 percent in 1960 to 76 percent in 1994. As the vast majority of mothers with school-age children entered the labor force, it became awkward for even the most sympathetic welfare advocates to hold public assistance recipients exempt from the obligation to seek employment.

Adequacy

Adequacy refers to the desirability of providing a decent standard of physical and spiritual well-being, quite apart from concerns for whether benefit allocations are equal or differentiated according to merit. Thus, as Frankena explains, the quest for distributive justice involves

> . . . . *a somewhat vaguely defined but still limited concern for the* goodness of people's lives, *as well as for their equality. The double concern is often referred to as respect for the intrinsic dignity or value of the human individual. This is not the position of the extreme egalitarian but it is essentially egalitarian in spirit; in any case it is not the position of the meritarian, although it does seek to accommodate his principles.*[45]

Standards of adequacy vary according to time and circumstances. In medieval times, serfs were usually provided with the necessities to keep them healthy and productive. At the turn of the twentieth century, $624 a year was estimated as a "living wage" for a family of five in New York City.[46] By 1996, the poverty level for a family of four was $15,600. In addition to the economic aspects of material existence, standards of *spiritual* well-being also vary. In the Middle Ages these standards had a basically religious connotation: The vicissitudes of life on earth were suffered for spiritual salvation in the hereafter. Today, spiritual well-being is more a secular concern; it involves, for instance, the sense of being able to control one's destiny, freedom of expression, self-realization, security, and happiness.

The value of adequacy is expressed rather faintly in public assistance and honored more in the breach than in reality. Nevertheless, its presence is reflected in the fact that grant levels are not set arbitrarily, but are based on state estimates of the costs of basic needs (even though the grants rarely approach the levels of these estimates).

Overall, as a benefit allocation mechanism, public assistance is more responsive to concerns for equity than for adequacy and equality. This emphasis stems, at least in part, from the broader societal context in which the program operates.

In capitalist society the value of equity is generally accentuated—those who work hard deserve to be rewarded. According to normative standards, the capitalists are those reaping the just fruits of their labor. Socialist societies theoretically place greater stress on the value of equality. As Marx wrote, "The secret of the expression of value, namely that all kinds of labor are equal and equivalent, because, and so far as they are human, labour in general cannot be deciphered, until the notion of human equality has already acquired the fixity of a popular prejudice."[47] Once the notion of human equality has achieved the status of a "popular prejudice," differential treatment of dissimilar people is significantly reduced if not completely abolished because, judged by the most important of characteristics—their humanness—everybody is the same.

From this somewhat lofty perspective, the "why" of policy design may be analyzed in terms of the quest for distributive justice as it is manifest in the differential realization of adequacy, equity, and equality.[48] Although a policy may emphasize any one of these values, the emphasis is often tempered by the demands of the other two values as efforts are made to approximate distributive justice.

Individual and Collective Values in Public Assistance

Moving down a rung, a much larger range of social values enters into the consideration of choice. For instance, the values of privacy, dignity, work, and independence may influence the criteria of eligibility, the forms of social provision, and the design of delivery and finance arrangements. To illustrate, we list in Table 3.2 our four dimensions of choice and some of the competing values that influence them. These four value dichotomies are suggestive and hardly exhaust the range of possibilities. They were selected because the range of values represents variations on central issues of policy choice exemplified in the polarity of individualism versus collectivism. These issues concern the ways and extent to which expressions of individual interests are given free rein or are harnessed in the service of the common good. As Marshall explains:

> The claim of the individual to welfare is sacred and irrefutable and partakes of the character of a natural right . . . but the citizen of the Welfare State does not merely have the right to pursue welfare; he has the right to receive it, even if the

TABLE 3.2   Dimensions of Choice and Competing Value Orientations

Individualist Orientation	Dimensions of Choice	Collective Orientation
Cost effectiveness	Allocation	Social effectiveness
Freedom of choice	Provision	Social control
Freedom of dissent	Delivery	Efficiency
Local autonomy	Finance	Centralization

pursuit has not been particularly hot . . . But if we put individualism first, we must put collectivism second. The Welfare State is the responsible promoter and guardian of the welfare of the whole community, which is something more complex than the sum total of the welfare of its individual members arrived at by simple addition. The claims of the individual must always be defined and limited so as to fit into the complex and balanced pattern of the welfare of the community, and that is why the right to welfare can never have the full stature of a natural right. The harmonizing of individual rights with the common good is a problem which faces all human societies.[49]

Cost effectiveness may be applied to each dimension of choice. When applied to the basis of social allocations it is measured by the extent to which each dollar of benefit is allocated to those most in need—that is, those least able to purchase what they need in the open marketplace. The guiding thought is that there be no waste of resources. With the cost-effectiveness criterion, individual treatment varies according to individual circumstances. Implementing this value requires a high degree of selectivity in determining those who are eligible for benefits. Applied in the extreme, this value can produce invidious distinctions among people, dividing the community into groups of the dependent and the independent, the incompetent and the self-sufficient.

Social effectiveness may take different forms. One way it is measured in allocative decisions is by the extent to which all individuals are treated as equal members of the social body. Here the notion of effectiveness is related to the fact that nobody who is potentially eligible will feel inhibited about applying for benefits because of shame, stigma, or the organizational rigamarole that is often required to implement selective procedures. Allocations are universal: An individual's special need or defect need not be exposed for scrutiny in order to become eligible for benefits. The "badge of citizenship" is sufficient basis for entitlement. In what was once AFDC and is now the TANF program, for example, the basis of social allocations—a thorough and probing means test of every applicant—is clearly influenced more by concerns for cost effectiveness than social effectiveness.[50]

Titmuss has observed that the apparent strain between cost effectiveness and social effectiveness may be a function of the short-range perspective of using cost-effectiveness calculations, especially for medical benefits, where policy objectives include prevention as well as treatment. For example, if access to medical care entails a means-test investigation that is demeaning, time-consuming, or otherwise inconvenient, clients may procrastinate about seeking aid until the symptoms are so advanced that they can no longer be ignored. At this stage the cost of treatment is usually more expensive. In the long run, cost effectiveness and social effectiveness can be brought into harmony when the universal allocation of medical care saves more through prevention than selective allocations save by limiting treatment only to those in dire need.[51]

Freedom of choice is reflected in provisions that offer recipients considerable latitude to exercise their individual preferences. Thus, for example, when social provisions are in the form of cash, a high degree of consumer sovereignty is preserved. *Social control,* on the other hand, is reflected in provisions that limit individual choice. With in-kind provisions, recipients are limited to whatever specific benefits (housing, medical care, counseling, therapy, advice, information, etc.) are offered. Of course, they have the freedom to take it or leave it, but that is where the choice ends. In some social welfare programs, social provisions are linked so that freedom of choice in one area of provision is bought at the price of social control in another. This is the case in public assistance, where the allocation of financial aid has been tied to increasing levels of social control. For example, in AFDC, recipients initially were given cash grants and could exercise a degree of choice in meeting their daily requirements for material existence. Under the Family Support Act of 1988, cash assistance in AFDC was linked to participation in work training programs, and, in some states, to educational programs as well.[52] By 1996 when AFDC was supplanted by the TANF program, cash benefits were tied as incentives to a variety of behavioral expectations such as going to school, living at home (for unwed teenage mothers), participating in work training, and identifying the child's father. In a curious twist, these behavioral incentives are strongly supported by conservatives, who traditionally have disavowed the collectivists' conviction that government might improve the human condition through social engineering.

Freedom of dissent and efficiency are values that influence whether the delivery system is designed primarily along democratic or bureaucratic lines. Blau states the choice succinctly:

> *Bureaucratic and democratic structures can be distinguished . . . on the basis of the dominant organizing principle: efficiency or freedom of dissent. Each of these principles is suited for one purpose and not for another. When people set themselves the task of determining the social objectives that represent the interests of most of them, the crucial problem is to provide an opportunity for all conflicting viewpoints to be heard. In contrast, when the task is the achievement of given social objectives, the essential problem to be solved is to discover the efficient, not the popular, means for doing so.[53]*

In the TANF program, the delivery system is organized primarily along bureaucratic lines. Clients do not vote to establish the level of their grants or eligibility criteria. In other social welfare programs, however, social provision is so loosely formulated that the local delivery system is charged with the dual purpose of deciding on specific objectives and then carrying out those decisions. For instance, the War on Poverty and Model Cities programs of the 1960s required substantial citizen participation in program planning and implementation. These systems thus incorporated democratic as well as bureaucratic elements in their structure. The problem in these systems, it often turned out, is that neither value was served very well, or one value was emphasized at the expense of the other.[54]

Local autonomy and centralization are values that find expression in the financing and administration of programs. Strains between these values are most likely to emerge when program costs are shared intergovernmentally or, in the private sector, between nationwide and local voluntary organizations. Cost-sharing arrangements are implemented through federal grants-in-aid that vary along a continuum from broad purpose block grants to special-purpose categorical grants. The block grant is a lump-sum national contribution for local programs. It carries few specifications or requirements on how the money should be spent beyond requirements that it be applied to a general program realm such as health, community development, or education. This insures a high degree of local autonomy. At the other end of the continuum is the special purpose grant with detailed standards. Here, local discretion regarding the use of funds is restricted according to precise federal criteria. In most cost-sharing arrangements, the methods of finance fall somewhere midway on the continuum, reflecting the mutual desirability of local autonomy and national planning.

For example, although based on categorical principles, the AFDC program contained elements of both values. The federal funders attached various conditions to these categorical grants concerning citizenship, "statewideness," and the provision of services. Yet, local autonomy prevailed in at least two crucial aspects of the program. States were free to exercise broad discretion in defining the criteria of need and the amount of financial assistance that is provided to recipients. The centralist thrust of the program was mitigated in part because, as Burns explains, "to prescribe in the federal act both the standards of need which determine eligibility and the minimum level of living to be assured all eligible applicants raises major issues regarding federal interference in an area which traditionally has been thought of as peculiarly a matter for local determination."[55] When AFDC was supplanted by TANF in 1996, the funding arrangement changed from a categorical to a block grant, giving states much greater latitude to determine how funds are spent. Various conditions, nevertheless, were attached to the block grants concerning citizenship, time limits, and work requirements. (See Chapter 8).

Theories, Assumptions, and Social Choice

The subtle and complex relationships between value preferences and social welfare policies offer one level of insight into the "why" of social choice. Another dimension of analysis that has a bearing on this question involves theories and assumptions about how clients, delivery systems, methods of finance, and types of social provisions function, both independently and in concert. Much of this kind of theory-derived knowledge is fragmented and only partially verified. This is not to deny the effect of social science knowledge on choice, but rather than overestimate what is known, we use the term *theory* to cover the influence and support that social science insights render to policy choices. We classify as *assumptions* those suppositions for which there has been little systematic effort to obtain and codify evidence. In the general sense the term *assumptions* is used to designate theories "writ small."

To illustrate, let us look at public assistance. At least three assumptions under-pinning major policy choices in this program have been seriously challenged by subsequent evidence. First, the 1962 "service" amendments were supported by the belief that the clinical model of casework service would bring about change in the economic dependency of individuals in poverty. Implicit is the theory that poverty is mainly a function of individual deficiencies, deficiencies that can be transformed and alleviated through the casework process. This theory was rela-tively new. Until the 1950s, assistance recipients were generally considered "vic-tims of external circumstances, such as unemployment, disability, or the death of the family's breadwinner," who "needed to be 'relieved'—not treated or changed."[56]

In 1971, after reviewing studies of casework efforts to treat and rehabilitate those on public assistance, Carter concluded:

> It becomes clear that it is time to reassess the purposes of casework services offered welfare recipients and other low income groups for whom problems identified for alleviation are complex and interrelated with other personal, family, and commu-nity or societal problems . . . there are serious questions as to what behavioral changes can be set in motion without provision first being made for a decent level of living and access being provided to a range of social resources within the agency and the community.[57]

Second, the separation of income maintenance from the administration of social services was predicated on the assumption that services would be improved because the caseworker–client relationship would no longer be tinged by the coer-cive undertones emanating from the worker's discretionary authority over the client's budget. Clients, presumably, would be free to accept or reject services as needed, and caseworkers, released from the task of administering grants, would have more time to engage in a voluntary service enterprise. This is a plausible line of reasoning, but one open to critical examination. Neither the strength of the case-worker's coercive powers, and their effects on relationships with clients, nor the extent of client initiative to seek services when routine caseworker visits were ter-minated, was clearly discernible. It is quite possible, as Handler and Hollingsworth suggest, that the coercion argument was exaggerated and, more important, that in the absence of routine home visits welfare clients would be reluctant to seek help from an unknown official. Thus, "requiring welfare clients to take the initiative may have the effect of cutting off a reasonably valuable service that most clients, in their own words, seem to like."[58] Indeed, research findings on this issue reveal that AFDC recipients made higher demands for services and expressed greater satisfaction when service and income maintenance were combined.[59]

As a final example, we turn to the work-incentive program established under the 1967 social security amendments—a case that, perhaps, offers a lesson for the most recent work-oriented reforms in the TANF program. The perversely accurate acronym for the Work Incentive Program, WIP, conveys the image of an instrument used to drive beasts of burden. Through some creative bureaucratese it was quickly transformed to WIN (Work INcentive). An objective of the 1967 amendments was to swing AFDC services away from traditional social case-work toward more practical and concrete work-oriented provisions. This shift in emphasis from welfare to workfare then reflected, and continues to reflect, two assumptions: (1) that jobs are available for anyone who really wants to work, and (2) we know how to change deleterious patterns of behavior. The problem is primarily seen again as individual deficiency—the lack of skills and adverse attitudes toward work—although of a different nature than those amenable to psychiatric casework. The solution is to equip people for jobs and motivate them to seek employment.

Although facts about WIN are not decisive, what is known suggests that its assumptions, and the assumptions of workfare approaches more generally, are unrealistic. Levitan and Taggart indicated that of the 167,000 people who enrolled in WIN through March 1970, more than one-third dropped out of the program and, all told, only 25,000 got jobs. Those who moved on to work were "creamed" from the pool of applicants—those moving into jobs were those best prepared for jobs. This group included a high percentage of unemployed fathers receiving AFDC-UP who probably would have found employment sooner or later without social assistance. In light of the program's "conspicuously unspec-tacular performance," the study observes, "the wisdom of expanding WIN is questionable, and the theoretical arguments for such a move are even more dubious."[60]

A subsequent analysis of the WIN experience suggests that the program's shortcomings endured to the end. In 1982 only 3 percent of the AFDC clients reg-istered for the WIN program in New York State were placed in a job; an additional 5 percent found employment through their own efforts. In a distinct echo of Levitan and Taggart's findings, the 1982 study observed that "those who eventu-ally are served generally represent the easiest to employ—those most likely to get jobs without the help of special services."[61] Although recent findings on work

---

CAPSULE 3.5:   Tireless Tinkering with the Poor

Unfortunately, the sorry history and limita-tions of day care and work training as "solu-tions" to the welfare problem could not be faced by the administration's welfare special-ists in 1970 . . . But after a few years it will inevitably be discovered that work training and day care have had little effect on the num-ber of welfare dependents and no depressing effect on public relief costs. Some new solution will then be proposed, but the more realistic approach would be to accept the need for more welfare and to reject continued fantasiz-ing about day care and "workfare" as miracle cures.

Gilbert Steiner, *The State of Welfare*, 1971.

programs in the five states that formed a model for the Family Support of 1988 are somewhat more encouraging, a substantial proportion (from 40 to 80 percent) of participants remained unemployed after six to fifteen months. The extent to which this type of program can ameliorate the circumstances of welfare recipients, therefore, remains uncertain.[62]

The two assumptions that have girded workfare policies since the mid-1960s continue to brace the TANF initiatives of the 1990s—a line of reforms aptly characterized by Gilbert Steiner as "tireless tinkering with dependent families."[63]

We should point out that in these examples the influences of value and theory on policy have been treated separately as a matter of analytic convenience. In reality, theory and value do not separate quite so neatly. Social facts do not organize themselves into a coherent framework simply by being observed; a theoretical viewpoint is required. But if theory informs the ordering of social facts, what is it that informs theory? On this issue Gunnar Myrdal's insight is worth noting.

> *Prior to answers there must be questions, and the questions we raise stem from our interests in the matter, from our valuations. Indeed, our theories and all our scientific knowledge are necessarily pervaded by valuations. . . . Value premises are required not only in order to enable us to draw practical and political inferences from observations and economic analysis, but . . . in order to formulate a theory, to direct our observations, and to carry out our analysis.*[64]

Summary

In this chapter we have outlined an analytic approach to the study of social welfare policy. The essence of this approach may be summarized as follows:

1. Viewing social welfare policy as a benefit allocation mechanism requires four types of choices, those pertaining to allocations, provisions, delivery, and finance.
2. Understanding these four dimensions of choice requires knowing the basic alternatives associated with each.
3. Understanding why given alternatives may be preferred over others requires explicating the values, theories, and assumptions implicit in policy design.

The implication here is not that certain choices are inherently preferable to others. Different choice preferences will be registered by different policy planners, depending on the values, theories, and assumptions given the most worth and credence. Our objective in the following five chapters is to take each dimension of choice, delineate the basic policy alternatives, and examine the interplay of values, theories, and assumptions.

Notes

1. Eveline M. Burns, *Social Security and Public Policy* (New York: McGraw-Hill, 1956), ix.

2. T. H. Marshall, "Value Problems of Welfare Capitalism," *Journal of Social Policy,* 1(1) (January 1972), 19–20.

3. For further discussion of social and economic markets, see Neil Gilbert, *Capitalism and the Welfare State* (New Haven: Yale University Press, 1983) and Neil Gilbert and Barbara Gilbert, *The Enabling State: Modern Welfare Capitalism in America* (New York: Oxford University Press, 1989).

4. For an early analysis, see Ken Judge, "The Mixed Economy of Welfare: Purchase of Service Contracting in the Personal Social Services" (Canterbury: Personal Social Services Research Unit, University of Kent, Discussion Paper, 195, 1981).

5. Robert Reich, *The Next American Frontier* (New York: Times Books, 1983), 247.

6. For a review of this development, see Alfred Kahn and Sheila Kamerman (eds.), *Privatization and the Welfare State* (Princeton, NJ: Princeton University Press, 1989); and Norman Johnson (ed.), *Private Markets in Health and Welfare* (Oxford, England: Berg Publishers, 1995).

7. Gilbert and Gilbert, 129.

8. U.S. Bureau of the Census, *Statistical Abstract of the United States, 1992* (Washington, D.C.: Government Printing Office, 1992).

9. Marshall, "Value Problems of Welfare Capitalism."

10. For example, see Richard Titmuss, *Commitment to Welfare* (New York: Pantheon Books, 1970), 124; and Martin Wolins, "The Societal Function of Social Welfare," *New Perspectives,* 1(1) (Spring 1967), 5.

11. Mayer Zald (ed.), *Social Welfare Institutions* (New York: John Wiley & Sons, 1965), 4.

12. Neil Gilbert, *Welfare Justice: Restoring Social Equity* (New Haven, CT: Yale University Press, 1995).

13. Lawrence Mead, *Beyond Entitlement: The Social Obligations of Citizenship* (New York: Free Press, 1986).

14. See, for example, Amitai Etzioni, "What Community? Whose Responsiveness?" *Responsive Community,* 1(2), 1991, 5–8; and Mary Ann Glendon, *Rights Talk* (New York: Free Press, 1991). The Communitarian principles for improving the moral balance between rights and responsibilities are set forth in the "Responsive Communitarian Platform," *Responsive Community,* 2(1), 1992, 4–20.

15. The analytic questions with which we will deal have also been explored by Martin Rein, *Social Policy* (New York: Random House, 1970); Titmuss, *Commitment to Welfare,* 130–36; Kahn, *Theory and Practice of Social Planning,* 192–213; and Gilbert Steiner, *The State of Welfare* (Washington, D.C.: Brookings Institution, 1971) 1–30.

16. This case analysis draws substantially on material originally presented in Neil Gilbert, "The Transformation of Social Services," *Social Service Review,* 51(4) (December 1977), 624–49.

17. Martha Derthick, *Uncontrollable Spending for Social Services Grants* (Washington, D.C.: Brookings Institution, 1975), 8.

18. David Super, Sharon Parrott, Susan Steinmetz, and Cindy Mann, *The New Welfare Law* (Washington D.C.: Center on Budget and Policy Priorities, 1996).

19. Alan Pardini and David Lindeman, *Eight State Comparative Report on Social Services,* Working Paper No. 21 (San Francisco: Aging Health Policy Center, University of California, 1982).

20. A prominent example of the extreme faith on which the movement for intensive services by trained caseworkers relied is expressed in the design of a study that compared special intensive services by professional caseworkers with fifty multiproblem families over 2 1/2 years to a control group receiving routine services by staff without professional training. The primary assumption on which the study is based is that some degree of variation in social casework skills can have a significant impact on the severe problems created by economic deprivation. The results of this study showed no significant differences between the two client groups and was deemed inconclusive due to methodological flaws. But it is in the methodological design that faith is revealed. The goals of the service and how workers' activities related to these goals were defined

in such general terms as to be unmeasurable. See Gordon E. Brown (ed.), *The Multiproblem Dilemma: A Social Research Demonstration with Multiproblem Families* (Metuchen, NJ: Scarecrow Press, 1968).

21. Derthick, *Uncontrollable Spending for Social Services Grants,* 9.

22. President's Commission on Income Maintenance, *Background Papers* (Washington, D.C.: Government Printing Office, 1970), 307.

23. Joel F. Handler and Jane Hollingsworth, *The Deserving Poor: A Study of Welfare Administration* (Chicago: Markham Publishing, 1971), 127.

24. While efforts were made to upgrade services, the results were seriously limited by the dearth of trained social workers available for these jobs and turnover difficulties in departments of public assistance. A study of turnover in public assistance agencies in New York City during 1964 indicates that 30 percent of the workers resigned within nine months of their appointment. Lawrence Podell, "Attrition of First-Line Social Service Staff," *Welfare in Review,* 5(1) (January 1967), 9–14. In 1966 the national turnover rate for public assistance agencies was 22.8 percent. This figure is almost double the national turnover rate of all professionals in civil service positions on a federal, state, and local level at that time. Further comparisons along these lines are reported by Irving Kermish and Frank Kushin in "Why High Turnover? Social Work Staff Losses in a County Welfare Department," *Public Welfare,* April 1969, 138. A survey of 766 AFDC recipients in the summer and autumn of 1967 gives evidence of a very low level of social service activity in the field. "For the majority of AFDC families, social services means a visit of a caseworker a little more than once every three months for a little more than thirty minutes per visit, with an occasional client's call to her caseworker." Joel F. Handler and Ellen J. Hollingsworth, "The Administration of Social Services and the Structure of Dependency: The Views of AFDC Recipients," *Social Service Review,* 43(4) (December 1969), 412.

25. Derthick, *Uncontrollable Spending for Social Services Grants,* 19.

26. Mildred Rein, "Social Services as a Work Strategy," *Social Service Review,* 49 (December 1975), 519.

27. Derthick, *Uncontrollable Spending for Social Services Grants,* 19.

28. Social and Rehabilitation Service, Department of Health, Education, and Welfare, *Social Services U.S.A.,* Oct.–Dec. 1975, Publication No. SRS 76-03300 (Washington, D.C.: National Center of Social Statistics, 1975), 7.

29. *Washington Social Legislation Bulletin,* 31(32), April 23, 1990, 125.

30. The evolution of caretaking services is discussed in Robert Morris and Delwin Anderson, "Personal Care Services: An Identity for Social Work," *Social Service Review,* 49 (June 1975), 157–74.

31. Gilbert Y. Steiner, *The State of Welfare* (Washington, D.C.: Brookings Institution, 1971), 106–10.

32. There were ways to circumvent this restriction. In practice, for example, it was not uncommon for a donation to be made by a United Fund Organization with the request that the contribution be used to support a particular type of activity in a specified community, one performed only by an agency affiliated with the United Fund Organization. In this fashion, private donations could be covertly earmarked as the local share for a designated agency. See, for example, Booz, Allen, and Hamilton, *Purchase of Social Service— Study of the Experience of Three States in Purchase of Service by Contract Under the Provisions of the 1967 Amendments to the Social Security Act,* Report Submitted to the Social and Rehabilitation Service, January 29, 1971 (distributed by National Technical Information Service, U.S. Department of Commerce), 40–42.

33. Lester Salamon and Alan Abramson, *The Federal Budget and the Non-Profit Sector* (Washington, D.C.: Urban Institute Press, 1982), 64.

34. Derthick, *Uncontrollable Spending for Social Services Grants,* 100–1.

35. Alva Myrdal, *Nation and Family* (MIT Paperback Edition) (Cambridge, MA: MIT Press, 1968), 1.

36. U.S. Bureau of the Census, *Statistical Abstract of the United States* (Washington, D.C.: Government Printing Office, 1995), 388.

37. U.S. Social Security Administration, *Social Security Bulletin,* 58(4) (Winter 1995), 167.

38. More precisely, the block grant allocation is based on the highest level of each state's spending calculated on their AFDC expenditures in 1994, 1995, or the average expenditure from 1992 to 1994. In addition, the Act provides for a contingency fund of $2 billion to meet any increase in needs experienced by the states. Super, et. al., *The New Welfare Law.*

39. Jocelyn Guyer, Cindy Mann, and David Super, *The Timeline for Implementing the New Welfare Law* (Washington D.C.: Center on Budget and Policy Priorities, 1996), 2.

40. Aristotle, *The Politics* (Modern Library Edition) (New York: Random House, 1943), 260–63.

41. Gregory Vlastos, "Justice and Equality," in Richard Brandt (ed.), *Social Justice* (Englewood Cliffs, NJ: Prentice-Hall, 1962), 32.

42. Cited in Karl de Schweinitz, *England's Road to Social Security* (Perpetua Edition) (New York: A.S. Barnes and Co., 1961), 123.

43. U.S. Department of Health, Education and Welfare, *Work in America* (Washington, D.C.: Government Printing Office, 1972).

44. See, for example, William Shannon, "A Radical, Direct, Simple, Utopian Alternative to Day-Care Centers," *New York Times Magazine,* April 30, 1972; and Sheila M. Rothman, "Other People's Children: The Day Care Experience in America," *Public Interest,* No. 30 (Winter 1973), 11–27.

45. William Frankena, "The Concept of Social Justice," in Richard Brandt (ed.), *Social Justice* (Englewood Cliffs, NJ: Prentice-Hall, 1962), 23.

46. See Robert Hunter, *Poverty,* Peter d'A Jones (ed.) (Torchbook edition) (New York: Harper & Row, 1965), 51–52.

47. Karl Marx, *Das Kapital,* Friedrich Engels (ed.), Vol. 1 (Gateway Edition) (Chicago: Henry Regnery Co., 1959), 33–34.

48. For example, see Richard Titmuss, "Equity, Adequacy, and Innovation in Social Security," *International Social Security Review,* 2 (1970), 250–67.

49. T. H. Marshall, *Class, Citizenship, and Social Development* (Anchor Books Edition) (New York: Doubleday, 1965), 258–59.

50. An analysis of cost effectiveness as it is expressed in different income-maintenance strategies is provided by James Cutt, "Income Support Programmes for Families with Children: Alternatives for Canada," *International Social Security Review,* 23(1) (1970), 100–12.

51. Titmuss, *Commitment to Welfare,* 69–71.

52. "Learnfare: Policy Implications," *Youth Law News,* May/June, 1989, 12–13.

53. Peter Blau, *Bureaucracy in Modern Society* (New York: Random House, 1956), 107.

54. Various studies on the War on Poverty and Model Cities have documented this result. See, for example, Ralph Kramer, *Participation of the Poor* (Englewood Cliffs, NJ: Prentice-Hall, 1969); Neil Gilbert, *Clients or Constituents* (San Francisco: Jossey-Bass, 1970); Neil Gilbert and Harry Specht, *Dynamics of Community Planning* (Cambridge, MA: Ballinger, 1977).

55. Burns, *Social Security and Public Policy,* 231.

56. Davis McEntire and Joanne Haworth, "Two Functions of Public Welfare: Income Maintenance and Social Services," *Social Work,* 12(1) (January 1967), 24–25.

57. Genevieve Carter, "Public Welfare," in Henry S. Maas (ed.), *Research in the Social Services: A Five Year Review* (New York: National Association of Social Workers, 1971), 224.

58. Handler and Hollingsworth, "The Administration of Social Services and the Structure of Dependency," 418. For a comprehensive historical review of the issues in "separation of services," see Winfred Bell, "Too Few Services to Separate," *Social Work,* 18(2) (March 1973), 66–77.

59. Irving Piliavin and Alan Gross, "The Effects of Separation of Services and Income Maintenance on AFDC Recipients," *Social Service Review,* 51 (September 1977), 389–406. Also, see Bill Benton, Jr., "Separation Revisited," *Public Welfare,* 38(2) (Spring 1980), 15–21.

60. Sar Levitan and Robert Taggart, III, *Social Experimentation and Manpower Policy: The Rhetoric and the Reality* (Baltimore: Johns Hopkins, 1971), 53.

61. Mary Bryna Sunger, "Generating Employment for AFDC Mothers," *Social Service Review,* 58(1) (March 1984), 32.

62. Judith Gueron, "Reforming Welfare with Work," *Public Welfare* (Fall 1987), 13–25.

63. Steiner, *The State of Welfare.*

64. Gunnar Myrdal, *Value in Social Theory,* Paul Streeten (ed.) (London: Routledge and Kegan Paul, 1958), 254–55.

Chapter **4**

The Basis of Social Allocations

"I suppose you mean that you have no money to pay wages in," said I. "But the credit given the worker at the government storehouse answers to his wages with us. How is the amount of the credit given respectively to the workers in different lines determined? By what title does the individual claim his particular share? What is the basis of allotment?"

"His title," replied Doctor Leete, "is his humanity. The basis of his claim is the fact that he is a man."

EDWARD BELLAMY
Looking Backward, 1888

In his classic utopian novel, *Looking Backward,* Edward Bellamy views the "good society" as a place where every individual can claim an equal share of the goods and services produced by the nation. Citizens are guaranteed a comfortable standard of living from, as Bellamy puts it, "cradle to grave." Entitlement does not depend on being rich or poor, single or married, brilliant or dull, healthy or ill; instead, a person's entitlement is his or her humanity.[1] In Bellamy's vision, social allocations are arranged according to the principle that everyone deserves an equal share, with one exception. That is, Doctor Leete explains, "A man able to do duty [i.e., work] and persistently refusing is sentenced to solitary imprisonment on bread and water 'til he consents."[2] Although this may seem rather harsh, in Bellamy's society work roles are structured to dignify every task and to allow a choice of occupations broad enough to suit individual preferences. Nevertheless, as an introduction to the allocative dimension of choice in social welfare policy, there is perhaps some small comfort in noting that even in a utopia of rationality, harmony, and consensus, problems of social allocation are not entirely amenable to neat, unqualified solutions.

Who Shall Benefit?

In the real world few social welfare policy issues engender more vigorous debate than who shall benefit and the manner in which entitlement is defined. The rules used to determine who benefits from any social welfare policy may be predicted on a wide and diverse range of criteria ranging from the unusual (Native American blood quantum) to the mundane (amount of money earned). We refer to the general principles that underlie these criteria as the bases of social allocations.

Attempts to develop principles of eligibility traditionally begin with the distinction between universalism and selectivity. *Universalism* denotes benefits made available to an entire population as a basic right. Examples are social security for the elderly and public education for the young. *Selectivity* denotes benefits made available on the basis of individual need, usually determined by a test of income. Examples include public assistance and public housing for the poor.

The social policy literature contains an ongoing debate between proponents of universal and selective principles.[3] Universalists view social policy as society's proper response to those ordinary life problems faced by all members of the community—not just the poor, the disabled, or those facing special hardships. For universalists, all citizens are "at risk" in the sense that all of us, at one time or another, face a variety of common social needs. The proper aim of the welfare state, accordingly, is to organize broad programs of response, without differentiating among rich or poor, men or women, or other citizen categories.

Young people, for example, need care and education. Those who are ill need health care. The elderly, disabled, and unemployed need income support. Universalists favor public arrangements that address these needs on the basis of a general entitlement, as a social right comparable to the political rights we take for granted. Social insurance, public education, health care for the aged—programs available without regard to income—stand as the models for a proper welfare society.

Universalists also emphasize the value of social effectiveness as manifest in the preservation of dignity and social unity that result when people are not divided into separate groups of givers and receivers. In their view, programs based on economic determinations are divisive, accentuating differences in society that frequently take on moral as well as economic meanings. Those who receive benefits often feel *demeaned,* even when their rights to benefits are clear. Receiving food stamps, for example, or being assigned to a special class for the educationally impaired, is for many a sign of failure, an embarrassing, stigmatizing experience. "Invidious rationing for the poor," as Alvin Schorr puts it, "does not seem a sound principle for a welfare state."[4]

Universalists, finally, argue the *political* advantages of social programs based on inclusiveness, citing the strength throughout the world of policies aiding broad populations. Universal programs, admittedly, cost more, but they are far more popular than means-tested programs that focus on marginal social groups. The history of social provision in the United States—AFDC being the most notable example—vividly demonstrates the political vulnerability of programs exclusively for the poor.

Selectivists see the world very differently. They view the appropriate scope of social policy in terms of carefully targeted beneficiaries. Families or individuals demonstrating need, they believe, should have priority for assistance. Rather than sponsoring universally available entitlements, selectivists favor benefits that are restricted. Underlying this perspective is the view that a proper social policy, especially in an era of fiscal constraint, must be a limited social policy, that people who can afford to meet their own needs should not receive government handouts, and that taxpayers should focus their help on that margin of the population legitimately unable to fend for themselves.

Means-testing, obviously, is a direct way of confining social benefits. Circumscribing eligibility according to need, selectivists argue, reduces overall spending, overcomes the tendency for welfare to benefit the politically powerful middle class, and ensures that available funds focus on those in the most dire straits. Why after all, should money be wasted on people not in great need, or in no need at all?

But neither side is quite satisfied to let the debate rest here. Each lays claim to at least a share of the values claimed by the opposition. Universalists, for example, claim cost effectiveness because broad prevention programs such as comprehensive prenatal health care or generally available preschool programs can avoid future problems—and their associated costs—in a way that case-by-case eligibility determination cannot. In the long-run cost accounting of "an ounce of prevention,"

CAPSULE 4.1: Targeting within Universalism

We can draw two conclusions from the history of social provision in the United States. First, targeted antipoverty efforts have generally been inadequately funded, demeaning to the poor, and politically unsustainable. Second, some kinds of (relatively) universal social policy have succeeded politically. And within the framework of universal programs, less privileged people have received extra benefits without stigma. I call this pattern "targeting within universalism" and suggest it could become the basis for a revitalized strategy against poverty.

Those who want to help the poor should not try to devise new programs finely targeted to low-income people or the "underclass." They should forget about reforming means-tested public assistance programs. Rather, they should aim at bypassing and ultimately displacing "welfare" with new policies that address the needs of the less privileged in the context of programs that also serve middle-class and stable working-class citizens.

Theda Skocpol, "Sustainable Social Policy: Fighting Poverty Without Poverty Programs," *The American Prospect*, 2, Summer, 1990, 59, 67.

then, universalists infer an economic saving to the larger community. As a bonus, universal allocations are said to be less expensive to administer than selective allocations because they do not require constant screening, checkups, and benefit adjustments to ensure the proper level of assistance.

Universalists also argue that broad-scope policies, properly constituted, can be redistributive, concentrating assistance on those with the greatest needs. This is Theda Skocpol's argument in Capsule 4.1. For example, "tax backs" can be employed to shift the burden of universal benefits to the economically better off. That is, by including the value of universal benefits in taxable income, richer individuals and families wind up supporting a disproportionate part of the costs involved.[5] Many countries, for example, including the United States, include at least a portion of the value of social security benefits in taxable income. And increasing numbers are beginning to tax children's allowances. In this fashion, programs for everyone are substantially financed by those most able to pay.

Universal services, on the pay-out side, provide a basic level of assistance to all while concentrating additional help on those in greatest need. In this way, programs for the poor, as Nicholas Lemann states, can "be contained (to some extent camouflaged) within programs to help the middle class."[6] Many countries follow this approach, modifying programs of universal scope to address the needs of the poor. In the U.S., for example, social security's benefit structure is "tilted" to

---

CAPSULE 4.2:   The Fine Feathered (Gallic) Nest

Scarcely three days old, Thomas Meilleroux slept softly in Paris's Hôspital Saint-Vincent-de-Paul, a pink shell of tiny fist tucked under his head. He had every right to wear an air of blissful unconcern. The moment Christine, his mother, announced her pregnancy, social security mailed a thick folder, the *carnet de maternité.*

It brought medications, exams, childbirth classes, and—from the sixth month—a monthly pregnancy allowance of 812 francs (about $135 U.S.). Afterward: ten visits to a physical therapist to tone the stretch-marked tummy. "They make it so easy, you don't even have to think," says Christine. "I never paid a cent."

Now our little bundle of *joie* is three months old. Young Thomas happens to be a firstborn. If he were a second child, Christine would collect a hundred-dollar-a-month family allowance until his 18th year. Were he the third, she'd pocket $200. For a fourth, $330. Single parents, low-income families, and handicapped children get more.

The goal is to raise the birthrate and ensure a decent living standard. But the biggest benefit of the free care lavished on expectant mothers (and a legally enforced maternity leave of at least 16 weeks at 80 percent pay) is an infant-mortality rate of 7.6 per thousand, among the world's lowest—well below the United States' 10.4.

The basic family allowance is not tied to income. Even the matron who shops for her precious heirs in Christian Dior Bébé collects. After all, *c'est son droit*—it's her right.

In France social welfare is not a charity but a right of citizenship inviolable as the August vacation.

Cathy Newman, "The Fine Feathered Nest—'La Protection Sociale'," *National Geographic,* July 1989, 130.

disproportionately help low-income earners. In Great Britain public health home visits for new mothers are universal, with additional visits focused on those mothers, and children, at greater risk. In France (see Capsule 4.2), lone parents, low-income families, and disabled children receive, in addition to the standard family allowance, a special targeted supplement.

Selectivists claim their own version of social effectiveness. If society seeks to move toward greater equality, they argue, offering benefits to the poor alone is bound to be more effective than allocations for everyone. Provisions targeted on the needy—whether through education, health care, child care, or housing—clearly reduce the inimical discrepancies that produce tension and hostility in our society. Given vast unmet needs, equity would seem to demand that the poor receive first call on scarce public resources.

These are some of the general issues that provide a framework for the universal-selective debate. To place this debate in a substantive context, let us illustrate how the choice between universal and selective principles translates into specific policy proposals. And let us also examine the values and assumptions that underlie these principles when they are applied.

Universality and Selectivity in Income Maintenance

In the decades-long dialogue concerning income-maintenance programs, numerous reform measures have been put forth by academicians and politicians.[7] These proposals can be analyzed from different perspectives. For example, they can be placed along a continuum of generosity, depending on where they define the poverty level and the proposed amount of financial aid they offer. Alternatively, they can be viewed according to their decision-making structure, varying by the degree to which policy is centralized or localized. Most recently, debate has centered on issues of moral values and reciprocity, with conservatives arguing for a reformed system of public aid focusing on jobs, time-limited assistance, and the reduction of teen pregnancy.

In the years of debate over the "proper" basis for allocating cash benefits, a variety of program reforms have been advocated. In the 1960s and 1970s, the choice between universalism and selectivism was debated in terms of two broad program options: guaranteed income programs (frequently referred to as negative income taxes) and children's allowances (sometimes called family allowances). In the 1980s and 1990s, the nature of the debate changed as efforts were made to find compromises between universalism and selectivity, and variant programs such as the Earned Income Tax Credit achieved considerable success.

Guaranteed income programs are defined by two characteristics: the provision of a defined minimum subsidy for families with little or no income and the utilization of a formula to determine how much this subsidy decreases as earnings increase. This formula represents what economists call a negative tax. Most proposals suggest administering the guarantee through the Internal Revenue Service, using the same procedures by which personal income taxes are collected and refunds distributed. Simply stated, the income tax structure would become a two-way operation with money flowing to the government from people with incomes above a certain level and money flowing from the government to people with incomes below that level. In either case, the amount paid in or out would be graduated according to income. An essential feature of the plan is that the allocation of benefits is tied directly to an income test and is thereby based on the principle of selectivity.

Schemes for a children's allowance, on the other hand, usually involve the provision of a *demogrant*, "a uniform payment to certain categories of persons identified only by demographic (usually age) characteristics."[8] More than sixty nations throughout the world, including most of the industrial West (but not the United States) offer some form of children's allowance as an integral part of their welfare system. (The United States, however, provides a dependents exemption as part of its federal income taxes, which achieves some of the same purposes.) The development of children's allowances has achieved widespread support for various reasons, among them the fact that children represent a substantial proportion of the poor and, wherever one places the blame and however one perceives the causes of poverty, children are clearly innocent victims. An essential characteristic of the demogrant is that benefits are allocated to *all* families, regardless of economic circumstances, thereby reflecting the principle of universality.[9] Table 4.1 shows your child allowance variations.

To illustrate the issues that arise in applying the universal-selective framework, the basic features of two classic income-maintenance proposals will be described. The first is the negative tax program tested experimentally in the mid-1970s in Seattle and Denver.[10] The second is the children's allowance proposal developed in 1974 by Martha Ozawa, one of the foremost advocates of this type of program in the United States.[11]

Seattle and Denver Income Maintenance Experiments

The Seattle and Denver Income Maintenance Experiments (SIME/DIME) were the largest and most carefully controlled income-maintenance experiments in history. The sample enrollment in the experiment included 4,706 families, 44 percent assigned to the control group and the remainder divided among eleven experimental groups. Each experimental group received one of three guaranteed levels of annual income—$3,800, $4,800, and $5,600—and was taxed at varying rates. Four negative tax rates were used: two constant tax rates (one of 50 percent and the other of 70 percent) and two varying tax rates that started at 70 percent and 80 percent and declined as income increased. Using the 50 percent constant tax rate and the $5,600 subsidy as an example, a recipient family with no earned income would be paid $5,600 a year. For each dollar earned, their grant would be reduced by 50 cents. With this negative tax rate, an income of $11,200 is the break-even level, the point at which the grant drops to zero.

Children's Allowance

The Ozawa proposal, formulated in 1974, involved an allotment of $60 a month for each child, with payments independent of family income or other eligibility conditions. Under the proposal, the allowance itself constituted taxable income. When translated into dollars and cents, this meant that families of equal size received exactly the same benefits. Depending on their income, however, these families ended up returning different amounts of the allowance to the government through their income taxes. A family with income low enough to fall below the federal tax threshold, for example, would not have their allowance taxed at all, whereas a family in the 15 percent bracket would have a portion of the allowance "taxed back." Households with higher incomes, in higher tax brackets, would find their allowance reduced by greater amounts.

TABLE 4.1   Child Allowance Standards in France, Japan, Sweden, and the United Kingdom, 1995

France

Age: Under 18 (20 for students, apprentices, vocational trainees, or disabled).
Coverage: Payable monthly to families with two or more children.
Benefit amount: $124 for two children; $159 for third and each subsequent child; plus a $35 increase for each child aged 10–15; and $62 for each child beyond age 15. Young child allowance is $178, payable beginning with the fifth month of pregnancy until the third month after birth without means test, then until age 3 subject to a means test. Additional allowances payable depending on means test, single parenthood, etc.

Japan

Age: First child under 4 and second and subsequent child under 3.
Coverage: Payable monthly to residents with one or more children who meet an income test. Requirements for a family of four: income below $36,540 a year.
Benefit amount: $51 for first and second child; $102 for third and each subsequent child.

Sweden

Age: Under 16 (20 for students).
Coverage: Payable monthly to all residents with one or more children.
Benefit amount: $100 for first child; $200 for second; $326 for third; $479 for fourth; and $598 for five or more children.

United Kingdom

Age: Under 16 (19 for full-time students in nonadvanced education).
Coverage: Payable weekly to residents with one or more children.
Benefit amount: $16 for first child; $13 for each additional child; plus supplement of $10 for the first child of a single parent.

Source: Ilene R. Zeitzer, "Social Insurance Provisions for Children with Disabilities," *Social Security Bulletin, 58*(3), Fall 1995, 32–48.

In this fashion, the net gain received by the allowance varies by income. The significance of this arrangement is that it makes the children's allowance a benefit that is universal at the point of distribution, but selective at the point of consumption. This is not an attribute only of children's allowance. When we consider how benefits are financed, some form of selectivity creeps into virtually all universal schemes. As Reddin has demonstrated, universal benefits are "those in which the universal gene is dominant but where there are also variant forms of 'recessive' selective genes incorporated in the structure."[12]

More recent proposals have suggested repealing the existing federal income tax exemption for children and replacing it with a children's allowance.[13] This would have a decided redistributive impact because the exemption—$2650 per child in 1997—benefits upper-income parents far more than lower-income parents. Parents in the 39.6% income tax bracket, for example, receive tax relief worth $1049 (39.6% of $2650) per child whereas parents in the 15% bracket receive just $397. And poor parents, those earning so little that they pay no taxes, get no benefit. Eliminating the exemption would save approximately $22 billion annually (1989 calculations), a sum that, transformed into a universal allowance, could provide *all* parents approximately $300 per child per year.[14]

The Negative Income Tax in Action: The Earned Income Tax Credit

The pros and cons of negative income and child allowance proposals have been strongly argued for some time. Neither plan, however, proved politically popular. Rather than making sweeping comprehensive changes in our system of social welfare, citizens and elected officials have generally been content to live with a variety of separate programs geared to specific needs and segments of the population, and reflecting different principles and values. Although our political system has avoided grand new schemes of comprehensive reform, both the negative income tax and the children's allowance have been incorporated, in modest and camouflaged forms, into our ongoing social policies.

The case of the personal exemption has been described. Tax-paying families have long received exemptions for each of their dependents, providing a significant form of income support that varies with family obligations. The Internal Revenue Code also contains a viable negative income tax in the form of the Earned Income Tax Credit (EITC). The credit, first enacted in 1974, contains many of the key characteristics of guaranteed income schemes. It provides a basic income subsidy to low-income families, it utilizes a formula to determine how subsidies decrease as earned income increases, and it is administered through the tax code. The EITC is different from a guaranteed income plan, however, in that it covers only *part* of the population (i.e., low-income wage-earning families). People who don't work are not covered.

Under EITC provisions, a family with two children earning under $8,425 (1996 figures) gets roughly a 40% tax credit—that is, a 40 cent subsidy for each dollar they earn (Figure 4.1). The credit reaches its maximum, $3,370, for earnings ranging from $8,425 to $10,999. As income rises above $11,000, the credit is reduced by 21 cents for each dollar earned, ultimately phasing out at $27,000. What makes the arrangement a negative tax is its *refundability*. That is, when the value of the credit exceeds the amount of taxes owed, the worker receives a cash rebate.[15]

The EITC only covers workers, so unlike the SIME/DIME demonstration, it has a salutary impact on employment. In this sense, it is akin to a wage subsidy, concentrating its benefits on those who are poor *even though* they work. Up to a point at least, the more people work, the *more* they get—quite the opposite of other negative tax and guaranteed income plans. According to David Ellwood, the EITC avoids the "conundrums" of welfare:

> *The rewards of work are increased, not diminished. Benefits go only to those with an earned income. People are helped without any need of a stigmatizing, invasive, and often degrading welfare system, and their autonomy is increased, not decreased. Since it truly would be part of the tax system, people would not be isolated. The negative impact on the work effort of the poor is likely to be small if it exists at all, but the benefits to the working poor may be large. And employers*

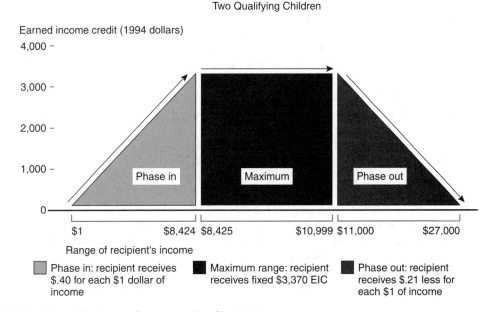

FIGURE 4.1 The Earned Income Credit, 1996.

Source: Congressional Research Service, 1996.

would have no reason to change their hiring practices. Their cost of doing business would essentially be unchanged except for slight additional administrative costs for employers who provided negative withholding.[16]

Since it is restricted to working families, the EITC is hardly the broad-brush measure proposed in the 1960s and 1970s by negative tax advocates. Moreover, EITC benefits are more modest than the most proposed negative income tax guarantees. Nevertheless, the EITC exists and the negative income tax doesn't. For all practical purposes, indeed, the negative income tax idea has faded to near oblivion, and is not likely to be revived as part of any income strategy in the near future. Refundable credits on the EITC model, on the other hand, constitute an antipoverty measure with substantial promise. Combined with the income tax exemption, it offers a mechanism for significant income support—especially for low-wage earners. Were the EITC further liberalized and tied more firmly to family size, it could go even farther in reducing poverty in this country.

Social Effectiveness and Cost Effectiveness

When the abstract principles of the universal-selective debate are applied to choices among concrete alternatives, such as the income-maintenance schemes just described, or to existing programs such as social security or public aid, the discussion generally centers on considerations of social effectiveness and cost effectiveness, the definition of these values, and assumptions regarding policy elements that facilitate and impede their realization.

Measures of cost effectiveness in income maintenance are usually determined by comparing the total costs of the alternative schemes, the extent to which the allocated funds fill the poverty gap, and the amount of "seepage" to the nonpoor. Implicit in this is a definition of income maintenance that seeks to improve the lot of the statistically defined poor (those people with annual incomes below the federally defined poverty line).

On the basis of these criteria, the negative income tax is clearly superior to child allowances. That is, benefits akin to SIME/DIME provide higher levels of assistance to the poorest families with little seepage to working- or middle-class income groups. The same is true of today's public assistance programs. While universal benefits, available to citizens of all income classes, certainly help to alleviate poverty, they are relatively inefficient in doing so. That is because only a small portion of their overall value assist the poor. This is especially true for children and families. A recent calculation by Irwin Garfinkel, for example, found that single parent families—a group particularly vulnerable to poverty—receive a share of universal benefits about equal to their percentage of the overall population. In stark contrast, as Table 4.2 indicates, they receive a full 75% of targeted, means-tested transfers.

Selecting the poor for benefits, not unexpectedly, is an efficient antipoverty strategy. However, this advantage is hardly impressive if the goal of public policy is to improve the lot of children in general, an important objective given the fact

TABLE 4.2 **Public Benefits to Families with Children, 1992, in Billions of Dollars**

	All Families	Single-parent Families
Universal Programs		
Cash	$ 50	$12
In-kind	$230	$58
Selective Programs		
Cash	$ 32	$25
In-kind	$ 95	$70

Source: Irwin Garfinkel, "Economic Security for Children," in Garfinkel et al. (Eds.) *Social Policies for Children*, 1996, p. 38.
Note: Universal cash programs include social security, unemployment insurance, and workers compensation. Universal in-kind programs include K–12 education and Medicare. Selective cash programs include AFDC, SSI, and General Assistance. Selective in-kind programs include Medicaid, Food Stamps, Housing, Head Start, and Foster Care.

that working and middle-class families, as well as the poor, frequently require additional income to insure the welfare of their members. From this viewpoint, cost effectiveness is defined quite differently and universal schemes may be preferable. As Cutt points out:

> *Universal schemes may be considered to be redistributive in a horizontal sense—from the childless to those with children—and therefore may be seen as having a broader objective than a selective scheme, specifically the alleviation of need among children in any income group, rather than the more tightly focused alleviation of need in families defined as poor in a statistical sense."*[17]

On the other side of the ledger, *social* effectiveness tends to be identified with the universal approach, although here, too, a definitive case is lacking. Estimates concerning the social effectiveness of income-maintenance schemes are based on certain assumptions about the potential consequences of the alternative approaches. These consequences include the effects on work, childbearing, family stability, stigmatization, and social integration. To illustrate these factors, let us review some relevant research findings.

Work Incentives

All social welfare benefits, to some extent, provide an incentive for the very circumstances they are established to ameliorate. Unemployment insurance makes it easier to be unemployed. Public assistance makes it easier to support a child without working. In this sense there is a germ of truth in the contention of Charles Murray and other conservatives that welfare "causes" dependency.[18] To the extent that they eliminate some degree of economic stress, therefore, both SIME/DIME and children's allowances have some negative effect on the incentive to work.

The engineers of welfare reform in the 1960s and 1970s were sensitive to these "perverse incentives" and sought to arrange payments in ways that would minimize them. Since the disincentive to work in a guaranteed income arrangement such as SIME/DIME was great because the basic payment in a zero-work/zero-income situation was high, these programs sought to reduce benefits only fractionally in response to work earnings. That is, the "tax" on work implicit in the benefit formula was kept low so as not to discourage recipients from getting jobs.

One of the most perplexing issues in the design of negative income tax schemes is the impact of different tax rates on work incentives. Simply put, how does a 50-, 60-, or 70-cent reduction in grant payments for each dollar of income earned affect a beneficiary's motivation to work? And how do these effects differ for grants offering low and high levels of support? The issue is complex because the lines of influence may flow in both directions. That is, high tax rates may be an inducement as well as a deterrent to greater work effort. The popular belief is that the person who gets to keep only 50 cents on a dollar is less inclined to work than the person who keeps 90 cents. However, assuming the desire for a certain standard of living, an individual who keeps only 50 cents may work harder and longer just to maintain his or her position, whereas the person who keeps 90 cents initially has more money to spend and may opt to enjoy more leisure time rather than supplement his or her income by additional work. That is to say, except for extreme cases where the tax rate approaches 100 percent, the point at which a worker may decide that the additional income is not worth the effort is indeterminate.

Regarding the ordinary federal income tax, for example, there is little evidence to support the belief that high tax rates necessarily have a deleterious influence on work. After reviewing a number of studies, economist George Break concluded that:

> . . . neither in Great Britain nor in the United States is there any convincing evidence that high levels of taxation seriously interfere with work incentives. There are, in fact . . . a number of good reasons for believing that considerably higher taxes could be sustained without injury to worker motivation.[19]

In the SIME/DIME experiments, however, the evidence was not quite so encouraging. In the first edition of this book we reported that the initial findings of one experimental negative tax program showed that "families receiving assistance worked just as hard as ever—and there were even some indications that they had been stimulated to work harder." The early findings also suggested that psychological barriers or disincentives to work were not evident even for those families whose earnings increased to the point where they were no longer eligible for assistance.[20] However, further research revealed that these conclusions were somewhat premature. The preliminary findings reported in the early 1970s were sharply contradicted after a longer period of study of a much larger sample in the SIME/DIME programs.

Findings indicate that, compared to the control group, families receiving the guaranteed-income grant worked significantly fewer hours per year. Although changes in work effort varied with the amount of the grants and the negative tax rates, an estimate of the nationwide effects of a SIME/DIME program suggested that a guaranteed income at 75 percent of the poverty line and a negative tax rate of 50 percent would reduce work effort about 6 percent for husbands, 23 percent for wives, and 7 percent for female heads of families.[21]

There are a number of reasons to believe that these findings underestimate the work reduction that would actually take place. One cannot discount the possibility that simply knowing they were part of an important social experiment may have influenced the participants' behavior. The *Hawthorne effect*, a well-known phenomenon in social research, suggests that in the process of becoming actively engaged in an experiment participants develop a commitment to its success, and an inclination to behave in ways that do not disappoint the investigators.[22] Moreover, the limited scale of SIME/DIME could not simulate the effects of a nationwide program with millions of participants who might well organize to lobby for higher benefits. The relatively brief duration of the experiment no doubt inhibited tendencies to reduce work effort and risk losing a job that the participant would need when SIME/DIME grants ended. There is also a reasonable possibility that a guaranteed minimum income would invite early retirements. Compensating for these and other factors that might have biased the SIME/DIME measurements, Martin Anderson estimated that any such scheme, nationally implemented, would result in a minimum 29 percent reduction in the work effort of low-income workers.[23] What this means is that a guaranteed income for everyone would result in public money replacing a considerable amount of income that recipients would otherwise have earned themselves. This not only makes for a costly program, it makes for a morally questionable one. A society that prizes independent effort and initiative is not likely to value public policy that appears to undermine the work ethic.

Yet questions of the extent to which income guarantees affect work cannot be put to rest on the basis of the findings of a few studies. The economic variables involved in the SIME/DIME experiment must be checked against studies of other programmatic arrangements, different population groups, and varying economic and cultural conditions. In recent years, several careful studies have reviewed both the combined and the separate effects on work behavior of welfare benefits, the earned income tax credit, job-training programs, and the minimum wage. Most conclude that significant financial disincentives continue to undermine work behavior by AFDC-eligible adults. Full-time working mothers earning $5.00 an hour (an amount above the minimum wage), for example, earned $10,400 in 1996, just 69% of the poverty line for a family of four, and an amount nearly equivalent to the combined value of AFDC and food stamps available in most northern urban centers. Although work may be important to poor families for any number

of good reasons—self-esteem chief among them—it rarely provides a financial advantage (at least in the short run) over welfare. According to Kathryn
Eden, indeed, a working mother would have to earn about $16,000 annually
(nearly $9.00 an hour) just to *maintain* the living standards of a welfare-reliant
counterpart.[24]

Childbearing

Whereas a guaranteed income can be faulted for sapping the work effort, children's allowances may be problematic in different ways. As Burns notes, a major
objection "to the adoption of a children's allowance system—and to many people
the most formidable—is the belief that it would stimulate procreation."[25] The
assumption is that the children's allowance acts as a "baby bonus," encouraging
population growth. On this issue, the experiences of Western industrialized countries such as France and Canada are informative.

In the mid-1930s France's birth rate fell below the level necessary for replacement of the population. Because of this, emphasis was placed on the potential
demographic impacts of a number of social security measures. One result was the
Family Code of 1939, which initiated children's allowances for the entire population with the explicit goal of increasing the birth rate. To what extent were the
desired results achieved? Five years prior to World War II, France averaged
630,000 births a year. In the five years after World War II, the annual average
increased to 856,000 births. Although there was a slight decline in 1953, the rate
per thousand remained fairly constant through the mid-1960s, while the total population rose.

At first glance the data appear to support the contention that the family
allowance successfully encouraged an increase in the birth rate.[26] However, as
Schorr points out, during the same period, the United States—with no children's
allowance—also experienced a dramatic rise in the birth rate, whereas the birth
rate in Sweden declined throughout the 1950s *despite* its allowance system.[27] And
although families with three or more children gain the major benefits of the
French arrangements, after World War II, more families in France had one to three
children and the number of larger families decreased proportionately. French
demographers, therefore, have been cautious in their interpretations of the influence of allowances on population growth. At best, they view the program as contributing "to a general natalist spirit which is now a force in itself."[28]

By the mid-1960s, however, this "natalist spirit" slackened and the French
birth rate declined precipitously, even with a children's allowance among the
most generous in the industrial countries. In 1983 the birth rate had fallen to 1.8
per woman, well below the 2.1 rate necessary to maintain a constant population
size.[29] In the early 1990s, the "birth dearth" remained of considerable concern to
French policymakers, despite even further liberalizations of the family allowance.

In Canada, where a modest family allowance program was started in 1945, the
birth rate has virtually paralleled that of the United States. Although such paral-
lelism contradicts the argument that the Canadian allowance significantly affected

childbearing, Moynihan has observed that in the program's first year of operation "the monthly production of children's shoes rose from 762,000 to 1,180,000 pairs."[30]

The effect of children's allowances on family size, of course, depends to some degree on the magnitude of the allowance. Although most all of the industrialized countries have some sort of payment, benefit levels tend to be small—generally under $2,000 per child per year in U.S. currency terms. Although this is modest, it is not an inconsequential supplement for low-income families. But it is hardly likely to appreciably influence family-size decisions.

In light of existing evidence, then, assumptions about the effects of children's allowances on family size must be viewed with a healthy skepticism. Undoubtedly, support based on family size provide some people some incentive. However, to generalize from the few to the many underestimates the complexity of human motivation. Decisions concerning family size reflect fundamental conditions of human existence. In these matters the influence of aid benefits must be weighed in the larger context of desires for self-betterment and a variety of other social/psychological factors (not the least of which is the need to be well thought of by others) that come to bear on people's decisions to have children.

The impact of *selectivist* income maintenance on childbearing, while hotly debated, is also uncertain. One of the primary critiques of AFDC has been that it provides a substantial baby incentive aid since eligibility is linked to the existence of a dependent child, and the level of benefit is linked to the number of children. Critics like George Gilder—who long has argued that public aid fuels illegitimacy—succeeded in recent years in getting laws passed permitting a "family cap" on welfare, i.e., disassociating the level of welfare aid from the number of children in the household. Nevertheless, social science research has produced little support for the baby incentive hypothesis. While out-of-wedlock rates have escalated dramatically since the mid-1960s, the availability of welfare payments seem to have had, at most, a negligible effect. (See capsules 4.3 and 4.4.)

Family Stability

Although children's allowances do not appear to constitute a potent stimulus to procreation, levels of financial support associated with guaranteed-income

---

CAPSULE 4.3:   An Irresistible Offer

The welfare system makes an irresistible offer to every eligible female over the age of 16. It says to every teenager, 'You may be poor, you may have family problems, and you may be discouraged about your future. But if you have a baby right now, we will give you your own apartment, free medical care, food stamps, and a regular income over the next 20 years. If you have another baby soon after, we will increase your allotment.'

George Gilder, *Visible Man*, 1983.

CAPSULE 4.4: A Not So Irresistible Offer

Seventy-nine prominent researchers in the areas of poverty, the labor market, and family structure said today that research does not support recent suggestions by Charles Murray and others that welfare is the main cause of rising out-of-wedlock births. At the same time, the researchers said, there is "strong evidence" that living in poverty harms children and that eliminating welfare for poor children would "do far more harm than good."

According to the researchers, most studies have found that welfare benefits have either no significant effect, or only a small effect, on whether women have children outside of marriage. When inflation is taken into account, they noted, the value of cash welfare benefits such as Aid to Families with Dependent Children

has fallen over the past 20 years. At the same time, out-of-wedlock childbearing has increased. If welfare benefits were the main cause of out-of-wedlock births, they said, the decline in benefits should have prompted a decrease or a slower increase in out-of-wedlock births.

The researchers cited several plausible explanations for rising rates of births outside of marriage. Among them are changed sexual mores, decreased economic opportunity for low-skilled workers, more women in the labor market, and deteriorating neighborhood conditions. Rather than denying welfare benefits to poor children, the researchers called for a variety of improvements in programs assisting poor families.

Press Release, "Researchers Dispute Contention That Welfare Is Major Cause Of Out-of-Wedlock Births," University of Michigan Research and Training Program on Poverty, The Underclass, and Public Policy, June 23, 1994.

schemes can have other effects on family life. There are competing hypotheses about the exact nature of these effects. Because financial stress is one of the major factors increasing the risk of divorce,[31] access to reliable financial aid is likely to help stabilize family life. On the other hand, it has been suggested that providing mothers an assured source of support outside of marriage reduces the material incentives to get or stay married.[32]

These hypotheses were examined in the Seattle and Denver Income Maintenance Experiments, with results that lend credence to the proposition that a guaranteed-income decreases marital stability. Compared to the control group, divorce in the experimental group at the $3,800 level of support was 63 percent higher for African Americans, 184 percent higher for Caucasians, and 83 percent higher for Mexican Americans. Overall the rate of marital dissolution for experimental families was approximately twice that of control group families.[33]

Amid these startling figures, however, there were some anomalies. It is puzzling, for example, that the marital dissolution rates at the highest support level ($5,600) were less than those at the lower levels of support. According to theory, the opposite should have occurred. That is, if the degree of economic independence available outside marriage contributes to the risk of divorce, then these risks should increase at higher levels of financial support.[34] Also, although the SIME/DIME findings reflect the short-term consequences of guaranteed incomes, the program's long-term effects on marital stability remain unknown. It is conceivable, for instance, that after the initial round of divorces the remaining pool of married couples and those who remarry would experience lower divorce rates than the current level.[35]

Stigma and Social Integration

One of the most forceful claims for universal schemes is that they avoid stigmatizing recipients. The assumption of the stigmatizing effects of the means test is held so firmly by so many that it has almost come to be considered fact. To achieve selectivity without stigma, Titmuss proposed the elimination of the means test and its "assault on human dignity" by employing, instead, a needs test applicable to specific categories, groups, and geographical areas.[36] To this suggestion, Kahn responded:

> *It has yet to be demonstrated . . . that a needs test to open special services to disadvantaged and perhaps socially unpopular groups will not carry some of the consequences of the means test. Nor, apparently, have even the most egalitarian of societies found it financially or politically possible to completely drop means test selectivity. . . .*[37]

Precisely what is it about the means test that, presumably, results in an assault on human dignity? Perhaps this result is inferred because means tests are frequently applied to socially unpopular groups such as the poor who may feel stigmatized even *before* they make an application for benefits. Certainly, college students, a privileged group, appear to carry the means-test burden lightly in applying for financial aid. In some cases they have been known to express a strong preference for means-tested selection over other bases of allocation. Moreover, average citizens experience a form of means test every year when their taxes are due without apparent damage to their sense of self-worth. Indeed, the social-psychological effects of the means test may be less inherently painful than is commonly assumed, even for the poor. Several studies have found that the means test *per se* is not a significant source of irritation to public assistance recipients.[38]

If this evidence is at all persuasive, and we think it is, then why the dogged persistence of this assumption? Why is the means test so often the bugaboo of allocative choices? The answer is twofold. First, discussions of the means test tend to confuse the principle with the practice. Distinctions between the means test as an allocative principle and the actual administration of the means test are important considerations. As we have suggested, the principle may be quite innocuous where worth and self-esteem of individuals are concerned. It is in the *application* of this principle that the potential for denigration exists. For example, when the methods of determining eligibility include unscheduled home visits at all hours of the day and night, the message conveyed to the recipient is that he or she is untrustworthy and no longer entitled to a private life. Such procedures are clearly damaging to a person's sense of competence and self-respect.[39]

Practices of this nature support the belief in the stigmatizing effects of the means test and create much of the disapproval. However, what is actually at issue in these cases is not the principle but its application. There is no reason why the principle could not be operationally defined according to a simple and dignified procedure whereby applicants declare their needs and resources without fuss and prying. The means test need not be mean-spirited.[40] A distinction, for example, can be drawn between the typically probing *means test,* which demands a complete disclosure of income and assets, and the narrower, more dignified, *income test,* which is concerned only with the applicants' current income, usually verified through their tax returns.[41] Income-tested programs, such as the Earned Income Tax Credit, apply selectivity without stigma.

The second reason that means-tested schemes frequently are maligned relates to their broader societal effects. By their very nature, means-tested programs divide society into distinct groups of givers and receivers. Although the argument against selectivity usually blends this divisive outcome with the notion that receivers are stigmatized, these effects can be weighed independently. That is, even if stigma did not attach to recipient status, the case remains that selective programs have a divisive influence on the social fabric, fracturing society along sharp lines according to income. The poor become a distinct recipient class, whereas the near-poor, working class, and middle class fall together on the donor side of the transaction. This is an arrangement ill-suited to the creation of social harmony. In contrast, universal schemes such as the children's allowance facilitate social integration by emphasizing the common needs families face in a variety of economic circumstances. Of the various issues we have discussed, this integrative function poses one of the most frequently voiced arguments for the social effectiveness of the universal approach to social allocations.

Another Perspective on Allocation: A Continuum of Choice

At the beginning of this chapter we suggested that the universal-selective dichotomy represents a preliminary effort to analyze the choices related to social allocations. For the remainder of this chapter we examine social allocations from other perspectives. Our purpose is to expand and refine the analytic concepts that may be brought to bear on this dimension of choice.

Although the universal-selective dichotomy serves as a useful starting point in conceptualizing eligibility, the bases of social allocations are more intricate than these ideas imply. In reality, abstract dichotomies are usually less useful than continua of choice. Thus, there are many policies where benefits are made accessible to people in *selected* categories, groups, or geographic regions without recourse to an individual means test. Up until now we have used "selectivity" in the narrow sense to designate means-tested allocations. Yet, as Titmuss points out, selectivity may be based on differential needs without the requirement of a means test.[42] The dilemma, however, is that once the concept of selectivity is pried loose from strictly economic means-tested considerations, its definition may be expanded to cover innumerable conditions, even some generally interpreted as universalistic, in which case the term's meaning is dissolved. For example, some veterans' benefits, housing-relocation allowances, special education classes and employment and college admission preferences involve eligibility standards based on other than means-related criteria. In fact, once we yield to the broader definition of selectivity, even children's allowances may be included because they are limited to families with at least one child. To conceive of these as examples of "selectivity," however, adds little to our understanding.

The problem, then, is to identify a broader range of eligibility alternates than are provided by "universalism" and "selectivity" (in the narrow means-tested sense) while still maintaining a degree of abstraction that permits generalizations that tell us something meaningful. Undoubtedly there are many ways to conceptualize allocative principles. Our view is to consider the different conditions under which social provisions are made accessible to individuals and groups in society. From this perspective, the criteria for social allocations may be classified according to four allocative principles: attributed need, compensation, diagnostic differentiation, and means-tested need.

Attributed Need

Eligibility based on attributed need is conditional on membership in a group of people having common needs that are not met by existing social or economic arrangements. Under this principle, "need" is defined according to normative standards. Need may be attributed to as large a category as an entire population, such as in the case of health care in England, or to a delimited group such as working parents, or residents of "underclass" neighborhoods, or school children with limited proficiency in the English language. The two conditions that govern this principle are (1) group-oriented allocations that are (2) based on normative criteria of need.

Table 4.3 identifies several federal policies with eligibility premised on the basis of attributed need. WIC, enacted in the 1960s to promote improved nutrition for women, infants, and children, is made available to pregnant women, nursing women, infants, and young children who are nutritionally at-risk. The concept of "risk," hard as it is to exactly define, does provide a broad gauge for attributing need to a specific group. The Family and Medical Leave Act of 1992, similarly, ensures workers the opportunity to attend to the care of a newborn baby or a dependent parent or spouse without the fear of losing their jobs.

Compensation

Eligibility based on compensation is conditional on membership in groups of people who have made special social and economic contributions— such as veterans or social insurance contributors—or who have unfairly suffered harm at the "hands of society," such as victims of racism or sexism. The two conditions that govern this principle are (1) group-oriented allocations that are (2) based on normative criteria for equity.

TABLE 4.3   Allocative Principles in Selected Federal Policies

Conditions of Eligibility	Federal Policy	Eligibility Criteria
Attributed Need	The Family and Medical Leave Act of 1992	Workers caring for dependents
	Older American Act	The elderly
	Community Action Programs: Head Start, Legal Aid	Residents of low-income neighborhoods
	WIC	Pregnant or nursing women and children nutritionally at-risk
Compensation	Social Security (OASDI)	Earnings-based, reflecting contributions, with adjustments benefiting low-income retirees
	Affirmative Action	Race- and gender-based
Diagnostic Differentiation	Ryan White Care Act	Metropolitan areas with high risks of AIDS/HIV
	Education for All Handicapped Children Act (PL 94-142)	Special needs children (i.e., children with severe disabilities)
	Medicare Nursing Home Care	Degree of functional disability as measured by impairments in Activities of Daily Living (along with means test)
Means-Tested Need	SSI	Elderly and disabled poor

The most controversial compensation-based program—Affirmative Action—originally advanced by federal executive action during the 1970s in an effort to compensate for the past exclusion of African Americans from the normal channels of access and opportunity, has evolved into a broad array of race and gender preferences for advancing access to higher education, jobs, and public contracts.

Diagnostic Differentiation

Eligibility based on diagnostic differentiation is conditional on professional judgments of individual cases where special goods or services may be needed, as in the situation of the physically or mentally impaired. The two conditions that govern the principle are (1) individual allocations that are (2) based on technical diagnostic criteria of need.

Means-Tested Need

Eligibility based on means-tested need is conditional on evidence regarding an individual's inability to purchase goods and/or services. The individual's access to social provisions is limited primarily by his or her economic circumstances. The two conditions that govern this principle are (1) individual allocations that are (2) based on economic criteria of need.

Allocative Principles and Institutional-Residual Conceptions of Social Welfare

Before examining these allocative principles further, let us return briefly to an issue raised in Chapter 1 concerning alternative conceptions of the institutional status of social welfare. We reintroduce this issue because the bases of social allocations are closely associated with the institutional and residual conceptions introduced at that time. The purpose of this discussion is to help clarify how these conceptions are linked with policy design.

As noted, the institutional conception posits social welfare as a normal ongoing first-line function of society, whereas the residual view sees welfare as a temporary necessity when the normal channels for meeting needs fail to perform adequately. The fundamental distinctions concern the causes and incidence of unmet needs and problems in society. To what extent do these unmet needs represent a failure of "the system" and to what extent do they represent a failure of those afflicted? To what extent are problems characterized as deviant or special cases rather than as normal occurrences? Answers to these questions are reflected in choices regarding the bases of social allocations as suggested in Figure 4.2. Here the allocative principles are arranged along a continuum in terms of the degree to which they may be identified with institutional or residual conceptions of social welfare.

Allocations made on the basis of attributed need assume that needs are normal occurrences in society that are attributable to system inadequacies. Under these conditions, eligibility is determined according to an organic status such as citizen, child, working mother, resident, and the like, rather than on the basis of an individual's attributes derived by a detailed examination of physical and psychological disabilities or evidence of special circumstances. Policies designed along these lines exemplify the institutional conception of social welfare in seeking to create stable, ongoing arrangements for meeting normal needs.

At the other end of the continuum, where means-tested need is the allocative principle, the problem addressed is usually considered a special circumstance

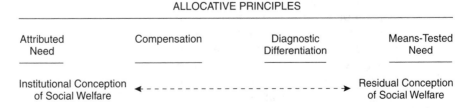

FIGURE 4.2   Allocative Principles and Conceptions of Social Welfare.

arising out of individual deficiency. To be poor is not an organic status defined in terms of an inherent set of rights and obligations, such as those for working mothers, but rather as a relative condition that is determined by calculating all of the income and resources available to an individual against an arbitrary level of economic well-being. Resulting policies exemplify a residual safety-net conception of social welfare that affords temporary support until the individual is "rehabilitated," educated, retrained, or otherwise made self-sufficient.

The principles of compensation and diagnostic differentiation fall midway between the institutional and residual conceptions. The principle of compensation is closer to the institutional view because it implies a systemic failure or "debt." Here, eligibility is determined according to organic status. Diagnostic differentiation is closer to the residual view because it is associated with individual disabilities and requires a more or less mechanical assessment of the applicant's special characteristics for eligibility.

This paradigm suggests that the residual conception of social welfare will persist as long as diagnostic differentiation and means-tested need (i.e., allocative principles that seek to differentiate among individuals) are incorporated in the design of social welfare policies. Under these principles, no matter how benign the operational mechanism for eligibility determination, unmet needs will be attributed more to chance or individual disability than to institutional strains or failures.

There will always be cases, of course, in which it is both necessary and desirable to differentiate among individuals in allocating social welfare benefits. Although the balance, over time, has shifted toward a larger institutional role for social welfare, it is unlikely that the residual functions will ever disappear. However, this does not mean that the negative aspects of the residual functions must endure. If attributed need and compensation are expanded as bases of social allocation, an adequate institutional core of social welfare may emerge. Then, as Shlakman suggests, the residual function becomes smaller and more manageable, and "it has a potential for emerging as the most flexible, most professionally oriented service, providing for the peculiarity of need and exceptional circumstances that cannot be met effectively by programs based on presumed average need."[43]

Operationalizing the Allocative Principles

This fourfold classification of allocative principles simplifies the structure of choice in the interest of order. To compensate for the distortions that occur whenever complex reality is compressed into theory requires at least a brief glimpse at some of the problematic facets of these principles. Differences among the conditions that govern the principles are not always self-evident. For instance, distinctions between normative definitions and technical assessments of need are often clouded. Is the allocation of special education slots for learning-impaired students based on valid technical measurements of academic potential, or on middle-class cultural norms? The technical assessment of social-psychological needs is a sensitive business in which science, art, and prevailing norms intermingle. Diagnostic differentiation encounters a serious dilemma when ostensibly objective individual assessments result in allocation patterns detrimental to minority populations.[44]

The principle of compensation is invoked to redress inequities imposed by historical injustices and to reward contributions to society made by individuals and groups. But the restoration of equity to "victims of society" may be deferred because these cases are controversial or simply not recognized by the public. Are innercity residents entitled to a special travel subsidy if public transportation is not available to their areas of employment because middle-class residents drive to work on publicly subsidized highways? To what extent are the hardships visited on past generations a legitimate debt to present generations? Is it equitable to compensate past inequities through the creation of new inequities? These questions suggest some of the complex interplay among values and social choice that attach to the principle of compensation.

Even the relatively straightforward principle of means-tested need becomes entangled in a web of value-laden choices at the point of application. First, of course, a standard of need must be operationally defined. Here it is interesting to note how the "iron law of specificity" operates in matters of social policy. The "iron law" holds that policy makers (1) experience discomfort with the uncertainties that attach to broad problems, such as racism, unemployment, and poverty; (2) ease the discomfort by employing arbitrary but plausible surrogates of such problems; (3) treat these surrogates as substitutes for the problem in subsequent policy decisions; and (4) reinforce the surrogates through continued use, ignoring alternative problem definitions.[45]

Consider the notion of poverty and how closely it has become associated with the federal poverty index. Based on the cost of a 1963 subsistence food budget multiplied by a factor of three, and updated annually for inflation, the poverty line is concrete, plausible, and convenient to use, but it overlooks the existential quality of poverty as a condition of life.[46] Compare the poverty index to Robert Hunter's observation, "To live in misery we know not why, to have the dread of hunger, to work more and yet gain nothing—this is the essence of poverty."[47]

Here we need a major caveat lest the "iron law of specificity" be taken too literally. That is, specificity operates only if the issue of choice is one on which it is possible to achieve fundamental agreement among the parties involved. (It might be the U.S. Congress, a presidential commission, a citizen's organization, or a local social agency board of directors.) More precisely, it must be a question of choice where there is substantial uncertainty. (Such a situation is more likely to involve the definition of a problem such as poverty, crime, or unemployment than the character of its solution.) If the situation is marked not so much by uncertainty as by strongly opposing views, then specification is likely to have the reverse effect, making agreement more difficult to achieve. In these cases, particularly when controversial solutions are being offered, there is a certain expedience to abstraction, which we will discuss in the next chapter.

Once the standard of need has been settled in means-tested allocations, there still remains the problem of determining how individuals measure up to this level.

CAPSULE 4.5:   How Poor for Public Housing?

While advocacy groups and Federal officials urge that the homeless, the disabled and the poorest of the poor be given priority for scarce public housing vacancies, officials of many large urban housing projects are arguing that they need a broader mix of incomes, including more low-income working families, to insure social stability in their developments.

The debate has sharpened as the Federal Government has reduced its role in providing new housing and the nation's stock of privately owned low-income housing has declined because of gentrification, the demolition of many single-room-occupancy hotels and the conversion of many apartments to condominiums. Meanwhile, the number of low-income households and homeless people has grown, putting more pressure on the nation's existing stock of 1.4 million public housing units as housing of last resort.

The recent trend toward giving preference to those least able to care for themselves has won the support of many advocacy groups for the mentally ill, people with disabilities and the infirm. On the other side are public housing managers and many tenants' organizations, who say they are sympathetic with the shelter needs of the very poor and infirm but believe it is unfair to force public housing communities, many of which are already under extreme pressure because of crime and poverty, to take in even more people least able to help themselves.

Their argument is that public housing's role today should be what it was when it was first created 50 years ago: an agent of social change that provides transitional housing for poor people, including the working poor.

George Sternlieb, a professor of urban affairs at Rutgers University, said the debate over housing policy reflected a clash of conflicting values.

"It's a very difficult dilemma," he said. "If you want to preserve these public housing developments as stable communities, the managers need to be able to control the selection and eviction of their tenants. But we also have to find the room to address today's tragedies—the growing numbers of homeless and people without shelter."

William Schmidt, "Public Housing: For Workers or the Needy?" *The New York Times*, April 17, 1990, A1.

The scope of economic resources that are weighed in eligibility formulas is open to question. Should it include the value of assets as well as income? Should it include items of sentimental as well as economic value (wedding rings, for example)? What about insurance payments, children's college accounts, the value of the tools of one's trade, or the income of relatives (distant or close)? When eligibility determination does include relatives' income as a resource, and the relatives are held liable for support, then in effect they too must be subjected to a means test. Under Medicaid, for example, nursing home eligibility requires that the value of certain assets be under a certain level—around $60,000. If the assets of the applicant—or the applicant's spouse—exceed this limit, then they must be "spent down" to the qualifying level. (Certain property—such as a home, household possessions, and one car—are exempt from the valuation.) For the most part, however, adult children are not legally responsible for their parents, and their own income and assets are not counted in the determination of their parents' aid eligibility.

The question of what resources should be included in a determination of income is one of the essential issues in measuring poverty. Specifically, should the dollar value of in-kind social welfare benefits (such as food stamps and public housing) be counted as a component of income? This issue arose during the 1980s as the proportion of in-kind benefits in the federal budget more than doubled. Critics have argued that excluding the substantial value of these benefits in calculating the income of the poor inflates the poverty statistics. Estimates made by the U.S. Bureau of the Census for 1995, for example, indicate that the official poverty rate would be reduced by a quarter (13.8% to 10.3%) if an "expanded" definition of income—one counting not only cash income but also the market value of food stamps, housing, and Medicaid—were employed.[48]

There is, however, another important facet to the issue of specifying poverty. The poverty line, in a very important sense, is a *relative* measure. That is, people with incomes below a certain level are perceived to be poor relative to those with incomes above that level. If in-kind benefits are to be figured into the incomes of those *below* the poverty line, then perhaps they should be figured into the incomes of those *above* the line as well. After all, employer-paid benefits for working people, such as health and dental insurance, contributions to retirement plans, and paid vacations, are substantial portions of the "pay" of regular workers.

Having reviewed some of the problems associated with operationalizing the principles that underlie social allocations, there is one final qualification concerning this dimension of choice. That is, in practice these allocative principles are not mutually exclusive even though their underlying premises may seem incompatible as, for example, in the joint employment of attributed and means-tested need. On the contrary, various combinations of allocative principles are found in the design and application of social welfare policies, reflecting the tug, pull, and eventual compromise over competing values. We will illustrate this point with reference to two rather different types of social welfare programs: social security—the Old-Age, Survivors, Disability, and Health Insurance program (OASDHI)—created under the Social Security Act, and the Community Action Program, legislated under the Economic Opportunity Act.

In social insurance, eligibility for benefits is predicated on the dual principles of attributed need and compensation. Here a persistent issue is the balance between adequacy and equity in the benefit-allocation formula.[49] The benefit to which a retiree is entitled under old-age insurance is designed, in part, to replace previous earnings as reflected in the contributions made to the social insurance system. To the extent that benefits reflect past contributions, a degree of equity is introduced into this system—workers who paid in more over the years of their employment are entitled to larger benefits in the years of their retirement. However, eligibility is also based on the principle of attributed need. As Hohaus explains, social insurance "aims primarily at providing society with some protection against one or more major hazards which are sufficiently widespread throughout the population and far-reaching in effect to become 'social' in scope and complexion."[50] In the case of old-age insurance, the attributed need of the retired elderly is for an *adequate* standard of living.

Thus, although social security seeks to compensate retirees in proportion to their contributions, it also seeks to provide a level of adequacy for low-income workers whose contributions were minimal. For this group, strictly applying the principle of compensation would result in benefit levels far below even the meager standards to which the individual was accustomed prior to retirement. In most social insurance programs, the dual allocative principles of attributed need and compensation result in a system in which the relationship between benefits and contributions exists in an ordinal sense, but is limited in a proportional sense, as efforts to express equity are modified by concerns for adequacy.

In the development of the Community Action Program (CAP) during the 1960s, the principle of attributed need was widely employed as the basis for social allocations. Initially, people became eligible for a variety of CAP-funded goods and services by virtue of their residence in designated low-income neighborhoods.[51] Once the program began operating, however, these normative assessments of need were often modified. Levitan documents how CAP-funded neighborhood health centers that intended to provide free health care services to *all* target-area residents eventually incorporated a means test into allocation procedures, as did CAP-funded Neighborhood Legal Aid, Head Start, and employment opportunities programs.[52] In certain instances neighborhood residents supported means tests as an additional basis for allocations, especially in cases where the services were relatively inelastic. A limited number of slots for Head Start students in a summer program is a good example. Neighborhood applicants included large numbers of both poor and nonpoor residents. The poor were not convinced that attributed need was the most suitable allocative principle under such circumstances. For the Community Action Program, then, attributed need became a preliminary screening device, a necessary but not sufficient condition for determining eligibility.

Despite some of their untidy features, the four allocative principles—attributed need, compensation, diagnostic differentiation, and means-tested need—provide a useful framework for conceptualizing policy alternatives. Consider, for example, the provision of preschool day-care center services, a program increasingly demanded by students and working parents. To whom and on what basis should these services be available? The four allocative principles offer an orderly framework for conceptualizing alternatives. As indicated in Table 4.4, eligibility at one extreme might incorporate all families with young children, based on a community-felt need for an institutional arrangement to allow fathers and mothers greater freedom during the early years of childrearing. However, such a diminution of childrearing responsibilities is unlikely to receive normative sanction in a child- and achievement-oriented society. A more plausible condition of eligibility might require casting attributed need, not into the mold of "untrammeled freedom," but rather in the image of freedom to achieve commonly valued objectives such as a career or an education. In this case, eligibility would be limited to working parents and/or students. Other options might involve day-care entitlements on compensatory and diagnostic bases. Finally, there is the means

TABLE 4.4   Alternative Criteria for Allocating Day-Care Services

Conditions of Eligibility	*Alternative Criteria for Allocations*
Attributed Need	All families Single-parent families Families with working parents Families with student parents
Compensation	Minority families Military families Families of workers in specified occupational groups
Diagnostic Differentiation	Families with physically or emotionally disabled parents Families in short-term crisis situations
Means-Tested Need	Families whose earnings and resources fall beneath a poverty standard

test, which could be used independently or in combination with any of the other principles to restrict subsidies to low-income families.

Who Wants to, Who Actually Benefits?

So far we have focused on a question that receives much attention in the design of social welfare policies: Who is to be *eligible* for benefits? But there is another side to this issue that is often ignored or misinterpreted by social welfare policymakers. It seems fitting that we address this question: Who *wants* to benefit?

In selecting the basis of social allocations there is a strong tendency to proceed on the assumption of receptivity. That is, those who qualify as recipients are expected to desire and readily accept the assistance offered. Eligible clients or consumers who don't are often labeled "hard-to-reach" or "resistant," and attention is then directed to developing specially responsive service structures that take account of the ethnic, linguistic, or other "barriers" that impede program participation.[53] However, these are not problems of eligibility determination, but rather of service delivery, a subject covered in Chapter 6.

Still, the assumption of receptivity, even with special delivery efforts, bears closer scrutiny than it is usually given. For a variety of reasons, those eligible for benefits may be uninterested in becoming recipients. They are hard to reach because they do not *want* to be reached. The costs of program participation may be perceived as outweighing the benefits. People may be aware of their eligibility but may avoid services they view as demeaning or stigmatizing. They may not wish to reveal information. They may be fearful of participation. For instance, although it meant a considerable loss of federal funds, citizens in one city refused to have their neighborhood designated part of a Community Action Program target area, in part because they believed the CAP was a scheme for racial integration.[54] Religious, political, or cultural convictions may also inhibit involvement.

Often the issue of who benefits is not determined so much by who *wants* to benefit, but rather, who is *able* to benefit. Individuals with severe emotional problems, addictive behaviors, or antisocial attitudes, whatever their desires or needs, may be "bad" candidates for assistance because they are not likely to make good use of whatever help is offered. Counseling programs offered in a mental health agency, for example, may simply not be able to meet the intense needs of the severely mentally disabled. Similarly, job training may not work for disturbed or hostile teenagers. Indeed, those with the greatest needs may have the least chance of success, even when significant resources *are* invested. Considerable evidence has accumulated over the years, for example, that employment programs have only minimal impact on the most poorly educated, least job-ready AFDC clients.

Service-providing organizations, seeking to make the most efficient use of their own limited resources, frequently avoid clients who are less than likely to benefit from their programs. This avoidance of the hard-to-serve is widespread in several social service sectors. For many years, for example, critics have charged vocational rehabilitation and job-training organizations with "creaming" their prospective clientele—focusing their efforts on those most likely to succeed while disregarding the least skilled, the least able. The Job Training Partnership Act, for example, legislated in 1982 to assist the economic have-nots, is generally agreed to have mainly served those who were very close to being "job ready," rather than the hard-core poor.[55]

Not everyone needing help can be served, and human service organizations must make determinations of how to best employ their scarce resources. It makes little sense, for example, to assign one of a very few units of transitional housing earmarked for the homeless to individuals who have little potential for permanent independence and self-sufficiency. In fact, providers of transitional housing generally screen for candidates who *are* likely to ultimately make it on their own—motivated people who will meet with social workers, attend training classes, save money, and seek out jobs and permanent accommodations. The hard-core homeless, those with drug, alcohol, and mental health problems, are not likely to be selected even when they possess the interest and motivation to apply for transitional housing. This creates a discouraging irony. The creaming phenomenon often means focusing on those most likely to benefit—those most likely to make it on their own, without help—and ignoring those least likely to succeed, those frequently with the greatest objective needs.

Finally, the question of who benefits can be examined in terms of generational equity. Although volumes have been written advancing assorted theses concerning the winners and losers in the welfare contest, one fact that is abundantly clear is that welfare is not simply a matter of public charity to the poor. Social security and Medicare—the universal programs that compose the major segment of the U.S. welfare state—principally serve the middle class. Even selective, means-tested programs are distributed broadly, with nearly a quarter of the population receiving cash entitlements at one time or another over a typical decade-long period.[56]

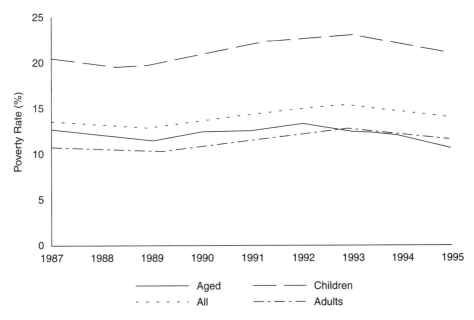

FIGURE 4.3 **Poverty Rates Over Time, By Age Group**

Source: U.S. Bureau of the Census, Current Population Reports, Series P60-194, *Poverty in the United States: 1995* (Washington, D.C.: U.S. Government Printing Office, 1996).
Note: Children = age 17 and under; adults = age 18–64; aged = age 65 and over.

Particular issues of social allocation—be they described in class, race, ethnic, or gender terms—are persistent concerns of social policy practitioners and analysts. Each generation defines these issues in its own way, reflecting its own unique demographics, its own economic circumstances, and its own needs and perspectives.

As we approach the third millennium, much of the social allocation debate has come to focus on the results of past social policies and the inequities they seem to have produced. In examining welfare state outcomes as a whole, for example, the various principles underlying social allocations have certainly resulted in clear winners and losers. One of the most resounding successes has been the dramatic decline in poverty among the elderly. One of the most distressing failures has been the deteriorating well-being of children and adolescents.

The contradictory results of the U.S. welfare state for young and old, it must be noted, largely reflects the fundamental bifurcation of income-support policy into universal and means-tested components. The elderly, covered by universal old-age insurance, plus universal medical insurance through Medicare, have had the material circumstances of their lives substantially bettered. In 1982 poverty rates for the elderly in the United States dropped below those for the overall population for the first time in history. And in 1995, as Figure 4.3 indicates, they registered below the rate for the working age (18–65) population. Indeed, counting the value of in-kind benefits, the poverty rate for those over 65 dropped below 6 percent by the mid-1990s. For children, however, the scope of poverty has been *enlarging* over the past decade, with young children the worst off. The 1995 poverty rate for children under 18 was 20.8 percent. For African American children in single-parent homes, it was 45.1 percent.[57]

Although not all of the dire circumstances facing children today reflect public policy choices—divorce, unwed parenthood, and unemployment are certainly independent factors—choices concerning social allocations and benefit eligibility have been of critical importance. Means-tested benefits—highly vulnerable to swings in ideological currents and political alignments, as well as constrained federal and state budgets—have shrunk both in terms of coverage and benefit levels. Critical programs such as preventive health and legal services have been restricted, and the real (spendable) value of AFDC/TANF payments has dropped in almost all states.

Whereas universal programs proved resilient to the cutbacks of the 1980s and 1990s, means-tested ones did not, and programs intended for poor families were particularly vulnerable. The repeal of AFDC in 1996 is likely to accelerate decline in already meager family incomes. This is why most of the major ideas recently advanced for "generational equity," for improving the life chances of children, have focused on broad and comprehensive programs, such as school reform, an expanded Earned Income Tax Credit, and universal child support and early childhood education arrangements.

The issue of how benefits are allocated cannot be carried much farther at this point without some reference to the substance of benefits, what it is that clients actually receive. In this next chapter we turn to this issue and examine the nature of social provisions.

Notes

1. Edward Bellamy, *Looking Backward* (New York: New American Library, 1960), 75. Originally published 1888.

2. Ibid., 95.

3. See the articles by Theda Skocpol and Robert Greenstein in Christopher Jencks and Paul Peterson (eds.), *The Urban Underclass* (Washington, D.C., The Brookings Institution, 1991), 411–59. See also Irwin Garfinkel, "Economic Security for Children: From Means Testing and Bifurcation to Universality," in Irwin Garfinkel et al. (eds.), *Social Policies for Children* (Washington, D.C.: The Brookings Institution, 1996), 33–82.

4. Alvin Schorr, *Common Decency* (New Haven, CT: Yale University Press, 1986), 31.

5. Sheila B. Kamerman and Alfred J. Kahn, "Universalism and Income Testing in Family Policy," *Social Work* (July–August 1987), 277–80.

6. Nicholas Lemann, "Target Practice," *The New Republic* (November 11, 1996), 29.

7. See James C. Vadakin, "A Critique of the Guaranteed Annual Income," *Public Interest, 11* (Spring 1968), 53–66; Edward Schwartz, "A Way to End the Means Test," *Social Work, 9*(3) (July 1964), 3–12; James Tobin, "The Case for an Income Guarantee," *Public Interest, 4* (Summer 1966), 31–41; Alvin Schorr, "Against a Negative Income Tax," *Public Interest, 5* (Fall 1966), 110–17; Irwin Garfinkel, "Negative Income Tax and Children's Allowance Programs: A Comparison," *Social Work, 13*(4) (October 1968), 33–39; Helen O. Nicol, "Guaranteed Income Maintenance: Another Look at the Debate," *Welfare in Review, 5*(6) (June/July 1967), 1–13; Alvin Schorr, "To End the 'Women and Children Last' Policy," *The Journal of the Institute for Socioeconomic Studies,* IX:2 (Summer 1984), 58–78.

8. Eveline M. Burns, "Where Welfare Falls Short," *The Public Interest,* 1 (Fall 1965), 88.

9. Not all children's allowance programs are universal in the sense that they cover all families in the country. In some countries, such as France, eligibility for the children's allowance is employment-related and financed through payroll taxes imposed on the employer, rather than out of general funds.

10. For a description and analysis of these experiments, see Mordecai Kurz and Robert Spiegelman, *The Design of the Seattle and Denver Income Maintenance Experiments,* Center for the Study of Welfare Policy Research Memorandum, No. 28 (Menlo Park, CA: Stanford Research Institute, 1972) and Martin Anderson, *Welfare: The Political Economy of Welfare Reform* (Stanford, CA: Hoover Institution Press, 1978).

11. For several proposals, see Alvin Schorr, *Poor Kids* (New York: Basic Books, 1966).

12. Mike Reddin, "Universality versus Selectivity," *The Political Quarterly,* January/March 1969, 14.

13. Daniel R. Meyer et al., "The Effects of Replacing Income Tax Deductions for Children with Children's Allowances: A Microsimulation," *Journal of Family Issues,* 12(4) (December 1991), 467–91.

14. Ibid.

15. U.S. General Accounting Office, *Earned Income Credit, Targeting the Working Poor,* Report Number GAO/GGD-95-122BR, USGPO, March 1995.

16. David T. Ellwood, *Poor Support* (New York: Basic Books, 1988), 115.

17. James Cutt, "Income Support Programmes for Families with Children—Alternatives for Canada," *International Social Security Review,* 23(1) (1970), 104–5.

18. The classic case is Charles Murray, *Losing Ground: American Social Policy 1950–1980* (New York: Basic Books, 1984).

19. George Break, "The Effects of Taxation on Work Incentives," in Edmund Phelps (ed.), *Private Wants and Public Needs* (New York: W. W. Norton, 1965), 65.

20. Fred Cook, "When You Just Give Money to the Poor," *The New York Times Magazine,* May 3, 1970, 23, 109–12. A more detailed breakdown of these findings is presented by David N. Kershaw, "A Negative Income Tax Experiment," *Scientific American,* 227(4) (October 1972), 19–25. For a description of the research design used in this study, see Harold W. Watts, "Graduated Work Incentives: An Experiment in Negative Taxation," *The American Economic Review,* 59(2) (May 1969).

21. Michael Keelye, et al., "The Labor-Supply Effects and Costs of Alternative Negative Income Tax Programs," *Journal of Human Resources,* 13(6) (Winter 1978), 3–26. See also Henry J. Aaron, "Six Welfare Questions Searching for Answers," *Brookings Review,* 3 (Fall 1984), 13.

22. A description of the Hawthorne effect can be found in almost any textbook on social research methods. This phenomenon derives its name from the study of the Hawthorne Plant of the Western Electric Company in which the effect was first identified. See F. J. Roethlisberger and W. J. Dickson, *Management and the Worker* (Cambridge, MA: Harvard University Press, 1939).

23. Martin Anderson, *Welfare: The Political Economy of Welfare Reform* (Stanford, CA: Hoover Institution Press, 1978), 104–27.

24. Kathryn J. Eden, "The Myths of Dependence and Self-Sufficiency: Women, Welfare, and Low-Wage Work," *Focus,* 17(2) (Fall/Winter 1995), 4. See also Jason DeParle, "Better Work than Welfare," *The New York Times Magazine,* December 18, 1994, 43–49, and Sheldon Danziger and Robert Plotnik, "Poverty and Policy: Lessons of the Last Two Decades," *Social Service Review,* March 1986, 36–50.

25. Eveline M. Burns, "Childhood Poverty and the Children's Allowance," in Eveline M. Burns (ed.), *Children's Allowances and the Economic Welfare of Children* (New York: Citizen's Committee for Children of New York, 1968), 12.

26. Walter Friedlander, *Individualism and Social Welfare* (New York: The Free Press, 1962), 161.

27. Alvin Schorr, "Income Maintenance and the Birth Rate," *Social Security Bulletin,* 28(12) (December 1965), 2–10.

28. Alvin Schorr, "Income Maintenance and the Birth Rate," 4. Additional evidence on this issue is presented by Vincent Whitney, "Fertility Trends and Children's Allowance Programs," in Eveline Burns (ed.), *Children's Allowances and the Economic Welfare of Children,* 123–39.

29. Richard Tomlinson, "The French Population Debate," *The Public Interest*, 76 (Summer 1984), 111–20.

30. "The Case for a Family Allowance," *The New York Times Magazine*, February 5, 1967, 71.

31. Phillips Cutright, "Income and Family Events: Marital Stability," *Journal of Marriage and the Family*, 33 (May 1971), 291–306.

32. William J. Goode, "Marital Satisfaction and Instability: A Cross Cultural Analysis of Divorce Rates," *International Social Science Journal*, 5 (1982), 507–26.

33. Michael Hannan, Nancy Tuma, and Lyle Groeneveld, "Income and Marital Events: Evidence From an Income Maintenance Experiment," *American Journal of Sociology*, 82 (May 1977), 186–211.

34. Ibid. For additional discussion of the implications of these findings, see Maurice MacDonald and Isabel V. Sawhill, "Welfare Policy and the Family," *Public Policy*, 26 (Winter 1978), 107–19.

35. The short-term versus long-term effects of SIME/DIME on marital stability are analyzed in James W. Albrecht, "Negative Income Taxation and Divorce in SIME/ DIME," *Journal of the Institute of Socioeconomic Studies*, 4 (Autumn 1979), 75–82.

36. Titmuss, *Commitment to Welfare* (London: George Allen and Unwin Ltd., 1968), 122.

37. Alfred Kahn, *Theory and Practice of Social Planning* (New York: Russell Sage, 1969), 203.

38. See, for example, Joe Handler and Ellen Hollingsworth, "How Obnoxious is the 'Obnoxious Means Test'? The View of AFDC Recipients" (Madison: Institute for Research on Poverty Discussion Paper, University of Wisconsin), January 1969; Richard Pomeroy and Harold Yahr, in collaboration with Lawrence Podell, *Studies in Public Welfare: Effects of Eligibility Investigation on Welfare Clients* (New York: Center for the Study of Urban Problems, City University of New York, 1968); and Martha Ozawa, "Impact of SSI on the Aged and Disabled Poor," *Social Work Research and Abstracts*, 14 (Fall 1978), 3–10.

39. A penetrating description of the ways administrative practices are used to intimidate and deter public assistance applicants is presented by Frances Fox Piven and Richard Cloward in *Regulating the Poor: The Functions of Public Welfare* (New York: Pantheon Books, 1971), 147–82. Also see Betty Mandell, "Welfare and Totalitarianism: Part I. Theoretical Issues," *Social Work*, 16(1) (January 1971), 17–25.

40. For a discussion of income testing see Sheila Kamerman and Alfred Kahn, "Universalism and Income Testing in Family Policy: New Perspectives on an Old Debate," *Social Work*, 34(4) (July–August 1987), 279.

41. For example, see George Hoshino, "Can the Means Test Be Simplified?" *Social Work*, 10(3) (July 1965), 98–104.

42. Titmuss, *Commitment to Welfare*, 114–15.

43. Vera Shlakman, "The Safety-Net Function in Public Assistance: A Cross-National Exploration," *Social Service Review*, 46(2) (June 1972), 207.

44. For further discussion of some of the complexities in the application of this principle, see Joseph Eaton and Neil Gilbert, "Racial Discrimination and Diagnostic Differentiation," *Race, Research and Reason*, Roger Miller (ed.) (New York: National Association of Social Workers, 1970), 79–88.

45. The "iron law of specificity" is based on our experiences participating in and observing the behavior of numerous planning and policy-making bodies. To see it operate in a microcosm (for those who doubt its power), we would suggest that at the next meeting in which you participate where a policy decision is pending on a fairly abstract issue, and there is some floundering, deliberately make a proposal that is simply plausible and contains some specification of the issue in concrete units, such as amount of dollars, units of service, numbers of people to be served, and the like. Then mark the time it takes for the discussion to shift from philosophy to considerations of whether the decision should involve a little more or a little less of the concrete units in your proposal.

46. For further discussion of the poverty index, see Mollie Orshansky, "Measuring Poverty: A Debate," *Public Welfare*, 33 (Spring 1975), 46–55; Peter Townsend, *Poverty in the United Kingdom: A Survey of Household Resources and Standards of Living* (Berkeley, CA: University of California Press, 1979); The Heritage Foundation, "How 'Poor' are America's Poor," September 21, 1990;

Robert Greenstein, "Attempts to Dismiss Census Poverty Data," Center on Budget and Policy Priorities, September 28, 1993; and Constance F. Citro and Robert T. Michael, *Measuring Poverty: A New Approach* (Washington, D.C.: National Academy Press, 1995).

47. Robert Hunter, *Poverty,* Peter d'A. Jones (ed.) (New York: Harper & Row, 1965, originally published 1904), 2.

48. Eleanor Baugher and Leatha Lamison-White, U.S. Bureau of the Census, Current Population Reports, Series P60-194, *Poverty in the United States: 1995,* USGPO (Washington, D.C., 1996), xii.

49. See, for example, Richard Titmuss, "Equity, Adequacy, and Innovation in Social Security," *International Social Security Review, 23*(2) (1970), 259–68.

50. Richard Hohaus, "Equity, Adequacy, and Related Factors in Old-Age Security," in William Haber and Wilbur Cohen (eds.), *Social Security: Programs, Problems, and Policies* (Homewood, IL: Richard Irwin, 1960), 61.

51. Drawing boundaries is a recurrent problem with this method of allocation. Exactly where any given central city low-income neighborhood begins and ends is a matter that even carefully designed empirical research rarely settles to everyone's satisfaction. For a technical analysis of this issue, see Avery Guest and James Zuiches, "Another Look at Residential Turnover in Urban Neighborhoods: A Note on 'Racial Change in a Stable Community' by Harvey Molotch," *American Journal of Sociology, 77*(3) (November 1971), 457–71. We should add that methodological efforts at boundary definition in most Community Action Programs were superficial.

52. Sar Levitan, *The Great Society's Poor Law* (Baltimore: Johns Hopkins, 1970).

53. For example, see Oliver Moles, Robert Hess, and Daniel Fascione, "Who Knows Where to Get Public Assistance?" *Welfare in Review, 6*(5) (September/October 1968).

54. Neil Gilbert, *Clients or Constituents* (San Francisco: Jossey-Bass, 1970), 75.

55. Kirk Victor, "Helping the Haves," *National Journal,* April 14, 1990, 898–901.

56. Howard Chernick, "Wide Cast For Safety Net," Economic Policy Institute Briefing Paper, November, 1995.

57. Baugher and Lamison-White, *Poverty in the United States: 1995.*

Chapter *5*

The Nature of Social Provisions

The only crucial question becomes one of waste or economy. The two alternatives for redistributional reforms, in-cash or in-kind, therefore have to be compared as to their effectiveness in relation to financial outlays. Just because both systems are costly, they must be scrutinized as choices. It would be an illusion to pretend that both lines could be followed. No budget could expand widely in two different directions.

ALVA MYRDAL
Nation and Family, 1941

The strain between collective and individualist tendencies is nowhere more apparent than in choices concerning the forms of social provision. Two forms of provision demark the traditional line of thought and debate in this policy dimension: benefits in-cash versus benefits in-kind. Should needy families be provided a monthly income to cover their basic needs or should help be given as food and fuel, clothing, and shelter? Should children be guaranteed education in the basic public schools or should their families receive cash, or an equivalent voucher, providing them options in the educational marketplace? The choice poised in these questions, although fairly simple to comprehend, is quite another matter to resolve.

Basic Forms: Cash Versus In-Kind

One of the earliest arguments in favor of in-kind benefits was advanced in the 1930s by Swedish economist Alva Myrdal in the context of that country's debate over the nature of child welfare provisions. For Myrdal, benefits in-kind were superior to in-cash children's allowances because of economies of scale. That is, public enterprise, presumably efficient in the manufacture and distribution of mass-produced goods and services, would provide shoes or clothing or similar products at low cost. The alternative—cash grants that could be used to purchase privately produced goods—was viewed as far more expensive. In the state planning perspective of the period, a uniform benefit, mass-produced and centrally distributed, was seen as eliminating many of the wasteful, duplicative, aspects of competition in the open marketplace.[1]

Myrdal also suggested that assistance in-kind was more effective than cash subsidies because benefits landed squarely on their targets. If the policy goal, for example, was to enhance child welfare, the question of effectiveness becomes: How much of the benefit directly serves this objective?[2] Using this criterion, the drawback of cash is clear—money subsidies can not be controlled at the point of consumption. There is no way to guarantee that a children's allowance (or any cash subsidy) will not be incorporated into the general family budget and used to purchase a variety of items, only a portion of which may apply directly to the intended purpose.

The argument advanced by the classic theorists of welfare economics, on the other hand, posit that cash provisions are optimal because cash gives its users maximum choice, therefore "maximizing their utility" (i.e., their happiness). Theoretically at least, it can be demonstrated that, given $50 to spend freely, an individual will invariably achieve a higher level of satisfaction ("welfare") than one given $50 worth of goods and services specified by someone else. This position, of course, assumes a consumer who is rational and capable of judging precisely what is in his or her best interest. It further assumes that maximizing the preferences of individuals also serves the good of the broader community—that the choices made by consumers for their own welfare aggregate together to advance the common welfare.[3]

The case for the superior effectiveness of in-kind benefits, on the other hand, hinges on their ability to advance specific community concerns. With public control, food, medical care, school lunches, and other common objectives can be distributed directly. Given free choice, recipients of welfare benefits can purchase booze, satellite digital TV, or $100 Nike Air Jordans; benefits in-kind, restricting such "bad" choices, insure that public judgments about appropriate consumption are advanced.

Some of the hazards of cash benefits are apparent from the results of the Experimental Housing Allowance Program (EHAP) conducted by the U.S. Department of Housing and Urban Development during the 1970s and 1980s. An elaborate social experiment executed over an eleven-year period, EHAP involved 30,000 households in twelve sites across the country. The impact of unrestricted housing allowances on patterns of housing consumption was one of several questions analyzed in this experiment. In Pittsburgh and Phoenix, the sites chosen to explore the issue, 1,800 low-income households received housing allowance grants over the course of three years. Findings revealed that only very small portions of these allowances were actually spent on housing. Just 10 percent in Pittsburgh and 25 percent in Phoenix were applied to housing costs.[4]

For most recipients, the allowances served principally as a general income supplement.

To make sure that social provisions further the purposes for which they are designated, Myrdal called for "increasing control from the consumption side" (i.e., stipulating the forms of public benefits). She posited this kind of "social engineering" as a manifestation of benign social policy based on cooperation and group loyalty. For Myrdal, the in-kind approach rested on "social solidarity and the pooling of resources for common aims" rather than just the "insurance of individual interests."[5]

Hence, the core of the argument—the imposition of social controls to harness individual interests to the collective good. As Holden puts it, "only through in-kind assistance is society able to exercise a measure of control over the final utilization of the tax dollar. . . ."[6]

The term *social control*, of course, has a distinctly negative connotation, and critics of social welfare have always charged that the welfare state is nothing but a device for regulating the conduct of the poor and underprivileged, a repressive mechanism that "keeps people in their place," maintaining conformity to an unjust order. The frequency with which this indictment is made does not constitute proof of guilt. Yet, to be sure, the charge is not without substance, neither today nor 100 years ago. As Briggs notes,

> *Many of Bismarck's critics accused him, not without justification, of seeking through his legislation to make German workers "depend" upon the state. The same charges have been made against the initiators of all "welfare" (and earlier, of poor law) policy. Yet it was Bismarck himself who drew a revealing distinction between the degrees of obedience (or subservience) of private servants and servants at court. The latter would "put up with much more" than the former because they had pensions to look forward to. "Welfare" soothed the spirit, or perhaps tamed it.*[7]

In general, social welfare professionals find social control a disagreeable element of policy. We mention this because the objectionable functions associated with, and the resistive feelings aroused by, the term should not paralyze our faculty to weigh the case for provisions in-kind. Social controls are required to regulate a complex and highly interdependent society. Regulation that replaces the power of the individual with the power of the community, Freud observed, "constitutes the decisive step of civilization."[8] The issue is not whether we will have controls but whether they will be designed to realize our ideals of human dignity and justice or to serve pernicious ends—to soothe or to tame the spirit.

Clearly, Alva Myrdal proposed social controls for estimable purposes. Yet the dilemma of social control exercised through in-kind benefits is that, although it may facilitate the realization of collective aims, it also restricts the freedom of the consumer, rich or poor. Myrdal recognized these objections. However, she suggested that at least in regard to provisions for children, in-kind benefits posed no constraints on consumer sovereignty because "children rarely have much voice in decisions about the use of the family income."[9] This defense is hardly persuasive, however, especially in the contemporary cash-kind debate. As Friedman points out:

> *The belief in freedom is for "responsible" units, among whom we include neither children nor insane people. In general, this problem is avoided by regarding the family unit as the basic unit and therefore parents as responsible for their children.*[10]

While advocating benefits in-kind, nevertheless, Myrdal's position was less than doctrinaire. And even she was not completely persuaded by her own argument that such benefits didn't limit freedom of choice. Hence her counsel to exercise caution when applying the in-kind principle, especially for inexpensive items that often are imbued with personal meaning:

> *Clothing falls in that category and it thus seems to be difficult to subsidize in-kind. Here personal taste is delicate and social prestige has become involved. Even if some class equalization in clothing, especially for children, is judged desirable, it would probably be extremely unwise to force any uniformity on families. . . . It would be cheaper, perhaps extremely rational but still a bit inhuman, to provide layettes, bedding, and baby carriages for all newborn children. All these cost items, invested with so much tender care, are certainly not appropriate for communalization.*[11]

As a final qualification, Myrdal advised that a serious preference for benefits in-kind should be entertained only *after* an adequate family income was established. In circumstances where it wasn't, she considered cash assistance an "appropriate deviation" from the in-kind principle.

In the context of the 1990s, many of Myrdal's assertions seem naively quaint. First, the alleged cost savings of publicly produced benefits in-kind has been universally challenged. Time and again, state monopolies have been shown to be relatively costly providers of goods and services—be they steel, garbage collection, education, or day care. And although economies of scale may apply to certain forms of technology, it is certainly questionable in the case of social services such as casework and vocational counseling.[12] This is because social services tend to draw on what Thompson describes as "intensive technology," techniques employed to change and aid the client, with the precise treatment based on constant feedback.[13] This type of technology, tailored to individual cases, substantially hinders standardization.

With social provisions more amenable to standardization, such as clothing, the sacrifice of freedom of choice in favor of a regimented universal product is bound to be discomforting. Moreover, although these benefits in-kind may theoretically eliminate some of the "wasteful" attributes of multiple providers, the market competition associated with cash benefits can generate innovations that result in significant cost reductions over the long haul.

Where economies of scale are not clearly operative, the issue turns on the question of whether cash subsidies and private competition are really preferable to provisions in-kind and publicly run bureaucracy. Examining this choice in the context of education, Milton Friedman opts for grant subsidies rather than in-kind provisions because

> [Grants] would bring a healthy increase in the variety of educational institutions available and in competition among them. Private initiative and enterprise would quicken the pace of progress in this area as it has in so many others. Government would serve its proper function of improving the operation of the invisible hand without substituting the dead hand of bureaucracy.[14]

The primary appeal of the argument for cash benefits, then, is in its reliance on consumer sovereignty. There is a compelling quality to the argument for an individual's freedom of choice. In essence it posits the right to self-determination, the right to use one's resources for whatever the psychological or material benefits derived, and, conversely, the right to command one's resources toward whatever future is desired. It is the right of individuals to exercise self-indulgence as well as self-denial.

This viewpoint relies heavily on the faith that the market is responsive to consumer demands. On this point, those favoring collective interventions are not convinced. John Kenneth Galbraith, for example, argues that the consumer "is subject to forces of advertising and emulation by which production creates its own demand." According to this proposition, which he labels the "dependence effect," consumer wants are not determined independently. Rather, the producers of goods and services also manufacture consumer *desires*.[15] The counter-argument is that producers cannot determine consumer wants; they merely provide information about what is available and endeavor to convince the consumer of its worth and value.[16] Whether or not the "dependence effect" is as consequential as Galbraith would have, his proposition discloses one of the hidden perils of unqualified acceptance of the market mechanism: namely, consumer awareness and skills must be taken into account when considering voluntary exchanges in pursuit of rational self-interest. Rational choices require objective information about the

---

CAPSULE 5.1:   "The Cash Constituency"

Milton Friedman is widely regarded as the godfather of the negative-income-tax idea. He proposed it in his 1962 conservative manifesto "Capitalism and Freedom." George McGovern endorsed it in 1972 as the major domestic initiative of what is widely regarded as the most left-wing major-party Presidential campaign of modern times. Liberals used to like it for conferring dignity and independence on the poor. Conservatives liked it for wiping out bureaucracies and interfering as little as possible with the free market.

Source: Michael Kinsley, "The Ultimate Block Grant," *The New Yorker,* May 29, 1995, 37.

items to be consumed. Such knowledge is often expensive and difficult to obtain. The predicament is more intense for the poor and ill-educated. As Rivlin explains,

> *Unless he knows what he is buying, a consumer cannot chose rationally. Yet, in the social [welfare] area, it is very difficult for him to find out anything about the quality of service before he uses it. Moreover, the costs of shopping around or sampling the merchandise of a hospital or a school may be prohibitive.*[17]

A multitude of studies examining Medicaid, for example, have demonstrated that no-strings cash transfers can hardly optimize the health of socially disadvantaged children. An open-market approach to health services is clearly an insufficient means, by itself, to improved health care, because personal factors ranging from a lack of knowledge about health care and language problems to an inability to obtain child care, transportation, or time off from work to keep medical appointments, potently deter the full and effective use of health care resources.[18]

Other arguments are advanced in favor of cash. Cash, clearly, is convenient to use. Providing cash rather than in-kind benefits saves substantially on administration because it involves little in the way of processing or regulatory costs. Cash is said to remove the stigma attached to in-kind provision, allowing the poor the dignity of managing their own lives. Finally, cash provides the most *efficient* means of reducing income poverty. According to Gary Burtless, distributing all public assistance to the poor in the form of cash would "completely eradicate poverty as officially measured and do so at less cost" than the current mix of programs. This is so because in-kind programs—in comparison with cash—don't directly raise the income level of their recipients; their value never directly enters the budget of the poor.

This "efficiency" argument, of course, is somewhat misleading because one's "welfare" demands more than simply an income above the poverty line. If all antipoverty programs were "cashed-out" (i.e., converted to their dollar equivalents) and then distributed on the basis of need, we *would* eliminate "official poverty" but we would certainly aggravate the problems that in-kind benefits address—poor health, malnutrition, and inadequate housing. This is because cash means consumer choice, which means people spending their dollars in their own fashion, which means that targeted public interest priorities may not be advanced. It also reflects the fact that cash assistance, even when it brings recipients to income levels near the poverty line, does not provide coverage anywhere near to what in-kind programs—especially medical programs—currently provide. Elderly people in nursing homes, for example, often receive Medicaid benefits at levels many times the poverty line. The acutely ill often receive health care benefits worth even more.

Benefits in-kind, then, promote a more genuine concept of "welfare" than cash alone. Food stamps may not efficiently reduce income poverty, but they directly increase a household's food consumption. At the very least, the social control of consumption insured by the in-kind approach offers a degree of protection to the unwary and the ignorant. From this perspective it might be said that it is not so much freedom to choose that is reduced by in-kind help as freedom to err or to choose poorly on the basis of limited knowledge. The response to this might be that, without freedom to err, self-determination is a hollow construct. What the collectivist sees as the desirability for social protection, the individualist views as a paternalistic infringement on individual responsibility.

The cash-versus-kind issue pitches the discussion of social provisions at a fairly high level of generality. From this level we can observe contending arguments, but no general solution is visible. To draw a general conclusion about the primacy of either cash or in-kind benefits would involve imposing an absolute standard in a realm of policy choice where relativity is the more appropriate stance. Much depends on the esteem in which individual freedom and consumer choice are held compared to social control and the collective good. But even the most ardent supporters of consumer choice bow to the necessity of collective interventions under certain circumstances, such as for the mentally incompetent or where the market is inoperative because of technical conditions.[19] And those who prescribe benefits in-kind are sensitive to both the need for adequate cash support and the social and psychological benefits of self-expression and autonomy derived from consumer choice. For them, as Mencher suggests, "the problem is not the potential conflict between individual rights and social controls but the maintenance of maximum opportunity for individual choice as an integral part of the system of government responsibility."[20] To achieve this balance, a mixture of different forms of social provision that offer varying degrees of consumer sovereignty and social control must be considered.

Alternative Forms: An Extension of Choice

We have discussed the nature of social provisions in terms of two basic benefit forms, cash and kind. The forensic utility of this classification affords reasonably firm lines for debate. Yet to think of social provisions in these terms alone oversimplifies the realties that policymakers face in practice. Finer distinctions are possible and desirable for analytic precision.

Social benefits may come in a variety of forms, from those that serve to enhance individual power to provisions in the form of concrete goods. Embedded in these varied forms is a dimension of transferability—the extent to which the provision allows for consumer choice. For example, public housing units, home repair services, cash supplements for housing, and rent vouchers offer varying degrees of freedom of choice to the consumer. Conversely, they ensure to varying degrees that the provision will not be used for anything other than its intended purposes. In terms of form and transferability, social provisions may be broadly classified into six categories: opportunities, services, goods, vouchers and tax credits, cash, and power.

Opportunities are incentives and sanctions employed to achieve desired ends. Although this is the vaguest type of direct provision, it is not unimportant; much social policy is concerned with the creation and distribution of opportunities.

Unlike goods and services, opportunity benefits involve the provision of civil rights or an "extra chance." Sometimes the extra chance is built into the basis of social allocations, as in the additional points afforded veterans on civil service exams and the special efforts of schools to recruit underrepresented students. In these cases the nature of the provision considerably overlaps the basis of social allocations. Opportunities ultimately lead to the acquisition of other benefits. However, opportunities have no immediate transfer value inasmuch as they must be utilized within the context that they are offered. A recipient of opportunity X cannot trade it for opportunity Y, or for goods, services, or other social provisions.

Services are activities performed on the client's behalf, such as in-home care, personal counseling, case management, and job training. These provisions are nontransferable in terms of their immediate market value to recipients.

Goods are concrete commodities such as food, clothing, and housing. These benefits have limited transfer value, generally confined to marginal channels of exchange such as pawn shops, flea markets, and informal barter.

Vouchers and tax credits are benefits that have a structured exchange value and may be transferred for resources within a delineated sector. Tax credits, for example, can be used to offset day-care expenses; food stamps can be exchanged for a variety of food products. Such provisions offer greater degrees of freedom of choice than goods or services. As a form of social provision, vouchers have special appeal because they preserve a modicum of consumer sovereignty (within a sector) while allowing for the exercise of social control (between sectors). Thus, they attract a range of proponents with both collectivist and individualist predilections.[21]

Cash benefits, programs such as public assistance, children's allowances, and social insurance, provide unrestricted purchasing power. Any tax arrangements that let individuals and families keep more of their own income also qualify, serving as indirect cash benefits. These provisions, of course, all have universal exchange value, offering the most latitude for consumer choice.

Power involves the redistribution of influence over the control of goods and resources. It can be achieved, for example, through policies that transfer policy-making authority to a particular group of people. In the 1960s and 1970s, for example, federal policy often required representation of the poor, clients, and other disadvantaged people on the boards of agencies that dispensed social welfare benefits, such as the Community Action Agencies established during the War on Poverty. Here, social provisions were incorporated into policy decisions about the structure of the delivery system (which we will examine in Chapter 6). Although such power cannot be "spent" in the same way as cash or credits, it offers a higher degree of latitude to command social and economic choices than provisions in the form of goods, services, or opportunities. In this sense, power has a fluid exchange value.[22]

In addition to these forms of provisions, there are social interventions that indirectly assist individuals and groups. A good deal of important social welfare policy, rather than providing tangible benefits to specific individuals in need, establishes programs that are instrumental in the development and implementation of benefit programs. *Instrumental provisions* are those that encourage more efficient and effective arrangements among agencies that supply direct social welfare benefits.

To illustrate, let us consider Title III of the 1973 amendments to the Older Americans Act, which established more than 600 Area Agencies on Aging (AAAs) throughout the United States. These agencies, which still exist, have responsibilities for planning, pooling, and coordinating local resources to produce a comprehensive service system for the elderly. The AAAs also are expected to function as advocates for the elderly, monitoring and evaluating relevant policies and programs. In this fashion, AAAs furnish indirect forms of aid in their jurisdictions.

Although instrumental provisions influence the distribution of social benefits through planning and coordination, there appears to be a tendency among indirect service agencies, such as AAAs, to move into the provision of direct services. There are several reasons for this sort of functional drift, not the least of which is that it strengthens the agencies' ties to the elderly constituents who receive immediate and concrete benefits from the direct services offered.[23]

Instrumental provisions are important in molding the process through which policy choices concerning tangible social welfare benefits are made. Because they are most pertinent to the process of social welfare planning, we will engage in a more detailed discussion of instrumental provisions in Chapter 9, where policy choices concerning the question, Who plans?, are examined. For the remainder of this chapter we will discuss the nature of social provisions that offer direct forms of aid to individuals and groups.

Vouchers: Balancing Social Control and Consumer Choice

Recently there has been an increasing interest in the use of vouchers. Compared to government cash or kind provisions, social benefits in the form of vouchers possess a special attraction—they preserve consumer choice while allowing a degree of social control. This ensures that benefits serve a publicly defined purpose, be it the provision of food, shelter, education, health care, or some other vital service.

The food stamp program is the largest and best-known voucher arrangement in the United States. Public assistance recipients and other low-income persons are eligible for food coupons with a designated cash value that may be used to purchase food products at supermarkets. Starting as a pilot project in 1961, food stamps grew at a phenomenal pace after the program was enacted nationally in 1964. Between 1967 and 1975, the number of participants soared from 1.5 million to 19.3 million, at which time the program came to be known in Congress as the "food stampede."[24] From 1975 to 1995, program costs nearly septupled from $4.4 to $27.5 billion.[25]

One of the first *educational* voucher schemes was devised by Milton Friedman in 1955.[26] Instead of directly financing and operating public schools, government, he proposed, should distribute vouchers to parents that could be used to purchase education at the schools of their choice. By introducing the competition of the economic market, school programs would presumably become more innovative and the overall quality of education would improve. Because it was also possible, of course, that some schools might effectively deny access to the poor by charging more than the cash value of vouchers, by employing admissions tests that reject weak students, or by misleading the unsophisticated consumer about the quality of their programs, later voucher plans, such as those developed by Christopher Jencks and his associates in the 1970s, included a series of protective regulations guarding against discriminatory admissions policies and requiring that precise information on educational programs be made available to aid parents in the intelligent exercise of choice.[27]

One of the first voucher experiments, conducted between 1972 and 1977 at the Alum Rock Union Elementary School District in northern California, sought to demonstrate the advantages of competition and consumer choice in education. When the Alum Rock demonstration was launched, its design was closer to Jencks' regulated plan than Friedman's *laissez-faire* approach. The Alum Rock voucher concept, moreover, was restricted in a number of ways: choice was limited to the thirteen of the district's twenty-four public schools that elected to participate; enrollment ceilings were used to maintain a degree of balance between demand and supply; and teachers were assured they would not lose their jobs if their school did not attract enough pupils. Despite these modifications, the Alum Rock demonstration enhanced parental choice and promoted a significant degree of competition among schools.[28]

The findings from Alum Rock revealed that although the range of educational alternatives increased, geographical proximity was the predominant consideration for most parents. More than 80 percent of the participants selected the schools nearest their homes. And choices made among different miniprograms *within* schools favored traditional over new, experimental, modes of education.[29] On the matter of educational quality, data from several studies found no significant

---

CAPSULE 5.2:   The Friedman Vision

Government could require a minimum level of schooling financed by giving parents vouchers redeemable for a specified maximum sum per child per year if spent on 'approved' educational services. Parents would then be free to spend this sum and any additional sum they themselves provided on purchasing educational services from an 'approved' institution of their choice. The educational services could be rendered by private enterprises operated for profit or nonprofit institutions. The role of government would be limited to insuring that the schools met certain minimum standards, such as the inclusion of a minimum common content in their programs, much as it now inspects restaurants to see that they maintain minimum sanitary standards.

Milton Friedman, *Capitalism and Freedom*, 1962, 89.

differences among the academic test scores of students from voucher and non-voucher schools.[30]

In 1990, Milwaukee, Wisconsin, adopted the nation's first districtwide school voucher program, providing tax-free tuition vouchers enabling low-income children—almost entirely African American and Hispanic—to select either public or private (secular) schools. (Efforts to extend the plan to parochial schools continue to be challenged in the courts.) In 1995, vouchers worth $3,600 were provided and over 1,000 low-income students, 1 percent of the district student body, were participating. "Low income" was defined as households with incomes below 1.75 times the federal poverty index.

Despite considerable evaluative attention, the results of the Milwaukee experiment are ambiguous. John Witte, a researcher at the University of Wisconsin, has generally given the voucher plan poor grades, concluding that participating students scored about the same as other students in math and reading performance. Voucher advocates, on the other hand argue that the Milwaukee experiment proves that school choice results in higher parental satisfaction, better retention rates, and higher test scores.[31]

Although the voucher idea originated on the *laissez-faire* right, the concept has gained support across the political spectrum. African-American advocates in several large cities have embraced vouchers as a way to improve ghetto education by providing alternatives to what are perceived as inadequate, unresponsive public schools. Sectarian groups promote the idea as a way to assist parents who wish to send their kids to parochial schools. And many families—apolitical but education-minded—see vouchers as a device to gain more influence over the substance of the schooling their children receive.

Although public policy has become more amenable to vouchers—and to other kinds of educational options—the overwhelming majority of U.S. schoolchildren remain in their local public schools, partly because of the inertia of entrenched arrangements, and partly out of a very real fear that vouchers would significantly undermine public schools, resulting in even worse education for many children. Against those who see school choice as the means for innovation, efficiency, and consumer empowerment, these critics fear the creation of fragmented, divisive educational systems segregated by income and ideology and the destruction of one of the few institutions in our society bringing together children from different backgrounds and promoting a measure of social integration.

In the housing field, conservatives have long argued for vouchers that would allow low-income people to find their own housing in the private market. The federal Section 8 program, enacted during the Nixon administration, was the first significant voucher program in the housing field. Operating through local housing authorities, Section 8 provides eligible low-income renters a certificate that they can present to any landlord willing to take part in the program. Tenants then pay 30 percent of their monthly income toward the rent, with the federal government making up the rest. In return, landlords agree to federal guidelines that set limits on overall rental charges.

Programs such as Section 8 have many appealing features. They give renters a choice, vouchers can be used anywhere, enabling poor people to blend into ordinary communities. They expand opportunities for decent, appropriate housing. One commentator remarked that they turn "low-income renters into any army of deputies who monitor government spending. Their collective, self-interested discretion amounts to an invisible hand that decides whether the housing needs of the poor are most cheaply met through new construction, existing units, moderate rehabilitation," or other alternatives.[32]

The idea of housing vouchers has a special appeal given the disappointing record of federal housing policy over the past forty years. Government public housing strategies—especially innercity megaprojects—have often been fiascos, and HUD bureaucracy has been prone to inefficiency and scandal. Nevertheless, housing vouchers, though they serve 3.5 million poor U.S residents—remain limited in scope for one important reason: cost. A universal voucher system covering a major portion of the population currently in inadequate housing would be enormously expensive.

Substance of the Social Provision

Our categorization of benefit types in terms of form and transferability permits useful insights into the nature of social provisions, particularly for cash, vouchers, and goods that are fairly concrete. A broad variety of options is possible within each of these categories. For example, the provision of goods may include food commodities, clothing, and shelter; cash may be provided in modest or generous amounts; and vouchers may be designed to cover part or all of the costs of different goods and services. Despite the many alternatives, there is a palpable quality to these types of provisions that makes them readily comprehensible. The substance of these provisions is evident; most of the relevant qualities of the benefit become known as soon as the amount of cash, type of good, and credit or voucher sector are specified.

Consider, again, the school voucher. We can specify a cash value that can be exchanged only to pay for designated educational programs. Different programs might be housed in a single local public school, spread out among a few local public and private schools, or encompass all accredited schools in the country. The point is that once the value of the voucher and the sector in which it can be used are identified, the nature of the provision is substantially clear. It should be noted that with both cash and vouchers, our analysis of social provisions ends at the point that recipients obtain benefits. Subsequent choices concerning how these benefits are utilized involve individual transactions. What is ultimately purchased becomes a matter of individual choice much like any other.

For the other benefits categories—opportunities, services, and power—the substance of the social provision is more abstruse. To understand what is provided requires some probing. Consider a proposal to provide family counseling services. The type of service has been designated—counseling—but the substance of the provision remains ambiguous. It may emphasize information giving, insight therapy, behavior modification, or the alteration of environmental contingencies. It may center on individuals, family units, or groups. It may be short-term or long-range. And it may be conducted by personnel with a variety of backgrounds and training who base their practice on alternative theories of change.

Likewise, day care may involve a range of services, from custodial care to comprehensive child development, depending on staff-child ratios, staff qualifications, program content, and available equipment. Opportunity benefits in the area of employment may range from traditional systems of access to affirmative preferences to quotas. In college admission there is considerable debate regarding the substance of affirmative action provisions, running the gamut from special recruitment efforts to the modification of admission standards. The redistribution of power in various settings may cover a spectrum of influence, from that exercised by a citizens' advisory committee to community control of local institutions. Without clarifying the substantive aspects of services, opportunities, and power, we are severely limited in understanding precisely what it is that social programs provide.

Expediency of Abstraction

To prescribe that policy analysts should strive for precision in defining the nature of social provisions is not to deny the political function of abstraction. Although our major concern is with comprehending social welfare policy by dissecting the various dimensions of choice, we allow ourselves a momentary detour because, in the real world of policy choice, ambiguity in the design of social provisions serves an important purpose. This is critical to note, if for no other reason than to balance the analytic impulse to endlessly dissect social choices with the wisdom of practical experience. The advantages of leaving the nature of the social provision vague when strong contending views prevail concerning the specifics of policy solutions are numerous. One is that it allows those who formulate policies to secure broader support. When social provisions are defined at a high level of abstraction, different parties may read into them what they please, making agreement easier to reach. Upon implementation, additionally, there is greater flexibility and potential for experimentation. Once vague provisions are operationally transformed, of course, former advocates may find themselves startled at the substance of their creation, and may even end up seeking its undoing. Hence, there is a fragile quality to the political expedience of abstraction; it can smooth the way for passage of legislation without necessarily developing the commitments required to support a program over the long haul.

The classic example, the Community Action Program of the Economic Opportunity Act of 1964, spearheaded the War on Poverty under President Johnson. It took approximately six months for this program to move from the drawing board to enactment. John Donovan indicates that few single pieces of domestic welfare legislation of comparable importance had ever moved through

Congress with such ease and rapidity. He also observes, "there were only a few people in Washington early in 1964 who had any very clear notion of what community action in fact was.[33]

According to the bill presented to Congress, Community Action would

1. mobilize and utilize, in an attack on poverty, public and private resources of any urban or rural, or combined urban and rural geographical area, . . . including but not limited to a state, metropolitan area, county, city, town, multicity unit, or multicounty unit;
2. provide services, assistance, and other activities of variety, scope, and size to give promise of progress toward elimination of poverty through developing employment opportunities, improving human performance, motivation, and productivity, and bettering the condition under which people live, learn, and work;
3. be developed, conducted, and administered with the maximum feasible participation of residents of the areas and members of the groups [served] . . . ; and
4. be conducted, administered, or coordinated by a public or private non-profit agency . . . broadly representative of the community.[34]

This statement is seemingly innocuous, in part because of the legal syntax, but also because its deft phrasing is general enough to allow different minds to draw different conclusions about its intent. The task force responsible for drafting the antipoverty bill viewed community action as a mechanism for increasing the participation and power of the poor in the political life of the community. Daniel Moynihan notes, "the observation that Community Action Programs are a federal effort to recreate the urban ethnic political machines that federal welfare legislation helped dismantle, would not misrepresent the attitudes of the task force."[35]

During the congressional hearings on the antipoverty bill there was little explication of the idea that community action was intended to transfer power to the poor. One notable exception was the Attorney General Robert Kennedy who pointed out that the poor were powerless to affect the institutions that served them, and that community action could change this pattern.[36] New York City Mayor Robert F. Wagner opposed the provision giving decision-making power to the poor. He stated: "The sovereign government of each locality in which a Community Action Program is proposed should have the power of approval over the makeup of the planning group, the structure of the planning group, and over the plan."[37]

What emerged from the hearings was a number of interpretations, many of which implied that community action would provide primarily instrumental, opportunity, or service benefits.[38] Stressing the instrumental provision, Marion Crank, Speaker of the Arkansas House of Representatives, told the subcommittee, "The important new feature of Title II is that it will encourage a coordinated effort toward solving some of the serious problems in our area."[39] Emphasizing service provision, Robert C. Weaver noted, "The Community Action Programs will focus upon the needs of low-income families and persons. They will provide expanded and improved services and facilities where necessary in such fields as education, job training and counseling, health, and housing and home improvement."[40] But the nebulous quality of the provision was typified by comments of one Representative who referred to Title II as the "community facilities provision."[41] Under the circumstances, it is not surprising that the requirement for "maximum feasible participation," soon the *bete noire* of local politicians, slipped through the hearings virtually unquestioned.

Thus, depending on the viewpoints and preferences of those assessing the policy, it was assumed that community action would take one of three forms: an instrument to coordinate the planning and delivery of local services, an expansion in the level of services for the poor, or an increase in the decision-making powers of the poor to formulate and administer their own local programs. Community action was defined broadly enough to encompass all these interpretations. But two things were left unclear. The first was the order of priority. The possibility that the provisions might be mutually inconsistent was largely overlooked. No one, for example, dealt with the possibility that transferring power to the poor might militate against the increase of goods and services, and impede efforts at coordination. No guidelines were offered for trade-offs among different objectives. More significantly, there was little probing of the substance of these various social provisions. What *types* of services did the poor need and want? How *much* power and influence did "maximum feasible participation" imply? Did "participation" mean that the poor were to be advisors or to have a controlling vote? Serious consideration of these choices would, no doubt, have delayed passage of the legislation. Instead, it sailed through Congress in a haze of abstraction.

When it came to implementation, and efforts were made to specify and operationalize "maximum feasible participation," the program encountered heavy resistance. By 1965, when the first guidelines for involvement of the poor were issued, local mayors were already expressing considerable displeasure with the program and were demanding that local governments be given greater control.[42] The Bureau of the Budget also reacted by suggesting that the poor should be involved less as policymakers and more as community action personnel.

In 1966, Congress imposed its own restrictions on the use of community action funds, and by 1967 the Economic Opportunity Act was amended to clarify the substance of "maximum feasible participation." These amendments gave states, counties, and cities the power to incorporate local Community Action Agencies within their own governmental structures, or to designate other groups to fill this role. Although very few local governments chose to exercise this option, the amendments symbolized and reaffirmed the fundamental authority and control of local governments. In addition, these amendments limited the composition of Community Action Agency boards to no more than one-third poor people, with the remaining membership divided equally between public officials and representatives from the private sector. When the dust had settled, the definition of "maximum feasible participation" as power allocated to the poor had been carefully limited.

In 1974 the scale tipped even farther toward conservatism. The Office of Economic Opportunity (OEO), which financed and coordinated the Community Action Agencies, was dismantled. With its removal control of the Community Action Program was transferred to a new Community Services Administration (CSA), and its financial base experienced a precipitous decline.

Social Provisions as Reflections of Policy Values

As noted, choices concerning the form of social provision can largely be understood in terms of individualist and collectivist values, individualists disposed to consumer sovereignty, and collectivists toward social direction. Although this perspective affords a general level of explanation, particular social provision choices often get rather complicated.

Social provisions, for example, often directly reflect policy objectives. To fully comprehend why a policy design contains specific provisions requires insight into the assumptions that underlie policy objectives. Such insight requires that we understand policy objectives not simply as ends, but as means-ends relationships. That is, objectives articulate how the cause-and-effect relationships of social problems are perceived. They reflect, in essence, the theoretical outlooks of those involved in policy formulation.

In practice, of course, policy objectives are rarely stated in theoretical terms because that would tend to make decision makers appear unsure. The notion that "objectives are only theories" does find its way into many research and demonstration programs. But on the whole, program objectives are put forth with emphatic assurances that they provide valid solutions to clearly understood problems. To do otherwise—to candidly and skeptically advance programs as hypotheses—is to invite the wrath of advocates and to undermine the confidence of potential allies. If policymakers are tentative about a program, the public is not likely to be supportive. On the other hand, if their confidence is misplaced, and results are disappointing, they can lose credibility.

Although planners, administrators, and policy analysts may sympathize with the plight of elected officials, it is not their own. To be effective in what they do, they need a clear grasp of the theoretical quality of policy objectives. Moynihan's charge that the failure of professionals in developing the War on Poverty "lay in not accepting—not insisting upon—the theoretical nature of their propositions" may be inflated but it underscores the point.[43] That is, professional obligation entails the critical examination of the theories and assumptions that support the choice of different social provisions. As Suchman explains,

> *The process of seeking to understand the underlying assumptions of an objective is akin to that of questioning the validity of one's hypothesis. Involved is a concern with the theoretical basis of one's belief that "activity A will produce effect B." Such concerns are the earmark of professional growth. So long as one proceeds on faith in accepted procedures without questioning the basis for this faith, one is*

functioning as a technician rather than a professional. The future development of the various fields of public service as science as well as art will depend to a large extent upon their willingness to challenge the underlying assumptions of their program objectives.[44]

With this in mind let us take a final look at the Community Action Program. We have noted that its major thrust was posited in the form of instrumental, service, and power provisions, depending on the different perspectives involved. These different viewpoints did not derive from whim; in most cases they reflected certain theories and assumptions about the causes of and remedies for poverty.

There are many intricate theories of poverty, but the purpose of this discussion is to illustrate how theory applies to the analysis of social provisions. Rather than present the details of these theories, we will consider three independent variables around which many are organized: *resource deficiency, individual deficiency,* and *institutional deficiency.*[45]

From the viewpoint of resource deficiency, the lack of basic material resources such as health care, housing, and income is the primary characteristic of poverty and a major factor contributing to its development and perpetuation.[46] Simply put, this is a formal expression of the conventional assumption that "to get, you must first have." To the extent that CAP provisions were concentrated on special kinds of services, such as neighborhood health centers and day care, program objectives were based on the proposition that poverty could be reduced by changing the circumstances under which people live.

The theory of individual deficiency, in its most primitive form, is social Darwinist in origin: poverty results from personal defects, which make some less fit and less adaptable than others. A less invidious version of the theme focuses on the "culture of poverty;" poverty is explained in terms of a debilitating cultural and environmental milieu that incapacitates the poor. The defect is not biological; rather the values, norms, and behaviors of the poor are at fault. In either case, this perspective leads to the conclusion that poor people themselves must be changed.[47] To the extent that CAP provisions were concentrated on counseling, training, and educational services, program objectives were based on the proposition that reducing poverty required changing skills, values, and behaviors.

Poverty may also be explained in terms of institutional deficiency. The basic assumption here is that social welfare institutions not only fail to function properly, they operate in ways that sustain poverty.[48] This perspective finds expression in two provisions of the Community Action Program. The objective of the instrumental provision, with the CAP serving a coordinating and planning function, was to improve institutional performance by increasing the rationality, efficiency, and comprehensiveness of service provision. The institutional deficiency, here interpreted as a technical problem, is addressed through administrative channels. The provision of power, on the other hand, views institutional deficiency as a political problem. The objective, then, is to make social welfare institutions more responsive to the poor, not through technical rationality, but by increasing the poor's political capacity to influence these institutions. To the extent that the CAP was interpreted in these terms, program objectives were based on the proposition that reducing poverty required change in the institutional structures that contribute to its maintenance.

Which are the best or the preferred interpretations of the Community Action Program? On this question the analysis sheds little light. An explication of the theories and assumptions that underlie the choice of different social provisions does not create the rules for choosing. However, it does help to clarify *what* we are choosing. First, it offers a basis for making judgments about the coherence of policy design in terms of the complementarity of social provisions. Many social welfare policies have multiple objectives, requiring the delivery of more than one type of provision. In some cases, these objectives are incompatible because of their underlying assumptions. For instance, it has been suggested that the service and power objectives of the CAP were contradictory. The reasons for this can be explained by the different assumptions underlying each. To put it bluntly, if the poor suffer mainly from individual deficiencies (their need for services, for example), then increasing their power *vis-a-vis* service-giving agencies is to place the healer in the arms of the lame. However, if institutional deficiency is seen as the major problem, then offering increased services only buffers and protects the *status quo*.

The second function of this analysis is to specify the major independent variables on which we are putting our money, so to speak. Clarification of this point provides guidelines to assemble empirical data that bear on the validity of the assumptions and also furnishes referents for future policy evaluation. Social welfare policy is rarely based on evidence that is so clear and overwhelming as to be determinate. Nevertheless, it is pertinent to inquire about evidence that clearly ties a given provision to a specified outcome. Faith may be a potent sedative for uncertainty, but it is insufficient for the thoughtful design of social provisions.

Yet, the influence of sheer faith in underlying theories and assumptions cannot be ignored; although we emphasize empirical grounding, choices regarding social provisions are, often as not, light on evidence.[49] A prominent example is cited by Connery and others in discussing the major assumptions supporting the development of community mental health programs:

> *In 1963, when the basic legislation was being considered, it was noted that there were no American studies demonstrating that, when the quality of care was held constant, community-based treatment facilities functioned any better than those located in large hospitals. If this is valid, it would appear that the nature of mental health services and the investment of hundreds of millions of dollars throughout the country was substantially shaped on the basis of firmly held and persuasively argued beliefs that lacked a substantial empirical base.*[50]

We introduced this section by suggesting that understanding specific choices concerning social provisions required a grasp of the theories and assumptions underlying policy objectives. At this point we advise that a distinction be drawn between theories and assumptions (along the lines noted in Chapter 3) with theories deriving largely from empirical insights and assumptions being based on faith and ideology. Obviously, this distinction is often difficult to make and is always relative. Yet, heightened sensitivity to the "why" of social choice is enhanced by considering not only the cause-and-effect relationships that underlie policy objectives but also the degree to which these relationships are informed by theory or assumption—by the tenets of evidence or faith.

What Is Not Provided?

In analyzing the nature of social provisions, we have focused on delineating the form and substance of social welfare benefits. We have also sought to understand the reasons for social choices among alternatives with reference to broad value orientations as well as theories and assumptions underlying specific objectives. Overall, we have focused on what is provided. It may seem odd, therefore, to pose the question, What is *not* provided? This question requires that another class of latent assumptions be brought into the analysis of choice, assumptions that do not bear directly on the cause-and-effect relationships relating to specific policy objectives but to the design of social provisions in general. They have to do with assumptions about the availability of already existing resources that can be counted on to accompany the provision of social welfare benefits. One need not look very hard to find that social provisions frequently require supportive human services that are nonexistent and unlikely to develop within a reasonable period of time. Consider, for instance, the following four programs.

Public Assistance Social Work Services

It was estimated soon after the enactment of the 1962 social service amendments that 31,000 graduate social workers would be needed by 1970 to take full advantage of the new provisions for funding. At the time of this estimate, public assistance agencies employed less than 2,500 graduate social workers, and fewer than 3,000 graduate social workers were being educated annually for all public and private programs, most of whom were predisposed to work for private agencies.[51] Although the legislation contained provisions to increase the supply of qualified workers, they were severely inadequate for the task. Examining the record, Steiner notes:

> In some ways the services emphasis did not have a real test, but the disturbing factor is that it was always obvious that personnel to do the job were not available. . . . No one had ever claimed that just anybody could provide services. This is the way it worked out, however, and what the House Ways and Means Committee saw in 1967 was the big picture: five years of service, no results. Of course, there was no point in offering as an explanation the absence of trained personnel because there was no more likelihood that trained personnel could be provided in subsequent years than had been the case in previous years.[52]

Community Mental Health

Conservative estimates of the personnel requirements for staffing the nationwide network of centers proposed in the 1965 amendments to the Community Mental Health Centers Act showed a need for 30,000 professionals from the four basic mental health disciplines of psychiatry, psychology, social work, and mental health nursing. As reported during the congressional hearings, this figure equaled almost half the total supply of such professional personnel available at that time. Although federal grants were made available to train additional mental health professionals, the expansion of human resources in these fields is clearly subject to the strictures of prolonged training, especially for psychiatrists. This fact led one team of investigators to conclude that, "Even with money available to pay them, it seems highly questionable whether these professionals will be available in sufficient numbers to make the program a reality.[53]

Social Services

In the 1970s there was a surge of planning for the delivery of social services. One of the first large-scale planning efforts was introduced by the 1973 amendments to the Older Americans Act, which established a network of more than 600 Area Agencies on Aging responsible for developing annual plans for services to the elderly. An even more significant planning effort was set in motion through the 1974 Title XX Amendments to the Social Security Act. Under Title XX, the states were required to engage in a tremendous amount of work each year to produce a Comprehensive Annual Service Plan (CASP). In 1978, for example, Massachusetts had forty area planning teams that performed county needs assessments, conducted public hearings, and submitted 149 program proposals. This vast planning activity, annually involving hundreds of citizens, professionals, and elected officials in each state, placed a heavy burden on human resources in the social welfare system. A nationwide study of Title XX plans reveals little evidence, however, that annual planning generated much in the way of program change, reallocation of resources, or "fine tuning" of policies from one year to the next. The annual plan appeared to be a ritualistic activity justified more by tradition than by principles of prudent forecasting.[54] Recognizing this, in 1980 federal officials permitted states to shift from a one-year to a two- or three-year planning cycle. Also in 1980, federal regulations for the Older Americans Act jettisoned the requirement of annual planning by Area Agencies on Aging in favor of a three-year planning cycle.

Employment

An expanded role for job-training programs has been a goal of numerous federal and state policy initiatives since the 1960s. From the WIN program of 1965 (discussed in Chapter 2) to the welfare enactments of 1996, public assistance and employment and training policies have sought to broadly increase the ability, the "human resources," of disadvantaged youth and adults to enter the labor market and support themselves and their families. Commenting on this trend, Levitan and Taggart have pointed out that major obstacles to program success, not the least is the availability of job training personnel, are often overlooked.

> *One constraint is the lack of trained manpower to administer projects. Too often it is assumed that demand will create supply. As proof, many point to the fact that while there were only a handful of manpower "experts" ten years ago there are now many thousands. No doubt there has been an increase in competent personnel, but the administrative difficulties of the programs suggest that many of the instant experts are lacking adequate preparation. If the programs are continuously expanded, it is doubtful that personnel can be supplied to take care of needs.[55]*

This obstacle is not easily overcome. A study by Mary Sanger in 1984 revealed several major deficiencies in the WIN program including "poor administrative structure, inadequate funding for supportive services, and lack of staff training."[56]

In more recent years, it has been the lack of available support services that has received the most attention. Job training efforts, no matter how competent their staff, may be of limited utility if recipients are unable to obtain basic education, medical aid, child care, family planning and life-skills assistance, transportation, and counseling.

Dubinsky describes one training program that was forged in a cauldron of heated rhetoric and arduous negotiations between indigenous African American groups from Pittsburgh's poverty neighborhoods and local construction unions. Out of a hard-won struggle, a significant number of on-the-job training slots were finally secured. But when the program was implemented, the trainees often did not show up for work. At the point of success, major difficulties were encountered because necessary support services failed to materialize. Many job sites, for example, were out of reach of public transportation, and few trainees owned automobiles. Only as an afterthought, following a period of confusion and hardship for trainees and program officials, was this addressed through a special transportation contract with the city bus company.[57]

In the recent debate over welfare reform, the importance of support services has been endorsed by most analysts, although there is considerable disagreement concerning the mix and quantity of the services necessary to promote self-sufficiency. One of the most obvious needs, however, is child care. If women with preschool children are to participate conscientiously in work-training efforts, they need to have care for their kids. About 82 percent of AFDC recipients have children under the age of six, and most of these parents report they need reasonably priced child care in order to work. It is safe to conclude that a broad expansion in the availability of care is necessary if job-training programs are to succeed.[58]

Cash, Kind, and the Cycles of Public Assistance

The tension between cash and kind in all its practical and philosophical dimensions has been persistently illustrated in the evolution of U.S. public assistance. Should government provide direct cash aid to needy families, or should cash be accompanied (or replaced) by programs and regulations advancing community values? Should poverty be addressed by giving poor families money sufficient to insure the satisfaction of their basic material needs, or should cash benefits be conditioned by a variety of obligations, making assistance a "social contract" with "personal responsibility" for jobs, education, and moral conduct the *quid pro quo* for aid?

What is interesting is that the responsibility theme, at various times, has been embraced by both the left and the right. In the early 1960s, for example, welfare reform was staunchly tied to the provision of social services. Social workers and their allies argued that providing AFDC *without* supportive counseling and other social services was a shortsighted, unrealistic way to attack poverty. Social work leaders, led by the National Association of Social Workers, believed that welfare recipients faced human problems that required more than just cash assistance; the forces undermining self-sufficiency could not be addressed by the simple expedient of supplying money. Money was important, but it took face-to-face counseling and attention to individual client circumstances to produce long-term positive results.

CAPSULE 5.3: "Where Have You Gone, Florence Crittenton?"

Before the government offered cash payments to unmarried mothers, hundreds of private maternity homes provided vital services in every major city. These important institutions cared for tens of thousands of endangered women and children by building confidence, inculcating healthy new habits, actively discouraging illegitimacy, and working to integrate endangered families back into mainstream society.

Within two years of AFDC's enactment, the number of individuals receiving government public assistance had more than doubled, including lots of unmarried mothers. Maternity homes went into eclipse. Institutions that expected behavioral reform could not compete with no-strings checks.

It is time we fixed [this] error. Unwed motherhood should no longer generate entitlement to public cash aid or be perceived by teenage girls as the road to economic independence.

Young unwed mothers as a class should be viewed as persons peculiarly in need of supervision, education, discipline, and reform, and not as appropriate beneficiaries of unconditional cash payments. Group homes can play an extremely useful role in this area. They are a way for communities to provide care in the critical months before and after birth, and to instruct new mothers in child care and the responsibilities of parenting. They can assist placements for adoption. And they can be the means by which the community discourages further out-of-wedlock births.

George Liebmann, "Back to the Maternity Home," *The American Enterprise*, January/February 1995, 50–52.

In 1962, as we have discussed, the Congress endorsed this theory, and social services for the first time were legislated as a major strategy for welfare reform. Rehabilitation was the key word, and social services were funded to strengthen welfare families, reduce dependency, and help the poor gain the knowledge and skills necessary to adapt to the mainstream.

With the demise of the services approach of the Great Society, welfare reform in the late 1960s and early 1970s turned toward cash strategies. Negative income approaches were endorsed both by the left and right and Richard Nixon nearly succeeded in having his Family Assistance Plan (guaranteed annual income) enacted in 1970. Although social services were scarcely defunded, their value as an instrument for relieving poverty was deemphasized. In the legal theory of the decade, cash assistance increasingly was seen as a right, akin to a property right, or a civil right, and any insistence on social work services, jobs, or counseling was perceived as demeaning, even exploitative. And although the left viewed cash as a basic right of citizenship, the right saw it as a way to disentangle AFDC from the welfare bureaucrats. As Richard Nixon stated, "People should have the responsibility for spending carefully and taking care of themselves. Patronizing surveillance by social workers make children and adults feel stigmatized and separate. What the poor need to help them rise out of poverty is money."[59]

With the election of Ronald Reagan in 1980, the pendulum once again swung toward services—but services of a very specific type. With the increasing expectation that able-bodied recipients of aid should be required to work, or at least trained for work, the AFDC amendments of 1988—the Family Support Act—created the Job Opportunities and Basic Skills Training (JOBS) program to transform welfare into a transitional program geared toward jobs. Although JOBS funded a broad range of job-related services and created minimum requirements for caseload participation, its achievements have been unimpressive. By 1994, for example, only 13 percent of all AFDC adults were involved in JOBS programs, and most of these involvements were related to education, without a strong employment focus.[60]

By the mid-1990s, skepticism about cash welfare *and* job services had become a paramount theme of the right. Abandoning the consumer-choice pro-cash orientation of their conservative forebears, Republicans in the Congress crafted new welfare measures that harkened back to a Victorian paternalism in their effort to demonitize welfare. In repealing AFDC in 1996, the federal government ended sixty years of guaranteed cash support to poor families in favor of decentralized state-run programs emphasizing mandatory jobs (rather than job preparation or job training), school attendance, marriage (disallowing welfare payments to unmarried mothers under age 18 living alone), small families (permitting states to prohibit extra payments for additional children born on welfare), and short-term aid (time limits making public welfare a temporary, transitional, program on the way to work).[61]

Notes

1. Alva Myrdal, *Nation and Family* (Cambridge, MA: MIT Press, 1968), 133–53. A similar position is offered in Charlotte Whitton, *Dawn of Ampler Life* (Toronto: MacMillan of Canada, 1943). And for a utopian proposal where benefits in-kind are employed more generally as the foundation of a guaranteed standard of living, see Paul Goodman and Percival Goodman, *Communitas*, 2nd ed., rev. (New York: Vintage Books, 1960), 188–217.

2. The question of how *directly* the objective is served can be asked quite apart from the issue of how *well* the objective is served. The former involves effectiveness in terms of impact, the latter in terms of performance or ultimate outcome.

3. For further discussion of this assumption see James Buchanan, "What Kind of Redistribution Do We Want? *Economia*, 35 (May 1968); and Martin Rein, "Social Policy Analysis as the Interpretation of Beliefs," *Journal of the American Institute of Planners*, 37(5) (September 1971). These assumptions are critiqued in Gunnar Myrdal, *Value in Social Theory*, Paul Streeten (ed.) (London: Routledge and Kegan Paul, 1958), 137.

4. Raymond J. Struyk and Marc Bendick, Jr. (eds.), *Housing Vouchers for the Poor* (Washington, D.C.: Urban Institute Press, 1981).

5. Myrdal, *Nation and Family*, 151.

6. Gerald M. Holden, "A Consideration of Benefits In-Kind for Children," in Eveline M. Burns (ed.), *Children's Allowances and the Economic Welfare of Children* (New York: Citizen's Committee for Children of New York, 1968), 151.

7. Asa Briggs, "The Welfare State in Historical Perspective," in Mayer Zald (ed.), *Social Welfare Institutions* (New York: John Wiley & Sons, 1965), 62.

8. Sigmund Freud, *Civilization and Its Discontents*, James Strachey, (trans. and ed.) (New York: W. W. Norton, 1962), 42.

9. Myrdal, *Nation and Family*, 150.

10. Milton Friedman, "The Role of Government in Education," in Robert Solo (ed.), *Economics and the Public Interest* (New Brunswick, CT: Rutgers University Press, 1955), 124.

11. Myrdal, *Nation and Family*, 150.

12. See, for example, Shirley Buttrick, "On Choice and Services," *Social Service Review*, 44(4) (December 1970), 427–33; and Anthony Pascal, "New Departures in Social Services," *Social Welfare Forum* (New York: Columbia University Press, 1969), 75–85.

13. James Thompson, *Organizations in Action* (New York: McGraw-Hill, 1976), 17–18.

14. Friedman, "The Role of Government in Education," 144.

15. John K. Galbraith, *The Affluent Society* (New York: Mentor Books, 1958), 205.

16. See Friedrick Hayek, "The *Non Sequitur* of the 'Dependence Effect,' " in Edmund S. Phelps (ed.), *Private Wants and Public Needs* (New York: W. W. Norton, 1962), 37–42.

17. Alice M. Rivlin, *Systematic Thinking for Social Action* (Washington, D.C.: Brookings Institution, 1971), 137–38.

18. See, for example, Peter Marquis, et al., "Barriers to Child health Care," *Archives of Pediatric and Adolescent Medicine*, 149 (1995), 541–45.

19. A more detailed discussion of these conditions is presented by Milton Friedman, "The Role of Government in a Free Society," in Edmund S. Phelps (ed.), *Private Wants and Public Needs* (New York: W. W. Norton, 1962), 104–17.

20. Samuel Mencher, *Poor Law to Poverty Program* (Pittsburgh: University of Pittsburgh Press, 1967), 336.

21. For example, see Friedman, "The Role of Government in Education;" Buttrick, "On Choice and Services;" and Christopher Jencks, "Private Schools for Black Children," *The New York Times Magazine*, November 3, 1968.

22. At some point in the utopian future, status/prestige as a distinct category may be appended to this list of social provisions. In Bellamy's society in *Looking Backward* (see Chapter 3), the distribution of opportunities as well as goods and resources was more or less equal among the population. But here the link between status/prestige and wealth/power was

broken. Status positions and symbols that conferred honor and esteem with neither direct nor indirect material benefits (i.e., they had no market value) became the major form of social provision to compensate those who made special contributions to society.

23. Neil Gilbert and Harry Specht, "Title XX Planning by Area Agencies on Aging: Efforts, Outcome, and Policy Implications," *The Gerontologist, 19*(3) (June 1979), 264–74; Stephanie Fall Creek and Neil Gilbert, "Aging Network in Transition: Problems and Prospects," *Social Work, 26*(3) (May 1981), 210–16.

24. American Public Welfare Association, "The Fiscal Year 1980 Food Stamps Budget" *W-Memo,* April 5, 1979.

25. U.S. Department of Commerce, Bureau of the Census, *Statistical Abstract of the United States, 1981* (Washington, D.C.: U.S. Government Printing Office, 1981), 322.

26. Friedman, "The Role of Government in Education."

27. Christopher Jencks, et al., *Education Vouchers: A Report on Financing Elementary Education by Grants to Parents* (Cambridge, MA: Center for the Study of Public Policy, 1970).

28. Paul Wortman and Robert St. Pierre, "The Educational Voucher Demonstration: A Secondary Analysis," *Education and Urban Society, 9* (August 1977), 471–91.

29. David Cohen and Eleanor Farrar, "Power to Parents? The Story of Education Vouchers," *Public Interest, 48* (Summer 1977), 72–97.

30. See for example, D. Weiler (ed.), *A Public School Voucher Demonstration: The First Year at Alum Rock* (Santa Monica, CA: Rand Corporation, 1974); Wortman and St. Pierre, "The Educational Voucher Demonstration"; and R. Crain, *Analysis of the Achievement Test Outcomes in the Alum Rock Voucher Demonstration, 1974–75* (Santa Monica, CA: Rand Corporation, 1976).

31. See Paul Peterson, Jay Greene, and Chad Noyes, "School Choice in Milwaukee," *The Public Interest, 125,* Fall 1996, 38–56.

32. E. G. West, "Choice or Monopoly in Education," *Policy Review, 15* (Winter 1981), 103–17.

33. John C. Donovan, *The Politics of Poverty* (New York: Pegasus, 1967), 40.

34. U.S. House of Representatives, *A Bill to Mobilize the Human and Financial Resources of the Nation to Combat Poverty in the United States,* 88th Cong., 2nd session, March 1964, H. R. 10443, 17–18.

35. Daniel Moynihan, "What Is 'Community Action'?" *The Public Interest,* 5 (Fall 1966), 7.

36. U.S. House of Representatives, Economic Opportunity Act of 1964, *Hearing Before the Subcommittee on the War on Poverty Program* (Washington, D.C.: Government Printing Office, 1964), Part I, 305.

37. Statement of Robert F. Wagner before the Ad Hoc Subcommittee on the Poverty Program of the House Education and Labor Committee, April 16, 1964, 3–4 (mimeographed).

38. For a more thorough discussion of these various interpretations, see Moynihan, "What is 'Community Action'?".

39. Statement by the Honorable Marion H. Crank, Speaker of the Arkansas House of Representatives, before the Ad Hoc Subcommittee on the Poverty Program of the House Education and Labor Committee, April 10, 1964, 3 (mimeographed).

40. Statement of Robert C. Weaver before the Ad Hoc Subcommittee on the Poverty Program of the House Education and Labor Committee, April 16, 1964, 12 (mimeographed).

41. Quoted in Elinor Graham, "Poverty and the Legislative Process," in Ben B. Seligman (ed.), *Poverty as a Public Issue* (New York: Free Press, 1965), 251–71.

42. For example, see Advisory Commission on Intergovernmental Relations, *Intergovernmental Relations in the Poverty Program* (Washington, D.C.: Government Printing Office, 1966); and William F. Haddad, "Mr. Shriver and the Savage Politics of Poverty," *Harpers,* December 1965, 43–50.

43. Daniel Moynihan, *Maximum Feasible Misunderstanding* (New York: Free Press, 1969), 188–89.

44. Edward A. Suchman, *Evaluative Research* (New York: Russell Sage, 1967), 41.

45. For a concise review of the literature and an elaboration of these perspectives on poverty, see Martin Rein, *Social Policy* (New York: Random House, 1970), 417–45.

46. For an excellent example along this line of study, see Alvin Schorr, *Slums and Social Insecurity* (Washington, D.C.: U.S. Government Printing Office, 1963).

47. See Michael B. Katz, *The Undeserving Poor*, 1989, especially 9–36.

48. See, for example, Frances Piven and Richard Cloward, *Regulating the Poor* (New York: Random House, 1971) and Ian Gough, *The Political Economy of the Welfare State* (London: Macmillan Press, 1979).

49. Joel F. Handler and Jane Hollingsworth, *The Deserving Poor* (Chicago: Markham Publishing, 1971), 127.

50. Robert H. Connery, et al., *The Politics of Mental Health* (New York: Columbia University Press, 1968), 478.

51. Advisory Council on Public Welfare, *Having the Power We Have the Duty,* Report to the Secretary of Health, Education, and Welfare (Washington, D.C.: U.S. Government Printing Office, 1966), 79.

52. Gilbert Steiner, *The State of Welfare* (Washington, D.C.: Brookings Institution, 1971), 39.

53. Connery, et al., *The Politics of Mental Health,* 530.

54. Neil Gilbert, Harry Specht, and David Lindeman, "Social Service Planning Cycles: Ritualism or Rationalism?" *Social Service Review* 55(3) (September 1981), 419–33.

55. Sar A. Levitan and Robert Taggart, II, *Social Experimentation and Manpower Policy: The Rhetoric and the Reality* (Baltimore: Johns Hopkins, 1971), 85.

56. Mary Bryna Sanger, "Generating Employment for AFDC Mothers," *Social Service Review 58*(1) (March 1984), 32.

57. Irwin Dubinsky, *Operation Dig: A Black Militant Program to Train Trade Union Craftsmen* (Ph.D. dissertation, Graduate School of Public and International Affairs, University of Pittsburgh, 1971).

58. Denise F. Polit and Joseph J. O'Hara, "Support Services," in Phoebe H. Cottingham and David T. Ellwood (eds.), *Welfare Policy for the 1990's,* (Cambridge, Mass: Harvard University Press, 1989), 173–82.

59. Richard Nixon, quoted in Edward Berkowitz, *America's Welfare State From Roosevelt to Reagan,* 1991, 128.

60. U.S. General Accounting Office, *Welfare to Work: Most AFDC Training Programs Not Emphasizing Job Placement,* GAO-HEHS-95-113, May 19, 1995.

61. Douglas Besharov and Karen Gardiner, "Paternalism and Welfare Reform," *The Public Interest, 122,* (Winter 1996), 70–84.

Chapter **6**

The Design of the
Delivery System

"You're very strict," said the Mayor, "but multiply your strictness a thousand times and it would still be nothing compared with the strictness that the Authority imposes on itself. Only a total stranger could ask a question like yours. Is there a Control Authority? There are only Control Authorities. Frankly, it isn't their function to hunt out errors in the vulgar sense, for errors don't happen, and even when once in a while an error does happen, as in your case, who can say finally that it's an error?"

FRANZ KAFKA
The Castle, 1930

When Kafka's hero wanders through a bureaucratic maze, continually confounded in his attempts to make sense of the system, his fictional world is not far removed from the real-life experiences encountered by many applicants for social welfare benefits. The system for delivering benefits is closed to certain applicants; others enter it only to find themselves shuffled from agency to agency without ever receiving appropriate help. And many will ask in despair for a "control authority" through which to seek redress for their grievances. At times the answer they receive closely approximates the quotation above.

This situation does not necessarily arise out of authoritarian mentalities or bad intentions. Indeed, there is no way to avoid some measure of bureaucracy in structuring services. Organization, to a considerable degree, requires bureaucracy. But there are important choices to consider in designing organizational forms, choices that provide policymakers and planners with opportunities to avoid some of the more Kafkaesque aspects of service delivery. In this chapter we will examine some of the choices and uncertainties involved in the design of social services delivery systems.

142

The delivery system, as noted in Chapter 3, refers to the organizational arrangements that exist among service providers and between service providers and consumers, in the context of the local community. We focus on "the local community" because this is where providers and consumers usually come together.[1] Service providers may be individual professionals, self-help associations, professional groups, or public and private agencies acting separately or in concert to provide services in private homes and offices, community centers, welfare or mental health departments, hospitals, and so forth.

The number of choices involved in designing delivery systems is large. Consider, for example, the following seven options (which by no means exhaust the possibilities). Providers may:

Be administratively centralized	or	Decentralized
Combine services (e.g., health, probation, and income support)	or	Offer single services
Be located under one roof	or	Maintain separate facilities
Coordinate their efforts	or	Never communicate
Rely on professional employees	or	Employ consumers or para-professionals
Delegate authority to service users	or	Concentrate authority in the hands of "experts"
Be public administrators	or	Private contractors

Through the early 1980s, most of the literature on the design of social service delivery systems focused on the first six options, choices which concern structural arrangements to promote services coherence and accessibility. Since then, a new body of literature has emerged that is centered less around structural arrangements and more around questions related to service delivery under public or private auspices. In examining choices in the design of delivery systems, we will begin with the selection of administrative auspice—one of the most pressing issues in the planning and politics of services organization.

Privatization and Commercialization of Service Delivery

Analyses of auspice tend to focus on two levels of choice: (1) the broad issue of privatization, which addresses the alternative of having a service delivered directly by a public agency or indirectly through contracting with a private provider (voluntary and for-profit agencies), and (2) the narrower issue of commercialization, which addresses the choice between for-profit and nonprofit providers.

CAPSULE 6.1:   The Privatization Nostrum

Today, government is beset with cynicism, conservatism, and libertarianism. "Privatization" is the magic nostrum to cure our public ills and two administrations have been industriously, if not always coherently, engaged in dismantling the structure they were supposed to be managing. "Bureaucracy" and even "government" have become pejoratives instead of descriptive terms. . . .

The pendulum has swung before and it will swing again. The attractions of libertarianism, which views each human being as ensconced in a shell of isolation, will fade in the face of the world's great social problems of population, of environment, of energy, and the establishment of peace. We will learn again that we must live together, all jostled up on this little planet; and we will learn that government plays an essential and honorable role in the endeavor.

Herbert A. Simon and Victor A. Thompson, "Public Administration Revisited," *Society, 28*(5), July/August 1991, 44–45.

Privatization and the Future of Public Social Services

Since the early 1980s, there has been considerable growth in third-party purchase of service arrangements, through which public funds are used to pay for services delivered by private agencies.[2] This contracting for services is certain to increase under TANF block grants for welfare, with community-based organizations receiving preference as contract agencies.

Today's degree of enthusiasm for contracting out represents a level of commitment to community-based agencies that has not been seen since the community action movement of the mid-1960s. It is an enthusiasm inspired by the convergence of two popular assumptions—one suiting the free-market ideology of the right, the other satisfying the citizen participation/empowerment objectives of the left. Privatization is therefore linked both to the presumed advantages of the competitive marketplace and to the failings of public bureaucracies. Private agencies perform well because they offer the most efficient approach to the production and delivery of social services.[3] Public bureaucracies perform poorly because they enjoy a monopoly in their areas of service; public consumers, a captive audience, must take what is offered.[4]

Although a competitive market *does* provide strong incentives to adopt cost-effective practices, which reduce waste, the efficiency assumption nevertheless bears scrutiny. This is because the market metaphor does not exactly apply in the realm of social services contracting where the forces of competition responsive to consumer choice are undermined by third-party purchase of service arrangements.[5] Under purchase of service contracts, the entire transaction is perceived neither by the individual consumer, who does not pay for the service, nor the purchasing public body, which does not receive the service. Moreover, social service consumers are often vulnerable—children, elderly, and poor—and less than well

---

CAPSULE 6.2:   Public Service, Noble Purpose

The monopoly provision argument assumes that public organizations have no ways to call forth good performance from employees other than the incentives typically available to private firms. This view ignores the role that the larger and—I do not hesitate to use the word—nobler purposes of many public endeavors can play in spurring employees to better performance. For example, the vast majority of people in our society who risk their lives on behalf of others in the regular course of their jobs are government employees—police officers, fire fighters, soldiers, foreign service officers. Certainly not every public employee is motivated by saintly purposes, nor does every government agency have a large public purpose. But where public purpose draws people into government in the first place, it should be nurtured and consciously be made part of a strategy for public management, not dismissed as something for snickers or sarcasm.

Steven Kelman, "The Renewal of the Public Sector," *The American Prospect*, No. 2, Summer 1990, 53.

informed. In the absence of the market discipline imposed by knowledgeable consumers who pay for what they get, third-party contracting does not operate in the kind of environment that secures the cost and quality of services being delivered, a problem Hansmann describes as the "contract failure theory."[6]

Competitive bidding for third-party contracts has been used in efforts to address the problem of contract failure, which stems from the absence of competition and consumer choice. Evaluations of the competitive bidding mechanism in several service areas, however, suggest that the results neither reduce costs nor enhance quality.[7] "Proxy shopping," another method recommended to introduce the discipline of market competition into purchase-of-service arrangements, involves contracting only with service providers who can attract paying customers (who serve as proxy-shoppers for public agencies). The reasoning here is that if consumers who have shopped around with money in their pockets are willing to pay for the service, the cost and quality should be competitive with that of other providers.[8] Still, there must be enough suppliers to form a competitive market, which is often not the case when dealing with community-based agencies.

Even if competition can be introduced into purchase-of-service arrangements, the problem remains that the transaction costs of contracting are quite high; these costs include complicated measurements to determine the price of units of service being purchased and expensive procedures to then monitor the quality of what is delivered (these costs holding providers accountable are discussed in more detail in the next chapter).[9] One answer to this criticism is that the transaction costs of purchasing services from private agencies may be mitigated by contracting with community-based agencies. Why? The reasoning goes that community-based agencies will be accountable and responsive to their local consumer-constituency; these agencies are in essence local groups organized to serve their own communities. Thus, even though the consumers do not pay for the services they are receiving, they are nevertheless in a strong position to influence the quality of these services, often participating on the boards of the local agencies. Under these circumstances the transaction costs of contracting can be reduced because monitoring for quality would be conducted by the consumers who have the power to influence their local organizations.

Contracting, then, can be promoted not only as a method for efficient and effective delivery of services, but also as a mechanism for advancing the democratization of social services. Community-based agencies are mediating institutions—local, private, and responsive to the people served—that provide a cushion of civil society between the individual and the state. Seen in this light, minimizing the role of government in the delivery of social services will give "mediating institutions,

---

CAPSULE 6.3:   The New Parlance of Community

Civil Society

An intellectual revolution is underway concerning the nature of our social crisis. It is no longer credible to argue that rising illegitimacy, random violence, and declining values are rooted in the lack either of economic equality or of economic opportunity. These positions are still current in our political debate, but they have lost their plausibility.

America's cultural decay can be traced directly to the breakdown of certain institutions—families, churches, neighborhoods, voluntary associations—that act as an immune system against cultural disease. In nearly every community, these institutions once created an atmosphere in which most problems—a teenage girl "in trouble," the rowdy neighborhood kids, the start of a drug problem at the local high school—could be confronted before their repetition threatened the existence of the community itself.

When civil society is strong, it infuses a community with its warmth, trains its people to be good citizens, and transmits values between generations. When it is weak, no amount of police or politics can provide a substitute. There is a growing consensus that a declining civil society undermines both civility and society.

—Senator Dan Coats

Social Capital

By analogy with notions of physical capital and human capital—tools and training that enhance individual productivity—"social capital" refers to features of social organization, such as networks, norms, and trust, that facilitate coordination and cooperation for mutual benefit. Social capital enhances the benefits of investment in physical and human capital.

Our political parties, once intimately coupled to the capillaries of community life, have become evanescent confections of pollsters and media consultants and independent political entrepreneurs—the very antithesis of social capital. We have too easily accepted a conception of democracy in which public policy is not the outcome of a collective deliberation about the public interest, but rather a residue of campaign strategy. The social capital approach, focusing on the indirect effects of civic norms and networks, is a much-needed corrective to an exclusive emphasis on the formal institutions of government as an explanation for our collective discontents. If we are to make our political system more responsive, especially to those who lack connections at the top, we must nourish grass-roots organization.

—Robert Putnam

Senator Dan Coats, Can Congress Revive Civil Society?," *Policy Review,* No. 75, January/February 1996, 25.
Robert D. Putnam, "The Prosperous Community: Social Capital and Public Life," *The American Prospect,* No. 13, Spring 1993, 35, 41.

once again, the space to flower, reclaiming their rightful place at the center of a revitalized civil society."[10] In the mid-1990s, this "civil society" theme has engendered considerable discussion about ways to reinforce local community structures to build the "social capital" necessary to promote democracy, local networks, and responsive helping systems.

There is however another, less sanguine, view of the value and the potential of community-based agencies. Abstract discourse on civil society, local responsiveness, social capital, and citizen empowerment tends to ignore the harsh fact that there is often a dense concentration of social problems in communities with the highest proportions of residents in need of social services. Fred Wulczyn, finding that one out of eight children born in some of New York's poorest neighborhoods are admitted to foster care as infants, estimates that the cumulative rate of foster care placement in these communities may be approaching 20 percent.[11] Plagued by high levels of child abuse, family disorganization, and crime these communities not only have few natural "civic" resources, they would be extremely difficult to organize for constructive local agency participation.

Effectiveness and local responsiveness aside, however, the plain fact is that community-based agencies often deliver social services for lower costs than public bureaucracies. They deliver services for less because they *pay* their workers less. Public bureaucracies, after all, represent one of the last strongholds of the union movement in the United States. Community-based organizations can also often rely on volunteers, keeping their personnel costs down.

Ironically, efforts to revitalize civil society through support of geographically based mediating institutions are being promoted at the cost of functionally based communities of organized labor, which *also* constitute powerful mediating institutions of civil society. Indeed, in his classic analysis, Emile Durkheim noted, "A nation can be maintained only if, between the State and the individual, there is intercalated a whole series of secondary groups near enough to the individuals to attract them strongly in their sphere of action."[12] With organizations based on territorial divisions (villages, districts) becoming less important, Durkheim envisioned occupational groups emerging to fill the void and recreate a sense of social solidarity.

Philosophical arguments about the place of geographic- and functional-community institutions in civil society will not mitigate the increasing fiscal pressures on state public assistance agencies to contract out the delivery of services under TANF block grants. As policy analysts consider the shift from the public social services to community-based delivery structures, the assumptions underlining privatization should be carefully examined and the trade-offs should be made explicit, particularly the implications for organized labor. Private services may be less costly, but whether community-based agencies are more *effective* in delivering social services isn't at all certain. To date, research findings on the effectiveness of social services delivered under public and private auspices haven't yielded a definitive answer.[13] As Kamerman and Kahn observe, the evidence runs both ways, "varying with field, time, context, and scale."[14] Although private community-based agencies reside close to the people being served, are less bureaucratic, and are more responsive to local influences than public bureaucracies, this does not guarantee greater effectiveness in service delivery.[15]

Commercialization: Services for Profit

Prior to the 1960s, social services were delivered almost exclusively by public and voluntary nonprofit organizations. When they were addressed, questions of auspice addressed the relationship between public and voluntary nonprofit providers.[16] With today's increasing involvement of commercial agencies in the delivery of social services, new questions have emerged concerning how well social welfare objectives can be served by providers motivated by profit.

Social welfare advocates view the emergence of profit-oriented agencies with a jaundiced eye.[17] There is a strong suspicion that the profit motive is not morally compatible with the ethos of social welfare provision. Yet, moral objections would be difficult to sustain if it could be shown that profit-oriented agencies were the most effective and efficient means for delivering social services. If, on the other hand, profit-oriented agencies were shown to be *less* efficient and effective than nonprofit providers, moral objections would be unnecessary to deter the privatization of services. Assessing the efficiency and effectiveness of social services, however, is a complex business. Service objectives are often multiple and vague. They are no less important for these qualities, but they frequently defy precise measurement.[18]

Despite the difficulties of empirical measurements, there is a body of research comparing the relative effectiveness of profit versus nonprofit providers.[19] Some studies reveal that nonprofit providers are more sensitive to client needs; others show service areas in which profit-oriented agencies do the best job; still others find no significant differences between profit and nonprofit agencies. On the whole, findings on the relative merits of for-profit and nonprofit service providers, like comparisons between public and private providers, are indeterminate.

In the absence of decisive empirical evidence, theoretical analyses of the distinguishing features of profit and nonprofit organizations offer a variety of guidelines for choice. Theoretically, nonprofit organizations have greater public accountability than profit-oriented organizations because their structure of governance requires boards of directors composed of people who are expected to promote the broad interests of the community. In contrast, the directors of profit-making agencies are expected to protect the financial interests of owners. In nonprofits, therefore, there is less temptation to exploit vulnerable service consumers for material gain. Finally, there is a charitable ethos associated with nonprofits that is at variance with the capitalist spirit of profit-making enterprises.[20]

These differences suggest several practical conclusions for choosing between profit-making and nonprofit providers:[21]

1. Standardization of service—Services that involve uniform procedures and standard products, such as public health vaccinations, readily lend themselves

to the economic planning skills and business initiative of profit-making organizations. At the same time, the uniform character of these services allows the purchasers to monitor their delivery for potential abuses more easily than services that require a technology that is custom tailored to each case (such as therapeutic services).

2. Client competence—Many social services deal with client groups that are highly vulnerable to exploitation. Children, the mentally retarded, and confused and emotionally upset people do not have the ability to hold service providers accountable for the quality of their services. To the extent that public accountability and the charitable ethos influence the behavior of nonprofit agencies more than that of profit-making agencies, the nonprofit form is preferable for delivering services.

3. Coerciveness of service—Services invested with coercive powers, such as protective services for children and work with parolees, pose a significant threat to personal liberty. In these cases, the service provider's degree of public accountability is of foremost importance. With the clients' freedom at stake, the lack of public accountability of profit-making organizations would not seem to offer the most adequate form of protection.[22]

4. Potency of the regulatory environment—Profit-oriented and nonprofit providers would seem equally preferable in delivering services that are under sufficient public regulation to ensure the maintenance of standards and client protection. We should note, however, that the scope and potency of regulatory activity in the social services are limited.

Although these conditions tend to favor nonprofit agencies, there are clearly service areas where this general proposition does not hold, such as transportation for the handicapped and elderly. In choosing between profit and nonprofit providers, the essential issue is not to seek the universally superior form of organization, but to determine the particular conditions under which profit- or nonprofit-oriented agencies may best serve social welfare clients. In assessing these conditions we must consider not only the points noted, but also the nature of the purchase-of-service arrangement, especially the extent to which funding agencies can design grant requirements to ensure compliance with their objectives (an issue that will be addressed in Chapter 8).

Promoting Coherence and Accessibility: Service Delivery Strategies

Whether social services are delivered under public or private auspices, issues remain about how to structure the delivery system in ways that foster coherence and accessibility. Broadly speaking, efforts to promote coherence and accessibility address three kinds of questions concerning the structural arrangements for service delivery: (1) Where shall authority and control for decision making be located? (2) Who will carry out the different service tasks to be performed?

(3) What will be the composition (the number and types of units) of the delivery system?

Attempts to answer these questions often stir controversy as they respond to the tug and pull of conflicting social values. In addressing questions about where authority should be vested, for example, the value of consumer participation may be emphasized regardless of its impact on the efficiency of service delivery. Issues having to do with efficiency compete with other values that may be equally important to society, such as providing jobs for low-income people or insuring equity in the geographic distribution of services.

In the heat of controversy, criticisms of service delivery intensify. Such criticism tends to focus on the characteristic failings of local service-delivery systems, particularly *fragmentation, discontinuity, unaccountability,* and *inaccessibility.* These problematic facets of service delivery have been amply documented and analyzed.[23] Plans to reform the organization and the delivery of social services usually concern one or more of them.

For a description of these problems, consider the following hypothetical circumstances: A single unemployed mother with a substance abuse problem drops her daughter off at a day-care center and then goes to receive treatment at a drug abuse rehabilitation clinic, after which she spends the rest of the day in a TANF work-training program. If the day-care center, the clinic, and the work-training program are in different parts of town, operate on different schedules, and provide overlapping services, that's fragmentation. If there is no convenient means of transportation between the three agencies serving this client, no referral between the clinic and the work-training program, and no TANF benefits to pay for the day care, that's discontinuity. If the client is not admitted to the treatment or training program because of her place of residence, lack of medical insurance, or the like, that's inaccessibility. When any or all of these circumstances exist and the client has no viable means of redressing her grievances, the delivery system suffers from unaccountability.

These problems have many facets, are interconnected at some points, and span a broader range of issues than we have just described. Problems of fragmentation concern organizational characteristics and relationships, especially coordination, location, specialization, and duplication of services. (For example, are services available in one place? Do agencies try to mesh their activities?) Problems of inaccessibility concern obstacles to a person's entering the network of local social services. (For example, does bureaucratic selectivity based on income, age, success potential, or other characteristics exclude certain persons from service?) Problems of discontinuity concern obstacles to a person's movement through the network of services and the gaps that appear as an agency tries to match resources to needs. (For example, are there adequate channels of communication and referral?) Problems of unaccountability concern relationships among persons served and the decision makers in service organizations. (For example, are those needing help able to influence decisions that affect their circumstances? Are the decision makers insensitive and unresponsive to clients' needs and interests?)

CAPSULE 6.4:   Malign Neglect

"A guy I met told me about General Relief. He said there was an office on Soto and Olympic. I walked to Soto and Olympic from Skid Row [2 miles away]. They gave me a lot of papers to fill out. The worker told me I had to get a Social Security card because I had lost mine. She told me I also had to register at the unemployment office, do five job searches, and get back at 3:30 the next day. . . . They gave me a voucher to a hotel in Huntington Park called the Long-fellow [3.2 miles]. I didn't know where any of these places were, the unemployment office, the Social Security office, or anything. The worker told me the offices were downtown. She gave me nine bus tokens; that was sup-posed to last a whole week. I asked for food stamps for some way to eat. She said I didn't have the right kind of identification. So I had to go to the Longfellow to register by 5:00 P.M., otherwise I'd get locked out. The next day, since I didn't get food stamps, I had to go to one of the missions [5.5 miles]. After I ate, I had to find out where the Social Security office and the unemployment office was, the one on Broadway. I first applied for unemploy-ment. . . . After the unemployment office [1 mile], I walked to the Social Security office [1.5 miles]. I applied for a duplicate Social Security card. By this time I had been walking around downtown all day. I didn't have a watch so I didn't know what time it was. But I caught a bus to go out on Olympic to the wel-fare office. When I got there, it was 4:15 P.M. The woman that saw me gave me a note from the worker saying I should call her the next day about 2:30. It was as if she left the note before 3:30 P.M. because it said to be given to me when I came in for my appointment. So I called her the next day and she said since I didn't get there on time, I'd get a sixty-day penalty [suspension of benefits] and couldn't reapply for two months."

Jennifer Wolch and Michael Dear, *Malign Neglect*, 1993.

Phrased as policy issues, these problems confront policy planners and admin-istrators with choices that, although conceptually distinct, become confounded with one another in practice. That is, the ideal service-delivery system is one in which services are integrated, continuous, accessible, and accountable. Taken sep-arately, however, each of these elements strains against one or more of the others. We may summarize some of the choices as follows:

1. Reduce fragmentation and discontinuity by increasing coordination, opening new channels of communication and referral, and eliminating duplication of services (possibly increasing unaccountability and inaccessibility).
2. Reduce inaccessibility by creating new means of access to services, and dupli-cating existing service efforts (possibly increasing fragmentation).
3. Reduce unaccountability by creating a means for clients and consumers to have input into, and increased decision-making authority over, the system (possibly increasing fragmentation and discontinuity).

Problems in service delivery do not exist because there is a shortage of ideas about how to improve the situation. On the contrary, the technical repertoire of social planners and public managers includes a wide range of strategies for affecting the delivery of local services. It is matters of choice and uncertainty that need to be resolved. We approach this task in the following sections by identifying the choices among service-delivery strategies, analyzing the types of systemic changes related to different strategies, suggesting what needs to be known about the effects of these strategies, and explicating alternative theoretical paradigms that influence the selection of different strategies.

Proposals for reform invariably accompany critical analyses of service delivery. Although specific proposals for service delivery reform contain considerable variation, most correspond to one or another of six general strategies, each of which addresses at least one of the service-delivery questions mentioned earlier:

1. Strategies to restructure policy making authority and control:

   a. Coordination.
   b. Citizen participation.

2. Strategies to reorganize the allocation of tasks:

   a. Role attachments.
   b. Professional disengagement.

3. Strategies to alter the composition (i.e., number and types of units) of the delivery system:

   a. Specialized access structures.
   b. Purposive duplication.

Each of these strategies seeks to restructure local service systems to enhance service delivery. Coordination and citizen participation both impinge on the bureaucratic hierarchy of the system. Role attachments and professional disengagement alter the roles and status characteristics of actors in the systems. Specialized access structures and purposive duplication change the substantive composition of the elements in the system.

Strategies to Restructure Policymaking Authority

Coordination

Social workers and other professionals are quick to declare their faith in the generic, the whole person, and the comprehensive approach to service. They recognize the complexity of social causation and the interdependencies among the mental, physical, and environmental factors that influence clients' functioning and life chances. At the same time, the thrust of practice among professionals is toward specialization and the development of technical skills within narrowly defined areas of expertise. In one sense, services coordination helps to mitigate the strains created by the juxtaposition of specialization and the comprehensive approach in the professional value structure.

Coordination is a strategy aimed at developing an integrated and comprehensive social service system. Whereas innumerable arrangements have been suggested and tested for bringing some coherence to the natural fragmentation of services, three approaches capture most of the possibilities—centralization, federation, and case-level collaboration. These models are exemplified in different approaches to the organization of local social services in England and the United States.

The current structure of the British system is a product of the 1970 Local Authority and Social Services Act, which prescribed a major reorganization of local service agencies. The staffs and functions of children's and welfare departments, community development services, home-help services, and other local agencies were centralized under the auspices of newly created Local Authority Social Services Departments (LASSD). In turning to the LASSD as a mechanism for centralization, the British utilized what Simon recommends as being among the most powerful of coordinative procedures.[24]

At the same time that increased coordination through administrative unification offers a remedy for service fragmentation, it also gives rise to potentially dysfunctional consequences. For instance, services centralization tends to increase the organizational distance between clients and decision-making authorities. Centralization may lead to an internalization and perhaps heightening of what were previously *inter*organizational strains. The potential for *intra*organizational conflict is especially sharpened when a variety of heretofore autonomous agencies with different aims, technologies, and perceptions are cast into a unitary organizational mold, as in LASSD.[25]

In addition, the consolidation of services under one administrative structure limits service accessibility. The "single door" may in fact be at a number of centers dispersed throughout a community. It is a "single door" only in the sense that it functions according to the rules and regulations of one administrative authority, with intake into the services network concentrated in the hands of a relatively few gatekeepers. Such a "single door" can serve as a mechanism to rationalize service delivery from the standpoint of case referral and continuity, or it can act as a barrier to service for those who, inadvertently or by design, do not fit the administrative criteria for eligibility.

The second major approach to the coordination of services is through federation, which often involves the geographic centralization of different agency resources but not their administrative unification. In the 1960s and 1970s, continuous efforts along these lines were made under federal sponsorship through neighborhood service centers developed by the Community Action Program of the War on Poverty, City Demonstration Agencies organized by the Model Cities Program, and focal-point agencies authorized in the 1978 amendments to the Older Americans Act.[26]

Federative structures encompass a variety of more or less formal and binding arrangements. This variability is usually expressed by reference to the degree of time, resources, and decision-making authority invested by member organizations in the joint enterprise.[27] Warren distinguishes between a "federation" and a

---

CAPSULE 6.5:   One-Stop Shopping for AIDS Services

A unique clearinghouse providing social services for San Francisco patients infected with the AIDS virus will open its doors at noon today at renovated offices in the Mission District.

The Center for Positive Care, formed by a coalition of San Francisco AIDS service groups, is billed as "one-stop shopping" for AIDS services among the 15 agencies that are collaborating with it.

Each of the agencies will have an employee at the center, which will help guide clients through what it calls "the complex and often confusing" health care system.

"If someone needs to get on Medi-Cal, we'll have AIDS Benefits Counselors down the hall to the door on the right. If someone needs help with substance abuse, they can see the counselor from the Haight-Ashbury substance abuse program, down the hall to the left," said Dr. James Dilley, project director for the

University of California at San Francisco AIDS Health Project, a leading sponsor of the center.

"There are a tremendous number of people who are HIV-positive in this city. It is absolutely imperative that they get treatment as early as possible to postpone the symptoms of AIDS," said Bill Hayes of the San Francisco AIDS Foundation, one of the collaborating agencies.

Although open to all San Franciscans, the center is designed to improve availability of AIDS services to groups that have been missing out: blacks, Hispanics, women, drug users, young people and the homeless.

It will be open Mondays through Saturdays, operating 60 hours per week. The center's usual hours of operation will be from 9 A.M. to 8 P.M., except on Tuesdays, when it will open at noon, and Saturdays, when it will close at 5 P.M.

Sabin Russell, " 'One-Stop Shopping' For AIDS Services," *San Francisco Chronicle,* October 1, 1991, A20.

"coalition" in this way: the former is an ongoing collaboration with a formal staff structure that has some decision-making authority generally subject to ratification by component agencies; the latter is more *ad hoc* with no sharing or modifications of component agency decision-making authority.[28]

Federative arrangements require organizations to pool their skills, resources, knowledge, and staff in a cooperative venture. The costs to member agencies of such an undertaking frequently are less than the benefits of coordination.[29] By and large the goals and policies of local service agencies are not like interlocking pieces of a big jigsaw puzzle that, given time, patience, and a constructive mentality, can be fit neatly into the frame of a common cause. The fit, of course, can be accomplished but with costs to autonomy that many organizations are disinclined to pay. Thus, federative efforts often result in loosely knit coalitions that fall considerably short of the cooperative ideal.

In comparing centralization and federation strategies, the crucial distinction resides in the different control mechanisms employed in each. Federative structures involve voluntary collaboration of autonomous agencies: Cooperation is based primarily on reciprocity, and units are not bound to a formal hierarchy of positions, as they are under a centralized administration such as Britain's LASSD. Compared to bureaucratic authority, of course, reciprocity is a tenuous mechanism of control. It is operative, as Dahl and Lindblom note, "provided that the people have the same norms and conceptions of reality."[30] The federative model frequently takes the form of bilateral agreements among agencies serving overlapping clienteles. Because most agencies have a single function, individuals with multiple problems (e.g., alcoholism and mental illness; mental and physical disability; homelessness, poverty, and drug abuse) will find it difficult to deal with several separate and independent service systems. To tie these networks together, agencies frequently enter into cooperative arrangements specifying their respective roles and responsibilities for helping people in need.

During the 1980s, interagency agreements in the child and family field were frequently executed to coordinate services for multiproblem clients.[31] Collaboration among child welfare and mental health agencies became increasingly important because larger numbers of troubled children and adolescents were being placed in foster care and other types of out-of-home arrangements. Working together, mental health and child welfare officials have formulated agreements identifying their joint responsibilities, creating cross-system program models, pooling funds for common clients, and requiring cross-training of personnel.[32]

Case-level collaboration, the third coordinative model, involves decentralized interactions among service agencies and services personnel, rather than formal structured patterns of services unification or federation. Lacking a system of coordination from above, it is often the ground-level services worker who must connect the diverse components of the helping network. Such coordination from below is nothing new, of course. Service workers have traditionally had to insure that clients with multiple problems receive the various services they need, but the complexity of today's service delivery system increasingly demands caseworkers who have the sophistication and knowledge, and the mandate, to link clients to services in a timely and efficient manner.

Case management is one method for planning and delivering services to people who require assistance from several different sources. The case manager, a designated agency representative with cross-organizational responsibilities, works with clients in an ongoing relationship to develop a suitable service plan, to facilitate access to services, to monitor service delivery, and to evaluate service outcomes and client progress. Although "linkage" is clearly the key component, case managers must often serve as advocates and resource developers as well in order to insure appropriate services. The model is particularly suitable for vulnerable clients who, on their own, are able to maneuver in the service network.[33]

Case management is a primary element in the new welfare reform legislation.[34] It is also employed in complex agency systems such as child welfare where children are subject to fragmented services provided by schools, mental health services, juvenile courts, departments of social services, and other child and youth-serving organizations. Such organizational fragmentation is often aggravated by the differing orientations of service workers, health personnel, and judges, each of whom may deal with problems such as abuse and neglect by using their own theories and solutions. Pediatricians, for example, are mainly interested in the physical health of the abused child, whereas the emphasis of the caseworker is on adjudicating the child's dependency status. Similarly, the child welfare worker may find that the reluctance of some physicians to report findings of abuse obtained during physical exams undercuts their ability to investigate and prosecute child abuse.

As a coordinating mechanism, case management facilitates access to services. Although it often raises costs, especially if the case manager is effective in lobbying on behalf of clients, this approach can be viewed as cost effective because it leads to early identification of problems when they are, presumably, easier to treat. Moreover, case management can ensure greater efficiency in the use of services by eliminating duplication. In several welfare reform demonstrations, case managers serve a gatekeeping function, helping to focus limited services, such as child care, on those participants in greatest need.[35]

Citizen Participation

Unlike coordination strategies in which new relationships are forged among agencies, the strategy of citizen participation is aimed at redistributing decision-making power between agencies and clients. The rationale for citizen participation is that clients will be guaranteed responsive and effective services only if they are in positions of influence. Neither the good will of professionals, nor bureaucratic rationality, is considered sufficient to ensure that recipients' needs are met because both professionals and organizations have multiple objectives, their own survival in the system being foremost.

The redistribution of authority through citizen participation is distinguished according to different levels and types of participation. For example, Arnstein identifies nine levels of participation ranging from manipulation to citizen control.[36] Spiegel discusses types of citizen participation from the point of view of the level of government involved, the functional area in which decisions are made, and the degree of technicism involved in the decision.[37] Kramer approaches the analysis of this strategy by focusing on the functions and purposes of different types of citizen participation, which he describes as ranging along a continuum from receiving information, to advising, to planning jointly, to having complete control.[38]

Ignoring the various nuances, three modal types tend to emerge. First, there is *nondistributive participation* or pseudoparticipation. This may involve therapy, education, or plain deception; in any case, there is no perceptible change in the established pattern of authority. The second is *normal participation* (tokenism to critics), in which citizen influence on decision-making authority is clear and present but to a degree that makes only modest differences in final outcomes. The third type is *redistributive participation.* Here the shift in authority is such that citizen participants are able to exert substantive influence on decisions affecting the service delivery system.

Citizen participation is a strategy wherein the means represent a value in their own right, with that value being democracy. The basic assumption is that democratic services will be more responsive than a system in which decision making is solely the prerogative of professionals. However, it is possible that a system can be democratized and at the same time suffer a deterioration in the quality of service delivery. In such a case the strategy might be valid for broader political reasons but not for the objectives being considered here.

Although participatory democracy connotes the idealized New England town meeting where everybody had a right to vote (except, of course, women, slaves, and those too poor to own land), in practice citizen participation invariably requires the election or appointment of representatives. People simply do not have the time or the inclination to participate in every decision that affects them. The point is that, rhetoric notwithstanding, this strategy must come to grips with the notion of representativeness and the concomitant issues of *which* citizens will participate, on *whose* behalf, and *how* they will be chosen.

Participation was a prominent service delivery theme during the 1960s when the involvement of poor people became an intrinsic element of varied radical movements to organize the disadvantaged for social change (i.e., "power to the people"). Its legislative equivalent—"maximum feasible participation"— became not only a standard for the organization of community action boards under the War on Poverty, but also the ethos for redistribution of bureaucratic and political power in society. The participation ethos joined neighborhood activists, civil rights advocates, and cultural radicals in a short-lived movement for change that sought to bring the disenfranchised into positions of genuine inclusion in society.

At the level of service delivery, maximum feasible participation sought to decentralize decision making by requiring elections in low-income neighborhoods to select the boards of directors of community action agencies. The resulting experiences, however, suggest some of the problems of using this strategy. Neighborhood elections were conducted in several communities around the country, but turnouts were always disappointing, and always far below voter participation in regular municipal, state, and federal elections. In Pittsburgh, for example, less than 2 percent, and in Philadelphia, less than 3 percent, of eligible residents participated in such elections.[39] Kramer reports that "the numerous neighborhood elections in San Francisco and Santa Clara can best be described as pseudo-political processes."[40] In addition, it was not uncommon for citizen representatives to be appointed by social service agencies, or to be self-selected, rather than chosen through some type of electoral process.[41]

What continues to be lacking in many endeavors to select citizen representatives are mechanisms of accountability to ensure that the opinions and objectives of participants are valid expressions of local sentiment. In the absence of such accountability, the strategy of citizen participation has the potential for reproducing, on a different plane, the very difficulties it seeks to ameliorate. As Weissman observes, "Community control tends to become control of the community by some elements to the exclusion of others and does not necessarily lead to more effective services."[42] Under these circumstances, "welfare colonialism" may be replaced by an approach to local planning and decision making in which an elite group of citizen activists monopolizes the role of neighborhood spokesperson. In extreme cases, citizen activists may even become a new generation of political bosses, snatching much of the power and many of the prerogatives of the previous elites.[43]

In the post–War on Poverty era, participation models took on more conventional forms. Many of the block grants enacted in the 1970s and 1980s promoted civic mechanisms to encourage the involvement of the poor in service programs affecting their communities. The Community Development Bloc Grant, for example, provides for advertised public hearings, and many communities have established elaborate procedures involving advisory boards, need surveys, and service evaluations to insure client participation.[44] In addition, several pieces of major legislation have incorporated provisions to stimulate the involvement of service users. Federal child welfare legislation, for example, emphasizes opportunities for the participation of natural parents in deliberations concerning the legal status of their children. More recently, federal housing policies have been reformulated to involve tenants more fully in the management of public housing. Harking back to earlier community action models, HUD (Housing and Urban Development) has established alliances with nonprofit tenant activist groups, bypassing the traditional power centers of municipal housing professionals.

Strategies to Reorganize the Allocation of Tasks

Role Attachments

Social services, in the main, are performed by middle-class professionals. Although services are offered to the entire community, a disproportionate segment of the population in need comes from the lower socioeconomic classes. The class chasm between the servers and the served is viewed, according to role-attachment strategy, as an impasse to movement into and through local delivery systems. On the one hand, the middle-class professional may not understand the lower-class client's outlook on life, behavioral patterns, cultural values. Inarticulate by middle-class standards, clients may be perceived as recalcitrant or even threatening. The norms of professional objectivity and impersonal treatment, on the other hand, prescribe behavior that may be perceived by clients as unfriendly or officious. Given these mixed perspectives, problems of access and discontinuity occur because of social stratification rather than organizational structure.[45] The case is stated succinctly by Miller and Riessman:

> The agencies must take upon themselves the responsibility for seeing that the individual patient gets to the service, or gets from one service to another. Without the assumption of this responsibility, the concept of continuity of care or services will become a meaningless programmatic shibboleth. Nor can these problems be resolved through administrative improvements along. A human link is needed.[46] [Emphasis added.]

This human link, it has been argued, should be indigenous nonprofessional aides, persons who, by virtue of their styles and special skills, can bridge the gap between professional agencies and lower-class clientele, serving what Brager describes as a social-class-mediating function.[47] Certainly, other general economic and political values support the employment of indigenous nonprofessionals, but it is as expediters of service that such employment is relevant to a discussion of delivery-system strategies.

At least three potential problems may undermine this strategy. First, the employment of nonprofessionals may mean that clients receive services that are amateurish or of a lesser quality than those offered by professionals. Second, efforts to integrate aides into the delivery structure may engender stiff resistance from professionals. Pruger and Specht comment on the inevitability and the source of this resistance:

It is inevitable because it is rooted in the virtually irresistible structural forces that shape organizational behavior. . . . In the case of the organizationally-based professions, the forces that insure organizational discipline complement the pressures that induce professional reliability. And because much of the professional's self-image rests on this perception of his dearly bought competence, competitors arriving on the scene through nontraditional routes must almost certainly be considered impudent upstarts if not conscious usurpers.[48]

Finally, even when nonprofessionals are effective in linkage roles and are integrated into the service-delivery structure, the latter may vitiate the former. The effectiveness of the nonprofessionals will wane under pressures to resolve the strains between bureaucratic conformity and the free-wheeling style of the indigenous

---

CAPSULE 6.6: Trust and the Paraprofessional

The types of benefits most often noted by paraprofessionals revolved around the close and trusting relationships formed between paraprofessional and client. There was agreement among two-thirds of the paraprofessionals interviewed that spending time with the client was the primary contributor to improved client trust. Peer workers explained that they have more time than other program staff to spend with clients, and therefore are able to build a relationship before making suggestions or taking actions. As one paraprofessional commented, "It takes a long time, six or eight weeks, just to know someone before you can start to take action, and the case coordinator comes right in and tells them what has to be done." In order to ensure that peer workers have sufficient time to develop these critical relationships with clients, it is suggested that small caseloads (4–13 clients) be maintained.

Peer workers also stressed the importance of soliciting clients' self-identified needs and addressing those needs, in addition to the explicit program objectives. . . . Paraprofessionals acknowledged that social workers have a different role in the program and often have many more cases and pressing objectives to accomplish. . . .

"Perspectives of Paraprofessionals: A Survey of AIA Peer Workers," in Amy Price (ed.), *The Source* (National Abandoned Infants Assistance Resource Center), 4(2), Fall 1994, 5–6.

worker. Examining the integration of nonprofessionals into agency structures, Hardcastle concludes that "the diminution of the non-professional's indigenous qualities—the emphasis on primary role skills, extemporaneousness, and lower-class behavior and communication patterns—appears inevitable because of the essentially bureaucratic nature of the organization."[49] In addition, it is not surprising to find that once they are on the job, many nonprofessionals bend their efforts toward becoming professionals. They seek the financial and status rewards accruing to those who achieve higher degrees of usable knowledge and skill.[50]

The literature on cultural factors in service delivery, it should be noted, continues to emphasize the need for services personnel to be ethnically and culturally sensitive. This, however, does not require that personnel be of the same socioeconomic class, race, or culture as the client in order to be effective. A recent review of the literature by Snowden and Derezotes, for example, points out that the utilization of minority staff is associated with an increased number of minority clients. They caution, however, against concluding that majority staff can't work effectively with minority clients: Cross-race pairings can be, and often are, effective. Indeed, in certain cases they may be preferable to same-race pairings. When they go wrong for reasons related to race, this usually occurs in the early phases of the relationship.[51]

Professional Disengagement

Although the imperative of bureaucratic conformity may cramp the style of nonprofessionals, forcing them to adopt a professional or quasiprofessional *modus operandi*, it has been observed that the same imperative operates to inhibit professional functioning. For example, Levy describes a public welfare setting where the discrepancy between the needs of administration and those of clients poses an acute moral dilemma for many workers.[52] He suggests that the high turnover rate of workers in this setting was related to difficulties in reconciling their inner feelings with the stringent logic of welfare administration. Piliavin states the case more generally:

> Social work has acquired many of the earmarks of a profession, including a professional association that has developed and promulgated standards, goals, and an ethical code for those providing social services. The members of this association and other social workers guided by its framework of values encounter a dilemma unknown to their early predecessors; they find agency policies and practices frequently in conflict with avowed professional norms.[53]

To enhance service delivery, then, it would seem to be more effective to disengage from the bureaucracy rather than try to reform it. That is, professionals are advised to undertake private practice on a fee-for-service basis to circumvent the constraints to service delivery posed by agency policies; they are to change roles from bureaucrats to entrepreneurs. As many people who use social services could not afford to support a fee system, those who favor the move to private practice propose that the financial base for implementing this strategy be furnished through government grants (e.g., Medicaid) that give clients the opportunity to select the service provider of their choice.

Assuming that government financing through such voucherlike arrangements could somehow be accomplished, we see that this strategy has certain limitations. Private practitioners may have expertise in public welfare, corrections, relationship counseling, family services, school social work, services to the aged, and the like, but they cannot possibly be specialists in all of them. In this sense the private practitioner is subject to the same professional myopia as the agency-based worker, except that agencies may incorporate a variety of specialists. Just as in the case of the bureaucratic delivery of services, there is little to prevent private practitioners from imposing their particular brand of service—be it education, insight therapy, behavior modification, or some other technology—rather than dealing with the recipient's unique needs. And even for the least avaricious, the tendency to interpret client problems in terms of one's own expertise is reinforced under a fee-for-service arrangement. As a means of increasing accessibility to and coherence of the delivery system, the entrepreneurial model may prove less effective than agency-based practice.

Although there is little empirical evidence to support the presumed virtues of the entrepreneurial model, the move toward private practice has been gaining in popularity among professional social workers. According to a 1982 survey of 56,000 members of the National Association of Social Workers (NASW), 12 percent were employed under profit-making auspices, mainly private practice. This represents close to a fourfold increase over the 3.3 percent reporting similar employment in a 1972 survey.[54] And as noted in Chapter 1, current estimates indicate that close to 25 percent of NASW members are in private practice for at least part of their work week. There is some indication, in addition, that the proportion of professionals engaged in private practice increases along with experience and formal qualifications. A 1984 study in Massachusetts, for example, revealed that 45 percent of the state's 4,400 licensed independent clinical social workers—the highest of four levels of licensed social workers in that state—were employed in private practice on a full-time (19 percent) or part-time (26 percent) basis.[55]

The major assumption underlying this strategy is open to question. Although some professionals may function poorly in organizational settings, it is not necessary to conclude that organizational demands inherently limit professional functioning. Reasoned arguments can be made that there is much greater latitude for individual discretion to negotiate the constraints and opportunities of organizational life than many professionals exercise, mainly because they lack the expertise required to be effective in their roles as bureaucrats. Most professionals prefer to identify themselves as helpers and service givers, and training is consciously sought to prepare for these roles. They tend to ignore or reject the bureaucratic role that they must carry.[56]

Furthermore, it is possible to design agency-based practice in ways that tap the energies and resources associated with entrepreneurial activity. In the Kent Community Care Project, for example, British social workers are given a budget they may spend according to the needs and circumstances of each frail elderly

---

CAPSULE 6.7:   The Lure of Private Practice

Social workers enter private practice today for the same reasons that they have been attracted to the private practice of psychotherapy since the 1920s: to obtain more autonomy over their practice and to earn more money. The findings of a recent study of the goals of private practitioners in New England upon entering private practice bring the priorities of these social workers into stark relief. The most important goals indicated by the survey respondents, in decreasing order of importance, were to "do direct counseling," "maximize professional autonomy," "grow professionally," "be my own boss," "set my own hours," and "earn money." The least important goals indicated, in decreasing order of importance, were "help solve society's problem," "become more politically involved," "help economically disadvantaged people," and "work with ethnic minorities." It is important to note that these people had been well socialized into the social work profession; they had an average of ten years of post–M.S.W. social work experience prior to entering private practice.

Harry Specht and Mark E. Courtney, *Unfaithful Angels: How Social Work Has Abandoned Its Mission*, 1994, 125–26.

client. The objective here is to create a local network of supportive services that will allow the frail elderly to remain living in the community rather than being institutionalized, and at a lower cost to the public than would result from an institutional placement.[57]

Strategies to Alter the Composition of the Delivery System

Specialized Access Structure

The objective of this strategy is neither to change the combination of roles in the service delivery system nor to change authority relationships through centralization or federation. Its advocates believe that specialized professional–bureaucratic services perform important functions despite their weaknesses as delivery mechanisms. Instead of changing roles and the like, they want to change the composition of the delivery system by adding a new element, one that acts on other service agencies, to pry open their entry points, and to ensure that proper connections are made by clients. In a word, *access* is to be provided as a social service.

Traditionally, the provision of access was considered a marginal function carried out by agency staff rather than a separate function around which to organize a distinct set of services. As a marginal function, access is unduly restricted by the narrow perspectives of agency specializations, perspectives relating primarily to an agency's core function instead of the particular problems brought by clients. This phenomenon is a by-product of neither incompetence nor malice. It is a normal structural reality of specialized service organizations.

To facilitate client access to service while maintaining a relatively high degree of specialization, it has been proposed that a new structure be added to the delivery system, one characterized as a "professionally unbiased doorway."[58] This doorway is a special agency that offers case-advocacy, advice, information, and referral services to help clients negotiate the bureaucratic maze.

Although it is in many respects a persuasive strategy, the consequences of access agencies may be more wished for than assured. From the client's perspective, one effect of this strategy may be *increased* service fragmentation and complexity. Further, whereas access services are increasingly important in urban societies, they are among the least tangible of services. Thus the access agency may be perceived by clients as merely another bureaucracy to negotiate, another base to be touched before the proper resources are matched to their needs.

Access strategy is also likely to influence other service agencies in the delivery system. The addition of an access agency can result in other service-providing agencies diminishing their own access services. For instance, there is likely to be reduced pressures on these agencies to perform outreach or to make referrals to clients they are unable to serve. The extent to which the creation of the access agency lessens traveling time, expense, or confusion in the client's search for service is presently unclear. Moreover, the separation of assessment and diagnosis (access) from treatment (services) that occurs from this strategy may prove rather clumsy in practice.

Purposive Duplication
Purposive duplication entails recreating in a new agency any or all of the services available in the existing system. Purposive duplication is advanced in two forms that have a surface resemblance but are dissimilar enough to warrant distinction— *competition* and *separatism*.

Competition involves the creation of duplicate agencies within the existing delivery system to compete with established agencies for clients and resources. This strategy increases choice. More important, competition is expected to have an invigorating effect on agencies and professionals, sensitizing them to client needs and producing greater enterprise and creativity. The consequences of this strategy, however, are not always compatible with its motives. Instead of a healthy competition for clients and resources, internecine conflict may ensue between powerfully entrenched agencies and new agencies scraping for a foothold in the system. The outcome of such conflict is reasonably predictable.[59]

The duplication of services to stimulate competition may be achieved through *direct* or *indirect* methods. The direct approach involves the restructuring of the delivery system with the creation of new agencies. Community action funds, for example, were often provided to develop new agencies that offered day care, counseling, and community organization services to a community rather than to expand the service offerings of existing agencies. The indirect approach involves changing the form of the social provision. That is, social provisions are distributed to consumers in the form of vouchers for services.[60]

Separatism differs from competition in both the systemic location of new structures and their purposes. In the separatist design, new agencies are created and organized *outside* the established delivery system, which they do not seek to enter. Competition is likely to be an inadvertent and unplanned by-product of separatism, more so for resources than for clients. The intention is to form an alternative network that will serve certain disadvantaged groups who, because of their race, ethnicity, gender, sexual orientation, or socioeconomic status, are served poorly or not at all by the existing system.

While offering direct aid to clients neglected by the existing network of services, alternative agencies also perform other functions. As Miller and Philipp point out, they engage in unorthodox activities that help to clarify legal issues, offer a theoretical critique of conventional service paradigms, and provide a community of interest for new, often unpopular, client groups.[61] In recent years, for example, independent community-based services networks have developed for battered women, gays and lesbians, persons with AIDS, and newly arrived immigrant groups. Proponents of separatism emphasize that this strategy contains social and political values for disadvantaged groups that transcend the enhancement of service delivery.[62]

Duplicatory strategies, in either form, are enormously expensive. The money may be well spent if the new agencies become a dynamic force for desired changes in the delivery system and reach those who are excluded from services. Weighing against these benefits are the risks of expending scarce resources to produce fruitless conflict and to create even greater program fragmentation.

Unsettled Questions

We have identified six major strategies to foster coherence and accessibility of social services: changing patterns of authority by *coordination* and *citizen participation,* altering roles and status by *role attachments* and *professional disengagement,* and changing substantive composition by *development of specialized access structures* and *purposive duplication.* We have analyzed each for their expected benefits and to discover how they may exacerbate difficulties in other directions. All of these strategies are plausible ways to develop more effective service delivery; yet each has limitations and latent dysfunctions. And although some strategies may be complementary, others are just as clearly contradictory.

Before we can accurately judge the efficacy of any of the reform strategies, certain empirical questions must be answered. We will not attempt to detail all of these questions, but rather to identify several key issues requiring more intense investigation.

Coordination

Within what range and mix of services does coordination operate most effectively? At issue here are the criteria for selecting the number and types of service to be incorporated within a coordinating structure to produce minimum strain and maximum productive collaboration. There is substantial evidence, for instance, that certain service functions (such as social action and direct services) create disharmony and strain when joined.[63] We have little evidence, however, of what the optimal mix of services is and whether coordination is more likely to improve service integration when organized around a geographic base (all services in a designated neighborhood), a clientele with special demographic characteristics (such as the aged, adolescents, lone parents, and ethnic groups), functional areas (such as health and employment), or combinations thereof.

In addition, it is difficult to gauge what, if any, cost savings are achieved through coordination. Again, the evidence is sparse and tentative. The following conclusions drawn from a study of thirty service-integration projects illustrate some of the variables that enter into the measurements.

> *It may not be possible to justify services integration strictly in terms of total dollar savings. Centralized/consolidated operation of core services, record-keeping, joint programming, joint funding, joint training and/or central purchase of service arrangements on behalf of a number of service providers promote economies of scale, and coordinated staff utilization, funding, planning and programming, and evaluation help reduce duplication.*
>
> *Although there are some cost savings resulting from economies of scale and reduction of duplication, they do not appear (at least in the short-run) to equal the input costs of administrative and core service staff required to support integrative efforts. However, if one includes protection of public investment in services as a measure of efficiency, then a stronger case can be made for service integration on grounds of efficiency. If the public investment in one service (job training, for example) is to have lasting benefit only if another service (a job placement service, for example) is also provided, the cost involved in assuring that the client get the job placement services as well as job training may be justified in terms of protecting the investment in job training.[64]*

Purposive Duplication

Under what circumstances do the savings that accrue to a large-scale organization make the duplication of services practical? The research required to answer this question involves cost-benefit analyses of social service programs. A major argument against purposive duplication and in favor of coordination is the increased efficiency attributed to the latter. However, the gain in efficiency may vary from one type of service to another.[65] At the same time, coordination or administrative unification is usually achieved at the expense of diversity. Ultimately, value judgments will be made concerning the relative desirability of efficiency versus diversity in the delivery of social services. The more information available regarding the economic costs and social benefits of duplication, the better informed these value judgments will be.

Access Agencies

To what extent does the creation of an access agency facilitate entry into social services? One issue already suggested is that the addition of an access agency to the local service system may have the unanticipated effect of decreasing the net amount of information and referral provided within that system (because other agencies may diminish similar services they previously offered). This question remains open to direct empirical investigation. Another line of study involves an analysis of the percentage of those seeking assistance who actually receive services. It would be useful to know how many bases these persons touch before they receive help, and how this varies in the presence and absence of access agencies.

Role Attachments

What types of local nonprofessional workers are best suited to withstand the strains inherent in the performance of linkage functions between professional workers and the community served? At issue here is the fact that the term *indigenous nonprofessional* is applied to a variety of people with diverse values, commitments, aspirations, and reference groups. Workers in this category are likely to possess different capacities for coping with pressures toward bureaucratic conformity and professionalism. Accordingly, a useful line of investigation suggested in an exploratory study develops a typology based on the differences among nonprofessional workers.[66] It was found that certain types of nonprofessional staff members appear better suited than others to perform tasks such as outreach. Further investigation is needed to extend and substantiate these tentative findings.

Professional Disengagement

How does the move from agency-based to private practice affect access to and continuity of services offered? Although the disengagement strategy assumes that the delivery of social services will improve when the professional worker is freed from bureaucratic restrictions, little evidence exists either way. A line of inquiry might involve selecting a few cities for study in order to evaluate the effects of having similar services offered by private practitioners and agency-based practitioners with regard to the characteristics of the persons served, the percentage of referrals made, the percentage of follow-ups, and the like.

Citizen Participation

To what degree does substantive citizen participation in agency decision making increase accountability to those being served? As indicated, election and selection procedures for citizen participants are frequently such that those who actually participate are not accountable to the service users they ostensibly represent. We lack careful comparisons of the decision-making behavior of citizen participants and the expressed wishes and interests of the people they serve as well as delineation of selection procedures that produce participants with a high degree of accountability. One issue for further investigation involves the extent to which elected representatives (on a block, neighborhood, and citywide basis), appointed representatives, and volunteer (or self-selected) representatives differ in their accountability.

Each of these unsettled questions contributes to the uncertainty that surrounds policy makers who are concerned with selecting the right strategy to improve the delivery of social services. To conclude that more research is needed (which it is) is the unblemished mark of academicians (which we are). To this advice practitioners may nod abstractly in agreement while they continue to design and implement the policies that govern service delivery. This means that policy choices regarding service delivery may eventually benefit from future investigation, but they will not await the results; choices will be made based on the knowledge we possess, imperfect as it is.

Selecting Strategies

All the strategies discussed are plausible approaches to improving the delivery of services. All contain different limitations, and there is considerable uncertainty surrounding the consequences of each. Given these circumstances, how do administrators and planners choose? From a policy-planning perspective, the answer depends on the operational context in which choices are made, the values to be maximized, empirical evidence about the consequences of different strategies and, in the absence of compelling evidence, theories and assumptions about how delivery systems function. It is the latter aspect of choice—theories and assumptions—to which our analysis now turns.

Social service staff and organizations are the two major elements in the delivery system that can be manipulated to build coherent and effective connections between services and clients. Orientations that program planners bring to bear in considering service delivery, therefore, may be perceived as the result of the interplay of theories and assumptions regarding staff and organizations. Our purpose is to explain the ways in which these two major perspectives influence the selection of delivery strategies.

Social Service Staff: Perspectives on the Function of Professionalism

Broadly speaking, there are two perspectives on the function of social service professionalism: *status enhancement* and *service*. From the perspective of status enhancement, professionalism serves to protect and enlarge professional prerogatives and status. In contrast, the perspective of service views professionalism as a means to aiding those in need.

The service perspective corresponds to the model of a profession described by Greenwood in terms of five distinguishing attributes: (1) *knowledge* based on a systematic body of theory; (2) *authority* derived from and functionally specific to professional expertise; (3) *sanction of the community* to perform special services over which the profession has a monopoly; (4) *a regulative code of ethics* that compels moral behavior and prevents the abuse of the powers and privileges granted by the community; and (5) *a professional culture* consisting of values, norms, and symbols.[67] For Greenwood, the ethical code offers the clearest expression of the service perspective, requiring the "highest caliber service, irrespective of the identity and finance of the recipient," and the subordination of the practitioner's personal needs and interests to client welfare.[68]

These virtues notwithstanding, professionalization even at its best is frequently perceived as incompatible with a spirit of social reform. As stated by Wilensky and Lebeaux:

> *The notion that professionalism is corrupting because it brings economic rewards and social recognition, making its adherents fat, comfortable, and lazy, is much too simple. . . . More impressive is the argument that a professional absorbed in the technical side of his work aiming mainly at full use of his skills and training, preoccupied with that competent, efficient performance of which his professional colleagues would approve . . . does not have the time, energy or inclination necessary for social reform, for dedicated attention to the broader social purpose.[69]*

Others adopting the status-enhancement perspective see professionals driven less by service ideals than by self-interest. For Dumont, for example, the "personal dread of poverty, the insatiable appetite for wealth, the fascination with esoteric skills and complicated machinery, and the yearning for status and command of others" constitute the true motivations of professionals.[70]

In a less polemic vein, professional knowledge and expertise may be cast in the mold of credentialism,[71] especially in the social services where results and achievements are difficult to evaluate and a professional credential is often presumed to be synonymous with ability.[72] Professional authority is perceived as a mechanism of client control flowing from practitioners' monopoly over service rather than their presumed technical competence.[73] Community sanction of the professional's service monopoly is viewed as bestowed by established elites to whom the professionals are accountable, not by clients. The self-regulative code of ethics may be interpreted as a device to protect professionals from outside meddling and to reaffirm their claim to esoteric knowledge; they prevent "outside interference" by asserting that only professionals are competent to judge professional work.[74] And finally, the good intentions and altruistic motives emphasized by the professional culture are questioned.[75] It has been shown, for instance, that the difference between professionals and businesspersons lies in the different paths to achievement and recognition afforded by their occupational situations rather than in their motives.[76]

TABLE 6.1   Perspectives on Professionalism and Responses to
Service-Delivery Questions

Perspectives on Professionalism

Service Delivery Questions	Status Enhancement	Service
Where shall authority and control rest?	Citizen participation	Coordination
Who carries out different tasks?	Role attachments	Professional disengagement
What will be the composition of the delivery system?	Purposive duplication	Specialized access structures

These perspectives on professional functioning are rarely applied in their extreme forms. Most planners recognize that social service staff are motivated by mixed sets of inducements. It is not implausible, however, to presume that the extent to which this mixture is weighted in favor of one or another perspective is likely to influence strategy choices. This view suggests two broad propositions. First, to the degree that staff functioning is directed by desires for status-enhancement, efforts to improve or develop service delivery will rely on strategies that constrain, modify, or otherwise limit the prerogatives of professional staff by (1) redistributing authority from agencies to clients, affording them some direct control over professionals (i.e., citizen participation); (2) changing roles so that staff includes indigenous nonprofessionals who are better equipped for certain functions (i.e., role attachments); and (3) adding elements to the system that create competition among professionals, stimulating them to greater effort and eventually eliminating the less competent (i.e., purposive duplication). Secondly, to the degree that the service perspective informs the behavior of professionals, the choice of delivery strategies will be inclined toward giving professionals greater latitude by (1) redistributing authority in ways that consolidate and strengthen the hierarchy of professional control (i.e., coordination); (2) changing the professional role from bureaucrat to entrepreneur, thereby allowing professionals to ply their trade unencumbered by the prerequisites of organizational life (i.e., professional disengagement); and (3) introducing new access structures that support specialization and produce further refinement in the division of labor among professionals (i.e., specialized access structures). In Table 6.1 we summarize the propositions that are derived from the application of these perspectives to the service-delivery questions identified at the beginning of this chapter.

Organizations: Perspectives on the Structure of the Service Network

Theoretical perspectives on the structure of the service network (which is composed of the agencies in the delivery system) are another variable that may inspire different strategy choices. Here the concern is with the impersonal forces of organizational behavior in a systemic context rather than with the forces generated by professional behavior *per se,* although these phenomena are separable only in the abstract.

Two fundamental perspectives tend to direct perceptions of the organizational structure of services: the "rational" model and the "natural-system" model. According to Gouldner:

> *In the rational model, the organization is conceived as an "instrument"—that is, as a rationally conceived means to the realization of expressly announced group goals. . . . Fundamentally, the rational model implies a "mechanical" model, in that it views the organization as a structure of manipulable parts, each of which is separately modifiable with a view to enhancing the efficiency of the whole. Individual organizational elements are seen as subject to successful and planned modification, enactable by deliberate decision.*
>
> *The natural-system model regards the organization as a "natural whole," or system. The realization of the goals of the system as a whole is but one of several important needs to which the organization is oriented. . . . The organization, according to this model, strives to survive and to maintain its equilibrium, and this striving may persist even after its explicitly held goals have been successfully attained. This strain towards survival may even on occasion lead to the neglect or distortion of the organization's goals.*[77]

Thompson refined this formulation with the notion that the rational model involves a *closed-system* perception whereas the natural-system views organizations as *open* systems.[78] Each of these perspectives draws attention to certain aspects of organizational functioning and tends to neglect others. Needless to say, most planners and administrators know that organizations behave in accordance with both perspectives, although they are not always taken into account equally. There appears to be a strong susceptibility, reflected in the organizational literature, toward envisioning organizations as *either* closed or open systems rather than as systems that are partially closed, half-rational, and that sustain otherwise contradictory tendencies. This susceptibility occurs, Thompson suggests, because there is no convenient conceptual means of simultaneously thinking of a system as half-open and half-closed.[79]

The open-system perspective explains organizational behavior in terms of the organizational "task environment"—clients, funders, staff, equipment, competitors, and regulatory groups.[80] In applying this perspective, the elements originating outside the subsystem of existing service agencies can be viewed as key leverage points for change. To the extent that the professional looks at the service network from an open-system perspective, delivery-system strategies will follow along lines that (1) organize clients to demand a share of authority and control over services (citizen participation); (2) utilize more essential organizational resources (professional staff) outside of the service network hierarchy, making them elements of the task environment (professional disengagement); and (3) add new elements to the task environment that will compete with the service network for clients and resources or that will operate independently as mediators between the service network and clients (purposive duplication and specialized access structures).

However, if the professional views the service network more in terms of a closed system, attention, as Gouldner implies, will be directed to strategies that enhance the efficiency of the "instrument" by manipulating organizational components to place them in better balance or welding on additional parts to make the instrument more functional. Thus, the tendency will be to select strategies that (1) redistribute authority either by centralization or federation but with authority always remaining within the closed service network (i.e., coordination); and (2) incorporate roles to improve network functioning over which service organizations exercise authority (i.e., role attachments). In Table 6.2, propositions that may be derived from the application of these perspectives are summarized for the three kinds of service delivery questions.

Orientations to Service Delivery

The interplay of theoretical perspectives regarding the structure of the services network and the functions of professionalism generates four types of orientations toward service delivery: professional/bureaucratic, egalitarian/bureaucratic, professional/activist, and egalitarian/activist. The relationship between the structure of the service network and the functions of professionalism is illustrated in Table 6.3.

The reader should keep in mind that these orientations are ideal types. In reality, there are innumerable variations on each of these orientations, often with cloudy distinctions.

Professional/Bureaucratic. This is the orientation of the administrator who "runs a tight ship," who ensures that lines of authority within the system are clear

TABLE 6.2   Perspectives on Service Delivery

Service Delivery Questions	Perspectives on Service Delivery	
	Closed System	Open System
Where shall authority and control rest?	Coordination	Citizen participation
Who carries out different tasks?	Role attachments	Professional disengagement
What will be the composition of the delivery system?	Existing mix of units in the service network remains unchanged	Purposive duplication and specialized-access structures

and hierarchical. A high degree of reliance is placed on professional expertise as demonstrated by both credential and performance and on the rationality of bureaucratic organization. At the extreme, this orientation seeks to maximize the discretion of professionals and enhance the relationships of professionals within and between agencies. The organization and the professional are viewed as mutually supporting entities. When each is committed to the values of the other they constitute a formidable system of institutional control.

Egalitarian/Bureaucrat. In the egalitarian/bureaucratic orientation, the importance and the power of the principles of organization are valued as in the previous orientation. Solutions are based on a belief that whatever is done should be rationalized and brought under organizational control. Professionals, however, are not viewed as especially well equipped for service delivery—linking clients to resources. Rather, they are perceived as being primarily concerned with self-enhancement. Thus, the attachment of nonprofessional role functions is likely to be advocated.

Professional/Activist. This orientation relies heavily on outreach strategies, sometimes referred to as aggressive casework, case-finding, or health education, depending on the area of service. In our schema such approaches support special access and professional disengagement strategies. Here the belief in professionals is strong; it is the organization that is believed to be confining. With this orientation the proper role for administrators and professionals is "enabling"; professionals can provide good services, and the function of the organization is to develop the most effective means to help consumers use them, even at the cost of organizational power and control.

Egalitarian/Activist. The egalitarian/activist orientation, the polar opposite of the professional/ bureaucrat model, rejects professionalism and accepts an open-system perspective on organization. Neither the organization nor professionals

TABLE 6.3 Orientations to Service Delivery as a Function of Theoretical Perspectives

Perspectives on Service-Delivery	Perspectives on Professionalism	
	Status-Enhancement	Service
Closed system	Egalitarian/Bureaucratic (Role Attachments)	Professional/Bureaucratic (Coordination)
Open system	Egalitarian/Activist (Citizen participation; Purposive duplication)	Professional/Activist (Professional disengagement; Special-access structures)

are to be relied on; one must turn to different sources of legitimacy, wisdom, and policy. These sources may be alternative institutions such as free clinics and cooperative schools that duplicate existing agencies, or they may be the recipients of services—the people, the community, or the poor. These constituencies may be defined ethnically, geographically, or in any other way that suits the ideological tastes of the planner. In the extreme, this orientation is similar to Rousseau's doctrine of the "general will" with its implied reduction of government to a mere agent of the community's corporate personality.[81] This orientation's answer to all of the service-delivery questions is: "Ask the people what they want, and help them get it."

Is there an orientation of choice? As we have indicated, each of the strategies may mitigate some service-delivery problems and exacerbate others. There is no calculus for computing all of the social costs and benefits. Any service network, whether it is "establishment" or "people-run," may operate as a system that is too closed and unable to deal efficiently with elements in its task environment, or one that is too open and unable to deal efficiently with internal functioning. Any service network, whether it is highly centralized with firm boundaries or it is diffuse, loosely structured, and community-run, may be too weighed down by the methods and doctrine of professional personnel or may lack sufficiently clear professional standards of behavior and conduct.

No orientation is *ipso facto* superior to another. In selecting service-delivery strategies, policy planners are influenced by a combination of circumstantial factors, social values, empirical evidence, and theoretical viewpoints. At best, their choices are infused with much uncertainty.

In articulating how orientations toward strategy choices are informed by perspectives on the structure of service networks and the functions of professionalism, we sought to illuminate the contributions made by competing theoretical viewpoints. To fixate on any one strategy as a panacea for service-delivery problems is to prematurely foreclose other options that are untested and that may have untapped potential.

Conclusion: Rationing at Century's End

Most of the service delivery strategies we have described were formulated in the 1960s and 1970s, an era of notable expansion in social services. The presumption of growth, as Glennerster puts it, was deeply imbedded in the intellects of social welfare planners.[82] When social services expenditures began declining in the late 1970s, and political support arose for meeting service needs through the market economy, several new issues of choice surfaced. The privatization/contracting option has been described. A few comments on a second option, rationing, will conclude this chapter.

When social service budgets are reduced through legislative cutbacks, the burden of implementation falls on the organizations and professionals responsible for service delivery. At the juncture where clients' needs intersect with social service resources the issue is how to make do with less. The ways that service delivery systems respond affect the fundamental design of social welfare policy.

To some extent, agencies have always engaged in service rationing—the distribution of limited resources to meet social needs of greater proportions. However, during periods of expansion there is less pressure for careful thought about and stringent application of rationing methods. It is in periods of fiscal retrenchment that choices among these methods become pivotal.

Rationing may be accomplished through several processes. Ellie Scrivens has analyzed the dynamics of service rationing methods and divided them into two broad categories: demand inhibitors and supply inhibitors. Strategies that act to reduce demand erect physical, temporal, and social barriers to service. On the deterrence of physical barriers, Scrivens cites a report on the British social services in which it is observed that some of the buildings they occupy are "forbidding and the reception arrangements are often not such as to encourage anyone, let alone anyone in distress, to approach them.[83] Temporal barriers can be raised in the form of waiting lists, time-consuming application procedures, remote service locations, and inconvenient office hours. Clients also may be put off by social barriers that involve embarrassing eligibility requirements. The failure to communicate relevant information to clients about available services is another effective deterrent.

On the other side of the ledger, strategies to reduce the supply of services include restriction and dilution. With a restrictive strategy, eligibility criteria are tightened so that fewer clients needing a service actually qualify for it. This goal is accomplished by narrowing the rules governing eligibility and more stringently applying professional discretion in interpreting these rules. Strategies for diluting services decrease the amount and quality of provisions by cutting time spent with clients, prematurely terminating cases, lowering the qualifications of professional staff, and substituting volunteers for professionals.[84]

As long as demand exceeds supply, there will be some form of rationing in service delivery. Thus we must ask, "On what grounds might one choose among the various strategies outlined in this chapter?" Some of these strategies are objectionable because of their furtive character. They amount to what Lipsky calls, "bureaucratic disentitlement," where service delivery is curtailed not by open and formalized policy choices but rather by "low-level marginal decisions or nondecisions of low visibility."[85] The problem, as Lipsky sees it, is that through obscure actions and inactions social service agencies may devise allocative policies that are not open to public inspection. In choosing among rationing strategies, those based on explicit procedures open to public scrutiny, such as tightening formal eligibility requirements, offer greater protection to the public than veiled activities designed to discourage consumption and dilute services.

Notes

1. Whereas most services are designed for *delivery* (i.e., policy implementation) at the local level, designing and planning activities may or may not occur at the local level. Frequently, program designers and planners may be several steps removed from the local community, located as far away as the State house or the White House. The location of the program planners is a factor of major significance in *policy development.*

2. Alfred Kahn and Sheila Kamerman (eds.), *Privatization and the Welfare State* (Princeton, NJ: Princeton University Press, 1989); Neil Gilbert, *Capitalism and the Welfare State* (New Haven, CT: Yale University Press, 1983); Lester Salamon and Alan Abramson, *The Federal Budget and the Nonprofit Sector* (Washington D.C.: Urban Institute Press, 1982).

3. E. S. Savas, *Privatization: The Key to Better Government* (Chatham, NJ: Chatham Publishers, 1987); Neil Gilbert and Barbara Gilbert, *The Enabling State: Modern Welfare Capitalism in America* (New York: Oxford University Press, 1989); Ken Judge and Martin Knapp, "Efficiency in the Production of Welfare: The Public and Private Sectors Compared," in Rudolph Klein and Michael O'Higgins (eds.), *The Future of Welfare* (Oxford: Basil Blackwell, 1985).

4. Robert Bellah, "Community Properly Understood: A Defense of Democratic Communitarianism," *The Responsive Community* (Winter 1995/96), 49–54; Peter Berger and Richard Neuhaus, *To Empower the People: The Role of Mediating Structures in Public Policy* (Washington D.C.: American Enterprise Institute Press, 1977); Harry Specht and Mark Courtney, *Unfaithful Angels: How Social Work Has Abandoned Its Mission* (New York: Free Press, 1994), 152–76.

5. Burton Weisbrod, *The Nonprofit Economy* (Cambridge, Mass: Harvard University Press, 1988); Susan Rose-Ackerman, "Social Services and the Market," *Columbia Law Review,* 8(6) (1983), 1405–38.

6. Henry Hansmann,"Economic Theories of Nonprofit Organization," in Walter Powell (ed.), *The Nonprofit Sector* (New Haven, CT: Yale University Press, 1987), 29–32.

7. Mark Schlesinger, Robert Dortwart, and Richard Pulice, "Competitive Bidding and State's Purchase of Services: The Case of Mental Health Care in Massachusetts," *Journal of Policy Analysis and Management,* 5(2) (Winter 1986), 245–64; David Young, "Referral and Placement in Child Care: The New York City Purchase of Service System," *Public Policy,* 12(3) (Summer 1974), 293–328.

8 Rose-Ackerman, *"Social Services and the Market."*

9. Rosabeth Kanter and David Summers, "Doing Well While Doing Good: Dilemmas of Performance Measurement in Nonprofit Organizations and the Need for a Multiple-Constituency Approach," in Walter Powell (ed.), *The Nonprofit Sector: A Research Handbook* (New Haven, CT: Yale University Press, 1987), 154–67.

10. Charles Krauthammer, "A Social Conservative Credo," *The Public Interest,* 121 (Fall 1995) 16.

11. Fred Wulczyn, "Status at Birth and Infant Placements in New York City," in Richard Barth, Jill Berrick, and Neil Gilbert (eds.), *Child Welfare Research Review, 1,* (New York: Columbia University Press, 1994).

12. Emile Durkheim, *The Division of Labor in Society,* George Simpson (trans.) (New York: The Free Press, 1933), 28.

13. See, for example, Neil Gilbert, *Welfare Justice* (New Haven, CT: Yale University Press, 1995), 135–37; Neil Gilbert and Kwong Leung Tang, "The United States," in Norman Johnson (ed.), *Private Markets in Health and Welfare* (Oxford: Berg Publishers, 1995).

14. Kahn and Kamerman, *Privatization and the Welfare State,* 262.

15. As Peter Blau observed long ago, bureaucracy and democracy are different modes of social organization for decision making and implementation that are effective for different ends. See Peter Blau, *Bureaucracy in Modern Society* (New York: Random House, 1956).

16. See, for example, Ralph Kramer, "Public Fiscal Policy and Voluntary Agencies in Welfare States," *Social Service Review,* 53 (March 1979), 1–14, and Alfred Kahn, "A Framework for Public-Voluntary Collaboration in the Social Services,"

Social Welfare Forum 1976 (New York: Columbia University Press, 1976), 47–62.

17. Kurt Reichert, "The Drift Toward Entrepreneurialism in Health and Social Welfare: Implications for Social Work Education," *Administration in Social Work, 1* (Summer 1977), 129. See also, Mimi Abramovitz, "The Privatization of the Welfare State: A Review," *Social Work,* July/August 1986, 257–64.

18. For further discussion of problems in this area, see R. M. Kanter, "The Measurement of Organizational Effectiveness, Productivity, Performance and Success: Issues and Dilemmas in Service and Non-Profit Organizations," *Program on Non-Profit Organization Working Paper 8,* Institution for Social Policy Studies, Yale University, 1979.

19. Richard Titmuss, *The Gift Relationship* (New York: Pantheon, 1971); Cynthia Barnett, "Profit and Non-Profit Distinctions in Theory and in Fact: The Lack of Fit Between Theory and Empirical Research in Health Care Organizations," 1982 (mimeographed paper); Lenard Kaye, Abraham Monk, and Howard Litwin, "Community Monitoring of Nursing Home Care: Proprietary and Non-Profit Association Perspectives," *Journal of Social Service Research, 7*(3) (Spring 1984), 5–19; and Catherine Born, "Proprietary Terms and Child Welfare Services: Patterns and Implications," *Child Welfare, 62*(2) (March/April 1983), 109–18; Stephen Shortell, "Hospital Ownership and Nontraditional Services," *Health Affairs,* Winter 1986.

20. For elaboration on this point, see Neil Gilbert, *Capitalism and the Welfare State* (New Haven, CT: Yale University Press, 1983), 17–19.

21. Ibid. Also see Neil Gilbert, "Welfare for Profit: Moral, Empirical, and Theoretical Perspectives," *Journal of Social Policy, 13*(1) (January 1984), 63–74.

22. This concern, it appears, is not always decisive. For example, in recent years federal and state agencies have contracted with profit-making corporations to run prisons. See Harry Hatry, et al., "Comparison of Privately and Publicly Operated Corrections Facilities in Kentucky and Massachusetts," The Urban Institute, August 1989.

23. Harry G. Bredemeier, "The Socially Handicapped and the Agencies: A Market Analysis," in Frank Riessman, Jerome Cohen, and Arthur Pearl (eds.), *Mental Health of the Poor* (New York: Free Press, 1964); Richard Cloward and Frances F. Piven, "The Professional Bureaucracies Benefit Systems as Influence Systems," in Murray Silberman (ed.), *The Role of Government in Promoting Social Change* (New York: Columbia University, School of Social Work, 1966); Alfred J. Kahn, "Do Social Services have a Future in New York?" *City Almanac, 5*(5) (February 1971), 1–11; Irving Piliavin, "Restructuring the Provision of Social Service," *Social Work, 13*(1) (January 1968); William Reid, "Interagency Coordination in Delinquency Prevention and Control," *Social Service Review, 38*(4) (December 1964); Martin Rein, *Social Policy: Issues of Choice and Change* (New York: Random House, 1970); Gideon Sjoberg, Richard Brymer, and Buford Farris, "Bureaucracy and the Lower Class," *Sociology and Social Research, 50*(3) (April 1966), 325–37.

24. Herbert H. Simon, *Administrative Behavior,* 2d ed. (New York: Free Press, 1965), 238.

25. Peter Townsend, et al., *The Fifth Social Service: A Critical Analysis of the Seebohm Report* (London: Fabian Society, 1970).

26. See, for example, Neil Gilbert and Harry Specht, *Coordinating Social Services* (New York: Praeger Publishers, 1977), and Stephanie Fall Creek and Neil Gilbert, "Agency Network in Transition: Problems and Prospects," *Social Work, 26*(3) (May 1981), 210–15.

27. James D. Thompson, *Organizations in Action* (New York: McGraw-Hill, 1967); and Reid, "Interagency Coordination in Delinquency Prevention and Control."

28. Roland L. Warren, "The Interorganizational Field as a Focus for Investigation," *Administrative Science Quarterly, 12*(3) (December 1967), 396–419.

29. Reid, "Interagency Coordination in Delinquency Prevention and Control."

30. Robert A. Dahl and Charles E. Lindblom, *Politics, Economics, and Welfare* (New York: Harper & Row, 1953), 238.

31. Mary Richardson, et al., "Coordinating Services By Design," *Public Welfare,* Summer, 1989, 31–36.

32. Jane Knitzer and Susan Yelton, "Collaboration Between Child Welfare and Mental Health," *Public Welfare,* Spring 1990, 24–33.

33. Karen Orloff Kaplan, "Recent Trends in Case Management," *Encyclopedia of Social Work, 18th Edition, 1990 Supplement,* (Silver Spring, MD: National Association of Social Workers, 1990), 60–77.

34. Denise Polit and Joseph O'Hara, "Support Services," in Phoebe Cottingham and David Ellwood (eds.), *Welfare Policy for the 1990s,* (Cambridge, Mass: Harvard University Press, 1989), 191–92.

35. Ibid., 193.

36. Sherry Arnstein, "A Ladder of Citizen Participation," *Journal of the American Institute of Planners, 35*(4) (July 1969).

37. Hans B. C. Spiegel, et al., *Neighborhood Power and Control: Implications for Urban Planning* (New York: Columbia University, Institute of Urban Environment, 1968), 157.

38. Ralph M. Kramer, *Community Development in Israel and the Netherlands* (Berkeley: University of California Press, Institute of International Studies, 1970), 127.

39. Gilbert, *Clients or Constituents* (San Francisco: Jossey-Bass, 1970), 145; and Arthur B. Shostak, "Promoting Participation of the Poor: Philadelphia's Antipoverty Program," *Social Work, 11*(1) (January 1966).

40. Ralph M. Kramer, *Participation of the Poor* (Englewood Cliffs, NJ: Prentice-Hall, 1969), 127.

41. There is some evidence that local citizen elections may improve over time. Brager and Specht indicate that voter turnouts in Model Cities elections, while usually low, tended to be higher than turnouts for earlier elections sponsored by the Economic Opportunity Program. For example, nearly 30 percent of eligible voters participated in Trenton's Model Cities election in 1968. George Brager and Harry Specht, *Community Organizing* (New York: Columbia University Press, 1973).

42. Harold Weissman, *Community Councils and Community Control* (Pittsburgh: University of Pittsburgh Press, 1970).

43. Neil Gilbert and Joseph Eaton, "Who Speaks for the Poor?," *Journal of the American Institute of Planners, 36*(6) (November, 1970).

44. George Peterson et al., *The Reagan Block Grants: What Have We Learned?* (Washington, D.C.: Urban Institute Press, 1986).

45. Sjoberg, Brymer, and Farris, "Bureaucracy and the Lower Class."

46. S. M. Miller and Frank Riessman, *Social Class and Social Policy* (New York: Basic Books, 1968), 207.

47. George Brager, "The Indigenous Worker: A New Approach to the Social Work Technician," *Social Work, 10*(2) (April 1965).

48. Robert Pruger and Harry Specht, "Establishing New Careers Programs: Organizational Barriers and Strategies," *Social Work, 13*(4) (October 1968), 23–24.

49. David A. Hardcastle, "The Indigenous Non-Professional in the Social Service Bureaucracy: A Critical Examination," *Social Work, 16*(2) (April 1971), 63.

50. Charles Grosser, "Manpower Development Programs," in Charles Grosser, William E. Henry, and James G. Kelly (eds.), *Non-Professionals in the Human Services* (San Francisco: Jossey-Bass, 1969), 136–37.

51. Lonnie Snowden and David Derezotes, "Cultural Factors in the Intervention of Child Maltreatment," *Child and Adolescent Social Work, 7*(2), April 1990.

52. Gerald Levy, "Acute Workers in a Welfare Bureaucracy," in Deborah Offenbacher and Constance Poster (eds.), *Social Problems and Social Policy* (New York: Appleton-Century-Crofts, 1970); see also Harry Wasserman, "The Professional Social Worker in a Bureaucracy," *Social Work, 16*(1) (January 1971), 89–95.

53. Piliavin, "Restructuring the Provision of Social Service," 35.

54. "Membership Survey Shows Practice Shifts," *NASW News, 28*(10) (November 1983).

55. Thomas McGuire, Arnold Gurin, Linda Frisman, Victor Kane, and Barbara Shatkin,

"Vendorship and Social Work in Massachusetts," *Social Service Review,* 58(3) (September 1984), 372–83.

56. Robert Pruger, "The Good Bureaucrat," *Social Work,* 18(4) (July 1973), 27.

57. Interim results of the project are reported by Bleddyn Davies and David Challis, "Experimenting with New Roles in Domiciliary Service: The Kent Community Care Project," *Gerontologist,* 20 (June 1980), 288–99.

58. Alfred J. Kahn, "Perspectives on Access to Social Service," *Social Work,* 15(2) (March 1970), 99.

59. Rein, *Social Policy.*

60. For a description of this method, see P. Nelson Reid, "Reforming the Social Services Monopoly," *Social Work,* 17(6) (November 1972), 44–54.

61. Henry Miller and Connie Philipp, "The Alternative Service-Agency," in Aaron Rosenblatt and Diana Waldfogel (eds.), *Handbook of Clinical Social Work* (San Francisco: Jossey-Bass, 1983), 779–91.

62. Richard Cloward and Frances Piven, "The Case Against Urban Desegregation," *Social Work,* 12(1) (January 1967).

63. Edward J. O'Donnel and Marilyn M. Sullivan, "Service Delivery and Social Action Through the Neighborhood Center: A Review of Research," *Welfare in Review,* 7(6) (November/ December 1969), 95–102, and Neil Gilbert and Harry Specht, *Coordinating Social Services.*

64. Marshall Kaplan, Gans, and Kahn, and The Research Group, Inc., *Integration of Human Services in HEW: An Evaluation of Services Integration Projects,* An Executive Summary of a Study for the Social and Rehabilitation Service of the Department of Health, Education, and Welfare (1972), 11.

65. For an insightful analysis of the vital functions that may be served by duplication within systems, see Martin Landau, "Redundancy, Rationality, and the Problem of Duplication and Overlap," *Public Administration Review,* 29(4) (July/August 1969), 346–58.

66. Philip Kramer, "The Indigenous Worker: Hometowner, Striver or Activist," *Social Work* 17 (1) (January, 1972).

67. Ernest Greenwood, "Attributes of a Profession," *Social Work,* 2(3) (July 1975).

68. Ernest Greenwood, " 'Attributes of a Profession' Revisited," in Neil Gilbert and Harry Specht (eds.), *The Emergence of Social Welfare and Social Work,* (Itasca, IL: Peacock Publishers, 1981), 264.

69. Harold Wilensky and Charles Lebeaux, *Industrial Society and Social Welfare* (New York: Russell Sage, 1958), 330.

70. Matthew Dumont, "The Changing Face of Professionalism," *Social Policy,* May/June 1972, 32.

71. Marie R. Haug and Marvin B. Sussman, "Professional Autonomy and the Revolt of the Client," *Social Problems,* 17(2) (Fall 1969), 153–61; and Miller and Riessman, *Social Class and Social Policy.*

72. As Eaton found in a study of professional employees in two treatment-oriented organizations, one of the difficulties of service evaluation stems from the reluctance of professionals to make interpretations of evaluative research data and their disinclination to communicate the findings of evaluative research. Joseph Eaton, "Symbolic and Substantive Evaluative Research," *Administrative Science Quarterly,* 6 (March 1962), 421–42.

73. Haug and Sussman, "Professional Autonomy and the Revolt of the Client."

74. Everett C. Hughes, "Professions," *Daedalus, 92*(4) (Fall 1963).

75. Richard Cloward and Irwin Epstein, "Private Social Welfare's Disengagement from the Poor: The Case of Family Adjustment Agencies," in Mayer Zald (ed.), *Social Welfare Institutions* (New York: John Wiley & Sons, 1965), 628–29.

76. Talcott Parsons, "The Professions and Social Structure," *Social Forces* 17 (Fall, 1939), 457–67.

77. Alvin W. Gouldner, "Organizational Analysis," in Robert K. Merton, Leonard Broom, and Leonard S. Cottrell, Jr. (eds.), *Sociology Today* (New York: Harper & Row, 1959), 404–5.

78. Thompson, *Organizations in Action.*

79. Thompson offers a creative synthesis of these two models by suggesting that organizations be viewed dynamically as open systems striving

for the rationality, control, and certainty of a closed system. Thompson, *Organizations in Action*, 10.

80. Thompson, *Organizations in Action*, 27–28.

81. Harry Specht, "The Deprofessionalization of Social Work," *Social Work, 17*(2) (April 1972).

82. Howard Glennerster, "Prime Cuts: Public Expenditure and Social Service Planning in a Hostile Environment," *Policy and Politics*, Vol. 8, no. 4 (1980), 367–382.

83. Ellie Scrivens, "Towards a Theory of Rationing," *Social Policy and Administration*, Vol. 13, no. 1 (Spring 1979), 53–84.

84. For more detailed discussions of these strategies, see Abraham Deron, "The Welfare State: Issues of Rationing and Allocation of Resources," in Shimon Spiro & Ephraim Yuchtman-Yaar (eds.) *Evaluating the Welfare State: Social & Political Perspectives* (New York: Academic Press, 1983), 149–159; and R. A. Parker, "Social Administration and Scarcity," *Social Work Today*, Vol. 12 (April 1967), 9–14.

85. Michael Lipsky, "Bureaucratic Disentitlement in Social Welfare Programs," *Social Service Review*, Vol. 58, no. 1 (March 1984), 20.

Chapter *7*

The Mode of Finance: Sources of Funds

Taxes are a changing product of earnest efforts to have others pay them.

LOUIS EISENSTEIN,
The Ideologies of Taxation, 1961

Let me tell you how it will be/
there's one for you nineteen for me/
'Cause I'm the taxman. . . .
If 5 percent appears too small/
be thankful I don't take it all/
'Cause I'm the taxman. . . .

THE BEATLES (GEORGE HARRISON),
Taxman

People don't much care for paying taxes. Although Supreme Court Justice Oliver Wendell Holmes might have considered taxes "what we pay for a civilized society," most U.S. residents view them, at best, as a burden to be reluctantly endured. Taxes may constitute the basic foundation for health, education, and welfare policies, but taxes will never be in public favor.

Likeable or not, taxes—along with philanthropy and other sources of revenue—provide the essential fuel for social welfare endeavors. Our objective in this chapter and the next, therefore, is to examine the process of revenue raising in the United States, to explore some of the basic policy choices involved in financing welfare state programs, and to identify the implications of different funding sources and different systems of funding transfers. In social welfare, the things that money can do are substantially influenced by how that money is obtained.

Questions about the mode of finance interest administrators and planners more than they do direct-service practitioners. Administrators and planners are concerned with securing resources to sustain their programs. They need to understand the kinds of activities funders will support. Funders, whether they're legislators, foundation trustees, or executives of agency federations, are concerned with making choices among competing interests and programs to achieve *their* goals. In negotiations for program support, both funders and fund seekers address the questions of the previous chapters: Who is eligible for help? What is it they will receive? How will service delivery be organized?

The direct-service practitioner is usually less attentive to questions of finance than to other dimensions of policy choice. This is because financing choices appear remote from the exigencies of day-to-day practice, and their effects on client welfare are typically indistinct. Funding decisions for almost any kind of social welfare program—whether mental health, housing, or AIDS counseling—are likely to involve "big government" somewhere along the line. Because most programs of significance require the money, sanction, or surveillance of one or more levels of government, direct practitioners are likely to consider funding questions outside of their influence. This view, certainly, is not entirely unrealistic. Funding arrangements *are* complex, and final program decisions *are* frequently made by individuals and groups many steps removed from actual service delivery.

Nevertheless, it is critical that professionals concerned with social welfare have a working knowledge of the major issues, concepts, and values involved in the mode of finance. Whereas the vast majority of professionals may not directly participate in allocation decision making, in their roles as citizens, members of professional associations, and agency employees, they can affect how decision makers think and act. It is not unreasonable, then, to expect professionals, regardless of their specific job, to be able to respond thoughtfully to questions such as these: Should a public agency "purchase" services by entering into a contract with a voluntary or for-profit agency? If so, under what circumstances? Are block grants preferable to categorical funding? What are the constraints of voluntary financing? What assumptions support the use of contributory schemes and fee-charging arrangements? What are the distributional implications of different tax sources?

Two interrelated sets of choices are fundamental to the mode-of-finance dimension of policy design. These choices pertain to:

> *The source of funds.* Should financial support be derived from recipients in the form of user charges and certain earmarked taxes, from taxes that make up general revenues, from some form of social insurance, from voluntary contributions, or from some combination of these?
>
> *The system of transfer.* What arrangements should govern the flow of money from the level of government where it is raised to the level where it is used, the different levels of review between funders and providers, and the conditions placed on the transfer of funds?

We will discuss choices that inform the design of transfer systems in the next chapter; here we will examine alternative sources of funding and their implications.

Sources of Funds

Funds to pay for social welfare benefits are obtained in three fundamental ways—through taxes, through voluntary giving, and through fees. *Taxes* are compulsory and governmental. They constitute public levies on citizens and businesses, and they are the primary source of support for public social welfare activities. *Voluntary giving* involves private contributions. Whether described as charity (which connotes giving for the poor) or philanthropy (which connotes giving for a broader range of health, research, civic, and religious activities), contributions represent voluntary, uncoerced, donations. *Fees* constitute the charge for social welfare goods and services on the open market. The providers of these goods and services may be entrepreneurs who are selling products for profits, or nonprofit agencies that are requiring user fees in order to cover their expenses. In a few instances, public institutions (chiefly colleges and universities) also impose charges.

In the actual conduct of the welfare state, these three funding sources very often are intermixed. That is, the budgets of social welfare agencies and organizations frequently include revenues deriving from taxes, voluntary giving, *and* fees and charges. Although public agencies, for example, tend to be funded with tax dollars, they may rely on user fees (e.g., tuition) or private giving (e.g., PTA fundraising). Similarly, private nonprofit agencies have increasingly become dependent on tax support, supplementing their private revenue sources with contract funding from governmental bodies. And profit-making businesses frequently rely on payments from third-party insurers, public or private, for their income.

The pluralistic funding patterns of the welfare state—often described as the mixed economy of welfare—can create terminological confusion. To clarify the terrain a bit, the distinctive characteristics of the major social welfare auspices must be specified. In our discussion, *voluntary agencies* refer to charitable, nonprofit organizations that are financed, at least to some extent, with voluntary contributions. These organizations devote their resources to education, science, religion, art, culture, and charity and are therefore commonly perceived as serving a public, or community, interest. In this sense, voluntary agencies may be conceived of as privately administered public-interest institutions.

Public agencies, established by law, and directly accountable to elected officials, are supported by governmental funds. Their programs are often referred to as "statutory" or "legislative."

For-profit organizations, a relatively new phenomenon in many sectors of the U.S. welfare state, are providers that operate on an entrepreneurial basis, like any commercial business. The role of these organizations remains controversial despite the strong ideological and legislative support harnessed on behalf of "privatization" since the Reagan administration.

Issues of public versus voluntary versus for-profit financing and provision have been fiercely debated since the mid-1960s. Although the private sector (for-profit and nonprofit combined) has always played a significant role in the United

TABLE 7.1 Public and Private Social Welfare Expenditures (in Billions of Dollars)

	Public Spending	Private Spending	Total
1972	$ 190.3	$ 97.0	$ 287.3
1980	492.7	255.3	748.0
1985	732.6	471.2	1,203.8
1990	1,050.8	727.5	1,778.3
1993	1,363.9	887.6	2,251.4

Source: Annual Statistical Supplement to the Social Security Bulletin, 1996, 158–160.

States—far more so than in other welfare states—the overall ratio of private to public social welfare spending has been growing. From 1972 to 1993, as Table 7.1 indicates, total social welfare outlays increased from $287 billion to $2,251 billion, an increase of some 684 percent, while the private portion of the overall total increased from 34 to 39 percent. Much of this increase in private outlays represents the enormous growth in size and scope of private pensions and health insurance. A major part however, also reflects the growth of nonprofit social service agencies.

The Philanthropic Contribution

There are presently about 600,000 nonprofit agencies registered under federal tax code section 501(c)(3) as charitable organizations. The 501(c)(3) designation, synonymous with tax deductibility, covers a broad range of nonprofits, ranging from traditional social service agencies to arts, environmental, health, educational, and religious bodies.

Charitable organizations vary in their reliance on voluntary contributions. Although religious congregations depend almost entirely on private giving, for example, hospitals rely on charity for less than 5 percent of their funding. In the social services, private giving provides about a fifth of total revenues.[1] Although much of the support provided voluntary agencies is not of private origin, philanthropy remains the irreducible private core of private agencies.

As Table 7.2 indicates, philanthropy provides over $150 billion a year for community purposes, nearly 80 percent of this amount coming from ordinary individuals. Some donations are organized through the annual fund-raising activities of federations such as the United Way and the United Jewish Appeal, "umbrella organizations" that collect on behalf of member agencies. The United Way, for example, collects over $3 billion annually for its agency constituency, chiefly through workplace giving campaigns. Alternatives to the United Way—federations representing social action, environmental, ethnic, and women's causes—currently raise over $200 million annually in their own fund-raising drives. Overall, however, these federations tap only a small portion of individual giving. Most people contribute directly to the charity of their choice, and most of these contributions go to

**TABLE 7.2   Sources of Philanthropic
Contributions, 1995
(in Billions of Dollars)**

Foundations	$ 11.8	7.9%
Corporations	8.5	5.6%
Individuals	119.9	79.6%
Bequests	10.5	6.9%
	$150.7	100.0%

Source: American Association of Fund-Raising Counsel, *Giving USA,* 1997.

religious groups. The very rich give heavily to universities and hospitals although, as Table 7.3 indicates, human services donations are not insignificant.

After individual giving comes corporate and foundation donations, and bequests. Corporations gave over $8 billion to philanthropy in 1996, about 6 percent of overall giving. Although corporate giving aids the spectrum of nonprofit activities, elementary and secondary schools have been a major priority since the mid-1980s, reflecting businesses' concern with the capacity of U.S. workers to compete in the global marketplace. Although education has received the largest portion of corporate giving every year since 1978, the portion going to colleges and universities has been steadily diminishing. This trend toward corporate support of basic K-12 public education is likely to increase given the Clinton administration's efforts to improve public schooling.

Private foundations represent a unique creation of U.S. capitalism. Foundations are voluntary funding entities that primarily exist to give money to other nonprofit organizations. There are nearly 39,000 grant-making foundations operating today, holding $196 billion in assets and annually awarding approximately $11.8 billion for social welfare, scientific, and cultural activities.[2]

Voluntary Financing: Not Entirely a Private Matter

Reflecting its individualistic orientation, the United States is unique among all welfare states in the elaborate development of its voluntary and for-profit welfare sectors. The parallel development of the voluntary and the public sectors, furthermore, has created a social welfare system that is distinctly bifurcated—a system that is dynamic in its ability to change and innovate, yet difficult to manage and control. One critical aspect of this dual system lies in the nature of its funding. "Voluntary" financing of social welfare services is not really as private or as philanthropic as we might think. This is because money contributed to nonprofit organizations engaged in health, education, welfare, religious, scientific, or cultural activities reflects not only private generosity but also public policy priorities. Most notably, private contributions are untaxed—and have been since 1915 when Congress sought to promote philanthropy by making donations tax deductible. Private generosity, in this sense, is partially private altruism, partially a tax break.

TABLE 7.3   Human Services Philanthropy, 1995–1996

Andre Agassi
$1 million to the Las Vegas Boys & Girls Club

Mariah Carey
$1 million to the Fresh Air Fund

David Geffen
$2.5 million to the Gay Men's Health Crisis (NY)

Paul Newman
$2 million to establish the Barretstown Gang Camp at Barretstown Castle, Ballymore
Eustace, in County Kildare, Ireland

Henry and Lucy Moses Fund
$2 million to four New York City hospitals to help pay for uninsured patients

New York Times Neediest Cases Fund
This annual Christmastime fund raised $4.8 million for human services charities in New
York City

American Red Cross Disaster Relief Fund
$233 million for human services responding to Midwest and California floods, the
Oklahoma City bombing, and Tropical Storm Opal

Century 21 Real Estate
$5.8 million to the National Easter Seal Society

Reader's Digest Association, Inc.
$1 million to the Boys and Girls Clubs of America (GA)

Ronald MacDonald Children's Charities
More than $1.1 million to 45 children's organizations

George Soros
$50 million to create the Emma Lazarus Fund to help immigrants become U.S. citizens

Donald L. Saunders
$7.5 million to Combined Jewish Philanthropies, Mass.

James Michener
$1 million to the Bucks County Free Library

Frankie and Stan Harrell
$4 million to Metropolitan Ministries, Tampa, Fla., for Project Uplift, to provide care for
homeless and at-risk families and individuals

Source: American Association of Fund-Raising Counsel, GIVING USA, 1996, "The 1996 Slate 60," *Slate*,
December 2, 1996.

One study of the relationship between tax exemptions and voluntary giving,
for example, estimated that 96 percent of large-sum donors would substantially
reduce their contributions if tax benefits were removed.[3] Because "tax deductions
are a monetary ointment to salve the strains of charity," they provide an indispensable incentive for individuals to support the nonprofit services of their
choice.[4] Little wonder that attempts to limit the deduction are always greeted with
fierce denunciations by the beneficiaries of philanthropic *largess*— most notably,
universities, art museums, and scientific research institutions.

In addition to questioning the charitable impulse behind philanthropic giving, one should also question how "voluntary" contributions are in the first place.

CAPSULE 7.1:   Ted's Excellent Idea

"That list [the Forbes Magazine list of wealthiest Americans] is destroying our country. These new super-rich won't loosen up their wads because they're afraid they'll reduce their net worth and go down on the list. That's their Super Bowl.

Why isn't it better to be the biggest giver rather than the biggest hog? What difference does it make if you're worth $12 billion or $11 billion? With a billion dollars you can build a whole university. They are fighting every year to be the richest man in the world. Why don't they sign a joint pact to each give away a billion and then move down the Forbes list equally?

These big billionaires are busy letting go middle managers in their 50s, the day before their pension plans kick in. We're getting to be like Mexico and Brazil, with the rich living behind fences, like they do in Hollywood. The Federal Government, the state government, the municipal government—they're all broke. All the money is in the hands of these few rich people and none of them give any money away. It's dangerous for them and for the country. We may have another French Revolution and there'll be another Madame Defarge knitting and watching them come in little oxcarts down to the town square and BOOM! Off with their heads!"

Ted Turner, quoted in Maureen Dowd's column "Liberties," *The New York Times,* August 22, 1996, A23.

Community pressures to give, for example, whether at the office or elsewhere, can exert sufficient social coercion so that a choice *not* to give may be available only at great cost to the individual's prestige and social position. Such pressures, of course, do a disservice to the idea of voluntarism.

Functions of Voluntary Services

Ideally, philanthropic incentives encourage the development of pluralism in community services and provide opportunities for the religious, ethnic, and cultural interests of individuals and groups to flourish. This, the "value guardian" function of the voluntary agency, allows for the expression of particularistic and sectarian values in social welfare.[5] In its role of value guardian, the voluntary organization is one of the major social devices for mitigating many of the strains that exist in U.S. political life. The history of successive waves of ethnic and racial minorities who have been assimilated into U.S. society, indeed, can be written as a biography of their organizational lives.[6]

Writing in 1895, Charles Henderson characterized voluntary organizations as social units that are less permanent and rigid than formal institutions, and thus better able to meet the needs of particular classes or social groups. Of course, many voluntary organizations evolve into large bureaucratic agencies, a phenomenon of interest in the study of social movements.[7] But Henderson's comments on the functions of voluntary associations are still quite relevant:

> *[Voluntary associations] may be compared to the tenders which ply between the port and the great ships which are more at home on the deep sea than in the shallow harbor or to the skirmish lines which are thrown in advance of the main army.*

. . . It is said that these societies dissipate social energy, rival the home, sap the resources of the church, and multiply like a plague of locusts. Unquestionably, the objection is partly justified by facts. There are too many societies, especially too many bad ones. They overlap, duplicate, and interfere with each other. Some of them seem to be organized simply to advertise the benevolence of the executive secretary. . . . But the severest judgement of an abuse leaves the normal use untouched. The voluntary associations require criticism and regulation but the principle of their life is legitimate.[8]

In addition to supporting diversity and pluralism in community life, voluntary services provide an important vehicle for implementing new and possibly unpopular ideas. The flexible and changing characteristics of some voluntary agencies make them uniquely suited to this "vanguard" function.[9] This function was exemplified in the early 1960s by the Ford Foundation's sponsorship of the Grey Areas Projects, the demonstration program that paved the way for the President's Committee on Juvenile Delinquency, the Economic Opportunity Program, and Model Cities.[10] This is not to imply that governmental agencies are incapable of innovation and experimentation. On the contrary, most of the funds used for research, experimentation, and innovation in social welfare services come from public sources.[11] Nevertheless, voluntary agencies often are able to pursue ideas and initiatives that would be far too unpopular to secure government sanction.

CAPSULE 7.2: Philanthropical Correctness

In the decades following the Second World War, foundations served as leading instruments of the liberal consensus, using their position at the intersection of the elite worlds of government, politics, academia, and the press to remake America in their own progressive image. Foundations funded, in whole or in part, the early expansion of our system of public libraries, Jonas Salk's discovery of the polio vaccine, the writing of Gunnar Myrdal's *An American Dilemma,* the Public Broadcasting Corporation, the "Grey Areas" project that led to Model Cities, and the Michigan study that yielded Head Start.

What was striking about the foundations of the 50s and 60s, however, was not so much the merit of their ideas as the extent of their influence. John Gardner, president of the Carnegie Corporation from 1955 to 1965, served as Lyndon Johnson's Secretary of Health, Education, and Welfare, taught at Harvard and MIT, worked at the FCC and founded Common Cause. McGeorge Bundy, president of Ford from 1966 to 1979, was a former dean of the faculty of arts and sciences at Harvard and national security adviser under Kennedy and Johnson. With years of experience and contacts throughout interlocking worlds of the elite, Gardner and Bundy conveyed their ideas to academics, editors, members of congress, and presidents and, in many cases, saw them enacted into law.

David Samuels, "Philanthropical Correctness," *The New Republic,* September 18 and 25, 1995, 28–36.

Voluntary agencies also may function as "improvers" and "supplementors" of public services. They can serve as vigilant critics, ensuring the quality of public services. And, finally, they can support programs to meet needs that public agencies are unable or unwilling to undertake.[12]

The case of the Family Service Association of America (FSAA) provides a good illustration of the supplementary function performed by a voluntary agency.[13] The FSAA was founded in 1911 as the National Association for Organizing Charities (NAOC), an outgrowth of the Charity Organization Societies of the late 1800s. The primary function of NAOC was to coordinate the work of community agencies involved with charitable giving.[14] The organization was opposed to public relief giving.[15] In the first decades of the twentieth century, NAOC dropped its coordinating functions, concentrating instead on the rehabilitation of distressed families. In 1919 it became the American Association for Organizing Family Social Work, using the combined methods of relief giving and social casework.

When the Social Security Act was passed in 1935, the federal government undertook substantial relief-giving for special categories of the needy. The FSAA responded by abandoning the "quantitative" job of providing income relief in favor of the "qualitative" task of providing family casework. By 1953, FSAA had developed a "family-oriented" casework approach for dealing with social problems and, for a while, the difference between public and voluntary services seemed clear. But with the 1956 amendments to the Social Security Act, public welfare itself took on a family orientation and states were encouraged to grant assistance and "other services" to needy children, parents, and relatives "to help maintain and strengthen family life." The 1958 and 1962 amendments to the act further strengthened this orientation. By the mid-1960s, therefore, agencies such as FSAA once again began to reassess their functions *vis-à-vis* public services. While, no doubt, there were many other reasons for the change, in 1971 the Community Service Society of New York City abandoned its long tradition of family casework and took up a strategy of community organization for neighborhood self-improvement.[16] In 1973, member agencies of the FSAA in Chicago and Minneapolis also began to emphasize social advocacy.

More recently, as FSAAs have found it increasingly difficult to acquire governmental funds to support counseling and other community service activities, they have given greater attention to emergency and other short-term assistance, relying more heavily on fee-charging arrangements with private practitioners, and developing private services such as Employee Assistance Programs focusing on corporate settings.

Voluntary agencies increasingly serve another important function, one not noted in Kramer's system of classification, and that is their role as protector of the poor in an era of diminishing welfare state spending. When federal policy, in particular, threatens significant cutbacks—as occurred during the Reagan era in the mid-1980s and the Contract with America campaign in the mid-1990s—national attention turns to nonprofit organizations to protect the country's most vulnerable citizens from the results. Nonprofits, presumably more efficient, more sensitive, and more effective than their public counterparts, would step into the breach, offset public cuts, and rescue the poor.

The problem, however, is not only that public cutbacks *impair* private action—the first thing state and local governments frequently do is to pass their federal cutbacks along to private charities by reducing their contracts—but that the magnitude of government reductions simply overwhelms any potential remediation by community agencies. In 1995, for example, Lester Salamon and Alan Abramson estimated that balancing the proposed Contract with America cuts would require a doubling in private charitable contributions in a six-year period, not a likely scenario.[17]

Problems and Issues in Voluntary Financing

Even without such emergency demands, several problems arise in financing voluntary social welfare services. First, there is the fundamental question of the public-private relationship. Are there some community activities that should be *exclusively* private and voluntary? Are there others that should only be public? And if public financing of private endeavors is appropriate, how should we balance cultural pluralism and social equality? Should contributions to ethnically or religiously exclusive educational, health, and social welfare agencies, for example, be tax exempt? Should governments provide *direct* support for parochial agencies (such as Catholic schools) if they meet community requirements and standards? Does such support violate constitutional guarantees separating church and state? These issues become exceedingly complex when there is a "mixing" of voluntary and public funds.

Public support for voluntary agencies occurs in a variety of forms. The *tax deductibility* of charitable contributions has been noted. Direct *public subsidies*, largely unconditional lump-sum grants to voluntary agency programs, although uncommon today, were at one time quite the norm. They have come to be considered poor public policy, however, because, as an essentially "agency-oriented" means of financial support, they commit government to supporting *all* of the goals and purposes of an organization.[18] *Purchase of service contracting*, a newer option, is an arrangement whereby governments buy specific services, such as foster care, job training, or respite services. In some cases, governmental units may even contract with private agencies to perform "indirect" activities such as program development, social planning, eligibility determination, and services evaluation.

The Mixed Economy of Welfare

As discussed earlier, a major part of the funds expended by voluntary agencies *are* provided by government. America's second largest charity, Catholic Charities USA, receives 64 percent of its income from government. The number eight charity, United Cerebral Palsy, relies on public support for 81 percent.[19] In the overall social services arena, indeed, half the budget comes from public funds, as

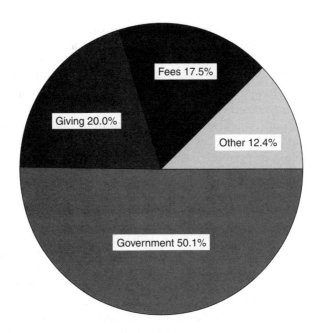

FIGURE 7.1   Sources of Funding for Social Service Nonprofits, 1995

Source: AAFRC, Giving USA, 1996, 39.

Figure 7.1 indicates. It is estimated, for example, that more than half of all Title XX social services funds are spent on services purchased from voluntary and for-profit organizations. Considering these trends, Ralph Kramer has stated: "It is ironic that a national coalition of non-profit organizations chose as its name 'The Independent Sector' when its constituents had become, more than ever, dependent on government."[20]

One major virtue of these subventions is that they enable governments to start programs quickly, utilizing the existing capacity of voluntary organizations while avoiding the rigidities of civil service and bureaucracy. Also, as noted in chapter 6, contracting reduces the costs of having to pay civil service salaries and being restricted to negotiating with public services unions. This is especially advantageous for experiments and demonstrations. Contracting also permits public officials to tailor programs to the special circumstances of hard-to-reach or minority populations. Relying on the access and expertise of existing community-based agencies, governments can be far more responsive to special population groups than if they tried to provide services in-house.

For the voluntary agency, the obvious advantage of purchase arrangements is access to the public coffers as additional sources of income. But they pay a price. To the extent that voluntary agencies are supported by government funds, they forfeit some degree of autonomy. Consequently, the ability of these agencies to function as agents for the expression of new or unpopular ideas, as critics of pub-

---

CAPSULE 7.3:   Fatal Embrace

"How [can we] protect [voluntary institutions] from the fatal embrace of government regulation? The problem . . . grows immensely when tax funds are channeled to them—in the name of accountability, equity, or whatever moral principle is supposedly to govern the expenditure of public money. . . . When such institutions are first 'discovered' and then funded by government, the very vitality that originally distinguished them from government agencies is destroyed. Indeed, they *become* government agencies under another name."

Peter Berger and Richard John Neuhaus, "Response," in Michael Novak (ed.), *To Empower People: From State to Civil Society*, 2d edition, 1996, 150–51.

lic services, and as the guardians of pluralistic values may be limited. Family-planning clinics funded with federal grant-in-aid funds, for example, are prohibited from providing information about abortion, a severe limitation on their ability to provide their clients a comprehensive set of options. In the extreme, voluntary agencies may simply become an instrument of government policy. The degree to which governmental constraints may be imposed, of course, depends in part on the method of financing that is employed. Indirect subsidies through tax deductions and vouchers are relatively benign and *laissez-faire*, whereas direct contracting through purchase of services arrangements hold the potential for considerable intrusiveness.[21] In the view of some, when voluntary agencies accept funds from government, they should be treated no differently than any other agency of government. According to Glasser, for example, the private agency that accepts public funds *should* forego privileges of autonomy.[22]

Accountability

The issue of governmental support places voluntary agencies in a paradoxical situation. Government controls are seen as undesirable, as contrary to the independence and the special role of voluntary agencies. On the other hand, reasonable controls must protect the use of public dollars. Government policymakers, under law, must be prudent in their use of tax revenue, and prudence demands reasonable mechanisms for accountability.

Even before the modern era of massive public contract financing, charitable trusts were held to be "in the public interest" and therefore subject to a degree of government regulation.[23] It is on this basis that voluntary funds have been restricted and some degree of public control exercised. Tax-exempt organizations must be chartered by state governments, and the states may require various kinds of accounting procedures and impose standards of practice. One important limitation is that "no substantial part" of the voluntary agencies' activities may consist of efforts to influence legislation.[24] This restriction accounts, in part, for the reluctance of many voluntary welfare agencies to become engaged in political action.

Public concern regarding the accountability of voluntary organizations, particularly philanthropic foundations, found legislative expression in the Tax Reform Act of 1969. Although not as severe as many critics of voluntary organizations desired, the act imposed several important limitations on voluntary organizations. Almost one-third of the act concerned foundations, establishing policies regarding the investment of funds, public reporting, and the amount of income that could be received on assets. In addition, the act required foundations to pay a 4 percent excise tax on their income and to dispose of at least 5 percent of their capital annually.[25]

The problem of establishing accountability for voluntary agencies can be understood in relation to a much older and more general notion known as "charitable immunity." Originating in centuries-old English law, this concept holds that charitable trusts cannot be held responsible for derelictions of duties to clients (negligence and neglect, for example), because without such immunity government intervention might eventually violate the intentions of the donors and limit the functions of voluntary charity.[26] The questions of charitable immunity and the extent to which bequests may be altered by action of government is significant. In 1995 alone, $9.8 billion was bequeathed to charitable organizations, with 90 percent of all bequests of $1 million and above going to education—especially universities.[27]

For many years, charitable bequests and legacies have been protected by this concept of immunity (sometimes referred to as "the dead hand") and have been allowed to follow donors' original purposes, even when some of these appear frivolous, discriminatory, or otherwise socially harmful. Whimsical examples from recent history include a trust fund for Christmas dinners ("one bushel of oats or a half bushel of corn chops") for hungry horses in Kansas City, a trust fund establishing "marriage portions" for poor young women about to be married, and a legacy providing "a baked potato at each meal for each young lady at Bryn Mawr."[28]

A more serious illustration is the case of Girard College. In this instance, the U.S. Supreme Court decided that the charitable bequest involved could not be used for tax-exempt purposes if the activities of the enterprise conflicted with the public interest by supporting discrimination against minority groups.[29] Here, the grip of "the dead hand" was loosened by another important legal concept, the *cy pres* (i.e., "as near as may be") doctrine, which holds that courts may modify bequests to be "as near as" possible to the original intent of the giver in light of social changes that have taken place in the community.[30]

Another case of this kind involved the Buck Trust controversy. This case provides an interesting test of the strength of the "dead hand" in respect to community definitions of "social need." In 1973, Mrs. Buck, following her husband's wishes, willed her estate, valued at that time at $10 million, to Marin County, California, "to be used exclusively for non-profit charitable, religious, or educational purposes in providing care for the needy." However, when Mrs. Buck died in 1979, her estate had vastly increased in value; by 1984, it was worth $360 million and was producing approximately $20 to $25 million a year. The San Francisco

Foundation, the administrators of the trust, challenged the "Marin only" provisions, arguing that the county (one of the wealthiest in the United States) was not able to make use of the funds.[31] Marin County, ultimately supported by the courts, argued for a strict construction of the will and its clear geographical limitation. Despite the fact that Marin County, by all statistical measures, had only a small amount of need—and a small population of the needy—the court decided that the definition of "need" was fundamentally subjective. Marin residents perceived of themselves as needy, the Buck instructions were clear, and the trust would not have to be shared with neighboring communities.

The vast increase in purchase-of-service contracting since the 1960s has made the accountability issue especially critical for state and local governments. Well over $1 billion worth of public services are purchased annually, providing government policymakers a flexible tool for delivering community services in a cost-efficient, responsive manner, often engaging clientele groups that might be reluctant to deal directly with public bureaucrats. But clearly, contracting brings with it accountability issues with respect to both fiscal and program standards. The typically diffuse goals and objectives of contract agencies, for example, make it difficult to determine effectiveness.

Public policymakers address accountability through the contract document itself, negotiating funding agreements that set forth the ground rules for the purchase of service. As in all contracts, there must be "consideration,"—in exchange for a budgeted allocation, provider agencies agree to deliver a specified quantity or services of a particular sort to an identified target group. Public control is then exercised through a variety of monitoring and evaluating procedures—audits, site visits, agency program reports, and the like.

"Accountability," of course, is a rather ambiguous term. And the conventional dichotomy of autonomy versus accountability—the need of private agencies for independence versus the need of public bodies to insure the proper use of tax dollars—often generates more heat than light. Nevertheless, it poses a real dilemma in today's mixed economy of welfare, a dilemma that typically is answered more on ideological than on technical grounds.

Who Determines Policy?

There is another side to the issue of accountability that concerns voluntary agency relationships, not with government, but with different socioeconomic groups. Tax-exempt support to nonprofit activities are distributed unequally within the population. Givers have different amounts to contribute and different views of how funds should be used. Nielsen, in his analysis of foundations, for example, describes one fundamental contradiction of voluntary philanthropy:

> *In the great jungle of American democracy and capitalism, there is no more strange or improbable creature than the private foundation. Private foundations are virtually a denial of basic premises: aristocratic institutions living on the privileges and indulgence of an egalitarian society; aggregations of private wealth*

which, contrary to the proclaimed instincts of Economic Man have been conveyed to public purposes. Like the giraffe, they could not possibly exist, but they do.[32]

Voluntary agencies themselves are an important part of the policy-making system of social welfare. Like many agencies, they become organizational vehicles for their professionals, board members, donors, and volunteers to exercise influence over community services. Consequently, voluntary social welfare agencies frequently reflect the interests of the economically advantaged. Elling and Halebsky argue, for example, that voluntary health services function to meet the needs of higher status groups in society. In a study comparing public and voluntary hospitals, they found the governmental institutions rated less favorably on several criteria. They draw the following conclusion:

> *In a democratic society, the political system, far from being the power instrument of the capitalist ruling class, as Marx maintained, has often been a major means of control and representation available to ordinary citizens. As changes in medical technology have encouraged the use of the hospital by all elements of society, "upper" elements have preserved the class structure of the community by organizing their own facilities outside of control of the masses and to some extent beyond their participation.*[33]

Since the 1960s, there has been great concern about community participation in planning and decision making in all forms of social welfare services. Voluntary as well as public agencies have been criticized for their failures to provide adequate representation of low-income groups and minorities on their boards, and some have reviewed their allocation and program policies in light of these criticisms.[34]

Extending the argument, some writers consider United Way's substantial control over workplace access and payroll deductions to be "a kind of monopoly [that] weakens the ability of the voluntary sector to protect pluralist values."[35] In recent years, opponents of this "monopoly" have developed two related strategies for dealing with the United Way's presumed elitism: *donor option* programs and *alternative funds.* In donor option programs, United Way contributors may designate their gifts for *any* charitable organization with tax-exempt status in their area, whether it's a United Way member agency or not. First endorsed by the Board of Governors of United Way in 1982, donor option plans are widespread today, providing significantly broadened freedom of choice to worksite employees.

Alternative funds provide a more radical means of raising and distributing voluntary contributions for community service organizations outside of the United Way network. Organizations such as United Arts Funds, National Network of Women's Funds, Black United Funds—and at least 100 others—are currently soliciting contributions for about 2,000 non-United Way charities. Women's funds, for example, gave away nearly $13 million in 1990 to programs dealing with violence against women, pornography, health and family planning, and employment. Some of these alternative funds are quite successful in their fund-raising efforts, some less so, and many have found it difficult to survive altogether. Interestingly, however, where alternative funds have developed, the local United Ways have usually experienced an *increase* in revenues, rather than a reduction. Perhaps the competition of the alternative fund heightens community awareness of social needs.[36]

Conservatives and Voluntarism

Voluntarism involves more than money—whatever its source. Classic voluntarism, the voluntarism of Tocqueville, of the Victorian Lady Bountiful, of today's weekend volunteer, involves action, good works, civic engagement. More than the citizens of any other advanced industrial nation, indeed U.S. residents donate money *and* time. They give to charitable organizations *and* they join churches, help with the local PTA, and serve on the boards of directors of local social services agencies.

For many conservatives, volunteer civic responsibility is the best way to approach social provision, representing a humane and effective alternative to the inefficient, bureaucratic, and bloated welfare state. This view, revived and reenergized in recent years in an influential body of literature from the political right,[37] has found voice—and expression—in national developments. Conservative regimes, such as the Reagan–Bush administrations in the United States and the Thatcher government in the United Kingdom, advanced the view that a large part of the welfare system *should* be the domain of the voluntary sector. Under Reagan, it was declared policy that public sector welfare activities should be substantially privatized, absorbed by "the voluntary spirit." As Lester Salamon points out, however, the Reagan administration never converted its commitment to private giving into a serious plan of action,[38] and, on balance, Reagan budget and tax policy negatively impacted the nonprofit sector.

Voluntarism *is* an enticing idea: get government off our backs and neighbors will help neighbors, families will pitch in, and the community will roll up its collective sleeves and get the job done. The only thing wrong with this idea is that it doesn't work. Despite the readiness of Americans to volunteer, one, as Figure 7.2 indicates, that is extremely impressive in the international context, citizens alone are insufficient. The welfare state developed because, in modern society, neighbors, friends, family, and local communities—the entire "thousand points of light" celebrated by President Bush—were *unable* to provide for contemporary social needs. That is not to say, of course, that public agencies and social welfare professionals should disregard private support systems and community groups. There is clearly major work to be done to better articulate the functions of human service professionals and the natural helping networks and voluntary activities of communities. However, it is quite another thing to reach into the dustbin of our Victorian past for discarded ideas as solutions to contemporary social problems.

Percentage of Population Volunteering, 1993

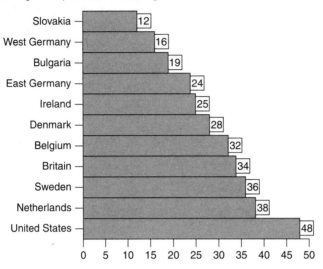

FIGURE 7.2   National Volunteers

Sources: *A New Civic Europe? A Study of the Extent and Role of Volunteering,* Volunteer Centre U.K.; *Giving and Volunteering in the United States,* Independent Sector, in *Giving USA, 1996,* 162.

Liberals and Voluntarism

The spirit of service—to neighbors, community, nation, or humankind—is far from a conservative monopoly. Tocqueville's pattern of volunteerism has been a U.S. phenomena, across the spectrum, from the start. But whereas conservatives tend to view private action as an alternative to public responsibility, liberals promote volunteer effort as a way to advance national goals. It was this spirit that framed John Kennedy's famous injunction, "Ask not what your country can do for you, but what you can do for your country."

Since the Kennedy years, Democratic presidents have promoted public efforts to stimulate individual volunteering. Lyndon Johnson initiated VISTA, an effort to replicate the Peace Corps on the domestic scene. In the 1970s and 1980s, new programs enlisted older citizens (RSVP) and young teachers. And in 1993 Congress and President Clinton created Americorps, the largest community service program since the Great Depression. Run by a federal Corporation for National and Community Service, Americorps has engaged close to 50,000 young citizens in service jobs that are part volunteer, part student aid. Participants earn a $4,725 scholarship for each year of service, plus a minimum wage stipend, while working for charitable purposes ranging from the Red Cross and Habitat for Humanity to jobs as teacher's aids in disadvantaged inner cities.

Contributory Schemes and Fee Charging

Those receiving social benefits may be asked to finance them in two ways: through "contributions" to statutory (i.e., public) social and health insurance programs, and through fees paid for services rendered. Public social security programs, although somewhat akin to private insurance, do not operate according to general marketplace rules of exchange. Rather, the conditions of exchange are regulated by government, reflecting recipient need as well as recipient contribution. And private profit, of course, is not allowed.

Social security, officially Old Age, Survivors, Disability, and Health Insurance (OASDHI), is the outstanding example of a contributory system in the United States. Its basic principle is that all those eligible for benefits at the time they withdraw from the labor force will have paid insurance-like "contributions" during their working years. Like any other insurance system, their investments "earn" entitlements to benefits. Social security, of course, is not like "any other" insurance system. First, despite the euphemism, "contributions" constitute a tax on both earnings (for employees) and payrolls (for employers); both workers and employers, therefore, are obligated to support the system. In 1997, approximately 98 percent of the U.S. work force was covered by a combination of social security and other governmental retirement systems. Second, unlike private insurance, OASDHI benefits are not paid on the basis of a written contract. Although there is a universally understood obligation for government to stand by its commitments, the exact nature of social security taxes and benefits are determined by Congress and change from time to time. And while there is an important relationship between contributions and benefits, Congress awards benefits on the basis of need as well as on the basis of contributions.

Fee charging, although associated with the buying and selling of goods found in the commercial marketplace, is not at all uncommon among voluntary—and very often public—organizations. Health care, notably, is primarily fee-for-service care, with payments provided by consumers in the form of insurance premiums, deductibles, and copayments. As a result, of course, the affluent receive excellent health care in the United States, whereas the less affluent—especially those having to rely on public assistance, or having no insurance at all—get less. Day care and private schools similarly rely heavily on user fees.

In the social services, fees, of necessity, are less available. Having a poor clientele to serve, social agencies must turn chiefly to charity and to government. Nevertheless, even agencies serving the disadvantaged often utilize fees and charges to cover part of the cost. Under these arrangements, fees may be calculated on a graduated "sliding scale" according to the user's economic circumstances. Rarely covering the entire cost of the services rendered, these fees subsidize poorer clients, and no one is turned away due to an inability to pay.

Sliding scale fees, for example, have long been used by family service associations, with charges for counseling sessions ranging from zero to $75 an hour, according to income. Mental health agencies similarly rely on payments, depending on the caseworker to negotiate an appropriate fee with the consumer. According to one analysis of fee-setting procedures, payment schedules generally "attempt to resolve the tension between consumers' expectations of paying fees for service, their ability to pay, the true cost of the service, and an agency's need to raise additional revenue."

Fee charging is also frequently introduced into public contributory programs. Medicare, the health insurance program for the aged under social security, gives beneficiaries an option to participate in a Supplementary Medical Insurance Program (Part B) which covers physicians' fees. In 1997, 97 percent of all eligible beneficiaries elected Part B, paying $43.80 per month for coverage. In addition, there is a deductible charge of $100 for physician's care. There is also a $760 deductible charge for hospital insurance under Part A, (which means that the recipient must pay this amount of the bill first before the program covers any costs) and a $190 copayment for hospital days sixty-one through ninety. In some health plans (such as Britain's National Health Service) members may be required to pay a fee that covers part of the cost for each episode of care, be it a visit to a dentist, prescribed medication, or a hospital stay.

Fee charging in the social services was promoted by the 1974 Title XX amendments to the Social Security Act, which allowed states to offer social services to nonwelfare families earning between 80 and 115 percent of their state's median annual income. These services could be offered for reasonable income-related fees on a subsidized basis. In 1975, approximately 21 percent of Title XX service recipients were in the "income eligible" category.[39]

Assumptions about psychological and behavioral dynamics underlie much of the debate concerning the use of contributory and fee-charging schemes. From the psychological point of view, it is argued that recipients are less likely to feel stigma or shame when they pay their own way, even if they are still partially subsidized. At the same time, the act of contributing is believed to enhance the individual's sense of social responsibility. This has been one of the major arguments for operating social security on a contributory basis. The behavioral rationale for contributory schemes and fee charging, as applied to service-giving programs, is that user payments restrain overutilization. That is, even small fees for doctor or therapist visits, or for prescriptions, are said to discourage unnecessary or excessive care.

There is little empirical evidence to support or reject these psychological and behavioral arguments. Recipients of social security benefits appear to feel a greater sense of entitlement to benefits than do recipients of other programs, but what part of this is due to having made contributions and what part is due to general public acceptance of the program is not clear. There are other well-accepted programs where beneficiaries do not make direct contributions (such as unemployment insurance, public education, and veterans' services), yet seem to develop the same sense of entitlement as OASDHI recipients.[40]

A sense of entitlement can be based on factors such as compensation or general public commitment to the program. Supplementary Security Income recipients receive better benefits, feel more entitled to them, and are socially perceived as being more deserving than recipients of TANF. Although contributory schemes may have some effect on the sense of entitlement, they are by no means determinative.

Similarly, it is not clear whether contributions and user-fees affect the consumption of benefits. Although fee charging may restrain excessive use on the part of consumers, even small fees may discourage utilization by those who are so needy that even a nominal charge can be a burden. Several studies of the effect of charges in prepaid health plans, for example, have found that even modest copayments for office visits significantly reduce the use of primary care services, although they appear to have no impact on visits to medical and surgical specialists.[41]

As Eveline Burns has indicated, contributions and fee charging are likely to have a responsibility-inducing effect only in small units where individual members can perceive the relationship between the organization's operations and the money they pay. She also noted, however, that contributions can result in *greater* consumer demand. The recipient's "belief that he has paid for whatever benefits he gets may . . . work in the opposite direction from that intended by those who view the contributory requirement as a brake upon unreasonable benefit increases or extensions."[42]

Public Financing: Not Entirely a Public Matter

Despite the importance of private and voluntary welfare, the essence of today's welfare state is principally one of public provision and public finance. Government remains the major source of funds for health, education, income maintenance, and welfare services, and the primacy of public financing means that social welfare policy choices are fundamentally matters of politics rather than matters of consumer choice or voluntary philanthropy.

In the same way that voluntary financing is not completely a matter of private philanthropy, public (or governmental) financing of social welfare services is not quite as public a business as it may initially appear. In the broadest sense, taxation is a central instrument regulating the interaction between government and the private economy. The core ideological debate between redistribution and social justice on the one hand, and the need for profit and economic efficiency, on the other, clearly comes into play here. In a narrower sense, tax policy directly impacts the private, nonstatutory, realms of social welfare. Tax exemptions for charitable contributions illustrate one way in which government uses its taxing powers to subsidize private welfare—the exemption provides a substantial public incentive for private generosity.[43] Other incentives—including the federal income tax deductions for catastrophic medical expenses, home mortgage interest, and child and dependent care expenses—all direct private activity in publicly specified ways. All of these represent private "welfare" elements in the public finance systems.

In Chapter 3 we introduced the concept of "tax expenditure" to denote these kinds of special features in the tax law that are designed to encourage certain kinds of behavior. Whether called tax credits, deductions, or exclusions, these provisions constitute a system of welfare that parallels regular social welfare spending. Although they are analogous to regular expenditures in that they represent a decision by government to direct resources to particular objectives, they are far less visible. Often, indeed, they are not identified and reviewed regularly as part of the regular (expenditure) budget.

The purpose of tax expenditures is not to finance government but rather to direct benefits in special ways. But although regular benefits—such as social security, TANF, or farm subsidies—are cash outlays, allocated through the annual budget process, tax expenditures occur when government *doesn't* tax at the level it normally would. They are, basically, targeted tax cuts. To subsidize child care for working families, for example, Congress authorizes direct spending in the form of cash payments to eligible families, and also provides program funding to day-care providers. In addition, it utilizes the tax system to help families with child-care expenses.

The use of the tax code as a system of special benefits has long been derided as welfare for the rich. And tax loopholes, many extraordinarily complicated, *do* frequently advance the interests of people with high incomes. In the federal system, nevertheless, two of the most significant tax expenditures—exclusions for income-transfer payments and employee fringe benefits—serve distinctly social objectives. The exclusion from income taxes granted public assistance and social security payments derives from the simple logic of protecting the limited income of the poor. It hardly makes sense, after all, to provide income support with one hand while taxing it back with the other. The exclusion, however, is not absolute. Because social security beneficiaries are often reasonably well-to-do, federal policy does tax a limited portion of the social security payments of the better-off elderly—currently 50 percent of any income over $32,000 for a couple, and over $25,000 for an individual.

Since 1942, employee fringe benefits—compensation received in the form of health and pension plans, special housing allowances, and employee-assistance services such as counseling, day care, and the like—have been *doubly* benefitted

---

CAPSULE 7.4:   The Leaky Bucket

The idea among tax theologians is that the income tax on individuals and corporations—before deductions, exclusions, and the like are factored in—represents a sort of ideal tax structure. The revenues due the Treasury under this ideal structure are like water that flows into a bucket. The deductions and exclusions are represented by holes punctured in the bucket. The holes have become quite large.

Paul Starobin, "Washington Update," *National Journal,* August 21, 1993, 2087.

under the federal tax code. First, the cost to employers of these benefits constitutes a deductible business expense. They can therefore be deducted from taxable income, appreciably lowering taxes owed. Second, employees benefit, because all compensation in the form of wages and salaries is taxed but compensation in the form of fringe benefits is not. This means that a valuable and costly form of remuneration is given to employees on a tax-free basis.

These provisions have been enormously successful in broadening our system of private welfare. Tax expenditures have promoted pension plans by making them less costly for employers to sponsor. The pension deduction—the second largest of the 109 items listed in the FY 1996 federal tax expenditure budget (some of which are enumerated in Table 7.4)—provided a huge tax savings for businesses, important benefits for employees, and, of course, corresponding losses (about $55 billion) in federal revenues.

Similarly, private health plans have been encouraged. Today, employers provide health insurance for over 60 million employees, deducting over $150 billion for these benefits, resulting, as Table 7.4 indicates, in a $64 billion tax loss to

TABLE 7.4 Revenue Losses From Major Social Welfare Tax Expenditures in The Federal Personal Income Tax, FY 1996 (in Billions of Dollars)

Tax Expenditure	Revenue Loss
Social security (OASDI) exclusion	$22.5
Individual retirement accounts	$ 7.8
Employer pension plans	$55.4
Exclusion of employer contributions for medical insurance and care	$64.5
Child and dependent care credit	$ 2.9
Charitable contributions	
for education	$ 1.9
for health	$ 2.4
for other purposes	$20.6
Earned Income Credit	$ 5.7

Source: *Budget of the United States Government, FY 1997*, Analytical Perspectives, Section 5, 1996, 62–64.

CAPSULE 7.5: Democrat and Republican Currencies

> Republicans give tax cuts;
> Democrats give 'programs.'
> Same currency, different voters.

Matthew Miller, "TRB From Washington," *New Republic*, January 29, 1996, 6.

CAPSULE 7.6:   Adopt-A-Tax

Among the more interesting and needed tax breaks passed [in 1996 were] those for adoption assistance that provide a tax credit of up to $5,000 per child for payment of qualifying adoption expenses such as adoption and legal fees. "Adoption is very expensive, and many people turn to adoption after spending tens of thousands on infertility," says Nancy Hurwitz, a Walnut Creek adoption facilitator.

Kay Read, a Walnut Creek resident who works in the systems division at Bank of America, knows about the typical costs—she has already spent about $15,000 for the not-yet-finalized adoption of her second child, a 3-month-old girl named Alexandra. "The tax breaks are wonderful but aren't enough," says Read. "Adoptions cost a lot of money and help society at large."

To encourage adoptions of children with special needs—a broad term for certain children who officials believe will be more difficult to find adoptive families for—the tax credit can be up to $6,000 for such adoptions. These adoption tax credits are in effect for tax years 1997 through 2001, unless you adopt a child with special needs, in which case the credit continues beyond 2001.

Eric Tyson, "Your Money Matters," *San Francisco Examiner,* September 29, 1996, B1.

government. Once again, in addition to providing a major business deduction, fringes provide an enormous break for employees. Because health benefits are tax-free, they constitute a favorable alternative to regular, taxable, wages. Workers furnished with $2,000 in medical coverage, for example, receive the full benefit value. If the $2,000 were provided in the form of salary, however, *that* would buy only $1,440 worth of insurance for a worker in the 28 percent income tax bracket.

The overall cost to the government of tax expenditures is considerable—approximately $410 billion in FY 1994, an amount equivalent to 32% of all federal revenues. In some areas of activity, indeed, the magnitude of tax expenditures approaches that of direct spending. In the federal budget category "education, training, employment, and social services," for example, direct outlays are just barely ahead of the amount given up in tax expenditures. In the housing field, homeowner deductions for mortgage interest, property taxes, and capital gains exemptions on home sales cost the federal government about $100 billion in taxes annually, five times the amount spent for low-income housing programs like Section 8.

Public objectives, it is clear, can be advanced by *both* tax expenditures and regular outlays. As noted, day care is a major area of federal and local activity under *spending* programs such as Title XX, the Elementary and Secondary Education Act, and Head Start, as well as under *tax* programs such as the dependent care credit. Although spending programs generally provide revenues directly to program and agency providers, tax credits and deductions give consumers additional purchasing power for use in the marketplace. In this way, they resemble vouchers, providing substantial freedom of choice to their users.

Are tax expenditures a good thing? Do they, on balance, help the poor? The answer to these questions is complex. Some tax expenditures clearly aren't redistributive. For one thing, only taxpayers benefit from them; if one's earnings fall below the tax threshold, then no benefit is available. Even socially oriented tax expenditures—such as those for day care, charitable contributions, and health plans—often wind up providing the most to those with the fewest needs. The dependent care credit, like the others, is tilted upward, with much of its benefits going to middle- and upper-income families.[44] Health plan tax expenditures also vary considerably in their impact, because younger workers, women, minorities, and unorganized workers, as a group, are less likely to be covered than older workers, men, Caucasians, and union members. In addition, the benefits of those who *are* covered are likely to be far broader for the second group.

The prevailing view of economists is that the overall system of tax expenditures is regressive. One recent calculation estimated that at least half their total benefit goes to the richest fifth of the population.[45] According to Isabel Sawhill, moreover, few tax subsidies are targeted so as to help those who need them most. They "neglect the housing, health care, and income security needs of low-income families while simultaneously providing billions to assist the affluent and the middle class."[46] This kind of "welfare for the rich" clearly diminishes the overall progressivity of the income tax. It accounts, in addition, for the fact that although income taxes remain the most redistributive form of taxation, their real rates vary only moderately among income groups. (Real, or "effective," rates refer to actual taxes as a proportion of overall income.) Despite the official 40 percent federal income tax bite on the marginal income of the rich, even the top 1 percent of taxpayers pay only one-fifth of their aggregate income to Uncle Sam.[47]

Tax expenditures have other weaknesses. First, they are a relatively hidden form of public support, which means that they generally avoid the review and scrutiny afforded direct spending. Many states and localities, for example, fail to identify tax expenditures in their annual budgets, and most exert little fiscal control over them in their committee deliberations. For the most part, tax expenditures are a form of entitlement, continuing unexamined from year to year to qualifying taxpayers.

A second problem is their impact on the tax base. By their very definition, tax expenditures remove funds from the public coffers. At last count, indeed, federal tax loopholes reduced almost by half the amount of income subject to taxation.[48] This means that taxes that in many instances would have been paid by the better-off are foregone. With less income taxed, less revenue is provided, meaning that tax-supported programs—social programs in particular—may be placed in jeopardy. A substantial portion of the present deficit problem, for example, is clearly the result of fewer dollars being available for public support. In recent years, indeed, there has been an enormous increase in the number and size of tax expenditures, resulting in a substantial gap between forfeited receipts and taxes actually collected, and an ever greater abandonment of the implication of the Sixteenth Amendment to the U.S. Constitution that federal taxes be paid on income from *all* sources.

The erosion of the tax base, in addition to reducing government revenues, also impacts differently on different groups. The charity deduction, for example, not only results in the federal government giving up many billions a year in revenue, it also draws resources to the particular charities—culture and research in particular—favored by the biggest givers. Without attempting to judge the relative value of differing nonprofit endeavors, it is clear that when J. P. Getty willed his fortune to a museum of classical art in Malibu, everybody paid for the project indirectly because of the taxes foregone. It is not the case, though, that everybody will benefit equally from what Getty's gift produced. In quite the same way, all citizens make up the taxes lost through the billions of dollars deducted for donations to religious institutions.

Types of Taxation

Taxes affect the distribution of resources in our society just as much as direct social allocations. Redistribution is therefore a double-edged sword, achieved by measures both of finance *and* expenditure. We have discussed the allocative ends of redistribution in the chapters dealing with the basis of allocation and the nature of provisions. Now we want to look in detail at some of these choices from the fund-raising viewpoint, specifically choices concerning the types of taxes levied and the unit of government levying them.

In the United States, as in most other industrial countries, taxes are imposed in a variety of ways. Most importantly, taxes are levied on income, both on individuals, through personal income taxes, and on corporations, through corporate income taxes. In the United States, individual income taxes are the largest single source of federal income, providing 44 percent of total federal revenue, with corporate income taxes providing an additional 12 percent. Taxes are also levied on the costs of things people buy (sales taxes), on earnings and payrolls (social security "contributions," or taxes), on the value of things people own (property taxes), and on estates and gifts.

One way to distinguish among types of taxes is to consider their effects in terms of continuum of redistribution. At the *progressive* end of the continuum are levies such as income taxes, which are proportionally higher for the wealthy than for the poor. The federal personal income tax, the most progressive tax in the United States, is an example, being levied in accordance with the "ability to pay." As income rises, in other words, so does the tax rate.

Most poor families are exempt from the federal income tax. Many, in fact, receive a tax credit (the Earned Income Tax Credit), which offsets a good part of their social security payroll taxes as well. When families cross over the tax threshold, $24,352 for a family of four in 1997, the initial rate is 15 percent. As income increases, so does the marginal rate, from 15 percent to 28 percent (at about $41,000) to 31 percent (at about $100,000). The top rate, 39.6% (levied on incomes over $271,000) has dropped considerably in recent decades. It stood at 91 percent in 1960, 70 percent in 1980, and 50 percent in 1986.

Although the federal income tax imposes heavier burdens on heftier incomes, the relationship between total income and taxes paid is neither simple nor direct.

A variety of complicating factors make total income, in and of itself, only a rough indicator of tax obligation. In addition to total income, for example, *type* of income, *family size,* and *spending patterns* all strongly influence the amount of taxes owed. Nevertheless, the federal income tax *is* modestly progressive. As Table 7.5 indicates, the top fifth of all taxpayers pay roughly 16 percent of their total income in federal income in taxes, while the bottom quintile receive a rebate (i.e., a negative tax) due to the Earned Income Tax Credit. Although the rate progression may not be as steep as many would desire, higher income groups do pay higher rates. When social welfare programs are financed by the income tax, then, the *source* of funding is progressive. Provisions so financed are therefore potentially redistributive, depending on the economic status of the major beneficiaries.[49]

A primary example of a *regressive tax* is the sales tax under which everyone is taxed at the same rate regardless of income. Most states have sales taxes ranging between 3 percent and 7 percent, resulting in the poor paying higher percentages of their incomes than the wealthy. As Table 7.5 indicates, poor taxpayers, those in the lowest income group, paid 2.4 percent of their total income for federal excise taxes in 1990, compared to just 0.5 percent for the top income group. Estimates of the impact of state and local sales taxes indicate a similarly disproportionate burden on the poor.

If social welfare programs are financed by sales taxes, then, the *source* of funding is regressive. Hence, the program is not likely to have a strong redistributive effect, although there may be a degree of redistribution introduced at its allocative end. Programs that are the most redistributive are those financed through progressive taxes and allocated to benefit lower-income groups.

Most taxes fall somewhere between the extremes of progressivity and regressivity. The payroll tax that finances social security is a good example. In 1997, all workers paid the same 7.65 percent of their earnings up to $65,400, with earnings above this limit untaxed. Thus workers who earned $65,400 a year paid the same annual social security tax ($5,003) as those earning $200,000 a year.

TABLE 7.5 Tax Burden of Major Federal Taxes by Income Group, 1990

Income Group	Personal Income Tax Burden	Payroll Tax Burden	Excise Tax Burden	Total Federal Tax Burden
Bottom Fifth	–1.5%	7.6%	2.4%	9.7%
Lower-Middle	3.5%	10.1%	1.4%	16.7%
Middle	6.7%	10.7%	1.0%	20.3%
Upper-Middle	9.0%	10.6%	0.9%	22.5%
Top Fifth	15.6%	6.8%	0.5%	25.8%
All	11.3%	8.6%	0.8%	23.1%

Source: U.S. Congressional Budget Office, The Economic and Budget Outlook: 1991–1995, January 1990, 86–87.

CAPSULE 7.7:   The Income Tax Amendment

The Congress shall have power to lay and collect taxes on incomes, from whatever source
derived, without apportionment among the
several States, and without regard to any census or enumeration.

16th Amendment to the U.S. Constitution, Declared in Force, February 25, 1913.

Clearly, regressivity at work. Nevertheless, social security is generally perceived as redistributive on its *allocative* dimension. That is, the benefits provided to those earning, and therefore contributing, the smallest amounts are more generous, proportionately, than to those who earned, and contributed, at higher levels. At present, for example, retired low-wage earners receive 57 percent of their former monthly wages whereas average earners receive 42 percent and high-income earners receive 24 percent. Some people, indeed, receive social security benefits without having made *any* contributions to the system. (All people over seventy-two are entitled to a minimum benefit whether they paid into the system or not.) The social security system is also redistributive *between* generations because payments to the presently retired come from the social security fund, which is supported by the current generation of workers.

Nonetheless, the regressive features of social security make it considerably less effective than the income tax as a means of redistribution. Unlike the income tax, the social security tax does not apply to total income (just to earned income), it is not graduated, and it does not take into account family size or extraordinary family expenses such as medical care and child care. Tax experts point out, in addition, that the employer's contributions to social security taxes are substantially passed on to consumers (through higher prices) and employees (through lower wages), further aggravating the regressive aspect of the program. For these reasons, many liberals support the idea of financing at least a portion of social security benefits through income taxes.[50]

What *is* the impact of the tax system on the distribution of income? Although economists have long debated this question—and the methodologies appropriate to answering it—the general consensus is that the tax system, on the whole, is slightly progressive. In assessing the period since 1950, for example, the late Joseph Pechman concluded that the overall progressivity of the U.S. tax system—federal, state, and local—has been declining, due to major reductions in the tax burden of the rich. Pechman states

> While the tax burdens of the bottom 90 percent of the income distribution did not change very much . . . , tax burdens of the highest income recipients fell because top federal income tax rates were reduced, the federal corporation income tax dwindled, [and] personal deductions, taxexempt bonds, and tax shelters proliferated.[51]

In 1981 and 1986, for example, President Reagan's supply side tax cuts reduced federal income top rates drastically, from 70 percent to 28 percent. Cuts in the tax rate for the rich at the federal level have been accompanied by major increases in state, local, and social security taxes, and user fees, that burden the poor disproportionately. Looking at federal taxes alone, as Table 7.5 indicates, shows a clear pattern of progressivity, with the poorest families paying 9.7 percent of their income in taxes compared to 20.3 percent for average families, and 25.8 percent for high-income families.

The Congressional Budget Office (CBO), in a series of studies examining the impact of federal taxes during the 1980s, indicated the strongly pro-rich tilt of Reaganomics. CBO figures show that by the end of the 1980s the poorest group of U.S. citizens was paying roughly 20 percent more of their earnings in taxes, and the richest group was paying about 20 percent less, than a decade earlier. This created the widest disparity between the family incomes of the rich and the poor since World War II. The CBO, indeed, reported that all but the richest U.S. families paid a higher tax share in 1990 than before the "tax-cuts" of 1981 and 1986.[52] These trends are continuing in the 1990s.

Social Earmarking

A broad body of policy analysis has examined social welfare financing in terms of "fairness," that is, in terms of issues of equity, redistribution, and antipoverty. More recently, the role of tax policy in influencing *other* aspects of social welfare has drawn considerable interest. Tax laws have been examined as a form of intervention ("social engineering" to critics) that can advance specific objectives in a variety of ways. The way taxes affect individual as well as organizational behavior, for example, has been increasingly recognized. So too has the way tax systems focus revenues on special social needs.

Tax revenues can be designated for either general or specific purposes. "General revenues," such as those provided by federal and state income taxes, finance the broad range of governmental operations. Special purpose taxes, often called "earmarked" or "dedicated" taxes, are restricted to narrowly specified activities. The social security payroll tax is the best known example, although in recent years policymakers at all governmental levels have enacted numerous self-financing programs (i.e., programs that provide their own revenues).

Pairing new taxes with new spending has been popular because it permits programs to be adopted or broadened without increasing budget deficits (at the federal level) or threatening spending limits (in the states). Earmarking, in addition, makes clear the connection between dollars raised and services provided. Taxpayers can see where their money is going, something that isn't possible with general taxes. Experience with social security—as well as excises such as gasoline taxes that are linked to road improvements—indicate that such designation, especially in times of fiscal austerity, may be one of the few ways available to expand governmental activities.

An increasing number of designated taxes have been earmarked for social welfare. Many states utilize alcohol beverage taxes for social programs, especially education. Some have financed programs for the blind with amusement taxes. And in several, alcohol and tobacco taxes support prevention and treatment efforts. Similarly, gambling taxes, lotteries, and other quasi-tax measures focus revenues on particular social ends. Since 1980, for example, a majority of the states have raised fees on marriage licenses, birth certificates, and divorce decrees to create Children's Trust Funds to support programs to prevent abuse, neglect, and family violence.[53]

At the local level, cities such as San Francisco and Boston have required commercial developers to put money into low-income housing and child-care trust funds on the principle that new office buildings create social needs. Other communities have added surcharges to property and sales taxes to support libraries and programs to serve the homeless, or have expressly created special taxing districts to finance programs for children. Although not dissimilar in their legal structure from school districts—and other special purpose districts—these taxing entities expressly generate revenues for health and social services. Palm Beach County voters, for example, created an independent taxing district in 1986, establishing a Children's Services Council as its policymaking body to plan, coordinate, fund, and evaluate programs for children. Among the priorities defined by the council in its first year of operations were substance abuse prevention, child care, and teen-pregnancy programs.[54]

Earmarking places the burden of program support on a clearly identifiable source of payment. We have noted some of the general implications of this arrangement for contributory programs, where the taxpayer is also the recipient of benefits, as in social security. In programs where tax payers *don't* benefit directly, earmarking may elicit less popular support, although creatively linking taxes and programs can substantially allay taxpayer resistance.

Attaching revenues to programs, however, can be hazardous if it undermines the ability of policymakers to utilize revenues flexibly for priority needs. Linking programs to special taxes makes an overall, integrated, planning, and budgeting process difficult to maintain. Earmarking, in addition, is not likely to help disadvantaged groups with poor reputations, or unpopular causes—voters are hardly likely, for example, to target taxes for welfare payments or affirmative action. Finally, the automatic nature of earmarking means that the magnitude and character of program spending may be driven by the amount of money generated, rather than by changing needs.

Taxes and Behavior

Traditionally, public policy attention has focused on the ways taxes influence economic (particularly saving and investment) behaviors. But taxes also affect important *social* behaviors, such as when people retire, how much they save for it, whether they have children or care for dependent relatives, their philanthropic activity, and so forth. In contrast to regulatory legislation (such as Prohibition) that directly outlaws certain kinds of behavior, taxes influence how people act through economic incentives. Certain activities are discouraged by making them costly; others are encouraged by making them inexpensive.[55] Activities that are socially detrimental can be reduced by heavy taxes; desirable behaviors can be promoted by light taxes, or no taxes at all.

Taxation, for example, has been used internationally as a means of population policy. Along with children's allowances, tax policies can reward larger families. In France and the Netherlands, most notably, tax rates at all levels of income are negatively correlated with family size.[56] Even in the United States, the federal income tax provides a modest reward for extra children through the personal exemption. Although taxes can further "populationist" policies, of course, they can equally promote "reproductive nonproliferation." In 1979, for example, China enacted its first baby tax on couples having three or more children, imposing wage reductions up to 10 percent for the birth of a third child and as much as 20 percent for a fifth child. Small families, conversely, were rewarded with low taxes *and* preferential treatment with respect to pensions, housing, jobs, and schooling.[57]

Income tax deductions can be used to encourage families to care for ill or dependent relatives. Long-term care is an overriding need of many older people. Although programs such as social security, Title XX, and Medicaid provide important public support, many families caring for their parents, or other relatives, still face enormous financial and emotional burdens. In recent years, the magnitude of these costs, and the belief that home care is better than institutional care, has resulted in many tax proposals. But only a few have been enacted. Most notably, Congress changed the child-care credit in 1971 into the dependent-care tax credit to encourage at-home care. Presently, about 10 percent of all claims are for adult (mainly elderly) dependents.[58] Several states also give tax relief to families caring for elderly relatives.

Tax policy can encourage other salutary behaviors. California, for example, permits taxpayers to deduct child adoption expenses that exceed 3 percent of their adjusted gross income; this limitation is waived for families adopting "hard to place" (disabled or older) children. Work behavior is frequently encouraged by making different kinds of work-related expenses deductible. And several states have devised tax schemes to help parents save for their children's college educations.

Just as tax policies encourage some activities, they discourage others. Excise taxes, in particular, are widely used to control behaviors that are viewed as harmful. In the United States, for example, excises on cigarettes and alcohol are levied at federal, state, and local levels. Although such taxes are often simply a way of raising additional revenue, or "punishing" people for bad conduct (thus the phrase "sin tax"), they also serve as a behavioral disincentive, rewarding those who eschew an undesirable, socially damaging product.

Most countries levy excises on alcohol, tobacco, and gambling. Beverage taxes are used worldwide to control alcohol consumption, and Finland, Czechoslovakia, France, Norway, Sweden, and Switzerland all explicitly utilize excises to reduce drinking. Furthermore, in these countries, and others, beverages are taxed differentially with the highest alcohol content subject to the heaviest levies in an effort to shift consumption from hard liquor to beer and wine.[59]

In the United States, the federal government has levied alcohol excises since the 1790s. Prior to the imposition of the federal income tax in 1913, alcohol excises constituted the federal government's main revenue source, supplying nearly two-thirds of all Treasury receipts. Despite periodic increases in alcohol excises in the years since, the overall trend, until quite recently, was steeply downward. Thus, in 1984, alcohol excises comprised less than 1 percent of all federal revenues. Since then, however, these low rates have received considerable criticism, largely as a result of increasingly clear evidence of the positive correlation that exists between social costs and drinking behavior. Although drinking habits are not easily changed, recent data suggest that alcohol taxes not only reduce alcohol sales and consumption, but also affect alcohol-related problems, such as auto fatalities and cirrhosis mortality. The effects are modest, but real.[60] Although critics argue that alcohol demand is relatively "inelastic"—that is, not responsive to price, especially for heavy users—support for tax increases has been growing. In 1984, for example, the federal tax on hard spirits was raised substantially, from $10.50 to $12.50 per proof gallon, and in 1991, it rose to its present value of $13.50 per gallon. States impose their own alcohol taxes on top of this.

Other detrimental behaviors can also be restrained. Cigarette taxes have increased as the association between tobacco and disease has become known. In 1982, the federal excise tax on a pack of cigarettes doubled from 8 cents to 16 cents; in 1993 it reached 24 cents. Moreover, all fifty states tax cigarettes, with the rates per pack ranging from a low of 2 cents (North Carolina) to a high of 40 cents (Connecticut). In addition, nearly 400 local governments levy cigarette taxes, ranging up to 10 cents per pack.[61] In Norway, taxation is near draconian, with 85 percent of the price of a pack of cigarettes composed of taxes and fees. In Canada, the price per pack is approaching $7 in some provinces.[62]

Much of the impetus for increased tobacco taxes has come from public health organizations, such as the American Medical Association, the American Heart Association, the American Lung Association, and the American Cancer Society. According to the Coalition on Smoking and Health, every 10 percent increase in the price of cigarettes decreases cigarette consumption among young people by about 4 percent. And the General Accounting Office, in a 1989 report that reviewed the impact of taxes on smoking, concluded that raising the federal cigarette excise tax by 20 cents would result in half a million fewer smokers, and 125,000 fewer "premature deaths."[63]

Taxes on beer, cigarettes, and gambling are often attacked for their regressive nature, and it is undeniable that they do impose a far greater burden on people with lower incomes. It is estimated, for example, that alcohol taxes absorb five times as much of the income of households with incomes under $15,000 than they do of over-$50,000 households. Nevertheless, it is shortsighted to dismiss the social value of excises. First of all, excise taxes can be enacted as part of broader tax packages that include balancing progressive measures. Second, excises can themselves be progressively structured—alcohol taxes, for example, can be linked to the price of the beverage so that, for example, drinkers of an expensive scotch such as Chivas Regal pay higher rates than those imbibing Bud Lite. Finally, although sin taxes may fall disproportionately on poor and middle-income U.S. residents, these groups make up most of the victims of cigarettes and liquor. Increased taxes *may* be burdensome; more importantly, however, they save suffering and lives.

Summary

The public, voluntary, and for-profit funding systems constitute a three-tiered "mixed economy" of welfare that provides a high degree of choice in meeting the social welfare needs of the U.S. public. The ways in which these financing arrangements operate have major impacts on issues of equity and accountability. Professional social service workers must be equipped with an understanding of these different funding arrangements because they constitute the critical foundation of the resources available to meet human needs.

Notes

1. American Association of Fund-Raising Counsel, *Giving USA, 1996* (New York: AAFRC), 37.

2. Ibid., 73–75. Figures are for 1995.

3. Gordon Manser, "The Voluntary Agency— Contribution or Survival?" *Washington Bulletin,* 22(20) (October 1971), 107; *Voluntary Giving and Tax Policy* (New York: National Assembly for Social Policy and Development, 1972).

4. William S. Vickrey, "One Economist's View of Philanthropy," in Frank G. Dickinson (ed.), *Philanthropy and Public Policy* (New York, National Bureau of Economic Research, 1962).

5. Ralph Kramer, *Voluntary Agencies in the Welfare State* (Berkeley, University of California Press, 1981), 193–211.

6. For example, see Oscar Handlin, *The Uprooted* (New York: Oxford University Press, 1964).

7. For example, see C. Wendell King, *Social Movements in the United States* (New York: Free Press, 1957).

8. Charles Richard Henderson, "The Place and Functions of Voluntary Associations," *American Journal of Sociology, 1* (November 1895), 334–39.

9. Kramer, *Voluntary Agencies in the Welfare State,* 173–192.

10. Peter Marris and Martin Rein, *Dilemmas of Social Reform: Poverty and Community Action in the United States* (New York: Atherton, 1967). For a dramatic account of how foundations undertake projects that the government may abjure because of political considerations, see Thomas C. Reeves, *Freedom and the Foundation: The Fund for the Republic in the Era of McCarthyism* (New York: Alfred A. Knopf, 1969).

11. Alvin L. Schorr, "The Task for Voluntarism in the Next Decade," presented at the Centenary Conference on Voluntary Organization in the 1970s, sponsored by the Family Welfare Association, University of Sussex, Brighton, England (June 1969). Schorr cites five pioneering ventures of the 1960s, which he notes were largely inspired and set in motion by government: the juvenile delinquency programs, community action, amendments to the Social Security Act, community care of the mentally ill, and the Model Cities Program.

12. Kramer, *Voluntary Agencies in the Welfare State,* 242–247.

13. This example is based on the article by Herman Levin, "The Future of Voluntary Family and Children's Social Work: An Historical View," *Social Service Review, 38*(2) (June 1964), 164–73.

14. Salvatore Ambrosino, "Family Service Agencies," *Encyclopedia of Social Work,* 17th edition (New York: NASW, 1977), 429.

15. Herman Levin, "Voluntary Agencies in Social Welfare," *Encyclopedia of Social Work,* 17th edition (New York: NASW, 1977), 1574.

16. "Social Work Unit Changing Tactics," *New York Times,* January 29, 1971, 1.

17. *Giving USA 1996,* 36.

18. Arlien Johnson, "Public Funds for Voluntary Agencies," *Social Welfare Forum, 1959* (New York: Columbia University Press, 1959).

19. The Non Profit Times, *The NPT 100—America's Biggest Nonprofits,* November 1996, 38–39.

20. Ralph Kramer, "Voluntary Agencies and the Personal Social Services," in Walter W. Powell (ed.), *The Handbook of Non-Profit Organizations* (Cambridge, MA: Yale University Press, 1985).

21. Elizabeth Wickenden, "Purchase of Care and Services: Effect on Voluntary Agencies," in *Proceedings of the First Milwaukee Institute on a Social Welfare Issue of the Day* (Milwaukee: School of Social Welfare, July 1970).

22. Ira Glasser, "Prisoners of Benevolence: Power vs. Liberty in the Welfare State," in Willard Gaylin, Ira Glasser, Steven Marcus, and David I. Rothman, *Doing Good: The Benefits of Benevolence* (New York: Pantheon Books, 1978), 110.

23. Austin W. Scott, "Charitable Trusts," *Encyclopedia of the Social Sciences,* Vol. III, Edwin R. A. Seligman et al. (eds.) (New York: Macmillan, 1937), 338–40.

24. The Tax Reform Act of 1969 made the prohibition on social and political action even more stringent for organizations classified as "private foundations" by removing the qualifying word, "substantial."

25. See *General Explanation of the Tax Reform Act,* 9162, H. R. 13270, Public Law 91-1972 (Washington, D.C.: Government Printing Office, 1970), 48–49.

26. For a detailed discussion of the concept of charitable immunity, see George W. Keeton, *The Modern Law of Charities* (London: Sir Isaac Pitman and Sons, Ltd., 1962).

27. *Giving USA 1996,* 42.

28. Warren Weaver, *U.S. Philanthropic Foundations* (New York: Harper & Row, 1967), 11 and 23; see also Julius Rosenwald, "Principles of Giving," *The Atlantic Monthly,* May 1929; and Wilmer Shields Rich, "Community Foundations in the U.S. and Canada" (New York: National Council on Foundations, 1961).

29. For a detailed history of the Girard College case, see Milton M. Gordon, "The Girard College Case: Desegregation and a Municipal Trust," *The Annals of the American Academy of Political and Social Science,* March 1956, 53–62.

30. For further discussion of *cy pres* see Keeton, *The Modern Law of Charities,* and Edith L. Fisch, *The Cy Pres Doctrine in the United States* (New York: Matthew Bender and Co., 1950), 141–42. On the general controlling legal principle as applied to Girard College, see "Validity and Effect of Gifts for Charitable Purposes Which Exclude Otherwise Qualified Beneficiaries Because of Race or Religion," in 25 ALR 3d 736 (1969).

31. For a discussion of varying conceptions of "social need" see Jonathan Bradshaw, "The Concept of Social Need," in Neil Gilbert and Harry Specht (eds.), *Planning for Social Welfare: Issues, Models, and Tasks* (Englewood Cliffs, NJ: Prentice Hall, 1977), 290–96.

32. Waldemar A. Nielsen, *The Big Foundations* (New York: Columbia University Press, 1972), 32.

33. Ray H. Elling and Sandor Halebsky, "Support for Public and Private Services," in Mayer N. Zald (ed.), *Social Welfare Institutions* (New York: John Wiley and Sons, 1965), 329.

34. For example, see the following: United Bay Area Crusade, *New Directions Report,* San Francisco, CA (June 1971); United Community Fund of Greater Toronto, *Reexamination Project,* Toronto, Ontario, Canada (May 1971); United Foundation, *Priorities Study,* Detroit, MI (April 1971); United Community Services of San Diego County, *UCS Implementation Program* (November 1971); and Bertram M. Beck, "The Voluntary Social Welfare Agency: A Reassessment," *Social Service Review, 44*(2) (June 1970), 147–54.

35. Stanley Wenocur, Richard V. Cook and Nancy L. Stekelee, "Fund-Raising at the Workplace," *Social Policy, 14*(4) (Spring 1984), 55.

36. John Pierson, "I Gave at the Office," *Foundation News,* September 1986.

37. See, for example, the articles in Michael Novak (ed.), *To Empower People: From State to Civil Society,* 2d edition (Washington D.C., AEI Press, 1996).

38. Lester Salamon, "Nonprofit Organizations— The Lost Opportunity," in John Palmer and Isabel Sawhill (eds.), *The Reagan Record* (Washington D.C., The Urban Institute, 1984) 261–285.

39. Neil Gilbert, "The Transformation of the Social Services," *Social Service Review, 51*(4) (December 1977), 628.

40. For an analysis of public views toward OASDHI and unemployment insurance, see Michael E. Schlitz, *Public Attitudes Toward Social Security 1935–1965* (Washington, D.C.: U.S. Government Printing Office, 1970).

41. Daniel Cherkin, "The Effect of Office Visit Co-Payments on Utilization in a Health Maintenance Organization," *Medical Care,* July 1989.

42. Eveline M. Burns, *Social Security and Public Policy* (New York: McGraw-Hill, 1956), 157.

43. Charitable contributions are allowed as an itemized deduction, generally up to 50 percent of a filer's adjusted gross income. Because lower income taxpayers generally select the "standard" deduction, rather than itemizing, the deduction is substantially restricted to richer individuals and families.

44. Douglas Besharov, "Fixing the Child Care Credit," *Harvard Journal on Legislation, 26*(2) Summer 1981, 509.

45. Daniel Weinberg, "The Distributional Implications of Tax Expenditures," *National Tax Journal, XL*(2), June 1987, 237–54.

46. Isabel Sawhill, quoted in Urban Institute, *Policy and Research Report,* Winter/Spring 1990, 28.

47. Joseph Pechman, "The Future of the Income Tax," *The American Economic Review, 80*(1), March 1990, 16.

48. Taxable income constitutes about 55 percent of total personal income. See U.S. Advisory Commission on Intergovernmental Relations, *Facts and Figures on Government Finance,* Table C41, 1990, 130.

49. For an assessment of the redistributive effects of tax and spending programs, see Joseph Pechman, *The Rich, the Poor, and the Taxes They Pay* (Washington D.C., The Brookings Institution, 1986) 19–30.

50. Joseph Pechman, *Social Security: Perspectives for Reform* (Washington D.C., Brookings Institution, 1968). Eveline M. Burns, *Social Security and Public Policy* (New York, McGraw-Hill, 1956). Richard M. Titmuss, *Essays on "The Welfare State"* (London, Allen & Unwin, 1958).

51. Pechman, "The Future of the Income Tax," 3.

52. U.S. Congressional Budget Office, "The Changing Distribution of Federal Taxes, 1977– 1990," U.S. House of Representatives, Ways and Means Committee, March 26, 1990. See also Citizens for Tax Justice, *Inequality and the Federal Budget Deficit,* March 1990.

53. Thomas Birch, *Children's Trust Funds: An Update,* National Committee for Preventing Child Abuse, 1984. See also Ronald K. Snells, "Earmarking State Tax Revenues," *Intergovernmental Perspective, 16*(4), Fall 1990, 12–16.

54. Healthy Children Report, *Special Taxing Districts for Children,* Harvard University Division of Health Policy, 1988.

55. Charles Lindblom refers to "tax inducements" and "tax punishments." See his "The Market as Prison," *Journal of Politics, 44*(2), May 1982.

56. Harvey E. Brazer, "Income Tax Treatment of the Family," in Henry J. Aaron and Michael J. Boskin (eds.), *The Economics of Taxation* (Washington, D.C.: Brookings, 1980), 223.

57. *International Family Planning Perspectives,* November 1979.

58. U.S. General Accounting Office, *Assessment of the Use of Tax Credits for Families Who Provide Health Care to Disabled Elderly Relatives,* August 27, 1982, 3.

59. Mavis M. Brown, Margo F. Dewar, and Paul Wallace, *International Survey of Alcohol Beverage Taxation and Control Policies,* 5th Edition, Brewers Association of Canada, November 1982, 378.

60. Philip J. Cook, "The Effect of Liquor Taxes on Drinking, Cirrhosis, and Auto Fatalities," in M. H. Moore and D. Gerstein (eds.), *Alcohol and Public Policy: Beyond the Shadow of*

Prohibition (Washington, D.C.: National Academy of Sciences), 256.

61. *The Taxation of Cigarettes, Alcoholic Beverages and Parimutuel Wagering Activity in California,* State of California Legislative Analyst, Sacramento, October 1981, 7, 9.

62. See, for example, "Canadians Fired Up Over Cigarette Tax," *San Francisco Chronicle,* May 16, 1991, and "A Clamor in Norway to Ban All Smoking," *New York Times,* May 4, 1991.

63. U.S. General Accounting Office, *Teenage Smoking,* GAO/HRD-89-111, June 1989.

Chapter *8*

The Mode of Finance: Systems of Transfer

"We are committed to getting power back to the states, we are committed to breaking out of the logjam of Federal bureaucrats controlling how we try to help the poor, and we believe you can trust the 50 states and the 50 state legislatures to work together on behalf of the citizens of their states."

NEWT GINGRICH
House Welfare Debate, August 1, 1996

"Subsidiarity enthusiasts are often quite two-faced. When there is a social problem they really think is pressing, they tend to lose their enthusiasm for turning it over to the states. Although crime is traditionally a matter for state and local governments, politicians in Washington compete vigorously to federalize the most categories of criminal behavior and spend the most out of the federal Treasury to build prisons. . . . Don't get me wrong. The states are nice to have around. I live in one myself. But 'turn it over to the states' is a trivial answer to any policy puzzle—even when it happens to be correct."

MICHAEL KINSLEY
"THE CASE AGAINST THE STATES,"
Time Magazine, January 16, 1995

The political system of the United States divides power in two major ways—horizontally, among the executive, legislative, and judicial branches, and vertically, among the different levels of government. In this chapter it is the *vertical* dimension that is of primary concern because financing the U.S. welfare state is substantially a matter of national, state, and local relationships. And although the federal level, given its national scope and institutional authority, is certainly preeminent among the three, jurisdiction over the public programs and services that meet this country's social needs is broadly distributed. Some programs are exclusively the responsibility of one level. Social security, Medicare, and veterans' programs, for example, are entirely federal in their funding and operations whereas General Assistance, libraries, and education are almost fully state and/or local. Other programs operate *intergovernmentally*, under combined authority. States, for example, share substantial authority with the federal government in Medicaid and Title XX whereas federal-city partnerships govern programs for housing and the homeless.

The balance of authority over social welfare programs typically parallels the balance of financial responsibility. Although numerous arrangements exist for transferring funds from their source of origin—the governmental unit collecting revenues—to the point of service delivery—the governmental unit spending them—it is usually the primary funder that exercises primary control. "He who pays the piper calls the tune" is quite the appropriate aphorism.

Two major questions of finance that are paramount in structuring intergovernmental arrangements for social welfare are how money flows and how money is conditioned. The question of *flow* deals with the fashion in which public moneys are transformed from being revenues to being outlays. This is often described in terms of funding streams. The question of *conditions* deals with the priorities, stipulations, and regulations that are placed on the flow of money from one governmental level to another.

Before one can understand the nature of these fiscal choices, however, their ideological context must be considered.

Centralization, Decentralization, and their Ideologies

Given the size and diversity of our federal system, the balance between centralization (power concentrated nationally) and decentralization (power devolved to state and local governments and institutions) is a perennial issue. In the design of social welfare policy, values and assumptions related to decentralization and centralization generally are expressed in choices concerning pluralism versus uniformity, small versus large. In the past twenty-five years, ideals of decentralization have been ascendant. Since the Reagan era, in particular, important service responsibilities have been returned to the level of the states and localities. Although these units have been generally eager to increase their program authority, they have been less prepared to cope with fiscal retrenchment and federal aid cutbacks, and their record with respect to social investment and social sensitivity has been mixed. Although the consequences for the poor of reduced federal control are far from uniform, the combination of decentralization and funding reductions has clearly harmed those dependent on public assistance and social services.

This is not to deny the values of decentralization. Local governments are often more knowledgeable than large centralized units about problems in their areas and more responsive to the special needs of their constituencies. In addition, small units can more easily experiment, and if they fail, all is not lost. Indeed, losses suffered through the failure of one unit's experiment may be compensated for by the lessons of successful alternatives. Finally, there is an existential quality about small decentralized units that is appealing. They lend themselves more readily to visions of the *Gemeinschaft* marked by warm meaningful relationships and a sense of belonging to a vibrant, caring, manageable community.[1]

Conservative theorists, in Europe and America, have articulated thoughtful visions of the role localities can play in the modern welfare state. The idea of "subsidiarity" has gained particular attention in Europe as social policy there has evolved into a three-tiered system of governance with new powers given to Europe-wide institutions such as the Council of Europe. Subsidiarity refers to the principle that although different public functions are appropriate for different governmental levels, action should be carried out at the lowest level where it can be performed effectively.

The devolution argument, as we have seen, is advanced not only by federalists who wish to see more authority given to states and localities but by conservatives who extol the responsiveness and efficiency of *private* institutions—individuals, families, voluntary associations, and the marketplace. Theorists from libertarian think tanks, for example, have called for limitations on *all* levels of government action through tax restrictions and the privatization of public functions. Both versions of decentralization see bigness as the enemy, both view society's smaller, more "organic," units as natural reflections of the true public interest.

Although many of these arguments are cogent, they often ignore the limitations of decentralization. As Chapter 2 indicated, the national welfare state emerged as a result of the incapacity of local institutions—public and private—to address twentieth-century problems of poverty and insecurity. In the United States, the federal government—not states, localities, private charities, or the marketplace—responded to the crisis of the Great Depression, securing broad economic gains for ordinary citizens. And it was the federal government again, in the 1960s, that advanced civil rights and social protections for the impoverished and the excluded.

National action has been necessary for many reasons. For one thing, localism can be parochial and oppressive. Privacy and freedom may shelter more securely in the cold impersonality of large centralized units. As McConnell argues:

> *Impersonality is the guarantee of individual freedom characteristic of the large unit. Impersonality means an avoidance of arbitrary official action, the following of prescribed procedure, conformance to established rules, and escape from bias whether for or against any individual. Impersonality, and the privacy and freedom it confers, may be despised, and the human warmth and community concern for the personal affairs of individuals characteristic of the small community preferred. Nevertheless, the values involved are different, and are to a considerable degree antagonistic.[2]*

The defense of minority interests within small units is often more difficult to achieve than within larger units. In small units it is easier to weld a cohesive majority that may disregard the interests of others or that bring great pressure for conformity to bear. "States rights" ideologies, for example, were long used to protect the power and privileges of whites in the South. Through the 1970s, indeed,

---

CAPSULE 8.1:   The State Record on Child Protection

At least 21 states are under court supervision because they failed to take proper care of children who had been abused or neglected, and many of them have flouted their obligations even after promising in legal settlements to protect the constitutional rights of foster children, court records show.

Judges across the country have found what Judge Thomas F. Hogan of Federal District Court here describes as "outrageous deficiencies" in child protection services. Child welfare officials in many states, swamped with work, are slow to investigate reports of child abuse and neglect. They often place children in unsafe or overcrowded foster homes and provide them inadequate medical care. They afford few of the social services needed to keep families together or reunite them. And they are delinquent in finding adoptive parents for children languishing in foster care.

The Federal Government provides $4 billion a year to the states for child protection services. The National Governors' Association recently urged Congress to let each state take its share as a lump sum, or block grant, with more freedom to decide how the money is spent. But the Clinton Administration says it would be foolish to reduce Federal supervision and enforcement, in view of the abysmal conditions brought to light in many lawsuits.

State responses to the suits vary widely. In Alabama, conditions for abused and neglected children have improved considerably as the state carries out a consent decree approved by a Federal district judge four years ago. Paul Vincent, director of the Alabama Division of Family and Children's Services, said the state now provided extensive training to foster parents and caseworkers, who in the past received "little or no formal training." "The kids are safer," he said. "Protective service workers are doing better jobs." In Missouri, by contrast, Judge Dean Whipple of Federal District Court found state officials in contempt for failing to carry out a court-approved consent decree protecting foster children in the Kansas City area. The failure, he said, resulted from the officials' "lack of commitment to make a good-faith effort to make the consent decree work."

Children removed from the homes of their biological parents are deemed to be in state custody, whether they live in state institutions or with foster parents. Federal courts have repeatedly ruled that such children are protected by the 14th Amendment, which says that no state shall "deprive any person of life, liberty or property without due process of law."

Robert Pear, "Many States Fail to Meet Mandates on Child Welfare," *The New York Times,* March 16, 1996, A1, A14.

"states rights" remained the battle cry of segregationists such as George Wallace, Orval Faubus, and the racist White Citizens' Councils. Up until the present time, indeed, African Americans and other minorities have looked to the federal government not only to support their rights against hostile or indifferent states and localities, but also to promote programs of social and economic assistance. Historically, larger centralized units have been more progressive and more likely to support reform.

National units, moreover, command greater resources; some problems are simply beyond the scope of secondary bodies. State and local revenue systems are often deficient. Constrained by regressive tax systems, the fear of losing businesses and affluent taxpayers to rival jurisdictions with lower tax rates, and an increasing proliferation of spending limits, they lack the wherewithal to address pressing needs. Their technical and administrative capacity, despite vast improvements since the 1960s, are often inadequate, with poorly trained and badly paid personnel more the rule than the exception. State and local units, by their very nature, can do little to effect problems of national scope. Generally speaking, for example, redistributive programs must be financed by progressive taxes levied by large governmental units. Only the federal government can levy taxes in all jurisdictions at once, so only the federal government is able to bring about significant redistribution in income or services.

The decentralization of authority also results in a troubling degree of variation in local social welfare efforts. Having significant diversity in state and local activities may reflect a salutary degree of pluralism, but it also blocks a national approach to problems and can result in substantial discrepancies in benefit arrangements from place to place. Perhaps the most dramatic example of this is the variation in public aid payments. In 1994, for example, maximum benefits for a family of three in Alaska were five times as high as in Alabama. Although the federal government modifies this discrepancy a bit through the food stamp program, which has uniform nationwide eligibility and benefit standards, the gap between high-payment and low-payment states in this, and other program areas, remains dramatic.[3]

The more general critique of decentralization, of course, is that it tends to reduce the emphasis on helping the poor. Historically speaking, in this country, and in others, it has been national leadership that has evidenced the greatest degree of concern with society's disadvantaged and vulnerable. Although it is difficult to characterize the multitude of state and local policies with glib generalizations, it is certainly clear that, for the most part, they have often been less-than-willing, and perhaps financially less-than-able, to undertake an effective social agenda.

How the Money Flows

How, exactly, *should* the United States face the question of dividing political, administrative, and fiscal powers and responsibilities among governments at different geographical levels? Should policymakers rely heavily on national decision-making, or should regional and local control be the rule? Can a system somehow combine the best features of both arrangements?

In establishing its own system of differentiation, the United States devised a unique answer to the question of structure and balance—American federalism. The federal division of powers between the national capital and the states, formulated in the Constitution in 1789, has remained the fundamental legal framework of local–national relations. The concept, of course, has evolved considerably over the years. At first it referred to an arrangement of "dual sovereignty" in which the different levels of government operated more or less separately, each with a large amount of autonomy. Today, federalism is characterized by a

---

CAPSULE 8.2:   The Decentralization Amendment

The powers not delegated to the United States by the Constitution, nor prohibited by it to the States, are reserved to the States respectively, or to the people.

10th Amendment to the U.S. Constitution, Declared in Force, December 15, 1791.

substantial measure of cooperative activity. Indeed, when we speak of federalism nowadays we are really speaking of *intergovernmental relations,* of different levels of government jointly formulating, operating, and financing domestic policies. The foremost instrument of modern federal relations is the intergovernmental grant-in-aid, commonly known as federal aid.[4]

Federal grant programs express the common interest of localities, states, and the national government in addressing common purposes in a cooperative fashion. The federal government, taking financial leadership, provides money to states and localities for the conduct of particular types of programs. In this fashion, federal aid is both a fiscal and a policy device for collective decision making. The *purpose* of aid programs is defined by Congress, often in very broad terms, whereas actual program *implementation* is the responsibility of states and localities. And because states and localities run the programs, and often share in their financing, they have a great deal of influence over their character. State and local participation, it is important to note, is fully voluntary. The core of the federal relationship, in other words, is built on cooperation, not coercion, on preserving local diversity within a framework of nationally shared values.

Although federal cash grants to states date back to 1879, their importance as a basic organizing instrument for social welfare didn't emerge until the New Deal. When the Social Security Act became law in 1935, for example, all but two of its dozen or so programs were organized and financed through grants-in-aid. Aid to Dependent Children, Aid to the Blind, and Old Age Assistance, the three programs that established the United State's basic public assistance system, were all formulated as grants-in-aid. Other titles of the act provided aid to states for maternal and child welfare services, for crippled children, and for vocational rehabilitation.

In the 1960s, the second major era in the development of the U.S. welfare state, Congress again relied on the grant-in-aid principle. Except for Medicare, all the principal social programs enacted as part of the Great Society followed the federal format—financial aid from Washington in exchange for program commitments by states and localities. Lyndon Johnson, like Roosevelt before him, used federal money to promote national purposes by enlarging and diversifying the scope of state and local programs. During the 1960s, however, greater stress than before was focused on antipoverty and urban programs, and more and more federal dollars went *directly* to cities rather than (as before) almost exclusively to states. In some instances, indeed, such as the community action programs of the War on Poverty, aid was funneled directly to private nongovernmental community organizations at the neighborhood level, bypassing both states *and* cities.

Today, the vast majority of America's social programs are multilevel partnerships. Only in a few areas of social welfare policy (mainly social insurance, programs for Native Americans, and veterans' affairs) does the national government have sole responsibility. States, for example, are the responsible program partner in mental health, social services, and Medicaid. Local governments take principal responsibility for operating aid programs in elementary and secondary education, community development, urban mass transit, and employment/training. State programs are generally administered at the federal level by the Department of Health and Human Services whereas city and county programs are generally administered by the Department of Housing and Urban Development.

As Table 8.1 indicates, grant policy has evolved somewhat fitfully over the past 40 years. During the years of the Great Society, the number, size, and relative importance of federal grants grew rapidly. Indeed, in 1964, 1965, and 1966 a total of 198 new federal grants were authorized. During the decade of the 1960s, grant outlays more than tripled, from $7 billion to $24 billion annually, making state and local governments increasingly dependent on federal aid as a source of revenue. The federal aid budget, measured in constant dollars, peaked in 1978 and then declined. Grant outlays in some program areas dropped quite dramatically. Between 1980 and 1985, for example, social services were reduced by 25 percent, urban renewal by 67 percent, and training and employment by 69 percent. By the middle of the Reagan years—1985—the overall level of federal aid as a portion of the federal domestic budget had fallen to that of the early 1960s.

But although the level of support has fallen, the principle of federal-state-local partnerships has never been stronger. Given the fundamentally centralizing trends that characterize modern society, this *is* surprising. The endurance of the states is *particularly* surprising, given the many predictions over the course of this

TABLE 8.1   Federal Grants-In-Aid, Selected Years

	Amount (in Billions of Dollars)	As % of Federal Domestic Outlays	As % of State–Local Outlays	Number of Grant Programs
1950	$ 2.3	11.6%	10.4%	60
1960	$ 7.0	20.6%	14.5%	130
1970	$ 24.1	25.3%	19.0%	400
1980	$ 91.5	23.3%	25.8%	540
1990	$122.0	18.7%	17.3%	450
1994	$217.3	22.3%	23.0%	640

Source: U.S. Advisory Commission on Intergovernmental Relations, *Significant Features of Fiscal Federalism, 1994*, Volume 2, USGPO.

century that their days as viable units of government were numbered. In 1933, for example, Luther Gulik, an eminent scholar of government, wrote:

> *In the state the appropriate instrumentality for the discharge of . . . important functions? The answer is not a matter of conjecture or delicate appraisal. It is a matter of brutal record. I do not predict that the states will go. I affirm that they have already gone.*[5]

Gulick's view represented a dominant theme of the Great Depression years, one which found the states unprepared to deal with the enormous economic and social problems facing the nation. The states, primarily rurally oriented, did not seem to have the financial, administrative, or leadership powers required to deal with the effects of the depression, which fell most heavily on urban areas. And the centralization of power that occurred under Roosevelt and, later Johnson, *did* significantly change U.S. politics, for a while at least, making "the White House, not the State House . . . the fountainhead of ideas, the initiator of action, the representative of the national interest."[6]

Transfers and Politics

The power to implement and administer programs, it must be noted, carries with it not only a degree of control over the nature of provisions, the bases of allocations, and the systems of service delivery, but also *political* power. The transfer of program funds confers the ability to dispense benefits to a constituency, to hire and appoint staff, and to award contracts. Apart from programmatic choices, therefore, the transfer of funds among governmental units represents the exchange of important political resources.

The Great Society, revenue sharing, and block grants all illustrate how political coalitions are a consideration in transfers. Both the Office of Economic Opportunity (OEO) and Model Cities, directed at urban areas, enhanced big-city mayors and their constituencies. In OEO, the system of transfer reflected the desires of the Democratic party to link itself with newly developing voting blocks in the cities, particularly with minority groups. Model Cities, a variation on this theme, pushed the development of new coalitions between low-income and minority residents and city hall. (We will point out in the next chapter how developments in Model Cities reflected the interest of the federal government in increasing the power of executive-centered government in cities.)

Revenue sharing and block grants, although not ignoring cities, usually had little in the way of a special urban emphasis. The term *general revenue sharing* refers to arrangements whereby the federal government makes grants to lower units of government with virtually no strings attached whereas block grants are federal aid programs that place only limited conditions on recipient units. The development of both kinds of programs during and after the Nixon era offers a final example of how the system of transfer reflects political coalitions.

In the 1970s and 1980s, the thrust toward decentralization was a clear political priority of Republican national administrations. The Republicans inherited a vast conglomeration of categorical programs from their Democratic Great Society predecessors. Because these programs were established in law, tradition, and experience, and were supported by an elaborate organizational and institutional apparatus, the Republicans had to live with them temporarily while attempting to contain and modify them with an eye to their reduction, and, at least in some cases, their ultimate elimination. Low-income and minority groups in urban areas did not represent a major segment of the Republican constituency. State governments were more likely to reflect Republican interests and to represent important parts of the Republican constituency. Therefore, revenue sharing with the states was of greater interest to Republicans than to Democrats.

We have described the flow of money as though it represents a simple exchange between two parties, but this is not always the case. Several actors may be involved, and the benefits to each may vary. For example, OEO legislation required that funds to local CAPs be approved by the state's governor. Thus, governors could exercise some control over the transfer. Similarly, in Model Cities, funds had to "pass through" the city, giving the mayors some control over expenditures. In both programs, "guidelines" (that is the rules set down on the basis of administrative discretion) required "sign-offs" from various local, state, and federal agencies, meaning that funding required their general approval.

Transfers and Policy Analysis

Although political considerations may influence choices concerning the units to which funds will be given, some degree of scientific analysis also enters into these decisions. That is, technically, there are some identifiable characteristics of units that can be utilized in selecting the one most appropriate to receive funds. These characteristics include the degree of expertise and resources required to administer a program, the appropriate governmental size given the substantive nature of the program, and the nature of the problem for which a programmatic solution is being sought. However, application of these technical considerations requires the utmost care and scrutiny. Often, for each logical reason given to vest a program in one unit ("They will be more efficient," is one example) another equally compelling reason can be found to vest it in another unit ("They are more committed to the policy goals," or "They are closer to the problem.").

Moynihan's observations on a report by the Task Force on Jurisdiction and Structure of the State Study Commission for New York City illustrate how technical considerations apply to the allocation of program responsibility. Regarding the allocation of services, the Task Force suggested that rat control services be a central function, whereas service centers to provide information on poison control should be a local responsibility. In both cases Moynihan argued the reverse arrangements to be technically superior. As for rat control services he notes:

> *Given stable food and harborage, the model urban rat lives and dies in an area extending at most a few hundred feet. . . . [T]he urban rat is preeminently a neighborhood type, preferring when possible, never even to cross the street. As for rodent control, opinion is universal (as best I know) that the fundamental issue is how humanoids maintain their immediate surroundings. I cannot conceive a municipal service more suited to local control, nor one which more immediately calls on those qualities of citizenship which the Task Force describes as constituting in some degree a "quasi-governmental responsibility" toward the community. It comes down, alas, to the question of keeping lids on garbage cans. What better issue for Neighborhood Service Representatives to take up?[7]*

On the other hand, Poison Control Centers provide services that require great knowledge about the chemical nature of different substances that people might ingest as well as possible antidotes in cases where the chemicals are poisonous. Quick access by day or night to a tremendous bank of information is required. In light of these requirements, Moynihan suggests:

> *At the very least it should be a city function, although a good case could be made for making it regional, or perhaps national: one telephone number anywhere in the nation, putting the doctor through to a laboratory/computer facility that would provide the information fastest. The idea that such a function could be broken down into thirty to thirty-five separate centers, in New York City alone, each to be manned day and night is . . . not persuasive.[8]*

Finally, a major consideration in the flow of funds is whether lesser units should operate programs for which they have no financial responsibility. Here, the issue is how careful a unit will be in spending funds that they do not have to raise, and whether they will act in the financial interests of the granting authority. For example, one general critique of public assistance financing is that the federal government gives almost a blank check to the states by paying the major costs of a program in which the basic determinants of costs—the number of recipients and level of benefits—are decentralized.[9]

How Transfers Are Conditioned

Conservatives favor *localism* in the allocation of government funds. This is the heart of the devolutionary strategy which has dominated federal domestic policy in this generation. For conservatives, it is the states and localities that should have primary responsibilities for directing and administering social welfare programs, not "big government" in Washington.

Devolution—in theory and in practice—is a reaction to the centralizing trend of sixty years of grant-in-aid policy. Beginning in the 1930s, the focus of federal aid moved increasingly toward establishing national standards in the provision of income support and social services. In the 1960s, the Great Society established a nationally directed urban-focused system of social welfare provisions that utilized grant funds as primary instruments for social reform. Great Society programs not only expanded the total sum of grant aid available, they also ushered in new goals and procedures that significantly altered the character and balance of intergovernmental relations.

In terms of ultimate purpose, the programs of the 1960s sought to guarantee minimum levels of opportunity and well-being throughout the nation. Comprehensive (if not precise) statements of national welfare goals were incorporated in a framework of grant-funded services for the disadvantaged, especially the urban disadvantaged. Although the Great Society recognized the importance of utilizing community organizations as program partners in the planning and delivery of services, these new programs incorporated extensive and detailed federal regulations and substantial program monitoring and oversight.

The ideology underpinning the aid transfer programs of the Great Society generation was decidedly centralist. Program direction as well as program finance shifted to Washington. The nation's obligation to eliminate poverty was asserted. Administrative procedures were formulated to insure that national purposes were properly carried out. Presidents Kennedy and Johnson both knew how very easily social programs could sway off target when carried out by states and localities that were not fully committed to social objectives. Memories of Jim Crow and anti-urban policy biases were still fresh in the minds of Washington policymakers. Grant policies were therefore carefully formulated to insure that benefits were effectively routed to the needy. Controls and guidelines were highly detailed.

By the mid- to late-1970s, the Great Society era had run its course. Although the programs it spawned were maintained, for the most part, their underlying spirit, along with their substantial reliance on federal leadership, faded away. Confronted with a series of major managerial problems, and a new farther-to-the-right philosophical *zeitgeist*, federal policies acquired a different face. Federal control and program expansion were replaced by "devolution, disengagement, and decremental budgeting."[10] The Great Society was replaced by the New Federalism.

The New Federalism of Richard Nixon and Ronald Reagan initiated a transfer system that was far more heavily reliant on states and localities. Whereas Great Society programs expressly advanced specific national purposes, New Federalism grants were formulated as a means of helping state and local government accomplish *their* objectives. Federal interventionism was abdicated in favor of decentralized policymaking. Federal spending, federal control, and federal regulation were all sharply reduced.

The contrast between Great Society centralization and New Federalism devolution can be clearly seen in the basic components of the intergovernmental transfer of funds. Financial transfers, whatever their philosophical rationale, always impose a set of reciprocal relationships—aid is never provided without conditions. The conditions that are required—often called "strings" or "controls"—govern how the aid can and cannot be used.

There are four fundamental types of federal aid conditions: *program conditions,* which define the purpose of the grant; *financial conditions,* which govern the matching arrangements; *beneficiary conditions,* which determine who is eligible to be assisted; and *procedural conditions,* which specify planning, administrative, and reporting procedures. In each area, the character of grant policy has changed markedly over the past thirty-five years as the respective roles of federal, state, and local governments have been redefined.

Program Conditions

Federal aid laws generally specify the kinds of activities they are intended to support. We therefore have grants for nutrition, mental health, runaway centers, drug and alcohol abuse, special education, foster care, medical care, cash support for the poor, and so on. Historically, the great majority of grant-in-aid programs have been defined rather narrowly, which is why they are often referred to as *categorical* (i.e., they are targeted on specific issues or population groups). According to one recent program inventory, over 95 percent of all federal aid programs remain categorically specific.[11]

Programs are categorical when their basic purposes are specified in detail. Categorical grants specify *who* is to be served, *what* benefits they are to receive, and *how* the delivery system is to be organized. For this reason, AFDC was frequently identified as the prototype categorical program, although the term applied to many others. Categorical programs may specify any number of conditions, including requirements regarding certification and licensing of personnel, how recipients are to be interviewed, and appeals machinery to handle client complaints. Categorical funding, very clearly, ensures that the unit of government providing revenue substantially controls its expenditure.

Since the Great Society, the federal aid system has become considerably *less* categorical. This shift is in keeping with the conservative critique of the welfare state, which supports a reduction in the scope of big government. For conservatives, big government, especially centralized government, threatens democracy and efficiency because basic decisions are made in Washington rather than in local communities where, it is said, the problems "actually are." For devolutionists, categorical aid is wasteful, supporting programs in which there is no compelling national interest, and creating excessive red tape, paperwork, and regulation.

One major objection to the categorical system has been principally managerial: the great number of specific programs are often-times difficult to administer effectively at the local level. It has been said that although individual programs make individual sense, the *aggregate* of programs produce administrative overload. Each program is usually separately administered. Coordination is absent. In many cases a mayor or governor may not even be aware of all the programs serving their jurisdiction. When they *are* aware, they often find themselves powerless to make the system work as a whole.

To deal with these concerns, the Republican presidents of the 1970s and 1980s sought to *decategorize* federal aid. When Ronald Reagan took office in 1981, a major plank in his domestic platform was to consolidate multiple, detailed, categorical grants into a limited number of broadly formulated "block" grants. Though many of Reagan's proposals weren't accepted by the Congress, seventy-seven categorical grants-in-aid *were* collapsed into nine block grants under the Omnibus Budget Reconciliation Act of 1981. For example, ten separate grants that provided state aid for addressing different aspects of alcohol, drug abuse, and mental health were combined into one new block grant, streamlining administration, reducing paperwork, and giving the states increased discretion to define programs as they chose. Thirty-seven categoricals in education were similarly consolidated, as were twenty-seven in health.

These new block grants defined goals broadly, giving local officials significant discretion within functional areas such as community development, employment and training, and social services. Although the federal government continues to provide some general direction on spending, recipients have considerable leeway in specifying program priorities as well as administrative and service-delivery arrangements. These features, of course, marked a significant retreat in federal intervention, with a commensurate increase in the role of states and localities.

Under Title XX, for example, over $2 billion a year in federal money is currently available to the states for "social services." Title XX is a block grant because these services aren't defined in programmatic terms. Instead of specifying money for family planning, homemaker services, marital counseling, day care, child abuse prevention, or any other specific activity, Congress simply requires priorities to be set by the states.

Similarly, the Job Training Partnership Act provides funds for "employment and training," however specified. The Community Development Block Grant program provides support for "community development," a term which can encompass anything from street repair to day-care services to low-interest facility loans for neighborhood nonprofits.

A more radical devolutionary reform—but one not nearly as successful as block grants—was General Revenue Sharing (GRS). Initiated in 1972, GRS constituted a major break with the categorical tradition in that it provided, for the first time, federal aid without *any* specification of program priority. In other words, revenue sharing was *unconditional* with regard to function. Depending on their preferences, localities or states could develop new programs, use the money for tax relief, or build new facilities. If they decided to develop new programs, or expand old ones, they could invest in health, recreation, police, sanitation, or code enforcement. For over a decade, GRS provided more than $6 billion a year—one-third to the states, two-third to local authorities—for their unhampered use.

The program, despite its appeal to conservatives, was abolished in 1987, as part of the effort to trim the federal deficit. This is rather ironic, given the Reagan administration's commitment to "returning power to the people," but it indicates the political vulnerability of grants that lack a clear program and client focus. GRS was extremely popular among state and local elected officials. It was, after all, money for nothing, grant aid for free. But revenue sharing was never terribly appealing in Washington.

Financial Conditions

The second major type of federal control relates to financing. In general, aid recipients must be willing to put up what is called a "local match." That is, states and localities must be willing to pay a share of program costs if they desire federal aid.

Matching serves a variety of purposes. For one thing, it reduces the cost burden on the providing unit. As important, matching helps to insure cooperation and efficient program management. A state or locality putting up its own resources is more likely to take its administrative responsibilities seriously than when simply using somebody else's funds.

Matching is also used to influence policymaking. Federal funds offer an important "carrot" by providing incentives for state and local involvement in particular programs. Because states and localities, through long periods of U.S. history, were reluctant to take on social responsibilities, federal aid was one of the major tools available to Washington to promote social welfare initiatives. States and localities are less likely to move into new areas of activity if they must pay the entire cost for such programs. But federal aid in the form of 50 percent, 75 percent, or even 100 percent grants may be difficult to turn down. The offer of ten federal dollars for just one raised locally is very enticing.

Different cost-sharing formulas apply to federal aid programs. In most cases, especially in the older categorical programs, the state/local share ranges from 10 to 50 percent. California, for example, split its AFDC costs 50-50 with the federal government. Under the maternal and child health act, states contribute $3 for every $4 they receive.

TABLE 8.2   Mode of Finance: Systems of Transfer

Funding Arrangements	Specification of Purpose	Role of States/Localities
Categorical grants	Specified narrowly	Strictly implementing federal policies and procedures
Block grants	Specified broadly	Establishing and implementing policy within a given functional area
General Revenue Sharing	Unspecified	Independent policymakers

Over time, however, state and local contributions have been diminishing. In the 1960s, to insure state and local participation in new social efforts, the federal government "sweetened the pot," offering higher and higher payment shares. The War on Poverty, for example, was 90 percent federal, 10 percent local. Public housing and Elementary and Secondary Education Act Title I grants were 100 percent federal, with recipient governments required to pay only the administrative costs. Food stamps operated the same way. Had Congress demanded more, full national coverage could not have been achieved, given the reluctance of many jurisdictions to contribute even small amounts to social programs.

The trend to minimize the local share continued under the New Federalism. GRS required no local share—it was "free" money. Block grants, for the most part, are the same. Title XX initially required a 25 percent state match, but that was eliminated in 1981. Nine of the thirteen block grants currently operating require no state/local funds.

Beneficiary Conditions

A third area of federal control concerns the definition of the beneficiary. Federal aid is often conditioned both with respect to the units of government that are eligible for assistance *and* the types of individuals who can receive benefits. Both conditions are often described in terms of *targeting*.

One way to distribute federal aid is proportionally, strictly in terms of population. Title XX social services operate this way. California has about 12 percent of the national population, so it gets 12 percent of the available funds. Every other state also gets funds proportional to its population. Clearly there is no targeting in this procedure, no special effort to focus help on those states with the greatest needs for services.

When the federal government desires to target aid on the neediest, it utilizes allocation formulas based on need. HUD housing grants, for example, frequently focus aid on communities with the worst housing stock. Education aid, such as Title I of the Elementary and Secondary Education Act, provides support to "districts serving areas with substantial concentrations of children from low-income families." Other programs concentrate funds on jurisdictions with high welfare rates, high unemployment rates, or low per capita incomes.

Targeting not only focuses aid on particular jurisdictions, it also focuses aid *within* recipient jurisdictions on particular populations groups. Many federal aid programs, for example, require means tests to determine client eligibility. All the public assistance programs are targeted on the poor. Other federal aid programs, such as Food Stamps, have been "assistance-linked," meaning that eligibility has been restricted to people eligible for AFDC, SSI, or other welfare programs.

Title XX, the social services block grant, *was* targeted on low-income people until the Reagan changes of 1981. Prior to that, states had to use at least 50 percent of all expenditures to assist welfare clients. Similarly, the mandate that 75 percent of Community Development Block Grant funds be targeted to low- and moderate-income citizens has been repealed.

Procedural Conditions

In addition to financial, program, and beneficiary conditions, aid legislation frequently contains a variety of *procedural* conditions relating to planning, audits, personnel, reporting, client rights, and the like. Some of these standards are "cross-cutting," meaning that they apply to all aid programs. All programs, for example, prohibit discrimination in hiring personnel and allocating benefits to clients. These civil rights requirements were expanded in the 1970s and 1980s to prohibit discrimination against racial and ethnic minorities, women, the disabled, and the aged. Other cross-cutting requirements exist for environmental protection, labor standards, merit personnel systems for selecting staff, and disclosure of information to the public.

Many conditions, however, apply only to specific programs. Some require citizen participation—Community Action mandated "maximum feasible participation" of the poor in formulating and running antipoverty programs. Others require advisory committees and public hearings. Under Model Cities, each city had to undertake a "comprehensive" planning process that involved community residents and public officials in producing detailed analyses of community needs and in describing one- and five-year plans of action. The 1987 McKinney Homeless Assistance legislation requires jurisdictions to submit comprehensive homeless-assistance plans that include statements of need, inventories of existing services and facilities, and remediation strategies that take account of needs of the homeless mentally ill, families with children, the elderly, and veterans.[12]

Some grants require procedures to ensure that funded activities are coordinated with related programs. Others call for appeal procedures for applicants who are denied benefits, for strict confidentiality standards, or for hiring employees with particular kinds of education. For many years, community mental health legislation required that only psychiatrists head up clinical programs; early social welfare programs promoted the use of social work professionals, especially in child welfare.

There is a large and varied body of regulation governing record keeping and program reporting. The federal government generally specifies report standards concerning expenditures and clientele. These demands may be relaxed or they may be rigorous. Probably no other grant condition excites more outrage and resentment than reporting requirements. Detailed report forms submitted in octuplicate on a monthly basis may often be a fact of bureaucratic life, but that hardly makes it palatable to action-oriented practitioners. At the same time, reporting requirements can also be frustrating to funders who depend on timely and appropriate information to determine the extent to which program goals are achieved.

Generally speaking, there are limits to the utility of reporting requirements as a mechanism to maintain control over expenditures, especially in large programs with ambitious objectives. In the Model Cities Program, for example, local Community Development Agencies were able to report their financial expenditures, but it turned out to be impossible to develop a system that could inform HUD of what they were actually accomplishing. Attempts to develop such an information system became bogged down in the uncertainty inherent in a complex, multifaceted program where broad latitude was given to local administrators. What information should be counted to measure program progress? How much weight should be given to the number of people and agencies participating in planning, or the quality of the process, or its outcome? What criteria are indicative of the quality or relevance of programs planned? All these factors relate to the goals of the Model Cities Program, but the goals as stated in the legislation were so vague, global, and comprehensive that in many respects they defied measurement.

In general, the Republican reaction to assertive nationalism has reduced the number of procedural "strings" attached to grant-in-aid programs. Title XX, for example, no longer required states to have an annual planning process, or to maintain formal procedures for the involvement of the public. Federal standards imposing fees to better-off clients were eliminated. All told, the federal regulations governing Title XX were reduced from fifty to eight pages.

The overall impact of the ideology of decentralization on the system of transfer, and on the welfare state in general, is difficult to assess. Most commentators point to the continuing vitality of intergovernmental policymaking and policy management and the continuity of aid programs themselves. A Brookings Institution study found that there was a "singular failure [of the New Federalism] to dislodge in any fundamental way the basic post–New Deal safety-net function of the federal government. Despite Ronald Reagan's intentions," the study continued, "the welfare state remains alive and well—not only in Washington but subnationally."[13]

Devolving Public Welfare

David Ellwood described the 1996 welfare reform bill as a compromise among four distinct strands of conservatism. *Work-oriented reformers,* emphasizing the critical importance of jobs and training, sought to build on The Family Support Act of 1988 by strengthening work requirements and supportive services such as day care. *Ideological critics,* seeing dependency and immorality resulting from misguided government programs, emphasized the importance of behavioral incentives—ending support for teen motherhood and out-of-wedlock births while encouraging school attendance, celibacy, and other positive behaviors. *Budget cutters,* the third group of reformers, viewed the welfare problem as one of excessively generous support, and therefore favored program cuts, time limits, and other measures to reduce spending. *Devolvers,* finally, saw the welfare problem in terms of excessive federal "command and control," intrusive red tape and regulations impairing the ability of the states to create welfare solutions crafted to their own circumstances. For devolvers, welfare reform required sorting out federal and state roles, with Washington providing resources, broad oversight, and central information gathering while the states were responsible for programmatic substance.[14]

Several of these themes have been addressed earlier in this book: work strategies in terms of services strategies (cash and kind); ideology in the values critique of public action; budget cutting as the traditional residualism of small government. The devolution theme, however, in many ways the centerpiece of the 1996 welfare enactment, needs some elaboration.

The Personal Responsibility and Work Opportunity Reconciliation Act of 1996 (Public Law 104-193) includes nine sections ("titles") addressing a range of low-income programs, from food stamps and day care, to child welfare, Title XX, and cash assistance to poor families with children. Its most dramatic element, Title I, transforms categorical AFDC into a new block grant, Temporary Assistance for Needy Families (TANF), providing the states broad powers to adopt welfare plans suited to their own circumstances. While far from eliminating federal influence over the welfare system, TANF incorporates a sweeping decentralization of authority, eliminating in one swoop a structure of federal legislation that over the course of 30 years had endeavored with at least some modest success to liberalize welfare arrangements and provide a measure of reliable economic protection to a great many poor Americans.

In some respects, the "devolution revolution" of 1996 was hardly a radical departure from previous arrangements. AFDC, for example, *always* followed a markedly decentralist orientation. As a grant-in-aid program, it was based on state action. (States weren't compelled to participate. If they did, they retained broad power over benefit levels and eligibility.) The federal role wasn't inconsequential but it was largely a funding role: AFDC committed the national government to match state spending for programs the states devised and operated. Federal requirements, of course, typically accompany federal funds, and the original 1935 Act specified at least a dozen stipulations.

Up until the mid-1960s, AFDC resembled the program enacted by the Congress thirty years earlier. States were in command, setting fundamental rules with minimal federal oversight. But under Lyndon Johnson's Great Society, and for nearly twenty-five years thereafter, AFDC came to incorporate an increasingly large number of federal conditions reflecting an evolving national sense of what constituted proper welfare policy.

The activist welfarism of the federal government was expressed in detailed stipulations on a broad number of subjects. Some of these stipulations sought to promote work. For example, to reduce the work disincentives built into AFDC, federal reforms in 1967 created the "$30 and one-third" rule requiring states to allow recipients to keep their initial $30 in monthly earnings, and one-third of remaining earnings, before their AFDC allotment was reduced.[15] Stipulations enacted in the 1980s conditioned the eligibility process as states were obligated to deny aid to families with assets over $1,000 and benefit levels were limited to 185 percent of the state-defined standard of need. The Family Support Act of 1988, in addition, required states to provide benefits to needy two-parent families, ending the optional status of the AFDC-UP program. The 1988 law also required that transitional child care and medicaid subsidies be made available to families who had worked their way off welfare.

At the same time, however, there were some devolutionary actions. Federal regulations were somewhat loosened in the 1980s, in keeping with the general tenor of the New Federalism, and a wide range of state welfare experiments were initiated after the Family Support Act liberalized the Section 1115 waiver program. By the time AFDC was repealed in 1996, indeed, forty-three states had been granted waivers from statutory regulations. At that point, the basic 1935 structure of categorical funding and federal oversight ended as Public Law 104-193 block granted public assistance, combining funds from AFDC, work programs, and the Emergency Assistance Program, terminating many long standing federal standards, and imposing a set of new, conservative rules.

AFDC to TANF

Title I of the new law, Temporary Assistance for Needy Families (TANF), replaced AFDC with a program far more responsive to state policy priorities. The federal allocation—$16.4 billion a year—is available for the states to use "in any manner reasonably calculated" (i.e., for any purpose that advances the general goals of the legislation, including, but not restricted to, cash aid, emergency assistance, child care, job training, education, and job subsidies). This provides states far greater discretion than under AFDC to organize their welfare programs in their own fashion. TANF, for example, permits the states the discretion to limit assistance to particular categories of poor families. States, if they wish, can prohibit cash payments to otherwise eligible legal immigrants, or to two-parent families, or, for that matter, to everyone. They can impose "family caps" on their aid formula, denying mothers additional benefits if they have children while on welfare. They can provide uniform benefit levels throughout the state ("statewideness") or they can match levels to the cost of living, paying more in areas with high housing costs. They can impose benefit penalties on new residents, giving them aid at the level of their home state, if lower. They can transfer some TANF funds to other programs, such as Title XX. They can do away with at least some of the broad civil rights protections for fair hearings that were part of federal welfare law since the 1960s. And they can structure service delivery pretty much as they choose. Under AFDC, public assistance was for the most part publicly administered. With AFDC's repeal, an array of new administrative options are available. Many states have started privatizing their job-training efforts and several are exploring the possibility of contracting with companies such as Lockheed Martin and Electronic Data Systems to manage their income-maintenance activities.

Broadly described, TANF provides increased flexibility to state governments, broadening their control over eligibility, benefit levels, and benefit duration, and freeing them of long standing federal mandates. Symbolizing the changed relationship between Washington and the states, TANF dramatically restricts federal administrative oversight. Although Congress specifies a number of functions in P.L. 104-193 for the federal Department of Health and Human Services (DHHS)—reviewing state plans and operations; monitoring state "maintenance of effort" levels; conducting research and analysis; providing technical assistance; disseminating information on "best practices"—it also cut DHHS oversight staff by 75 percent, eliminating 245 civil service jobs and dramatically reducing the capacity of federal officials to participate in meaningful program oversight.

The new law, nevertheless, is far from the block grant ideal advanced by devolution purists. Although TANF loosened some strings, it attached several new ones, as Tables 8.3 and 8.4 indicate. TANF, indeed, imposes a rather significant

TABLE 8.3   Federal Welfare Conditions, Old and New

	AFDC	*TANF*
System of Transfer	Categorical grant-in-aid	Block grants melding AFDC with JOBS and Emergency Assistance
Federal Funding	Entitlement: open-ended funding guaranteeing aid to poor families meeting state requirements	No Entitlement: fixed annual funding based on FY 92–94 levels, plus $2 billion contingency fund
State Funding	State matching required	State maintenance of effort required
Beneficiaries	Mandated Inclusion: all families below state eligibility threshold must be served	Mandated Exclusions: states must deny benefits to families not meeting job requirements and time limits; states can deny aid to other categories of poor families
Service Delivery	Public agency delivery by state and/or local units	States can select public operations or contracting out
Time Limits?	No	Yes, 5-year lifetime limit, with 20 percent exemption for "hardship cases" (earlier at state option)
Work Requirements?	Yes. WIN and, later, JOBS require states to offer work-training programs	Yes. Work or "work activities" within 2 years or loss of assistance
Statewide Uniformity?	Yes. "Statewideness" required	No. State can vary benefit levels geographically, such as between high and low cost areas
Family Cap?	No	Yes
Fund Shifting?	No	Yes. 30 percent can be shifted to child care and social services
Residency Requirement?	No. States can't deny or reduce benefits to new residents	Yes. Permits two-tier state systems giving lower rates to new residents
Due Process Protections?	Yes. Client rights to "fair hearings" required	Maybe. Client rights specified in vague terms

TABLE 8.4   TANF Prohibitions

Section 408 of PL 104-193 prohibits federal assistance for:
1. parents not cooperating in establishing paternity or obtaining child support;
2. teenage parents not living in adult-supervised settings and not attending high school or training programs;
3. individuals convicted of felony drug possession, use, or sale;
4. medical services; and
5. family assistance for more than five years over a lifetime.

array of moralistic "personal responsibility" rules on the states, prohibiting assistance for varying categories of the most "undeserving" poor (teen moms living in their own homes, teens not attending school, individuals convicted of drug felonies) and demanding increased state attention to programs addressing out-of-wedlock pregnancies and statutory rape. The new law, in addition, imposes a sixty-month lifetime limit on most beneficiaries (permitting states to impose even stricter time limits), and compels states to move an increasing portion of their caseload into work programs so that by the year 2002 fully half of all one-parent families, and 90 percent of all two-parent families, are participating. Contrary to typical block grant practice, finally, TANF requires a state "maintenance of effort" and it prohibits any state from spending more than 15 percent of its federal allotment on administration.

Rather than eliminating federal control, then, the new welfare law signifies a marked shift in the *character* of regulation. Under six decades of AFDC, federal law generally served as a liberalizing influence, a vehicle for guaranteed, nonpunitive public aid. To protect the rights of vulnerable parents and children, standards for state conduct were established, and the more egregious and demeaning features of local welfare administration were outlawed. In 1962, for example, Congress prohibited state eligibility conditions that denied assistance to out-of-wedlock children, requiring instead that "illegitimacy" be addressed through services and rehabilitation. Later in the 1960's, Congress, prompted by the U.S. Supreme Court, prohibited "midnight raids," bed and closet checks to see if the "man in the house" rule was being violated.

Under the new welfare initiative, federal regulations have morphed from the protective to the punitive, from an emphasis on rights to one on responsibilities. Rather than mandating an inclusive eligibility, the new law mandates exclusions and limits. Rather than advancing guarantees, federal funds are denied to several classes of the poor, with the states invited to establish their own restrictive practices and disqualification criteria.

Terminating the Guarantee

The most important federal guarantee was the pledge to contribute to the financial support of all eligible parents and children in poverty. For sixty-one years AFDC, and ADC before it, provided a modest income safety net for children and

---

CAPSULE 8.3:   Welfare Salvation

The Salvation Army has received $375,000 from the state to match welfare recipients with "mentor families" in churches and other religious groups to help recipients get and keep jobs.

The contract with the Salvation Army will be paid out of an $11 million federal bonus Michigan received for turning in its welfare plan to the federal government ahead of schedule. The bonus is part of the new welfare measure that sends federal dollars to states in block grants—along with broad flexibility in how to spend the money.

Under the contract, the state will refer all welfare recipients in two experimental areas to the Salvation Army, which will subcontract with churches and other religious groups to pair recipients with families. The idea is for the families to work together to erase barriers a welfare recipient might have to employment. Services that the mentoring family may provide could include budgeting advice, help with care or home repairs and goal setting.

"Around the Nation—Lansing, Michigan," *Welfare to Work,* 5(19), October 7, 1996, 343.

families by insuring federal open-ended matching grants to the states. No upper limits were placed on the size of the federal allotment; states determined how much of their own money to spend and the federal government automatically contributed its matching share. The portion paid by Washington varied. In AFDC's last year—FY 1996—it ranged from 50 percent for the highest per-capita income states to 78 percent for Mississippi, the poorest state.

The guarantee of open-ended federal matching made AFDC a federal entitlement—all families meeting the state's eligibility criteria had a statutory right to assistance. The entitlement, although modest, was important. It never covered all the poor; only those deemed income-eligible by the states were eligible. And it never carried with it standards for minimum benefit levels—assistance was typically insufficient to remove recipients from poverty. The matching arrangement, nevertheless, insured a basic level of material support. Families stranded by the economy, a lack of ability, or just bad luck had a right to aid. Matching also powerfully encouraged state spending because the more the state put in, the more Uncle Sam contributed. The open-ended character of the federal grant, furthermore, was responsive to changing situations of need. In prosperous times, caseloads were reduced and AFDC funding (federal *and* state) was reduced. In recessionary periods, caseloads increased and AFDC funding increased.

TANF, in ending the federal entitlement, subordinates assistance to the availability of funds. Rather than matching state spending, the federal government provides a fixed annual sum. Unconnected to state spending—and unconnected to changing levels of need—this allotment can easily result in benefit rationing in hard times. When more families meet the state need standard than are budgeted for, assistance is likely to be reduced or denied.

This financing change—the end of automatic care for dependent children—is the most potentially damaging element of the new block grant. Over the short run, TANF is likely to resemble AFDC. The federal allocation, based on spending over the period from fiscal years 1992 to 1994, is likely to be sufficient, because it is based on a recessionary period when jobs were scarce and welfare rolls were high. Many states, indeed, are likely to enjoy a financial windfall for the first few years because their federal allotment will exceed what is needed in a healthy economy. State spending, for a while, is also likely to suffice because the TANF "maintenance of effort" requirement is pegged pretty much at current levels. But the public aid safety net is not likely to remain intact for long. State policymakers, given unprecedented authority to design their own antipoverty programs, *may* in fact devise effective and humane welfare interventions. Without federal standards, however, and without a right to assistance, it is equally, if not more likely that they will cut benefit levels and narrow eligibility, especially if facing a period of economic downtown and reduced state revenues.

Time Limits

While the new law imposes a five-year limit on federal assistance, it permits states to exempt up to 20 percent of all welfare families for hardship. Given the fact that a major portion of the AFDC caseload has been composed of long-term users— one estimate is that about three quarters of those on aid in 1996 had been beneficiaries for over five years—there is considerable apprehension concerning the limit's implementation.[16]

First of all, there is a question of enforceability. It seems clear that, at least for the immediate future, there is no nationwide data keeping system able to track welfare recipients and the duration of their aid. A welfare worker trying to determine the eligibility of a new applicant, in other words, generally has no available source of information—other than the client him or herself—concerning aid received in other states. Even *within* states, information systems are often deficient.

Second, there is the question of applying the exemption. If and when the time limit is enforced—either at the five year point, or, at state discretion, earlier—there is bound to be significant hardship. One of the most critical choices facing state policymakers, therefore, is that of defining the nature and severity and consequences of that hardship. Who is to be permitted aid beyond the cutoff? What criteria will be employed to determine "worthiness" for long-term assistance? And what political factors will have to be factored into these decisions?

In the year following the enactment of PL 104-193, advocates representing needy groups around the country mobilized to protect their constituencies, as Capsule 8.4 illustrates. Among the most active groups—and the only one given explicit attention in the legislation—has been battered women, who argue that public assistance is an indispensable option for abused mothers, providing them perhaps their single alternative to victimization by a violent boyfriend or husband. Those representing moms with AIDS/HIV, and other chronic disabilities, argue that their conditions make work impossible, and therefore require lengthier periods of support. Grandparents caring for grandchildren constitute another group seeking special consideration under the hardship exception.

CAPSULE 8.4: Hardship Competition

The charter buses from New York City rumbled into Albany this week, carrying hundreds of advocates for the poor and disabled. Counselors for battered women and AIDS patients sat side by side, united in their opposition to Gov. George E. Pataki's welfare-overhaul plan. But when the lobbying began, long-time allies became reluctant rivals as they urged legislators to spare their constituents from welfare cuts.

The new Federal law that imposes a five-year limit on public assistance allows states to exempt 20 percent of welfare families from that limit. And as legislators weigh the merits of each group, advocates for battered women, advocates for foster parents and advocates for those infected with H.I.V., among others, find themselves competing for consideration. In their view, they are sparring for space aboard a metaphorical lifeboat, battling over who will

survive (and keep welfare benefits) and who will perish (and lose them).

"Welfare reform hurts all of us," said Lisa Cortes, the outreach coordinator for the Boriken Neighborhood Health Center in East Harlem, who helped organize the group trip to Albany on Tuesday. "But you can't help but think, 'Who is going to be saved?' "

With so few seats, the lifeboat is likely to fill up fast. Advocates for battered women, for instance, say that victims of domestic violence are the heads of about 30 percent of all welfare families and could easily consume the coveted exemption slots. Advocates for AIDS patients say that 20 percent of welfare recipients may be H.I.V. positive. Advocates for foster parents, on the other hand, say the number of foster parents caring for toddlers or children with disabilities is so small—fewer than 7,000 families—that no one would be hurt by their inclusion.

Rachel L. Swarns, "Welfare Family Advocates, Once Allies, Become Rivals," *The New York Times,* March 29, 1997, A1.

Race to the Bottom

It has been broadly hypothesized that the structure of the new welfare block grant will lead to lowered assistance levels and a denial of help to those very families least likely to be able to support themselves in today's economy. Critics have predicted that the disentitlement of welfare will subject public assistance to competitive cycles of state budget politics, resulting in a significant erosion in welfare spending over time. Social legislation is high-cost, politically unpopular legislation, and the taxes necessary to support it put generous liberally minded states at a disadvantage. High benefits mean high taxes, which not only produce dissatisfaction among residents but can scare off potential new sources of revenue—industries, new businesses, new residents. What's worse, liberal benefits may serve as a "welfare magnet," attracting service users from less welfare-minded areas.[17]

The old welfare system was designed to counter this tendency for states to minimize their benefits. Under AFDC, states knew that their own payments would elicit generous federal matching. Mississippi, for example, received more than four dollars in federal AFDC support for every dollar it put up. This provided a significant incentive—some might say "bribe"—for poorer states to maintain welfare levels at least minimum levels. Under the block grant, however, this incentive is gone—a fixed federal payment is assured irrespective of state spending levels.

In fact, the incentives structured into the new welfare system are likely to promote stinginess. Neither the federal nor the state allotments are indexed for inflation. There are real incentives to reduce caseloads and costs. Subject to normal budget processes, public assistance is likely to fare poorly in the competition for funds. States are not likely to spend more on TANF than the minimum required by PL 104-193. They could, of course, continue TANF as a *state* entitlement; they *could* guarantee benefits to all those not prohibited by federal law from receiving assistance. But this likelihood is slight. Facing other pressing needs, and often constrained by tax limits and balanced budget requirements, states are far more likely to reduce their obligations, seeking, perhaps, to eliminate their maintenance of effort mandate altogether. TANF is dissimilar from most block grants in that it *does* require state spending. Other block grants set no minimum, a model naturally appealing to state officials.

The outcome of these fiscal pressures, the "race to the bottom" predicted by many, occurs as states compete with one another to reduce benefits and limit eligibility in order to avoid welfare costs. The central fear of welfare reform's critics lies here, in the likelihood that, *sans* entitlement, TANF, at best, would reduce the state's ability to maintain help for the poor in an economic slump, and, at worst, would lead to a system of "spiraling parsimony," pushing large numbers of families and children into increased deprivation, homelessness, and suffering. One estimate, based on Urban Institute calculations, predicts the new welfare bill will result in 1.1 million additional children being impoverished. According to Senator Moynihan, "there are not enough social workers, not enough nuns, not enough Salvation Army workers to care for the children who [will] be purged from the welfare rolls."[18]

Job Hypotheses

Although the future of the 1996 welfare overhaul is hard to predict, it is clear that states will be undertaking numerous new responsibilities for planning, operations, and evaluation. These responsibilities include establishing new employment and service programs, allocating block grant funds among counties and municipalities, responding (or not) to the needs of groups excluded from aid, such as legal immigrants, and creating new data-management systems to monitor caseloads and to enforce the five-year limit on welfare receipt. Each of these tasks involves major challenges. For many states, however, these are not entirely new challenges, because many have for several years been using the leeway provided under Section 1115 waivers and the JOBS program to experiment with new welfare designs. Several states, for example, have implemented changes to increase work effort, including "triggers" that activate after two or three years, reducing or ending benefits for those not complying with the new work rules, and "disregards" that increase the amount of income a family may keep before being subject to the loss of benefits. As Table 8.5 indicates, time limits and family caps also have been emphasized.

The most ambitious changes have occurred in efforts to move clients from welfare to work. State plans have spawned a broad range of initiatives encouraging or mandating greater participation in education, training, or employment activities. Many of these initiatives began after 1988 seeking to increase the proportion of the AFDC caseload involved in the JOBS effort. Since 1996, states have

TABLE 8.5   Welfare Laboratories

Work First (Michigan). Mothers lose their welfare benefits if they do not obtain jobs, paid or unpaid, within six weeks of having a child.

Work Pays Demonstration Program (California). Adopted in 1992, WPDP reduced welfare payments 10 percent, reinstated the $30 and 1/3 rule (meaning that families can keep the first $30, and a third of additional work earnings, before benefits are reduced), increased child-care support, and expanded work and training opportunities.

LearnFare. Links benefits to school attendance. In some states, families whose children quit school or are frequently truant lose benefits. In others, welfare benefits are increased for teenage parents staying in school, or graduating, and reduced for those who drop out.

Social Contract (Michigan). Michigan has been experimenting with welfare reform since 1992. Its program requires recipients to participate in some combination of work, training, general education, or community service. Among the initiatives in the program are "license penalties"—fathers who don't pay their obligated child support, for example, can lose their drivers license and other professional licenses.

Illinois Model. Unmarried mothers under 18 must live with their parents and be enrolled in school or lose part of their grant. "Family cap" eliminates extra funding when families have additional children. Benefits can be obtained only if paternity is established within six months of birth.

Iowa Model. Welfare recipients are encouraged to work and build up savings through "individual development accounts" from which they can make withdrawals only to start a business, buy a home, pursue education or job training, or take care of a family emergency.

Welfare Restructuring Project (Vermont). Most recipients must do community service after 2-½ years of benefits. If a recipient is unable to secure a private sector job, the state provides ten months of employment in a public or nonprofit organization. WRP also provides substantial social services and work incentives.

Two-Tiered Residency. Several states restrict welfare benefits for recent arrivals from other states. In California, newcomers receive the benefits they would have gotten in their home state, if this amount is less.

WorkFirst (Mississippi). WorkFirst requires welfare recipients to accept any job offered or else lose all benefits. Employers hiring welfare recipients are provided a TANF subsidy of $3.50 an hour to which they must add $1.00 an hour. In this fashion, public assistance is turned into a wage subsidy program.

Diversion (Wisconsin). Touted by conservatives as a "welfare miracle," Wisconsin cut its welfare rolls by 55 percent from 1987 to 1997 through "diversion," a tough work program requiring nearly all recipients to work for their benefits on penalty (strictly enforced) of reduced (or eliminated) welfare checks. Wisconsin claims that 75 percent of those now off welfare have private jobs; critics argue that a major portion are poorer than ever, many in homeless shelters.

adopted a more punitive direction, using the leverage of aid cut-offs to demand work, shifting their emphasis from training and education to employment, and often providing expanded subsidies to private businesses to hire recipients.

One lesson from the last decade that *is* clear is that welfare-to-work programs are costly. It requires substantial time and effort—substantial resources—to successfully get people into the work force. States that take the task seriously find over the short run at least that work programs are substantially costlier than cash welfare.

Will TANF's strict emphasis on work make a difference? Will employment opportunities and support services keep pace with the numbers evicted from the rolls? Will the states be able to meet the federal demand that 50 percent of those on welfare be working 30–35 hours weekly (not just in training or in school) by 2002? There is little empirical basis for optimism. The basic tenet of the reform—that poor people who really try will get jobs and escape poverty—is unlikely to be realized. It is unlikely, first, because even in the most prosperous times a modest level of unemployment is built into the economy. In an era of downsizing and low-skill job export, there are simply not enough jobs for those needing them. It is unlikely, second, because employers are reluctant to hire workers with poor skills and questionable work habits. Welfare users are frequently without usable job-market skills, without self-discipline, without the necessary family and community supports to manage the child care and transportation necessary for regular employment. It is unlikely, third, because even full-time jobs at the wages welfare recipients are likely to command do not bring families above the poverty level.

Most of the evaluations of state welfare experiments point to the difficulty of the welfare-to-work transition. Recent Urban Institute evaluations of state waiver programs, for example, found that a significant portion of welfare recipients—typically those with the greatest social and educational deficits—face multiple barriers to employment, barriers that work-related programs rarely address.[19] These findings, coupled with the generally disappointing results of the JOBS program, auger poorly for the success of the hard-line approach embodied in TANF.[20]

Summary

Given the phase-in of TANF's job requirements, the five-year leeway before time limits lock in, and the generous nature of the block grant in its initial years, the new welfare system is not likely to produce immediate or dramatic results. But as the most able recipients enter the labor market, and caseloads are increasingly composed of the most disadvantaged, most challenged families, the situation will become far more problematic. According to one welfare scholar, the welfare systems will really feel the effects in the fifth to eighth year, when families reach the time limits and are severed from the rolls.[21] If states set lower than five-year limits, or cut recipients from the welfare rolls for other reasons—drug felonies, immigrant status, failure to cooperate with child support enforcement—then the crunch may come a good deal sooner.

The abolition of AFDC and its reformulation into fifty separate poor law operations signify a remarkable abandonment of a basic element of the U.S. welfare state. As noted in Chapter 2, all welfare states are facing great difficulties in maintaining their social protections, yet each has acknowledged the necessity to provide relief to those—able-bodied or not—who are unable to fend for themselves. Only the United States has declared, in stark terms, its unwillingness to assure basic help to its most impoverished, most vulnerable citizens. Reflecting persistent beliefs in individual responsibility, and the value of work and family, the 1996 welfare law is reminiscent of nineteenth-century "survival of the fittest" social Darwinism. Although perhaps unwilling to accept starvation or death, TANF does remove a key component of the United States' system of social protection, posing a real likelihood of grave distress for those affected, and substantial risks for social instability.

CAPSULE 8.5:   The Future of Welfare: Pessimistic Senarios

Congress can expect little from the states. Governors may promise great compassion for the poor, but anyone who has worked closely with state legislators can tell you that welfare families, people with disabilities, nursing home residents, the elderly poor and abused children usually score very low on the political scale. Financing for their needs is often shortchanged when it comes to providing dollars for competing highways, schools, businesses and farms.

—Fred Kammer

The politicians have gotten together and decided it's a good idea to throw a million or so children into poverty. But they can't say that. The proponents of this so-called "reform" effort have gone out of their way to avoid being seen for what they are—men and women of extreme privilege who are taking food out of the mouths of infants and children, the poverty-stricken elderly, the disabled.

The welfare legislation currently before Congress is in no way a reform measure. It will help no one. It is a form of officially sanctioned brutality aimed at the usual suspects—the poor, the black and the brown, the very young, the uneducated, immigrants. Somebody has to be the scapegoat and they're it.

The states will be given block grants and if that money (plus a small contingency fund) runs out because of rising unemployment, a recession, mismanagement, whatever—well, that will be too bad.

—Bob Herbert

This legislation does not "reform" Aid to Families with Dependent Children; it simply abolishes it.

It terminates the basic Federal commitment of support for dependent children in hopes of altering the behavior of their mothers. We are putting those children at risk with absolutely no evidence that this radical idea has even the slightest chance of success.

It is the first step in dismantling the social contract that has been in place in the United States since at least the 1930's.

—Senator Daniel Patrick Moynihan

Fred Kammer, President, Catholic Charities USA, "Block Grants Will Worsen Poverty," *The New York Times,* August 1, 1995, A15.
Bob Herbert, "In America: The Mouths of Babes," *The New York Times,* July 22, 1996, A15.
Senator Daniel Patrick Moynihan (D–New York), Senate Debate on Welfare, August 1, 1996.

CAPSULE 8.6:   The Future of Welfare: Optimistic Senarios

Welfare is implicated in America's gravest social problem, the existence of isolated, depressed neighborhoods, the vast majority either black or Hispanic, where intact families and working fathers are practically nonexistent. You can argue about welfare's role in creating this underclass, but there is little doubt that welfare *sustains* it.

Change the welfare system, and the underclass will change, too. The bill has one virtue that overrides its flaws: it will, finally, start the process by which America's underclass problem can be solved.

—"Sign It,"

In the last 50 years, we have spent $5.2 trillion on means-tested programs, that is programs where we were trying to help poor people. No society in history has ever invested more money trying to help needy people than the United States. And yet 50 years later what has been the result of all those good intentions? Well, the result of that investment is that we have more poor people today than when we started that program. They are more dependent on the government today than when we started the current welfare program, and by any defin-

ition of quality of life fulfillment or happiness, people are worse off today than they were when we started the current welfare system.

Our welfare program has failed. It has driven fathers out of the household. It has made mothers dependent. It has taken away people's dignity. It has bred child abuse and neglect and filled the streets of our cities with crime. And we're here today to change it.

Now let me outline the new program. We are giving the states the ability to run their own programs. We believe that the Federal Government does not have all the wisdom in the world and that states should run their program. We have taken a Federally run program, we have taken the funds that we have spent on that program and we have given that money to the states so that rather than have one program, each state in the Union can tailor its program to meet its individual needs. It's a program that asks people to work. It's a program that tries to make Americans independent. It is a program that for the first time uses work and family to try to help families escape welfare and to escape poverty in America.

—Senator Phil Gramm

"Sign It," *The New Republic,* August 12, 1996, 7.
Senator Phil Gramm (R–Texas), Senate Debate on Welfare, August 1, 1996.

Notes

---

1. For a creative explication of the decentralist position, see Paul Goodman, *People or Personnel* (New York: Vintage Books, 1968).

2. Grant McConnell, *Private Power and American Democracy* (New York: Alfred A. Knopf, 1966), 107.

3. Ford Foundation, *The Common Good: Social Welfare and the American Future,* May 1989, 63.

4. A brief historical review of U.S. federalism can be found in Daniel J. Elazar, "Opening the Third Century of American Federalism: Issues

and Prospects," in John Kincaid (ed.) *American Federalism: The Third Century,* The Annals, Volume 509, May 1990, 11–21.

5. Luther H. Gulick, "Reorganization of the State," *Civil Engineering* (August 1933), 420, as quoted in *The Book of the States,* 1976–77, Vol. 21 (Lexington, KY: The Council of State Governments, 1976), 21.

6. William E. Leuchtenberg, *Franklin D. Roosevelt and the New Deal* (New York: Harper and Row, 1963), as quoted in *The Book of the States,* ibid., 24.

7. Daniel P. Moynihan, "Comments on 'Re-Structuring the Government of New York City'," in *The Neighborhoods, the City, and the Region: Working Papers in Jurisdiction and Structures* (New York: State Study Commission for New York City, 1973), 15.

8. Ibid., 16.

9. Eveline M. Burns, *Social Security and Public Policy* (New York: McGraw-Hill, 1958), 230.

10. Robert Reischauer. "Fiscal Federalism in the 1980s: Dismantling or Rationalizing the Great Society," in M. Kaplan and P. Cuciti (eds.), *The Great Society and Its Legacy,* 1986, 179.

11. U.S. Advisory Commission on Intergovernmental Relations, *A Catalog of Federal Grant-in-Aid Programs: Grants Funded FY 1989,* M167, October 1989.

12. U.S. General Accounting Office, *Homelessness: McKinney Act Reports Could Improve Federal Assistance Efforts,* GAO/RCED-90-121, June 1990.

13. Timothy Conlan, *New Federalism: Intergovernmental Reform from Nixon to Reagan,* The Brookings Institution, 1988, 229.

14. David T. Ellwood, "From Social Science to Social Policy? The Fate of Intellectuals, Ideas, and Ideology in the Welfare Debate in the Mid-1990's," Center for Urban Affairs and Policy Research, Northwestern University, Evanston, Illinois, 1996, 23–24.

15. The "$30 and one-third" rule was revised significantly in 1981, 1984, and 1988. By 1996, at the time of AFDC's demise, the disregard was limited to four months; after that a $30 disregard continued an additional eight months. The work expense disregard was $90/month whereas the maximum child care allowance was $175/month per child, $200 for children under two. TANF repealed all federal disregard regulations.

16. U.S. General Accounting Office, *Welfare Waivers Implementation,* GAO/HEHS-96-105, 1996, 9.

17. Paul E. Peterson and Mark C. Rom, *Welfare Magnets* (Washington, D.C.: The Brookings Institution, 1990).

18. Daniel Patrick Moynihan, September 16, 1995 Speech, reported in *The New York Times,* August 2, 1996.

19. LaDonna Paretti and Amy-Ellen Duke, "Increasing Participation in Work and Work-Related Activities: Lessons from Five State Welfare Reform Demonstration Projects," Urban Institute, September 1995.

20. The Manpower Development Research Corporation, the principle evaluator of welfare-related jobs programs, takes a more sanguine view of the findings, interpreting most welfare-to-work projects as modestly cost-effective. See Friedlander, Daniel, *Five Years After: The Long-Term Effects of Welfare-to-Work Programs* (New York, Russell Sage Foundation, 1995).

21. Jill Duerr Berrick, quoted in "Reform Means Retaining Caseworkers as Counsellors, Job Developers," *Welfare to Work,* 5(18), September 23, 1996, 333.

$Chapter$ 9

Who Plans? Choices in the Process of Policy Formulation

The dispute between the modern planners and their opponents is not a dispute on whether we ought to choose intelligently between the various possible organizations of society; it is not a dispute on whether we ought to employ foresight and systematic thinking in planning our common affairs. The question is whether for this purpose it is better that the holder of coercive powers should confine himself in general to creating conditions under which the knowledge and initiative of individuals are given the best scope so that they can plan most successfully; or whether a rational utilization of our resources requires central direction and organization of all our activities according to some consciously constructed "blueprint."
—**FRIEDRICH A. HAYEK**
The Road to Serfdom, 1944

In preceding chapters we examined a series of choices affecting the design of social welfare policies. Generally speaking, these choices address questions of what is to be done, what alternative courses of action can fulfill social welfare objectives, and what their implications might be. In this chapter our attention shifts to a dimension of choice that is found, not in the product, but in the *process* of policy formulation. Although we have emphasized policy issues that relate to the product, it is important to recognize that the arrangements governing *how* decisions are made are as significant a policy choice as questions pertaining to their substantive content.

Planning Models

Many authors have modeled the policy formulation process as a series of unfolding stages. In most cases the neat sequential ordering of the process is qualified by

TABLE 9.1   Comparison of Models of Policy Development

Model A (Kahn) Planning Process	Model B (DiNitto) Policymaking Process	Model C (Freeman and Sherwood) Social Policy- Development Process
1. Planning instigators		
2. Explorations	1. Identifying policy problems	1. Planning
3. Definition of planning task	2. Formulating policy proposals	
4. Policy formulation	3. Legitimizing public policy	2. Program development and implementation
5. Programming	4. Implementating public policy	
6. Evaluation feedback	5. Evaluating public policy	3. Evaluation

the recognition that these stages exist in a state of dynamic readjustment, feeding back data that alter the preceding information while forming the groundwork for data to follow. For students new to the field of social welfare policy, these policy development models are sometimes confusing, varying not only with regard to the number of stages they employ, but with the terminology used to describe them. Nevertheless, most models share much in common. To illustrate this point, Table 9.1 compares three formulations found in the literature. Model A identifies a six-stage "planning process";[1] Model B a five-step "policy making process";[2] and Model C a three stage "social policy-development process."[3] Whatever the number of stages, each model relates a process of rational progression.

Our model, presented in Table 9.2, divides the policy formulation process into eight separate stages, providing a sense of the rich variety of professional functions and tasks involved. Five social welfare-related functions are identified: direct service, research, community organization, management, and planning. As indicated, these functions are often performed by the same worker; a planner, for example, may have both research and community organization responsibilities.

The policy formulation process outlined in Table 9.2 serves both to uncover incipient and unmet social needs and to identify methods of meeting them. The process might occur in a variety of settings—a small private agency, a large institution, or a national bureaucracy. The model, like the others, does not reflect the complex feedback interactions among stages nor does it specify who generates the initiative for carrying the process forward.

Problem Identification

The impetus for policy change usually reflects a recognition of an unmet or poorly met need in the community. The perception of particular needs and the formulation of appropriate responses are related to numerous political, economic, social,

TABLE 9.2   Professional Functions and Policy Formulation

Stage	*Professional Functions*
1. Problem identification	1. Direct service
2. Problem analysis	2. Research
3. Informing the public	3. Community organization
4. Development of policy goals	4. Planning
5. Building public support and legitimacy	5. Community organization
6. Program design	6. Planning
7. Implementation	7. Management and direct service
8. Evaluation and assessment	8. Research and direct service

and institutional forces. What people define as problems, commonly reflect their institutional positions. So, for example, concerns for organizational economy and harmony might guide the perceptions of agency managers more than their feelings of responsibility for improving services to clients.[4]

Tasks that must be completed during this stage are case-finding, recording examples of unmet needs, and identifying gaps in services. These are tasks that direct-service practitioners are singularly well positioned to perform. It is through their functions as advocates and social brokers for their clients that they will most likely be involved in the policy-formulation process. Scott Briar has discussed these functions as part of the direct-service workers' professional role, noting that these individuals bring to the task "a substantial body of knowledge with which to understand the dynamics of the welfare system and its constituent agencies."[5]

However, to use such knowledge in this process requires a professional orientation that views client service as a foremost professional responsibility. For many practitioners, a major dilemma arises when (as we discussed in Chapter 6) the requirements of bureaucratic conformity clash with this responsibility.

Problem Analysis

Having identified a problem, it is necessary to develop factual data about its magnitude, its severity, and the number of people it affects. The kind and quality of information gathering may change as the process evolves. Consider the following hypothetical case. A probation officer observes that children are being physically mistreated in the county's residential institution. Unable to make headway with the agency administrator (who is defensive and unwilling to condemn physical coercion by his subordinates), the probation officer brings the problem to the attention of a group of citizens who have organized to advocate for the needs of children. This citizens' committee sets up meetings throughout the county, inviting youths who have been at the institution to relate their experiences.

In this case, a fairly informal procedure—the community meeting—is used early in the process to generate raw data for the work of the citizens' committee. As these meetings progress, and the nature of the issues become clear, the committee might direct its energies toward bringing in a professional standard-setting agency or research unit to more systematically examine the probation program. Whatever the method employed, the basic task at this stage is to move from an expression of concern about unmet needs to an organized (frequently complicated and expensive) program of information gathering and analysis. Research skills are primary to this task.

Informing the Public

The public includes the various subsystems in the community that must be informed of a problem if improvements are to occur. The size of the public—as big as the community-at-large or as limited as an institution's top leadership—depends on the nature of the problem. The task is to present the problem in a form that will capture the interest and attention of the relevant parties. Such a task requires organizing skills and the use of appropriate media channels.

As in the problem analysis stage, no clear-cut time frame divides information gathering from informing the public. The use of testimony at community meetings, for example, interweaves public information with information gathering and analysis. Neighborhood surveys by resident volunteers can similarly uncover unmet needs while informing the public. Both research and organizing skills are required to implement such a survey.

Informing the public necessarily precedes developing policy goals even though the parties initiating change may have specific policy goals in mind. This is because any such goals can have little meaning to a public that is unaware that a problem exists.

Development of Policy Goals

The preceding stages create public awareness of a problem and information concerning its dimensions. Now the discussion turns to addressing the problem and meeting the need. At this stage many solutions may be suggested, all of which must be sifted, analyzed, and shaped in order to develop concrete policy goals. In the case of the probation department, these goals might include changing the attitude and behavior of residential center staff, moving residents out of the facility into community-based halfway houses, or attacking the need for incarcerating children and adolescents in the first place.

The key professional function at this stage is social planning. According to Kahn:

> *The planner's most serious decision and major contribution is what may be called the* formulation *or* definition *of the planning task. The "task" is formulated through a constant playing back between an assessment of the relevant aspects of social reality and the preferences of the relevant community. Each of these two factors affects and modifies the perceptions of the other. The task definition appears as an integration of the two. Much else in social planning follows from the outcome of such integration.*[6]

The outcome of this stage is a general statement of the broad-based objectives or goals to be achieved.

Building Public Support and Legitimacy

During and after the process of goal formulation, efforts must be made to maintain public support for the general course of proposed action. Those initiating the policy must identify groups in the broader system—political figures, professional groups, voluntary social agencies, and the like—that can lend support and legitimacy to the change objectives and can assist in translating those objectives into instruments for action.

Major tasks at this stage include the cultivation of leadership, coalition formation, and negotiation of agreement among potential supporters. Compromises may be made at this stage that modify the goal statement. Here, the organizer's skills in bargaining, exchange, and persuasion are essential to forge the support base. The culmination of this stage is the creation of a consensus platform containing the goals and objectives of the supporting constituencies.

Program Design

Once a general direction has been determined, the task of actually drafting a program design rests on the drawing board of the social planner. At this point, goals and objectives are transformed into operational guidelines for action—for example, statutes for the agenda of a legislative body or program proposals for consideration by an agency board of directors.

The plan of action or policies that are products of this stage describe the allocation of responsibility for the proposed program and the organizational structure, financing, and personnel requirements of program operations. These program elements vary with regard to the amount of detail they contain. Frequently, a program is designed to leave considerable room for interpretation by those responsible for its implementation.

Implementation

Depending on how detailed the program design is, a large part of the process of policy formulation may be left for this stage, when the concrete translation of action principles to programmatic elements is accomplished through practice, precedent, and experimentation. The 1974 Title XX amendments to the Social Security Act, which required each of the states to develop a Comprehensive Annual Services Plan involving social planning, problem analysis, and citizen participation, provide a good illustration. The specific ways in which these requirements were to be implemented were quite vague, leaving the substance of implementation decision making to state administrators.

The chief tasks at this point—getting the program organized, clarifying policy, producing the service or benefit, and delivering it to the client group—relate to administrative and direct-service functions. The courts may also enter the process at this stage and play a major role in the clarification of policy. It is by establishing a system of rights and guarantees through appeals and judicial precedents that a body of administrative procedure and law evolve.

Evaluation and Assessment

In a sense, the goals of social welfare policy are always receding. New programs create new expectations and uncover additional unmet needs. Programs themselves become a major element in the "demand environment" of policy. This continuing process is based in part on faulty assumptions of policy design concerning the resources needed to implement programs and the availability of resources and supportive services in the external system.

Individualist and Collective Approaches to Planning

For many years during the midcentury, planning—its hows and whys and by whoms—was one of this country's most politically divisive issues. At first, the debate followed the traditional contours of left–right, collectivist and individualist, politics. Hayek, for example, writing in 1944, saw the dispute between "modern planners and their opponents" not in terms of the desirability of planning *per se*, but in terms of the merits of alternative planning arrangements and the degree to which they allowed for the expression of individual interests, as opposed to the collective will. For Hayek, the question was whether smaller units of society—

CAPSULE 9.1:   Central Planning: The Critique

It is not difficult to see what must be the consequences when democracy embarks upon a course of planning which in its execution requires more agreement than in fact exists. The people may have agreed on adopting a system of directed economy because they have been convinced that it will produce great prosperity. In the discussions leading to the decision, the goal of planning will have been described by some such term as "common welfare," which only conceals the absence of real agreement on the ends of planning. Agreement will in fact exist only on the mechanism to be used. But it is a mechanism which can be used only for a common end; and the question of the precise goal toward which all activity is to be directed will arise as soon as the executive power has to translate the demand for a single plan into a particular plan. Then it will appear that the agreement on the desirability of planning is not supported by agreement on the ends the plan is to serve. The effect of the people's agreeing that there must be central planning, without agreeing on the ends, will be rather as if a group of people were to commit themselves to take a journey together without agreeing where they want to go: with the result that they may all have to make a journey which most of them do not want at all.

Friedrich A. Hayek, *The Road to Serfdom*, 1944, 61–62.

individuals and groups—were to be involved in determining their own interests or whether plans would be centrally and bureaucratically determined. It was the latter course—centrally planned change—that Hayek perceived as the "road to serfdom."[7]

Since the 1960s, this dispute has lost most of its edge. Certainly, the collapse of the planned "command economies" of eastern Europe and the Soviet Union eroded most of the world's faith in socialist arrangements that relied on centralized long-range schemas for economic and social development. Few modern planners anywhere in the globe still advocate unitary, nationally determined plans. But even before the great upheavals of 1989 and 1990 changed the face of Europe, skepticism had been growing concerning the utility of the planning model for directing activity at regional and local levels, and particularly in the area of social policy. As Paul Davidoff, an influential "advocacy planner" of the 1960s and 1970s put it:

> *A practice that has discouraged full participation by citizens in plan making in the past has been based on what might be called the "unitary plan." This is the idea that only one agency in a community should prepare a comprehensive plan; that agency is the city planning commission or department. Why is it that no other organization within a community prepares a plan? Why is only one agency concerned with establishing both general and specific goals for community development, and with proposing the strategies and costs required to effect goals? Why are there not plural plans?*[8]

CAPSULE 9.2:   Central Planning: The Defense

But the general mood of the ordinary citizens in the advanced Welfare State can be observed to be one of quiet satisfaction—although combined with a ubiquitous urge, but also a reasonable hope, to get more and more of the good things of life.

Behind this attitude is the reality that in the Welfare State a higher degree of harmony of interests actually becomes attained through cooperation and collective bargaining. When in recent years the Social Democrats in Sweden sponsored, and had a decisive influence in inaugurating, social security legislation affording insurance payments rising with a person's income up to a very high level—in unemployment, sickness, and old age insurance—this was an indication, among many others, that the present income distribution, including the expectation of how it is going to change, is widely accepted in that country as just and fair, even by those who are in the relatively lower income brackets.

This gradually accomplished harmony of interests is not the old liberalistic one, which was supposed to emerge out of the unhampered working of free forces in the market. Quite the contrary: it has, as a matter of fact, resulted from a long historical process, during which the market forces have been ever more intensely and effectively regulated by acts of public and private intervention, so that these, as they became more numerous and important, had to become coordinated and planned in an ever more comprehensive way.

Gunnar Myrdal, *Beyond the Welfare State*, 1960, 79–80.

Pluralistic planning occupies a middle-range position somewhere between the *laissez-faire,* highly individualistic approach that Hayek desired and the collectivist approach of the centralized unitary plan. The pluralistic approach conceives of planning as a contentious process involving the clash of different interests in the community but emphasizes the group (or microcollective) rather than the individualistic nature of these competing interests.

There is considerable distance on the spectrum of political thought between the nineteenth-century *laissez-faire* liberalism of Hayek and the twentieth-century liberalism of Davidoff. And, to be sure, their positions contain disparate views on various aspects of the social planning enterprise. Yet, their convergence of thought on two fundamental points is interesting. First, both favor diversity in place of the centrally produced plan. On this point Hayek's views are more extreme in favoring an approach that permits a diversity of individual choices. Davidoff's position favors pluralistic planning and the diversity of group choices. Second, they both have similar conceptions of the public interest. That is, both Hayek and Davidoff believe that the common good derives from contending individual and group interests.[9] This view rejects the idea of a more general harmony of interests that might be exemplified through broad scope national planning.

The Planner's Role

It is important to clarify the planner's role in the planning enterprise. The policy issue of who plans might be put to rest simply by saying that planners plan. But in so doing they are influenced and directed by their own values, knowledge, and inclinations as well as by the values, knowledge, and inclinations of other parties in the planning environment. The issue turns on the degree to which planning decisions are more or less influenced by the planner in comparison to the influence exerted by others. Thus, Who plans? is a relative matter that depends on the organizational arrangements among planners, political and bureaucratic leaders, and consumer publics. To whom is the planner primarily accountable? Whose values and interests guide the planning choices that are made? Efforts to answer these questions constitute the major choices that govern the planning process and the development of organizational arrangements to decide how policies are formulated.

Role refers to the ways in which the planner's responsibilities, expectations, and commitments are structured. There is a body of knowledge, skill, and expertise that all planners claiming "professional" status are expected to master. But in any given professional position there are specific tasks the worker must do, there are expected ways in which the professional must behave, and there are people to whom the professional is accountable. These components vary from job to job. Thus, in addition to a guiding set of professional ethics, there is some sponsor, usually an agency, and/or clients or constituents, to whom the planner is accountable.

The competing and oftentimes contradictory claims of profession, sponsor, and client frequently constitute a great source of strain (and sometimes conflict) for the planner.

The profession, placing importance on "professional standards," awards recognition to practitioners who promote these standards (e.g., seeing that only properly credentialed people perform professional tasks). The sponsor, having a greater interest in economy and efficiency than in standards, may constrain the planner to find the least expensive way of doing things. Clients and constituents, evaluating the planner in terms of what is produced for them, are not likely to have as great an interest in the maintenance of professional standards or in economy. (This is not to say, of course, that professional standards, economy, and effectiveness are necessarily contradictory.)

The social context of the planner's role, then, is one of the factors that determines the nature of the process to be followed. The planner's relationships with other actors (sponsors and clients) play an important part in determining the values and interests that will predominate in the planning process. To a large extent the planner is both committed and limited to working in certain ways by the nature of these relationships. Professionals involved in planning must be cognizant of the features of the social context that bear on the work.

The planner's role requires the integration of knowledge and skill to deal with both *interactional* and *analytic* functions. That is to say, it demands proficiency in both sociopolitical and technical tasks. These functions are different sides of the planning coin; each is important in bringing the process to fruition. Technical (analytic) tasks involve data collection, quantification of problems and analysis in light of the data, ranking priorities, specification of objectives, program design, and the like. Sociopolitical (interactional) tasks involve the development of an organizational network, which requires building the structure of a planning system within which communication and exchange of information among relevant actors takes place and planning decisions are made.[10] The ways in which these interactional functions are performed are the means of resolving the question, Who plans?

The distinction between the technical and sociopolitical aspects of the planning process may be illustrated by examining the planning requirements of the Model Cities Program. We use this example from the late 1960s because it was the last of the Great Society programs based on the belief that the federal government should support and encourage local communities to undertake systematic and comprehensive social planning. After 1970, there was a precipitous decline in the government's commitment to planning. Not until the 1990s was some renewed federal interest in community planning expressed with the adoption of the Empowerment Zone and Enterprise Communities program under the 1993 Omnibus Budget Reconciliation Act, which funds broad community-based strategic plans, drawing together resources from various federal funding streams and private sources. Much smaller than the Model Cities effort, the bulk of federal support for this program is concentrated in nine areas.[11]

Planning in Model Cities

Under Model Cities, all cities were invited by the Department of Housing and Urban Development (HUD) to submit applications for planning grants. In these applications, cities described their characteristics, social problems, and their "plan for planning." During the first application period in 1967, 193 cities submitted proposals. After a careful and complex scrutiny of the applications and the applicants, seventy-five cities were selected to receive planning grants.[12] A similar process was used the following year to select another seventy-three cities, bringing to 148 the total number of cities given grants.[13] The Model Cities experience for any given city was expected to last approximately six years (the first for planning and the next five for implementation).

The HUD guidelines for Model Cities participants were clear and firm on technical planning but vague and loose on sociopolitical planning.

Technical Approaches

The HUD planning model stipulated that cities follow a predefined, rational, analytic process in developing their Comprehensive Demonstration Plans (CDPs). Initially, this entailed a three-part CDP framework:

> *Part I was to describe and analyze problems and their causes, to rank problems in order of local priorities, and to indicate objectives, strategies, and program approaches to solving these problems. This document was to be submitted to HUD two-thirds of the way through the planning year. Based on these documents, HUD was to provide appropriate feedback to the City Demonstration Agencies (CDAs) that would be useful for the completion of Parts II and III.*
>
> *Part II was to be a statement of projected five-year objectives and cost estimates. This document was to be submitted at the end of the planning year, along with Part III.*
>
> *Part III was to be a detailed statement of program plans for the first action year, the costs involved, and administrative arrangements for implementation. This document was to be a logical extension of the analysis, strategies, and priorities outlined in Part I.*[14]

Toward the end of 1969 this framework was simplified by eliminating Part II and changing Part I to a Mid-Term Planning Statement (limited to seventy-five pages) that was to be submitted halfway in the planning year and then revised and merged with what was previously designated as the Part III document for the final submission—the CDP.

The extent to which cities were able to satisfy the requirements of the planning process has been detailed in a number of studies.[15] In general, the cities made considerable effort to follow the guidelines, but few were able to approximate the ideal process prescribed by HUD. In part, this is because the demands were strenuous even for those cities that commanded the required technical expertise. Their causal analyses of problems had a tendency toward infinite regress, and the problem-analysis approach often proved to be frustrating and unilluminating. Given the limited planning resources available, five-year projections could hardly secure the investment of time, effort, and commitment that planning for the following year's programs received; in fact, the Part II CDP submissions were often superficial. Moreover, many cities simply did not have the staff expertise to perform comprehensive planning according to HUD's model. Sixty-four percent, indeed, used private consulting firms to provide technical assistance during the planning period.[16]

Sociopolitical Approaches

Although the technical requirements of the Model Cities planning process were spelled out in detail, the sociopolitical aspects were left largely to local determination. The major prescription HUD offered was that ultimate administrative and fiscal responsibilities be vested in the elected local chief executive. Beyond this, the guidelines left considerable latitude for the types of linkages and relationships among groups that might develop to imbue CDP decision making with an element of social choice as well as technical procedure. The first Program Guide stated:

> [The CDA] should be closely related to the governmental decision-making process in a way that permits the exercise of leadership by responsible elected officials in the establishment of policies. . . . It should have sufficient powers, authority, and structure to achieve the coordinated administration of all aspects of the program. . . . It should provide a meaningful role in policy making to area residents and to the major agencies expected to contribute to the program.[17]

Although "a meaningful role in policy making to area residents" is an innocuous enough statement, the HUD administrative staff responsible for Model Cities vigorously promoted citizen involvement in decision making. (Model Cities staff came largely from outside of HUD; many were former Office of Economic Opportunity personnel.) First-round planning awards, for example, were often accompanied by stipulations that the cities strengthen their provisions for resident participation.[18] A study of the Planning Grant Review Project, the means used by HUD to select the cities that were to be funded for first-round planning grants, showed, further, that project staff gave highest ratings to those cities that later proved to be most successful at achieving high degrees of citizen participation.[19]

Although citizen influence in the planning process was emphasized, the guidelines for its achievement and the structure of relationships between professional planners, political leadership, and citizen groups were relatively vague. Overall, a number of planning arrangements emerged in which planners were accountable, in varying degrees, to different parties.[20] In general terms, these different patterns of relationships among planners, political leadership, and citizen groups are associated with the ways in which the "public interest" is defined.

Conceptions of the Public Interest

One justification for any form of social planning is that the decisions arrived at and the choices made will serve the common good, whether planners are primarily accountable to themselves, to political or bureaucratic leaders, or to the consumer public. It is true whether planning is done under public auspices or by private agencies. Take, for instance, the United Way of America. This private organization explicitly disclaims that their community planning reflects the special interests of particular groups and agencies. United Way literature prescribes that

> The process by which community resources . . . are marshaled and focused to bring remedies to problems . . . is essential to problem-solving. The process may be manifested in a variety of ways such as convening, facilitating, mediating, and conciliating. It usually requires that significant segments of the community agree that action is needed; and also on the nature of the action.[21] This is done to assure donors that their contributions are being used . . . not to solve one problem or support one group, but to meet priority human care needs.[22] [Emphasis added.]

The problem with claims that planning activities serve the public interest is that there are different conceptions of what the common good is and the means by which it is served. It is a matter of opinion whether, for practical planning purposes, "a total community point of view" is attainable or even desirable as a means of defining the public interest. Depending on how the idiom is interpreted, planning *pro bono publico* may be expressed through several sociopolitical processes, each of which involves different relationships among planners and other relevant parties in the planning environment. To illustrate, let us examine three conventional meanings of the term *public interest*. As described by Banfield, these are the *organismic, communalistic,* and *individualistic* conceptions.[23]

The Organismic View

According to the organismic view, there is an ideal public interest that transcends the specific preferences and interests of the individuals composing the public body. The public body is viewed as a unitary organism whose interests are greater or different than the sum of its parts. For example, in community planning the community is believed to have certain anthropomorphic needs and interests that are essential to its health; its arteries must be able to sustain a sufficient flow of goods and services; its tax base must be sufficient to nourish growth and provide maintenance; and police are needed to protect, social services to mend, and sanitation agencies to cleanse its parts. To stretch the analogy a bit farther, the planner's relationship to the community is akin to that of doctor to patient. In diagnosing the community's interests the planner is guided primarily by professional values and technical expertise. Although planners may be working for a public or private agency, their primary accountability is to the profession. In essence this conception of the public interest, in its purest form, gives rise to *technocracy*. This approach is often used by city and regional planning officials in developing long-term "master plans" governing physical development.

The Communalistic View

In the communalist view, one envisions a unitary public interest composed of the interests that all members of the public share in common. This single set of common ends is seen as more valuable in calculating the public interest than are the unshared objectives of individuals and groups. The public's common ends are embodied in political leaders and nonpartisan community institutions. This view of the public interest is associated with a planning process that includes, as Rothman notes, "legislators or administrators who are presumed to know the ends of the body politic as a whole and to strive in some central decision-making locus to assert the unitary interests of the whole over competing lesser interests."[24] In this context the planner is accountable primarily to political or bureaucratic leadership. Planning choices are guided by the values and interests these leaders express. (The United Way of America, as noted, operates primarily with this kind of planning perspective.)

The Individualistic View

In the individualist view, there is no single public interest. Rather, there are different publics with different interests. The unshared ends that are held by individuals and groups are seen as more consequential than shared ends in determining the common good. In this view the public interest is a momentary compromise arising out of the interplay among competing interests; it is constantly shifting as new groups make their interests known and respected. Individualistic conceptions of the public interest are associated with *advocacy planning,* an arrangement in which the planner is accountable to a particular group whose values and interests guide planning choices. The objective is to increase this group's participation and influence in the competitive process through which one or another particular point of view wins public support.

It was the intention of programs such as Community Action and Model Cities, of course, to give voice and representation in the political process to organizations representing the poor. As Moynihan's critique indicates, however, these federal efforts to balance the playing field frequently had contrary results.

Three Planning Models

Each of these conceptions of the public interest implies sociopolitical processes requiring different planning roles and different relationships among planners, political and administrative leaders, and consumer publics. In the organismic model, the planner is a *technocrat* accountable primarily to the profession and operating with a view of the public interest derived from special skills and

---

**CAPSULE 9.3: Community Action and the "Power"
of the Poor**

Over and again, the attempt by official and quasi-official agencies (such as the Ford Foundation) to organize poor communities led first to the radicalization of the middle-class persons who began the effort; next to a certain amount of stirring among the poor, accompanied by heightened racial antagonism *on the part of the poor;* next to retaliation from the larger white community; whereupon it would emerge that the community action agency, which had talked so much, been so much in the headlines, promised so much in the way of change in the fundamentals of things, was powerless. A creature of a Washington bureaucracy, subject to discontinuation without notice. Finally, much bitterness all around. Just possibly, the philanthropists and socially concerned intellectuals never took seriously enough their talk about the "power structure."

Daniel P. Moynihan, *Maximum Feasible Misunderstanding: Community Action in the War on Poverty,* 1969, 134–135.

---

professional knowledge. In the communalistic model, the planner is a *bureaucrat* accountable primarily to the political and administrative hierarchy and operating with a view of the public interest derived from institutional leadership. And in the individualistic model, the planner is an *advocate* accountable primarily to those who purchase his or her services and operating with a view of the public interest derived from group preferences.

These models, of course, represent ideal types, pure approaches on which reality often intrudes in a disconcerting manner.[25] Students of social planning typically find that inconsistencies are incorporated in the operations of individuals and organizations engaged in the social planning enterprise. As Banfield explains:

> *An institution may function as a mechanism which asserts at the same time different, and perhaps logically opposed, conceptions of the structure of the public interest. The members of a citizen board, for example, may endeavor to explicate the meaning of some very general ends which pertain to the body politic or ethos while at the same time—and perhaps inconsistently—seeking to find that compromise among the ends of individuals which will represent the greatest "total" satisfaction.*[26]

Alternative views of the public interest are sometimes held simultaneously because of the dynamic interplay of competing social values that are associated with these views.

Competing Values: Participation, Leadership, and Expertise

There is a continuing cycle of competition among three values that govern the management of community affairs, and that affect the degree to which different conceptions of the public interest are emphasized. These are the values of participation, leadership, and expertise. All three are prized values that compete for ascendancy in community life. These values and their significance for social planning have been extensively described in the literature.[27] Our interest is to point out the dialectical relationship among them and how this relationship affects community planning. Each value, when maximized, contains the seeds of its own undoing. Each generates conditions that will, in turn, encourage another of the values to emerge. Although policy planners have relatively little control over these dynamics, it is important to understanding the process.

Participation is a value that extols the virtue of each and every person joining meaningfully and directly in decisions that affect their welfare. In the extreme it supports a vision of a participatory democracy, championing schemes for community control and decentralization. In the 1960s and 1970s it was celebrated in the slogan "power to the people." Theoretically, this value is supported by findings from small group experiments and industrial psychology, which indicate that people who participate directly in the decisions that impinge on their lives are more likely to feel a part of their community. Decisions arrived at with a high degree of participation are more likely to be binding, and alienation and apathy are reduced.[28]

Countervailing theory contends that an urban industrialized society is too large and complex to allow the value of participation to operate in the extreme. Rather, participation must be organized and expressed through a system of representation. The New England town meeting might have been an appropriate decision-making device for a nineteenth-century small town America, but modern society needs electoral machinery for selecting representative leaders.

The value of participation in the management of community affairs always exists, although at some times and places it is more prominent. For example, the Jacksonian era, which followed the Revolutionary War, the Populist period of the late 1880s, and the period of social upheavals in the 1960s and 1970s, were times when issues of participation were paramount. In the mid-1990s, the value of participation is being expressed, not in the language of "power to the people," but in the more moderate and centrist discourse of communitarian theory, which promotes the revitalization of civil society (discussed in Chapter 3).

Participation becomes the primary value in community governance when leadership or expertise are perceived to be unresponsive. Then, decentralization, localism, and constituency satisfaction are likely to be the major programmatic goals of planning. Major evaluative concerns about programs will derive from the central question, Do the people like it?

Leadership as a value is the antithesis of participation because complex decisions must continuously be made and executed, and to do this, leadership is required. In a heterogeneous society such as ours, with a swarm of competing claims to the public interest, community decision making is bound to generate a hopeless drone of discussion and debate unless citizens can find leaders they trust, who they can hold responsible, and who have the ability to mitigate conflict and regulate competition with equity and dispatch. Unless the executive committee, the board of directors, the officers—in short, leadership—undertake these tasks for the community, chaos will reign. The extreme example of local leadership in government is the boss system and the political machine. Historically, both the nineteenth-century movement against the "long ballot" and the twentieth-century political reform movement were aimed at strengthening the power of governors and mayors.

When leadership emerges as the prime value in community life, centralization and growth become major programmatic goals of planning. The major evaluative question is, Does it work? But the capacity to rule and lead does not ensure the capacity to plan and implement. Leaders searching for ideas, concerned and constrained to rule with economy and efficiency, eventually turn to the repository of another set of values—the experts—for assistance.

Expertise is a value that makes rationality the supreme criterion for decision making. Theoretically, experts choose among programmatic alternatives on the basis of merit rather than politics. Expertise is an antidote to corruption, waste, and inefficiency in government. Historically, expertise in government, whether in the form of civil service, the merit system, or the nonpartisan city manager, has evolved as an antidote to unrestrained leadership. Presumably insulated from the vagaries of politics, experts are free to bring knowledge and skill to bear on the problem-solving process, enabling leaders to make the most sensible decisions for the community.

As the expert gains primacy, the planning enterprise moves to the touchstone of professionalism—technique. Refinement of professional skill, experimentation, coordination, and the attainment of improved methods of executive intervention become the major planning interests. Evaluative concerns deriving from this perspective focus on information about how and with what consequences different programs operate.

However, experts and leaders often succumb to their own ambitions. They may be inclined to preserve the status quo and to protect their privileged positions, whether as *eminences grises* to the ruling coalition, as the vanguard of an emergent technocracy, or as entrenched administrators of planning "empires." In time, experts may come to suffer from "hardening of the categories," leaders may become despots, and both may become major obstacles to innovation and change. The synthesis then transforms to a new thesis in the dialectic process. Technocracy and leadership may be challenged and community renewal brought about by new efforts to mobilize the disaffected, organize the disadvantaged, and from their ranks to draw fresh leadership. Sooner or later, these leaders will call on the experts for advice—and the cycle recurs.

The Cycle of Values

The political scientist, Robert Michels, saw this dialectic in the evolution of European socialist political parties earlier in this century. His "iron law of oligarchy" was based on the doctrine that history is a record of a continuous series of struggles over values, all of which culminate in the creation of new oligarchies

that eventually fuse with the old, "representing an uninterrupted series of oppo-
sitions . . . attaining one after another to power and passing from the sphere of
envy to the sphere of avarice."[29] His insights into this process are timely:

> *The democratic currents of history resemble successive waves. They break ever on*
> *the same shoal. They are ever renewed. This enduring spectacle is simultaneously*
> *encouraging and depressing. . . . Now new accusers arise to denounce the trai-*
> *tors; after an era of glorious combats and inglorious power, they end by fusing*
> *with the old dominant class; whereupon once more they are in their turn attacked*
> *by fresh opponents who appeal to the name of democracy. It is probably that this*
> *cruel game will continue without end.*[30]

Contemporary experience suggests the ways in which the dialectic of social
planning operates. In the years following World War II, the technician emerged as
the central figure in community welfare planning. The notion of a professionally
developed community "master plan" achieved broad support, but in the 1950s
dissatisfaction grew with this process of planning and its effects. Citizen participation, as a check on the professional planners, was a significant ingredient in the
seven-point Workable Program for urban renewal contained in the Housing Act
of 1954. Initially, participation involved the appointment of a citywide advisory
committee, generally composed of civic leaders, to work with planners; representation of the poor, the people who were usually most affected by renewal activities, was neither mandatory nor commonplace. But as experience with resident
opposition to renewal increased, agencies began to give greater consideration to
the involvement of neighborhood residents, although overall citizen participation
remained modest.[31]

Other efforts in the late 1950s and early 1960s gave citizens an increasingly
active role. These included the Ford Foundation Grey Area Projects, the planning
programs spawned by the President's Committee on Juvenile Delinquency, the
War on Poverty, and the Model Cities Program. All gave emphasis to the value of
participation *vis-a-vis* leadership and expertise. (It is interesting to note that at
their inception, *all* community planning programs seem to invoke all three values, although this kind of *tout ensemble* never comes off very well. One of the values is sooner or later elevated above the rest.) By the mid-1960s, the value of participation reigned; the expertise of professionals was rejected in favor of the
direct experiences of neighborhood residents.[32] Meanwhile, leadership fretted,
floundered, and failed to achieve consensus. By the end of the 1970s there had
developed a disenchantment with social planning of any variety. And although
"participation" as a formal element of the planning process has not been revived,
de facto arrangements in most large U.S. communities in the 1990s reflect significant social and economic diversity, well-organized and competing interest
groups, and decision-making systems that substantially incorporate a plurality of
concerns, including, to a degree unrivaled in the past, participation by neighborhoods (rich and poor), ethnic and racial and sexual preference minorities, and
women.

U.S. General Accounting Office, *Community Development: Comprehensive Approaches Address Multiple Needs but Are Challenging to Implement,* GAO/RCED/HEHS-95-69, USGPO, February 1995, 58–60.

CAPSULE 9.4: Pluralism and Consensus on Dudley Street

The Dudley Street Neighborhood Initiative (DSNI), begun in 1984, [soon] developed a comprehensive plan of action that included, among other goals, developing community pride, strengthening cultural diversity, improving residents' job skills, providing housing counseling, promoting human service programming and resource allocation, and developing new housing opportunities. According to neighborhood residents and officials from DSNI and other organizations, this plan achieved multiple purposes. Because it was developed through a consensus of the participating residents and the board, it had widespread support. It provided the board, staff, and residents with a long-term vision for the neighborhood's revitalization, thereby enabling those involved to remain focused on the agreed-upon goals. Thirdly, it demonstrated residents' commitment to city officials, foundations, banks, and other institutions. The city adopted DSNI's comprehensive plan as its official plan for improving the neighborhood.

As designed by local residents, DSNI's 31-member board of directors must have a majority of residents; the balance of the members must be representatives of community nonprofit organizations, development corporations, business and religious groups, and government agencies. In addition, the resident members must represent equally the neighborhood's major cultural populations—African-American, Latino, Cape Verdean, and White.

Currently, over 1,800 residents are voting members of DSNI. The governing body is the board of directors, first elected in April 1985 and elected every 2 years thereafter. The executive director and staff are charged with carrying out the board's mandates. As of January 1995, DSNI employed 16 full-time staff members. Staff resources are supplemented, when needed, by the voluntary contributions of residents and other individuals, local law firms, downtown Boston organizations, and several interns from local universities.

Shifting Power to City Hall

As federal interest in citizen participation subsided, the national government increasingly emphasized policy and planning processes that engaged state and local elected leadership. Despite the continued existence of a number of detailed categorical aid programs, and a not inconsequential number of guidelines and mandates, the intergovernmental system, as described in Chapter 8, has moved significantly toward decentralization. The most dramatic expression of this—block grants—has been noted. Block grants represent a vital shift in power over the use of federal funds. Eschewing the tradition of categorical centralization, they provide city and state officials—particularly mayors and governors—broad flexibility in spending federal funds.

The shift toward decentralization has also been marked in the HUD-administered programs. In 1970, under the Planned Variations experiment, HUD gave up much of its review and oversight responsibility in favor of mayoral decision making. Mayors, for example, were given the responsibility to review, comment, and sign off on all HUD programs serving their cities. This was not unimportant, because the growth of federal aid in the 1960s had resulted in mayors often being bypassed. Before the New Federalism, for example, local public agencies and private nonprofit organizations frequently received federal assistance over which local elected chief executives had little if any influence. Given the hundreds of centralized limited focus programs in existence, mayors often found it a formidable task simply to keep abreast of their amounts, purposes, and locations.

A further departure from the old model came with the passage of the Housing and Community Development Act of 1974. Like other block grants, this consolidated a number of categorical grants (urban renewal, neighborhood and public facilities, and economic development, along with Model Cities) into a single decentralized program. Although local officials had to direct programs to one of three national objectives (assisting low- and moderate-income people, reducing blight, and meeting urgent community needs), their discretion was quite broad. The balance of spending between housing development, social services, and economic development, for example, became largely a municipal decision. Especially since 1981, when Congress approved the Reagan-backed Community Development Bloc Grant (CDBG) amendments that eliminated detailed grant applications and citizen participation requirements, the program has operated with maximum local discretion.

Although officials in some cities have kept the CDBG planning process open to a broad spectrum of local interests, including residents of poverty neighborhoods, mayors and elected council members have a degree of freedom and flexibility in setting local priorities that provides at least a promise of overall, integrated planning. In this sense, intergovernmental *decentralization* has resulted in local *centralization* (see Figure 9.1). The workloads of mayors' offices, for example, have increased substantially. Special staff have been hired to develop, review, and assess projects, and to create the mechanisms and procedures to organize planning and program activities in conjunction with local agencies, nonprofit organizations, development and rehabilitation entrepreneurs, and target-area residents.

Figure 9.1 indicates the shifting locus of allocative decision making along two dimensions of the federal aid system. On the horizontal plane, the changes occur within the levels; on the vertical plane they occur between levels. At the federal level, reduced oversight and program-review responsibilities have substantially limited the national leadership role. Instead of a complicated system of federal

FIGURE 9.1   Impact of decentralization on allocative decision making.

grant reviews and an extensive number of precise guidelines, HUD-variety devolution has relegated basic decision-making authority to governors and mayors, enhancing their planning, coordinating, and service-delivery powers. Without strong federal emphasis on neighborhood involvement, in addition, the intensity of citizen participation has diminished. On the neighborhood level, CDBG, and other block grant programs, have resulted in greater power for traditional political leadership, and less focus on "indigenous leadership." From a focus on poverty and designated target neighborhoods (e.g., the Model Cities demonstration area), urban development has evolved into citywide programs with substantial involvement by chambers of commerce, banks, downtown developers, as well as a variety of housing and community development activists.[33]

As noted in the preceding chapter, the HUD experience is not unique. The Omnibus Reconciliation Act of 1981 transferred broad decision-making authority over federal aid programs to states while eliminating almost any system of accountability for how the monies are used. There are, of course, certain obstacles to the realization of federal decentralization goals. As Banfield points out, organized beneficiaries of the categorical grant system are not enthusiastic about changes that deprive them of their special status, dissolving their identities in a mass of supplicants through grant consolidation.[34] Members of Congress, too, often have a special affinity for categorical grants that can be tailored to suit particular groups of constituents. Moreover, the rhetoric of local control notwithstanding, it is unclear how anxious mayors and governors are to assume responsibilities that may prove politically awkward when the foil of federal control is removed.

Nevertheless, as a result of these alterations in the system of authority, two major changes have occurred in the nature of local social planning. First, mayors and governors are being held increasingly more accountable by their constituencies for their plans and programs. In the past, these officials could claim that they had little authority over the local agencies receiving federal funds, and that they were hamstrung by federally designed program guidelines. With decentralization, the accountability that was impaired by the exigencies of the categorical grant system has been considerably enlarged.

Second, citizen participation characterized by grass-roots organizations, created in Community Action and Model Cities neighborhoods, and later on by citizen participation requirements in such programs as Title XX and the Older Americans Act, has been deemphasized. As federal programs came to be designed for broader urban constituencies and whole states, the influence of neighborhood groups diminished. Instead, the focus of political activity shifted to the formal citywide and statewide political apparatuses, injecting a new vitality into urban politics. Although detailed federal participation requirements were largely deleted from grant legislation during the Reagan years, the tradition of citizen involvement continued in more conventional political forms through interest group activity, neighborhood meetings, direct contact with policymakers, electoral advocacy, and the like. Yesterday's poverty workers have become today's mayors and council members; yesterday's radicals have become today's establishment. In some ways, indeed, citizen action has moved from being on the fringes of social institutions to being right in the center of things. And this shift has had a profound effect on social planning and community organization.[35]

Social Welfare Planning: Drift or Design?

Where does the policy planner fit into all this? Does the planner gravitate toward executive leadership when leadership is in the saddle, and "back to the people" when the impulse for participation arises? Is there any meaning for professional planners in what we describe as the dialectical relationship among the values of participation, leadership, and expertise beyond, perhaps, the recognition that planning is a complex business?

Rein suggests that the conflicting values of participation, leadership, and expertise invest the planning enterprise with insoluble dilemmas.[36] From the dialectical perspective, however, the competition among values is not a dilemma but a dynamic, necessary, and continuously unfolding process that sustains democratic vigor in the planning endeavor. Policy planners should encourage rather than avoid the dialectical relationship among these values; no single value should become the professional's polestar. The contradiction among these values is a healthy stimulant to the profession; each value can become salient as emphases in the community change.

To conclude, we should like to emphasize our own view about the values described in this discussion. Shifts in the values that guide social planning bear careful scrutiny. In the short run, the change from participation to leadership was welcomed by many members of the planning profession who experienced some of the turbulence and frustration of the citizen participation era. They were inclined to embrace the value of leadership warmly. Leadership perpetually looks to expertise, and planners can expect to be well received.

Nevertheless, as local and state executives extend their spheres of authority, and as the number of planners on their staffs increase, the executive's ability to control planners may be reduced, laying the ground for technocracy. Instead of being advocacy planners for the poor, as they were in the 1960s, the planner-technocrats of the 1990s could become remote from the would-be beneficiaries of their enterprise. Only by continuing to work with representatives of different groups, including consumer publics, can this estrangement be avoided.

If one fact has been made clear in the evolution of social policy over the past half-century, it is that excessive faith in planning can be as damaging to the community's interest as an unquestioned belief in "the people." Professionals don't know everything; there are problems they can't solve; they are as much creatures of their values, their culture, and their generation as anyone else.

Notes

1. Alfred Kahn, *Theory and Practice of Social Planning* (New York, Russell Sage Foundation, 1969), 61.

2. Diana M. DiNitto, *Social Welfare: Politics and Public Policy* (Needham Heights, Mass.: Allyn and Bacon, 1995), 12.

3. Howard Freeman and Clarence Sherwood, *Social Research and Social Policy* (Englewood Cliffs, NJ, Prentice-Hall, 1970) 3–16.

4. Organizational maintenance and direct-service needs frequently make competing claims on social welfare administrators. This leads Etzioni to suggest that this type of position constitutes a case of institutionalized role conflict. Amitai Etzioni, *Modern Organizations* (Englewood Cliffs, NJ: Prentice-Hall, Inc., 1964), 82–85.

5. Scott Briar, "Dodo or Phoenix? A View of the Current Crisis in Casework," *Social Work Practice 1967* (New York: Columbia University Press, 1967); see also, Gordon Hamilton, "The Role of Social Casework in Social Policy," *Social Casework,* 33(8) (October 1952).

6. Kahn, *Theory and Practice of Social Planning.*

7. Friedrich A. Hayek, *The Road to Serfdom* (Chicago: University of Chicago Press, 1944), 32–42.

8. Paul Davidoff, "Advocacy and Pluralism in Planning," in Ralph M. Kramer and Harry Specht (eds.), *Community Organization Practice* (Englewood Cliffs, NJ: Prentice-Hall, 1969), 440.

9. Hayek, *The Road to Serfdom,* 56–65; and Davidoff, "Advocacy and Pluralism in Planning," 438–50.

10. Robert Perlman and Arnold Gurin, *Community Organization and Social Planning* (New York: John Wiley & Sons, 1971), 52–75; and Ralph M. Kramer and Harry Specht, *Readings in Community Organization Practice* (Englewood Cliffs, NJ: Prentice-Hall, 1969), 8–9.

11. U.S. General Accounting Office, *Community Development: Comprehensive Approaches Address Multiple Needs but Are Challenging to Implement* (Washington D.C.: U.S. Government Printing Office, 1995).

12. For a detailed description of this process, see Neil Gilbert and Harry Specht, *Planning for Model Cities: Process, Product, Performance, and Predictions* (Washington, D.C.: U.S. Department of Housing and Urban Development, U.S. Government Printing Office, 1970).

13. For further details on the Model Cities Program legislation, guidelines, and operational procedures, see the following: Neil Gilbert and Harry Specht, *Dynamics of Community Planning* (Cambridge, MA: Ballinger Publishing Co., 1977); Gilbert and Specht, *Improving the Quality of Urban Life: A Program Guide to Model Neighborhoods in Demonstration Cities,* U.S. Department of Housing and Urban Development, HUD PG-47, December 1966, and HUD PG-47, December 1967 (Washington, D.C.: U.S. Government Printing Office); Marshall Kaplan, *Model Cities and National Urban Policy* (Chicago: American Society of Planning Officials, 1971); Marshall Kaplan, Gans, and Kahn, *The Model Cities Program: A Comparative Analysis of the Planning Process in Eleven Cities* (Washington, D.C.: U.S. Department of Housing and Urban Development, U.S. Government Printing Office, 1970); and Roland L. Warren, "Model Cities' First Round: Politics, Planning, and Participation," *Journal of the American Institute of Planners,* 35(4) (July 1969), 245–52.

14. Summarized from Gilbert and Specht, *Improving the Quality of Urban Life.*

15. See footnote 13.

16. Gilbert and Specht, *Planning for Model Cities.*

17. Gilbert and Specht, *Improving the Quality of Urban Life,* 11.

18. See, for example, Marshall Kaplan, Gans, and Kahn, *The Model Cities Program;* and Warren, "Model Cities' First Round."

19. Gilbert and Specht, *Dynamics of Community Planning.*

20. For example, in the Marshall Kaplan, Gans, and Kahn study, *The Model Cities Program,* five types of planning systems are identified: staff dominant, staff influence, parity, resident influence, and resident dominant. Each of these systems

is characterized by different sets of relationships among planners, political leadership, and citizen groups, which are analyzed in Gilbert and Specht, *Dynamics of Community Planning.*

21. United Way of America, Report of Special Study Committee on the Role of United Way in Community Problem-Solving (Alexandria, VA: United Way of America, October 19–20, 1983), 8.

22. American Association of Fund-Raising Counsel, *Giving U.S.A.* (New York: American Association of Fund Raising Counsel, 1984), 82.

23. Martin Meyerson and Edward Banfield, *Politics, Planning and the Public Interest* (New York: Free Press, 1955), 322–29. These conceptions are similar, respectively, to the idealist view, the rationalist view, and the realist view of the public interest as analyzed by Glendon A. Schubert, *The Public Interest* (New York: Free Press, 1960).

24. Jack Rothman, "Three Models of Community Organization Practice," *Social Work Practice 1968* (New York: Columbia University Press, 1968), 38.

25. For an excellent analysis of the complexities and variations in these planning relationships, see Francine F. Rabinovitz, *City Politics and Planning* (New York: Atherton, 1969), 79–117.

26. Meyerson and Banfield, *Politics, Planning and the Public Interest,* 329.

27. For example, see Herbert Kaufman, *Politics and Policies in State and Local Government* (Englewood Cliffs, NJ: Prentice-Hall, 1964); Martin Rein, "Social Planning: The Search for Legitimacy," *Journal of the American Institute of Planners,* 35(4) (July 1967), 233–44; and George A. Brager and Harry Specht, *Community Organizing* (New York: Columbia University Press, 1973).

28. For example, see Eric Fromm, *The Sane Society* (New York: Holt, Rinehart and Winston, 1955); Ralph White and Ronald Lippitt, "Leader Behavior and Member Reaction in Three Social Climates," in Dorwin Cartwright, et al. (eds.), *Group Dynamics* (Evanston, IL: Row, Peterson and Company, 1953); Jacob Levine and John Butler, "Lecture vs. Group Decision in Changing Behavior," *Journal of Applied Psychology, 36* (February 1952), 29–33.

29. Robert Michels, *Political Parties* (New York: Dover Publications, Inc., 1915), 319.

30. Ibid., 408.

31. Peter Rossi and Robert Dentler, *The Politics of Urban Renewal* (New York: Free Press, 1961); James Q. Wilson, "Planning and Politics: Citizen Participation in Urban Renewal," in Jewel Bellush, et al. (eds.), *Urban Renewal: People, Politics, and Planning* (New York: Anchor Books, 1967); and Scott Greer, *Urban Renewal and American Cities* (Indianapolis: Bobbs-Merrill, 1965).

32. Neil Gilbert and Joseph Eaton, "Research Report: Who Speaks for the Poor?," *Journal of the American Institute of Planners, 36* (November 1970), 411–16.

33. William Frej and Harry Specht, "The Housing and Community Development Act of 1974: Implications for Policy and Planning," *Social Service Review* (June 1976), 275–92. See also, Richard E. Klosterman, "A Public Interest Criterion," *Journal of American Planning Association, 46*(3) (July 1980), 323–33.

34. Edward Banfield, "Revenue Sharing in Theory and Practice," *Public Interest, 23*(2) (Spring 1971), 33–45.

35. Harry Specht, "The Grass Roots and Government in Social Planning and Community Organization," *Administration in Social Work, 1*(3) (Fall 1978), 319–34. See also, Thomas R. Dye, *Politics in States and Communities* (Englewood Cliffs, NJ: Prentice-Hall, 1988).

36. Rein, "Social Planning."

Name Index

Subject Index

normal participation, 156
normative criteria of need, 101
numerical equality, 70

occupational welfare, 44, 47
Office of Economic
  Opportunity (OEO), 131,
  222–23, 255
Office of Human Development
  Services (OHDS), 62
Old-Age Assistance (OAA), 65,
  67, 220
Old-Age, Survivors, Disability,
  and Health Insurance
  program (OASDHI), 107,
  197–98
Older Americans Act (1965), 51,
  264
  amendments of 1973, 124,
  135
  amendments of 1978, 153
oligarchy, iron law of, 260
Omnibus Budget Reconciliation
  Act (1981), 60, 264
  (1993), 253
open-ended federal matching
  grants, 67
open-system perspective, 170
opportunities, provision of, 122
organismic view of public
  interest, 256
organizational structure of
  services, 169
Organization for Economic
  Cooperation and
  Development, 33, 44
Organization of Petroleum
  Exporting Countries
  (OPEC), 31

participation:
  as value, 258–59
  citizen, 152, 156–57, 164, 166,
  169–70, 261
  "maximum feasible," 130,
  157, 230
Peace Corps, 196
pension insurance, 28

pensions, 6
performance studies, 13, 15–16
personal responsibility, 137, 235
Personal Responsibility and
  Work Opportunity
  Reconciliation Act (1996),
  51, 59, 68, 232
perverse incentives, 94
philanthropy, 183 *see also*
  voluntary financing
Pitied But Not Entitled: Single
  Mothers and the History of
  Welfare (Gordon), 15
Planned Variations experiment,
  262
planning, 245, 265
  analytic tasks, 253
  individualist and collective
  approaches, 250, 252
  in Model Cities Program, 255
  interactional tasks, 253
  pluralistic, 252
  process, 246
  role of planner in, 252
Planning Grant Review Project,
  255
pluralistic planning, 252
Poison Control Centers, 224
policy, defining, 2
policy design, 103
policy formulation:
  direct practitioner's role in,
  20–21
  process of, 245–46
policy goals, development of,
  248
popular prejudice, 73
potential recipients, 59
poverty, 129
power:
  as social provision, 123
  political, 222
  resources theorists, 34
  vertical dimension of, 215
power to the people, 259
President's Committee on
  Juvenile Delinquency, 187,
  261

private institutions, 217
private sector, 52
privatization, 143–44, 147
problem analysis, 247, 255
problem identification, 246
procedural conditions,
  226, 230
process studies, 13–16
product studies, 13, 15–16
professional/activist
  orientation, 171–72
professional/bureaucratic
  orientation, 171
professional disengagement,
  152, 160, 164, 166, 169, 171
professional standards, 253
profit-oriented agencies, 53–54,
  148
profit vs. nonprofit providers,
  148
program conditions, 226
program design, 249
Progressive Era, 18
Progressive Policy Institute
  (PPI), 33
proportional equality, 70
provisions, social, 57, 116–20,
  123, 131–32
proxy shopping, 145
pseudoparticipation, 156
public agencies, 182
public assistance programs,
  29, 42–43, 59, 61, 69, 72,
  93, 123, 220
public financing, 199
public housing, 107
public interest, 56, 255–57
public sector, 52
public subsidies, 189
Public Welfare, 67
purchase-of-service
  arrangements, 63, 65,
  144–45, 149, 189, 193
purposive duplication, 152,
  163–65, 169, 171

quid pro quo, 137
quota hiring plans, 70